Unearthing St. Mary's City

UNIVERSITY PRESS OF FLORIDA

Florida A&M University, Tallahassee
Florida Atlantic University, Boca Raton
Florida Gulf Coast University, Ft. Myers
Florida International University, Miami
Florida State University, Tallahassee
New College of Florida, Sarasota
University of Central Florida, Orlando
University of Florida, Gainesville
University of North Florida, Jacksonville
University of South Florida, Tampa
University of West Florida, Pensacola

UNEARTHING ST. MARY'S CITY

Fifty Years of Archaeology at Maryland's First Capital

EDITED BY

Henry M. Miller and Travis G. Parno

Foreword by William M. Kelso

University Press of Florida

Gainesville · Tallahassee · Tampa · Boca Raton

Pensacola · Orlando · Miami · Jacksonville · Ft. Myers · Sarasota

26 25 24 23 22 21   6 5 4 3 2 1

Library of Congress Cataloging-in-Publication Data
Names: Miller, Henry M. (Henry Michael), editor. | Parno, Travis G., editor. | Kelso, William M., author of foreword.
Title: Unearthing St. Mary's city : fifty years of archaeology at Maryland's first capital / edited by Henry M. Miller, Travis G. Parno ; foreword by William M. Kelso.
Description: Gainesville : University Press of Florida, 2021. | Includes bibliographical references and index.
Identifiers: LCCN 2020041064 (print) | LCCN 2020041065 (ebook) | ISBN 9780813066837 (hardback) | ISBN 9780813057767 (pdf)
Subjects: LCSH: Excavations (Archaeology)—Maryland—Saint Marys City. | Historic sites—Maryland—Saint Marys City. | Saint Marys City (Md.)—History. | Saint Marys City (Md.)—Antiquities.
Classification: LCC F189.S14 U54 2021 (print) | LCC F189.S14 (ebook) | DDC 975.2/41—dc23
LC record available at https://lccn.loc.gov/2020041064
LC ebook record available at https://lccn.loc.gov/2020041065

The University Press of Florida is the scholarly publishing agency for the State University System of Florida, comprising Florida A&M University, Florida Atlantic University, Florida Gulf Coast University, Florida International University, Florida State University, New College of Florida, University of Central Florida, University of Florida, University of North Florida, University of South Florida, and University of West Florida.

University Press of Florida
2046 NE Waldo Road
Suite 2100
Gainesville, FL 32609
http://upress.ufl.edu

CONTENTS

FIGURES

TABLES

ACKNOWLEDGMENTS

After a half century of archaeology at St. Mary's City, there are many people to whom gratitude is merited. First is the late General Robert Hogaboom for his wisdom in insisting that solid research should always precede any interpretation at the museum. Next is a remarkable team of historians—the late Lois Green Carr, Cary Carson, Russell Menard, and Lorena Walsh—for leading the way in revealing the story of early Maryland and producing vital groundwork for archaeological interpretation.

Archaeological investigations spanning half a century involve many, many people. We are most thankful for the hundreds of students and professional archaeologists who have conducted the excavations, processed the artifacts, and aided in analysis. They are too numerous to name individually, but without their hard work, skills, and devotion, none of these findings would be possible.

The archaeology at Historic St. Mary's City has been funded primarily by appropriations from the State of Maryland, grants from the National Endowment for the Humanities and other agencies, project funding from St. Mary's College of Maryland, and private donations. In particular, the Maryland Legislature on behalf of the public has provided consistent support for the preservation, exploration, and interpretation of the state's first capital. HSMC executive director Regina Faden has given enthusiastic support and staff time for bringing about this book. To all of them, we are most appreciative for providing the means by which these fascinating and valuable explorations of the past could be first conducted and now shared.

We are thankful for the hard work of each of our coauthors, who volunteered their time, knowledge, and insights to produce the diversity of subjects covered by this volume. Their generous efforts are what made this book possible. In particular, we wish to acknowledge the vital role of Garry Wheeler Stone. Stone established the archaeology program at St. Mary's, instilling professionalism and keen attention to detail while developing the procedures by which early colonial sites could be deciphered. He is coauthor of several chapters, but his wisdom, respect for the evidence, and skills at integrating documentary and archaeological evidence influence every page.

Images are an essential element of any archaeological study, and we wish to acknowledge the superb photographic skills of Donald L. Winter for all of the artifact pictures. Many of the inked drawings are the product of James O'Connor.

We received valuable comments from three anonymous reviewers that significantly improved the volume content. Likewise, the staff at the University Press of Florida, especially Meredith Morris Babb, have provided excellent support in bringing this book to fruition.

We hope that these chapters will show respect for and bring recognition to the many people who over the centuries have lived and died at a place called St. Mary's City.

FOREWORD

This book is an anthology written by a number of the nation's leading historical archaeologists who creatively blend microscopic documentary history, meticulous archaeological excavation, artifacts, state-of-the-art earth science, and forensic anthropology to create an enlightened understanding of the story of the oft-forgotten mythological place known as St. Mary's City, Maryland. The chronologically arranged chapters describe and interpret the remains of various structures that once made up the townscape, from the time when St. Mary's City was a seventeenth-century colonial capital, to the time when the land became eighteenth- and nineteenth-century tobacco farms until the fields became a female seminary campus in the mid-nineteenth century.

One early chapter of particular interest to me takes the reader through a how-to exercise in uncovering and interpreting four of the early settlers' earthfast (post-in-ground) buildings. This exacting step-by-step excavation and analytical guide finally sets in print a process with which archaeologists studying earthfast houses in the Chesapeake region have struggled for at least 40 years. Another highlight is a chapter about the methodical interpretation of the archaeological remains, artifacts, and a probate inventory of an eighteenth-century gentleman immigrant who, on the backs of his enslaved workforce, transformed the former capital city land into a successful tobacco farm.

The chapter that details the results of seeking to understand seventeenth-century life by studying the dead is also of especial interest. Led by Smithsonian forensic anthropologists and St. Mary's City archaeologists, the researchers chronicle their excavation and analysis of the graves of high-ranking colonial individuals buried in rare sealed lead coffins. This painstaking process combines documentary history, archaeology, genomics, and cutting-edge skeletal biology that has set the standard for Chesapeake region burial studies ever since.

This impressive book fittingly ends with a chapter that considers archaeology an essential tool of heritage memory, "making history physical in a way that other disciplines cannot." I think that readers will learn, above all, that five decades of digging at the site of Maryland's first capital has indeed successfully turned a historical myth into compelling "reality" history.

William M. Kelso, (Hon.) CBE, FSA
Director of Jamestown Archaeology and Research Emeritus

1

Introduction to St. Mary's City History and Archaeology

HENRY M. MILLER

One of the first English settlements in what is now the United States was established in 1634 at a place known as St. Mary's City. Named for the Queen of England, the colony of Maryland was the vision of an English Catholic family in a Protestant world. St. Mary's City served as the capital of the colony until 1695, when the seat of government was relocated to present-day Annapolis and the land of St. Mary's City was converted to agricultural uses. For more than 200 years, the land was plowed, planted, and plowed again, burying the remains of the seventeenth-century capital beneath the loamy soil. Fortunately, the site was granted protection as a National Historic Landmark (NHL) in 1969, a status that honors the city's critical role in America's colonial beginnings. Today, the land within the NHL is owned by three stakeholders: Historic St. Mary's City Commission, St. Mary's College of Maryland, and Trinity Episcopal Church (see figure 1.1). Decades of investigation show that St. Mary's City is an immensely rich archaeological landscape with hundreds of sites identified thus far, dating before, during, and after the seventeenth century. In many areas, individual sites cannot be distinguished because the location was used repeatedly, creating a palimpsest of occupation spanning hundreds, or in some cases thousands, of years. Each successive occupation has left some trace of its presence, and this deep archaeological record makes St. Mary's an exceptional place to examine human life over a span of millennia. In the chapters that follow, we and our fellow contributors present some of the many stories that have been drawn from this research with a focus upon what life was like in colonial and post-colonial St. Mary's City.

Figure 1.1. Aerial view of St. Mary's City. The St. Mary's River is in the foreground and Chesapeake Bay in the background. (Courtesy of HSMC.)

The History of St. Mary's City

Credit for the vision of what would become St. Mary's City belongs to a Yorkshire farm boy named George Calvert, who rose from obscurity to a high station in early seventeenth-century England, serving as principal secretary of state under King James I. Calvert resigned his powerful position upon his conversion to the Catholic faith in 1624. As a reward for loyalty and service, the King made him the Baron of Baltimore in Ireland, and the new Lord Baltimore initially focused his efforts on expanding the King's realm in Ireland and Newfoundland. Calvert had long had an interest in English colonization, being an investor in the Virginia Company and the East India Company. His first effort to establish a colony was in Newfoundland at Ferryland in the early 1620s. Despite a huge investment, one brutal winter spent in Newfoundland in 1628–1629 caused Calvert to seek a warmer climate and he returned to England and began lobbying for a new colony near Virginia (Krugler 2004). This was finally granted by King Charles I in 1632, but George died two months before the charter received the official seal. The challenge of founding a new colony passed to the second Lord Baltimore, George's 26-year-old eldest son, Cecil.

After much difficulty, Cecil sent the first expedition to North America with about 150 people in November 1633. They arrived in the Chesapeake in early March 1634 in the midst of a land that had been populated for more than 10,000 years by a variety of Native American tribal groups (Potter 1993; Rice 2009). At the time of the first expedition's arrival, the people settled along the Potomac shore were Algonquian-speaking groups united into a chiefdom named for the most powerful tribe, the Piscataway. Their Iroquoian enemies called them the Conoy (Potter 1993:19). A group called the Yaocomaco, probably allied with the Piscataway, inhabited the area of what would become St. Mary's City. In 1634, they were consolidating their habitations in an effort to put distance between themselves and their Susquehannock enemies. The arrival of the English seemed to provide a useful opportunity: the Yaocomaco could obtain compensation from the English for land they were prepared to vacate, while positioning the English settlement as a buffer between themselves and the Susquehannock to the north.

When the Calvert expedition arrived in the region, they established a temporary camp along the Potomac River while Governor Leonard Calvert, brother of Cecil, obtained permission from the *tayac,* or leader, of the Piscataway to settle. Afterward, Calvert was taken to a village, called Yaocomaco, by Henry Fleet, an English fur trader who spoke several Algonquian dialects. After negotiations with the community's leaders, the Yaocomaco agreed to vacate half of the village to provide housing for the new settlers. The rest of the village remained occupied by the Yaocomaco until the corn crop was harvested in the autumn. Because of the efforts to first negotiate with the Piscataway before settlement, the founding of Maryland involved an unusually harmonious cultural interaction between newly arrived English and the native inhabitants, a factor of much significance in the initial success of the new colony (White 1910). The Yaocomaco were the latest in a long history of native people to inhabit the place that became St. Mary's City (see chapter 6).

Maryland was unique as the only colony founded by English Catholics and the first in colonial America to make religious freedom its official policy. The plan for the colony, labeled "the Maryland Design," included the concepts of liberty of conscience, the free exercise of religion, and a lack of religious test for office or voting. This was in direct opposition to the policies of England and the colonies of Virginia, Plymouth, and Massachusetts Bay, especially because it included Roman Catholics. The Lords Baltimore tried to create a new society in which religion would not be a source of conflict and hostility. Another policy that was essential for the others to be realized was having no official religion for the colony. Government and faith were separated in Maryland. As a result, the colony attracted Europeans from a diversity of religious backgrounds, including Anglicans, Anabaptists, Lutherans, Presbyterians, Quakers, Roman Catholics, and a few people of Jewish descent. The experiment of religious freedom ended after the removal of Lord Baltimore and the proprietary government in 1689. With the introduction of royal governance came the enforcement of Anglicanism as the state religion. Nearly 100 years later, however, the Calverts' policy of liberty of conscience would be reborn in the First Amendment to the United States Constitution.

Maryland thrived for the first decade as settlers turned to the production of tobacco for European markets. Most settlement in the colony was on rural plantations scattered along the region's rivers and creeks. Tobacco had rapidly become the foundation of the economy, despite Calvert's hopes for more agrarian diversity and industry. The intricate water highways of the Chesapeake allowed ships directly from Europe to collect the bulky tobacco casks from each plantation and sell needed manufactured goods to the residents. This system meant that economic centers were not needed, and none developed in the first century of settlement (Carr 1974). Only government business and courts spurred any clustered settlement, and as a result, the capitals of St. Mary's City and Jamestown were the only places with a measure of urban character in the region (figure 1.2).

St. Mary's City was slow to develop because of internal and external conflict. The hostilities of the English Civil War reached the colony in 1645 when a Parliamentary ship attacked and captured St. Mary's City, nearly destroying the enterprise. Fithian discusses the archaeological evidence of this conflict in chapter 8. Some stability was experienced after 1648, but the Battle of the Severn in 1655 again threw Maryland into turmoil as hostile Virginians took over the government. In a brilliant political move, Lord Baltimore persuaded the government of England's staunchly anti-Catholic Lord Protector Oliver Cromwell to return control of Maryland to Baltimore in 1657 (Krugler 2004). Energized by the restoration of Charles II to the throne in 1660, the colony began sustained growth that would continue unabated for centuries.

The capital of St. Mary's City likewise began expanding, and Lord Baltimore formally incorporated it as Maryland's first city in 1668. The government purchased Leonard Calvert's old house as the first state house in 1662, and a new brick state house and jail were commissioned in 1674. To accommodate a growing number of visitors, public inns (then called ordinaries) were established and innkeeping became a major industry of the settlement.

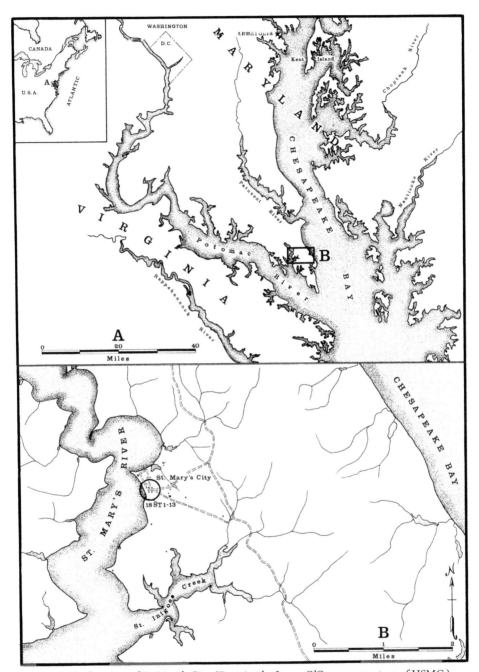

Figure 1.2. The location of St. Mary's City. (Drawing by James O'Connor, courtesy of HSMC.)

Touches of urbanity appeared in the community, including an operational printing press with the arrival in 1684 of William Nuthead, the Chesapeake's first printer, as well as the opening of one of colonial America's earliest coffee houses in that same decade. No precise estimate of the population is possible due to the loss of records, but by the late 1600s, a community of at least several hundred people had developed on the St. Mary's Townlands.

Sudden change arrived from political events echoing throughout the Atlantic World. A 1688 revolution in England overthrew the Catholic King James II and replaced him with his son-in-law and daughter, William and Mary. Based largely on unfounded rumors of a Papist plot involving Iroquois attacking Protestants, many Maryland Protestants rose up the following year, claiming the government of the Catholic Lord Baltimore would not protect them, and rebelled against Charles Calvert. They took control of the government and petitioned William and Mary to become a royal colony. The English Crown agreed, appointing Sir Lionel Copley as the first royal governor. Copley's first efforts included making the Church of England Maryland's official church, but he died in late 1693. The second royal governor, Francis Nicholson, took charge the following year, immediately acting to move the government from St. Mary's City to a Protestant stronghold called Arundell-town (later renamed Annapolis). This action both symbolically and practically removed the government from any association with the Catholic Lords Baltimore. As the provincial government relocated in 1695, most residents of St. Mary's City moved to the new capital, because providing services was their major source of income. While county government continued at St. Mary's into the early 1700s, all urban development was abruptly halted in 1695.

Largely abandoned, St. Mary's City retained its seventeenth-century infrastructure for a few decades afterward, but the wooden buildings and fences rapidly decayed without maintenance. By 1740, residents had demolished most of the structures and converted the lands of the former capital into agricultural fields. In a land sale to an individual named John Mackall in 1774, the entire area of the former city was consolidated into a single plantation. This plantation and its agrarian landscape remained in the possession of Mackall's descendants, the Bromes, for the next two centuries. The last seventeenth-century structure, the 1676 State House, survived as an Episcopal church until 1833, when it was demolished and a new church built from its bricks.

Marylanders remembered this was the state's founding site and first capital, and pilgrimages to it began in the mid-nineteenth century. Parno and Miller detail the nineteenth- and twentieth-century history of commemoration across the St. Mary's City landscape in chapter 16. As a belated commemoration of Maryland's 200th anniversary, St. Mary's Female Seminary for young women was established near the old State House site in 1840. The seminary had a troubled history of financial difficulty and administrative dysfunction, but it survived and by the mid-twentieth century became a Junior College and in 1965, St. Mary's College of Maryland (SMCM). Sivilich et al. combine the archaeological and documentary records to examine late nineteenth- and early twentieth-century life at the Seminary in chapter 15.

The anticipated growth of the newly created college and the resulting effects on the site of Maryland's founding became a matter of concern to local citizens led by a new resident: retired marine general Robert Hogaboom. This grassroots preservation effort resulted in the appointment of a special committee by Maryland's governor in 1965 to consider the future of the state's first capital. These deliberations led to the establishment of the St. Mary's City Commission by the legislature in 1966; it was renamed the Historic St. Mary's City Commission in 1997. The commission's legislated mission was and continues to be the preservation, study, and interpretation of the site for the benefit of the public. Details of this effort are provided by Parno and Miller in chapter 16.

Exploring Early Maryland

The first professional employee of the commission was historian Lois Green Carr. Beginning in 1967, she examined the surviving documents about the original settlement. As the commissioners already suspected, Carr found there were no period maps, detailed descriptions, or diaries, and only a scatter of letters and surviving land records pertaining to the first city. On the other hand, Maryland had a rich collection of legal records from the seventeenth century, and the Maryland Historical Society had purchased a remarkable collection of seventeenth- and eighteenth-century Calvert family documents called the Calvert Papers. It was obvious that much remained unknown about the former city, and vigorous historical, archaeological, and architectural research would be essential to produce a more complete understanding of the site and colony. This process was aided by a critical decision the new commission made in its first year that all museum development would be based upon and preceded by solid scholarship.

Before full-scale work on the seventeenth century could begin, however, development at SMCM necessitated the first archaeology sponsored by Historic St. Mary's City (HSMC). At the proposed site of a new dormitory, an archaeological survey revealed evidence of a colonial site. Archaeologist

Glenn Little was contracted to evaluate the site in 1969. He found the remains of a house built ca. 1725 and glass bottle seals identifying its owner, John Hicks. An intensive excavation followed with the discovery of the first colonial earthfast building identified in Maryland and the recovery of an impressive collection of ca. 1725–1750 artifacts. To better understand the site, Carr conducted an important study of the eighteenth-century neighborhood of St. Mary's City, with a focus upon household probate inventories (1973). The results of this important project are summarized by Stone and Israel in chapter 12 (see figure 1.3 for a map of sites discussed in this volume).

The Hicks site excavations were not the first archaeology in St. Mary's City, however. Colonial Williamsburg architectural archaeologists tested the site of the 1676 State House in 1933 to collect data for its reconstruction. The following year, the brick floor of the Van Sweringen site was uncovered as part of the public display for the 300th anniversary of Maryland's founding. This was the first exhibition of seventeenth-century archaeological remains in the state. Soon afterward, a young architectural historian named Henry Chandlee Forman began an investigation of St. Mary's City sites. He uncovered or tested the foundations of several structures, including the Van Sweringen Council Chamber, a large building he called Smith's Ordinary (later determined to be the Leonard Calvert House), the mansion of St. Peter's, and the 1660s Brick Chapel site. Forman had worked previously at Jamestown, and he combined that experience with his St. Mary's City findings in a book titled *Jamestown and St. Mary's: Buried Cities of Romance* (1938). This volume demonstrated that St. Mary's City contained an abundance of archaeological evidence, and its publication was very significant in inspiring the initial efforts to preserve St. Mary's. With his direct knowledge, Forman served as an invaluable consultant to the commission during its first decade.

In 1970, the commission hired two more scholars: Cary Carson, as a social historian to explore seventeenth-century architecture, and historical archaeologist Garry Wheeler Stone. Together, Carr, Carson, and Stone developed an innovative research program that combined documentary, architectural, and archaeological evidence to better understand early Maryland and its first city. Carr led the investigation of legal records, especially probate inventories, to reveal the lives of rich and poor settlers. She pioneered methods to statistically analyze inventory content, including some of the first use of computers for historical analysis (Carr and Walsh 1980). Carr and her colleagues conducted novel studies on a broad range of topics including colonial demography, the tobacco economy, immigrant opportunity, the beginnings of slavery, and the lives of seventeenth-century women (Carr 1974; Carr and Walsh 1977; Carr and Menard 1979; Carr et al. 1988; Main

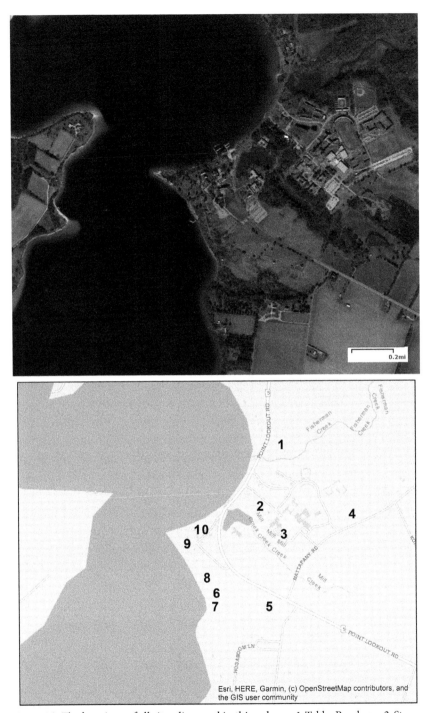

Figure 1.3. The locations of all sites discussed in this volume: *1*, Tabbs Purchase; *2*, St. John's; *3*, John Hicks; *4*, 18ST1-205; *5*, Chapel Site; *6*, Town Center–Leonard Calvert House, Pope's Fort, Smith's Ordinary, Brome House; *7*, Print House and Brome Slave Quarters; *8*, Van Sweringen's; *9*, Church Point, the Mulberry Tree, 1676 State House, Copley Vault, Trinity Church; *10*, St. Mary's Female Seminary. (Figure by Travis G. Parno and Henry M. Miller.)

1982; Menard 1975, 1977; Walsh 1977, 1985; Walsh and Menard 1974). One of the more remarkable finds was the only plantation account book from the seventeenth-century Chesapeake. Its analysis provided the first in-depth understanding of how plantations operated during the era, information synthesized in the award-winning volume *Robert Cole's World* (Carr et al. 1991); this topic was further developed by Walsh (2010). A synthesis of much of the HSMC historical research is found in Russo and Russo (2012).

Carson studied colonial architecture in both America and Britain, evaluating not only changes in construction but how buildings reflected shifts in social dynamics. Working with architectural historians of the Maryland Historical Trust, this team found that many homes attributed to the 1600s were actually of later construction. A new method of dendrochronology, or tree-ring dating, confirmed the later dates of structures (Heikkenen and Edwards 1983; Stone 1987). To the surprise of scholars, only three buildings survived in Maryland from the seventeenth century, with the earliest dating ca. 1684. These findings significantly altered the understanding of the region's architectural history, sometimes to the dismay of the homeowners (Ranzetta 2010:2–7). They also bolstered the archaeological findings from seventeenth-century sites at St. Mary's City and in Virginia. Instead of elegant brick edifices, excavations demonstrated that most colonists lived in cheap, earthfast buildings supported on wooden posts. Stone and Morrison describe evidence for earthfast construction at St. Mary's City in chapter 2. A group of scholars summarized these findings in the pivotal article "Impermanent Architecture in the Southern American Colonies" (Carson et al. 1981). Inspired by this architectural and historical research, a student in HSMC's 1974 Field School in Historical Archaeology, George McDaniel, began an investigation which led to his doctoral thesis and subsequent influential book (1982). McDaniel's study was the first to examine African American rural life and architecture in Maryland, not only recording homes that are now destroyed, but also interviewing elderly individuals who had dwelled in those buildings. He documented a people and way of life that had been largely ignored by historians.

Exploring the Seventeenth Century through Archaeology

Stone created the museum's archaeological research program and led the first exploration of seventeenth-century sites in Maryland using modern archaeological methods. The initial effort, however, demonstrated the unpredictability of archaeology. A house cellar depression visible on a seventeenth-century tract called Pope's Freehold (named for George Washington's first

American ancestor, Nathaniel Pope), was thought to be an early building. Excavation proved instead that it was an eighteenth-century home with its cellar filled by nineteenth-century trash (see figure 1.3). Nevertheless, this excavation of Tabbs Purchase spurred a number of important studies, one of which is reported by Miller in chapter 13. To conduct this excavation, Stone created the HSMC Field School in Historical Archaeology, in cooperation with SMCM and the Smithsonian Institution. This class is offered annually and is today the longest continuously running historical archaeological field school in the United States.

It was in 1972 that exploration of the first seventeenth-century site began at the St. John's plantation with the museum's second field school (see figure 1.3). Archaeologists found the remains of this 1638 house to be remarkably well preserved, and four years of excavation produced a plethora of new evidence about early Maryland. Its builder, Secretary of State John Lewger, had brought an English architectural style to Maryland. Modeled on hall-and-parlor houses in southeast England, St. John's featured complex joinery, a masonry foundation of cobblestones, a lobby entrance, and a central H-shaped chimney. Stone's doctoral dissertation unraveled the complex architectural story of this important site (1982). Researchers found that all subsequent structures erected there were built using the more cost-effective earthfast method. Mitchell et al. offer a summary of these findings in chapter 7. Stone also directed Maryland's earliest landscape archaeology on a seventeenth-century site at St. John's, focusing upon the identification of artifact distribution patterns and the variety of fences that had shaped spaces around the site through time. A related innovation during the St. John's project was the application of soil chemistry to a seventeenth-century site. Robert Keeler pioneered both distributional analysis and the soil chemical study in his doctoral dissertation (1978). Hurry and Keeler describe the notable findings from this analysis in chapter 3.

Artifacts from St. John's also provided the first insights into the material world of Maryland's seventeenth-century colonists and their new environment. When the excavations began, many of the artifacts, such as ceramics and tobacco pipes, were undefined, and much work was necessary to determine the origin and dates of their manufacture and use. As a result, the St. John's site became the "type site" for subsequent analyses of seventeenth-century sites in Maryland. It also became the first 1600s site in the state at which ceramic sherds were converted into vessels for more comprehensive analysis, leading to the development of a new analytical tool called the Potomac Typological System (Beaudry et al. 1983). Hurry presents some of these findings in chapter 5. Excavators recovered specimens of tobacco pipes made of local clay, most likely produced by Maryland Indians (Henry 1979). These proved a strong material indicator of the interaction between indigenous people and the colonists (see chapter 6). St. John's also yielded one of the largest samples of early turned window leads that were found to bear dates on their interiors, offering another useful analytical tool (Egan et al. 1986). Animal remains from St. John's gave the first insight about the changing diet of Chesapeake colonists and the nature of the natural environment, as detailed in Miller's doctoral dissertation (1984). Oyster shells recovered from St. John's were used to develop new methods of human subsistence and environmental analysis (Kent 1988; Kirby and Miller 2005).

The second major seventeenth-century site investigated by the museum was the Van Sweringen Council Chamber (see figure 1.3). Built as an office in 1664, the structure was acquired by Dutch immigrant Garrett Van Sweringen in 1677, and he made major improvements. He converted the building into the most elegant hotel in the colony, patronized by the elite, including Lord Baltimore and royal governors (Miller 2008). Among the more notable activities of Van Sweringen was his opening of one of the first coffee houses in English colonial America at the site in the late 1600s (King and Miller 1987). This was a site that provided essential services to elite travelers. Public inns or ordinaries were a vital element of the first capital, and their role in seventeenth-century entertainment is discussed by Parno and Riordan in chapter 10. Museum excavations began at Van Sweringen's inn in 1974 and a total of seven seasons of work were conducted at the site. The first five seasons formed the basis for Julia King's doctoral dissertation (King 1990), and the artifacts from the Van Sweringen site afforded development of a new analytic methodology for comparing archaeological midden deposits using plow zone samples (King and Miller 1987). St. John's and Van Sweringen's were the central learning sites where Historic St. Mary's City (HSMC) archaeologists acquired the skills to begin deciphering the archaeological record of seventeenth-century Maryland.

For the museum, the next step was to find the city. In 1974, despite having no original maps, incomplete land records, cursory descriptions, and limited archaeological data, Carr and Stone produced a hypothetical map of the city's seventeenth-century layout. This suggested a scattered village with little urban character, as the few period descriptions also implied. For the archaeologists, this map formed a critical model which could be tested with newly acquired archaeological evidence. The first major test came in 1981–1983 when a National Endowment for the Humanities grant funded a thorough search for the center of the city. Surface collection and the excavation of test squares found that the sites predicted to lie at the projected crossroads of the town were not there. Instead, materials clustered to the west, closer to the river and in the vicinity of the surviving 1840s Brome Plantation house.

Several years of intensive excavation successfully identified important buildings in that area (see figure 1.3). The first and perhaps most significant was the home of the first governor, Leonard Calvert, which later served as Maryland's first state house. Wesley Willoughby (2015) analyzed archaeological evidence from the site to demonstrate its role as a critical public building in the seventeenth-century city; he describes the results of this analysis in chapter 9. Work at the Calvert House also revealed a major surprise: a fort had surrounded the building. Dating to 1645, the fort is directly related to the English Civil Wars and is discussed by Charles Fithian in chapter 8. Nearby, excavators uncovered another building with its post molds filled with ash and charcoal, indicating destruction by fire. Artifacts suggested a brief occupation ca. 1660–ca. 1680, and this evidence allowed identification of the site as Smith's Ordinary, built in 1667 and burned down in 1678. Excavators next located a storehouse that belonged to French immigrant Mark Cordea named "Cordea's Hope" and a structure called "the Lawyers' Messuage," or lawyer's office (H. M. Miller 1986). When these buildings and associated fences were mapped, the archaeologists were surprised to find that these four principal structures—the Calvert House, Smith's Ordinary, Cordea's Hope, and the Lawyer's Messuage—had been placed to form a square at the intersection of the city's main streets. Instead of a random development, as historians had first suspected, the finding suggested at least a rudimentary level of planning.

As survey work continued, additional sites were discovered and added to the overall plan. Rediscovering the landscape through archaeology eventually allowed the first relatively accurate map of Maryland's first capital to be developed. These efforts revealed that nearly all the structures were made of wood with very few brick buildings. St. Mary's City was in essence a settlement built of earthfast architecture. Only four structures in the core area of the town were fully brick—the 1660s Chapel, the 1676 State House, and adjacent Prison are three of them. There is reference to a brick Jesuit "School of the Humanities," but its precise location is uncertain (Browne 1903:81). It may have been located on the remains of a brick structure of unknown function that has been found near the primary land entrance to the city. Although not yet intensively investigated, its brick foundation has been confirmed by both survey and testing (Riordan 1988). Just outside the city was one other brick building: Chancellor Philip Calvert's ca. 1678 Palladian-inspired mansion called St. Peter's (Riordan 2004a).

Southeast of the center of town sat a powerful symbol of Maryland's experiment in freedom of conscience: the Brick Chapel. The first wooden chapel was built on the site ca. 1635; it was burned down by soldiers in the 1645 attack on St. Mary's City. Political turmoil prevented any rebuilding until after the restoration of Charles II in 1660. Around 1665, the Jesuits began construction of the first major brick building in Maryland—a Catholic chapel. It was a unique symbol of Maryland's religious policy because it was a freestanding church, not part of a dwelling. Nowhere else in the English-speaking world at the time could such a Catholic church be built. From the mid-1660s to early 1700s, it was the centerpiece of the Catholic faith in Maryland. But on the order of Maryland's protestant governor in 1704, the door was locked and the building no longer allowed to be used for worship. A decade or so later, the Jesuits dismantled the Chapel, recycling most of its fabric. The Chapel was forgotten until 1938, when it was rediscovered by Henry Chandlee Forman during his architectural explorations at St. Mary's City (1938).

After testing in 1983, HSMC began investigating the Chapel in 1988, and excavators fully uncovered the foundations of the structure (Riordan et al. 1994). Well built of locally made bricks and roof tiles on a Latin cross–shaped plan, it featured plastered interior walls, multipart windows formed with specially made mullion and jamb bricks, and a floor paved with approximately 14 tons of stone apparently imported from Europe (Keys et al. 2016). The Chapel's facade and window mullions and jambs were also probably plastered. Architecturally, it was similar to contemporaneous Jesuit churches being built in other locations around the world. On the frontier of early Maryland, it was a very impressive structure that physically expressed the policy of religious freedom offered by the colony. Surprisingly, and despite intensive research, this prominent building is virtually undocumented historically. Only one brief description exists. In 1697, the anti-Catholic Royal Governor Francis Nicholson wrote that the Jesuits had "a good brick Chapel at St. Mary's" (Browne 1903:81). Based upon intensive excavation, the sparse documentary evidence, and architectural analysis, the Chapel was rebuilt in the early 2000s as an exhibit.

Archaeology in and around the Chapel also uncovered hundreds of human graves. The 3-foot-thick and 5-foot-deep foundations of the 1660s Chapel cut through a number of burials, indicating that they predated the mid-1660s. Most likely, these were related to interment in the ca. 1635–ca. 1660 period. Because the first chapel was built here, the location became recognized as a burial ground. No burial registers survive and the identities of the people buried here are unknown. Excavations and a ground-penetrating radar survey suggest there may be more than 400 burials, making it the largest seventeenth-century burial ground in Maryland. In preparation for reconstructing the Chapel, archaeologists cleared an exterior corridor 10 feet from the foundation and in the process excavated 66 graves (Riordan 2000). Archaeology has been able to identify only three people buried at the Chapel, and this is because they were treated differently from the hundreds of others interred here. Instead of a shroud and/or wood coffin, they were buried in lead coffins. Archaeologists discovered three lead coffins inside the chapel in 1990, the first such coffins found by archaeologists in North America. In 1992, HSMC began a major scientific investigation to identify these individuals and learn as much as possible about their lives and the seventeenth-century natural environment. Incorporating the skills of a wide range of scientists and engineers, this project succeeded in identifying the coffin occupants as members of Maryland's founding family—the Calverts. Bruwelheide et al. summarize this project and the invaluable bioarchaeological evidence assembled during it in chapter 11.

Precise placement of the Chapel and three other brick buildings on the archaeological map of the city led to a remarkable discovery. St. Mary's City had a layout far different from that suggested by the map hypothesized in 1974 (see figure 1.4). The brick buildings were placed at the same distance from the town square, and each structure served as a focal point for one of the four principal streets of the city. This arrangement and the associated streets formed two symmetrical triangles (see figure 1.5). Placing these four symbolically significant buildings at the nodes of the street system is the application of the concept of perspective, a Classical idea rediscovered during the Renaissance. Perhaps most notable about this plan is the placement of the government (State House and prison) and church (Chapel and the possible Jesuit school) on opposite sides of the city, in keeping with Lord Baltimore's policy of separating religion from government. Thus, archaeology discovered that the plan of Maryland's first capital was not that of a scattered village, but instead was a community laid out using Baroque design, the most sophisticated ideas of urban planning at the time (Miller 1988a, 1999).

Although the colony's first capital was never large, it featured a unique plan meant to create an impressive city as it grew. Sudden removal of the government in 1695 halted all development, and the very existence of this remarkably early urban planning effort in colonial America was soon forgotten. It seems to have had one enduring influence, however. When Governor Francis Nicholson designed the new capital of Annapolis in the late 1690s, he used the same Baroque planning ideas, but intentionally placed the State House and Anglican Church side by side on adjoining circles, with major streets radiating outward from these circles. This was in strong contrast to

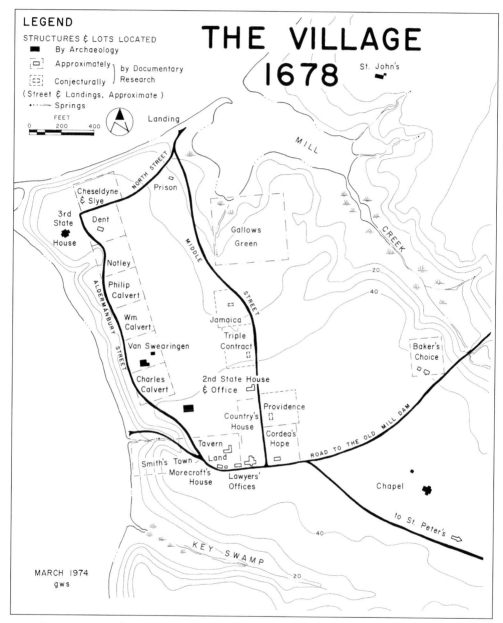

Figure 1.4. Map of St. Mary's City created in 1974 based on HSMC research into the early town's layout. (Map by Lois Green Carr and Garry Wheeler Stone, courtesy of HSMC.)

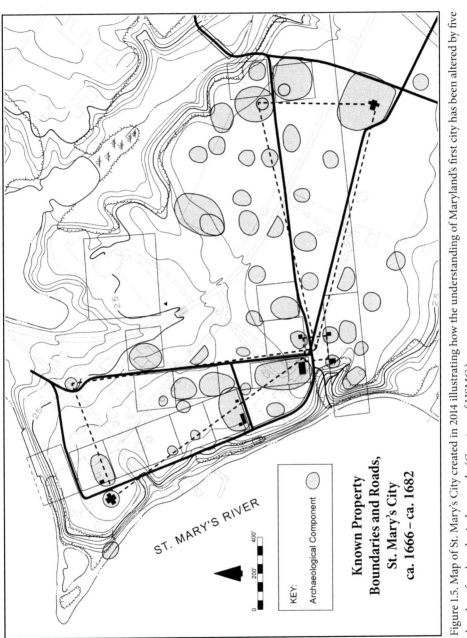

KEY:

◯ Archaeological Component

**Known Property
Boundaries and Roads,
St. Mary's City
ca. 1666 – ca. 1682**

ST. MARY'S RIVER

0   200'   400'

Figure 1.5. Map of St. Mary's City created in 2014 illustrating how the understanding of Maryland's first city has been altered by five decades of archaeological research. (Courtesy of HSMC.)

St. Mary's and symbolically expressed the new social order of Maryland with a formal state religion: the Church of England.

LATER SITES AT ST. MARY'S CITY

With the movement of the government to Annapolis in 1695, growth of the city ceased and it was largely abandoned. However, some people continued to live at St. Mary's City, gradually transforming the urban setting into an agrarian landscape. In addition to the John Hicks site previously noted, another major site was the Hicks-Mackall plantation (ca. 1754–1816). It was excavated in 2011–2014 to mitigate an area where the museum's new archaeological laboratory and SMCM buildings have been constructed. The next major plantation was established in 1840 by John Mackall Brome, who built his new house on top of the Leonard Calvert site. The plantations built by the Hicks, Mackall, and Brome families controlled virtually all the land of the first city from the eighteenth into the mid-twentieth centuries. The plantations were worked by enslaved Africans and African Americans. Sites associated with enslaved communities, especially houses occupied by the enslaved people who worked the agricultural fields, can be more difficult to find than those of the plantation owners.

In this volume, we present two studies about the enslaved communities at St. Mary's City. The first addresses the fact that sites inhabited by enslaved workers often leave fewer archaeological traces on the landscape, meaning that some survey methods can miss them. Reconnaissance in an area targeted for SMCM development detected a site dating ca. 1780–1830, but very little historical evidence could be found to identify its occupants. Archaeological and documentary analysis concluded that the site was home to members of the enslaved workforce of the John Mackall plantation. In chapter 4, Mitchell and Miller use this site as a case study to evaluate the effectiveness of different survey methods in detecting sites with less archaeological visibility.

The enslaved people of the Brome Plantation are somewhat better documented. This community grew to 60 people by the time of the Civil War. Archaeology indicates they lived mostly in a row of quarters placed along a ravine. One duplex quarter survives, and excavations were conducted around it in 1992. Nearby stood a single quarter demolished ca. 1930; HSMC archaeologists excavated this former dwelling in 2000–2004. The archaeology of these quarters and the story of the Brome enslaved community was the subject of a doctoral dissertation by Terry Brock (2014) and he summarizes his findings in chapter 14. Brock not only examines the period of enslavement, but significantly, he traces how African Americans living in St. Mary's City used freedom after emancipation to improve their lives.

Nineteenth-century lifeways are also investigated at a tenant site by Miller in chapter 13. The lives of St. Mary's Female Seminary students in the late nineteenth century and early twentieth century are discussed in chapter 15. A concluding chapter examines how Marylanders have both remembered and forgotten St. Mary's City over the centuries since the government moved away in 1695, and the steps gradually taken to restore its place in history.

This volume offers a small sample of the many investigations conducted by archaeologists at St. Mary's City over the past half century. Those efforts, combined with the historical research by Carr and others, have transformed our understanding of early Maryland and the broader Chesapeake. Just as the historians develop new ways of studying documents, such as probate inventories, archaeologists at HSMC developed new methods to decipher the archaeological records created by the site's many inhabitants. That important process of making new discoveries and expanding the capability of historical archaeology continues at Historic St. Mary's City to this day.

PART 1

DISCOVERING
THE PAST

New Approaches and Methods

2

From Humus Mold to Stout Building

Reverse Engineering Post-in-the-Ground Structures

GARRY WHEELER STONE AND ALEXANDER H. MORRISON II

As archaeologists at a historic site, it is our responsibility to help visitors to envision the vanished past. Where were the dwellings, outbuildings, gardens, fields, and roads that framed their occupants' lives? The challenge is fascinating and daunting—none more so than reconstructing long-gone earthfast structures—buildings that left only disturbed dirt and humus casts of timbers. Varying in size and shape, these wooden members—posts, studs, stakes, sills, sleepers, puncheons, and palisadoes—were the framing of colonial buildings. While some St. Mary's City buildings had masonry foundations, many more had timber footings.

The dissection of earthfast structures is tedious, requiring precision and specialized study. The additional time required is productive. We have learned to recognize different ways of framing structures. Was the building constructed with preassembled sidewall frames or with individual pairs of posts with a connecting timber (called bent frames)? How was the building dimensioned? Was the carpenter skilled or unskilled? Did he make mistakes? Collecting the information needed to answer such questions requires a higher level of data collection than simply mapping and cross-sectioning features. The analysis of earthfast structures should begin in the field as soon as the structure is recognized. The best dimensions of an earthfast structure are taken directly from the dirt and not from the drawing board or computer screen.

At St. Mary's City, we learned how to interrogate timber molds by excavating a number of seventeenth-century sites, including St. John's, Garrett Van Sweringen's inn, William Smith's ordinary, and William and Dinah Nuthead's print shop. Most of these sites included not only a timber-framed principal structure, but also several outbuildings and numerous landscape features. In these excavations, we were able to investigate a variety of building types and construction techniques. We also studied the timber-framing of surviving historic Chesapeake houses such as Sotterley plantation, while keeping an eye on the work conducted by colleagues. Finally, there was much to be learned by practicing experimental archaeology while reconstructing timber-framed exhibits on the St. Mary's City landscape. These lessons were learned over many years. Over that time, we developed a rigorous methodology for excavating and understanding the archaeological traces of timber-framed buildings that is as useful today as it was nearly 50 years ago.

Our first seventeenth-century excavation was St. John's, the 1638 home of the colony's secretary and later the residence of Governor Charles Calvert. In 1972, when we started the excavation, we had no idea that we were taking the first step toward becoming experts in post-in-the-ground architecture. After all, St. John's was an English-framed house with sills supported by a stone foundation. We found the stone foundation and many post holes. Most were from fence posts, but others were from outbuildings with hole-set timbers. Still others were from additions and repairs to the main house (see chapter 7; Stone 1982).

As we began excavating at St. John's, we used standard procedures for working in a former agricultural field: (1) excavate the plow zone; (2) trowel-clean the subsoil surface; (3) map the exposed features; (4) excavate half of the feature and draw the cross section, and (5) complete feature excavation. All excavation was by cultural stratigraphy. Thus we excavated pits in multiple layers. For timber molds and holes, this meant carefully separating artifacts obtained from the construction period post hole fill from the demolition period artifacts obtained from the timber mold.

Our first modification to these procedures came in 1973, as we recognized that, at the bottom of the plow zone, the dimensions and shapes of timber molds and post holes frequently were distorted by rodents and tree roots. So, when better-defined feature shapes emerged during excavation, we began adding them to the square plan drawing in colored pencil. The soils at St. John's are a sandy loam and have suffered little erosion. In a more clayey soil where the top of the subsoil has been plowed away, timber molds and post holes may be better defined below the plow zone.

In 1974, we made our second change. Having discovered the post molds and holes of a 20-by-30-foot outbuilding in front of the St. John's dwelling, we uncovered all of the post holes and molds at one time, stretched strings to mark the exterior lines of the walls, and then dimensioned the structure, corner to corner and post mold to post mold. When diagonal measurements indicated that the building corners were not square, we set up a transit over

Figure 2.1. The 1650s storehouse/quarter at St. John's showing the pattern of post holes revealed by archaeology. Arrows indicate the main structural posts. (Courtesy of HSMC.)

one corner to measure the error (1 degree). The evidence of this building is seen in figure 2.1. Simon Overzee constructed the building shortly after 1655, most likely as a storehouse. The post mold/post hole relationships suggest that it was bent-reared (for more on the architectural analysis of the St. John's site features, see chapter 7).

Our 1970s archaeology was not undertaken in a vacuum. We benefited from Little's and Israel's earlier work at the John Hicks site (see chapter 12), prior and ongoing work in Virginia, and Cary Carson's architectural research. When Carson began advocating a publication on seventeenth-century architecture, we decided to determine the best method for excavating a building with hole-set timbers. In addition to our work at the St. John's site, we spent much of the 1970s and early 1980s excavating the Van Sweringen inn and outbuildings. The inn was home to Dutch immigrant Garrett Van Sweringen, his family, and their servants and slaves. As one of the most fashionable establishments in town, Van Sweringen's inn was the frequent site of meetings of the Governor's Council and visits from prominent guests. In addition to the inn itself, excavations at the site revealed kitchens, a dairy, and one of the earliest coffee houses in the English colonies (Miller 2008).

Our 1977 test case was the "Coffee House," an outbuilding behind Van Sweringen's inn. The building measured 18.5 × 21 feet and was supported by

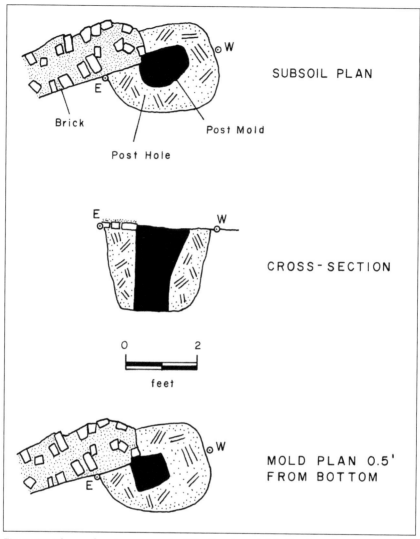

Figure 2.2. The southeast corner post of Van Sweringen's "Coffee House" excavated in half-foot increments to reveal how the post mold shape changes with depth. (Drawings by Alexander H. Morrison II and Chinh Hoang, courtesy of HSMC.)

timbers at the corners and smaller timbers in the centers of the long sides (only one of the latter had survived deep plowing). The "Coffee House" timber molds and holes were excavated in 0.5-foot horizontal slices; first, half of the mold was excavated 0.5-foot deep, then half of the hole, and then the section was drawn. Next, the other half was excavated, and the plan drawn. This process was repeated until the bottoms of the holes and molds were reached. This method was tedious and time consuming but yielded excellent evidence about the original building. It showed us that the timber shape seen on the surface of subsoil can be quite different from that of the original post, as seen in figure 2.2. Pulling the post, erosion as the timber rotted, or bioturbation can create a much different shape at the top that does not reflect the dimensions of the original post.

Furthermore, not all hole-set timbers were hewn to uniform dimensions. A surviving post-in-the-ground structure (Cedar Park, Anne Arundel County, 1702: Heikkenen and Edwards 1983:17) has square posts above grade and round posts below grade. Excavated examples of similar "club foot" posts are known, including at the circa 1690 Van Sweringen kitchen. At the Print House site, the hole-set wall posts were reared with their small, waney ends down (a waney post is one that retains a portion of the original rounded shape of the tree). So our recommendation is to determine the depth of the holes, choose a depth at which to re-plan the molds and holes (say, 0.5 feet above their bottoms), and cautiously begin sectioning one mold toward that depth. If the timber mold changes from square to round, gets smaller, or twists, then you may need to stop and re-plan the molds below surface disturbance as well as at 0.5 feet above the bottoms of the holes.

In 1980, we were faced with a huge challenge: the construction and interpretation of a representative Maryland plantation of the 1660s—the Godiah Spray Plantation. Historians Lois Carr, Lorena Walsh, and Russell Menard provided the needed agricultural, demographic, and economic modeling; Cary Carson and colleagues provided information on Colonial architecture; Housewright John O'Rourke reinvented clapboard construction; and we provided details on post-in-the-ground construction. As our work at St. John's and Van Sweringen's did not provide adequate prototypes, we looked to the work of our Virginia colleagues. Fraser Neiman's excavations at the Clifts Plantation were informative. Post hole orientation showed that the manor house of ca. 1670 had been "bent" reared, while a quarter of ca. 1690 had been constructed with preassembled sidewall frames, both reared in the same direction (Neiman 1980a). These two principal methods of erecting earthfast buildings are shown in figure 2.3.

We based the plantation exhibit buildings on surviving early buildings in England and Maryland and archaeological evidence of hole-set posts. The buildings were constructed with the same tools that were used in the seventeenth century: felling and broad axes, adzes, saws, augers, and chisels. Walls and roofs were covered with 5-foot clapboards riven (split) from white oak with froe and club. Building construction was both living history and experimental archaeology. As we reared the plantation dwelling and tobacco houses, we realized that our reconstructions were taking too long.

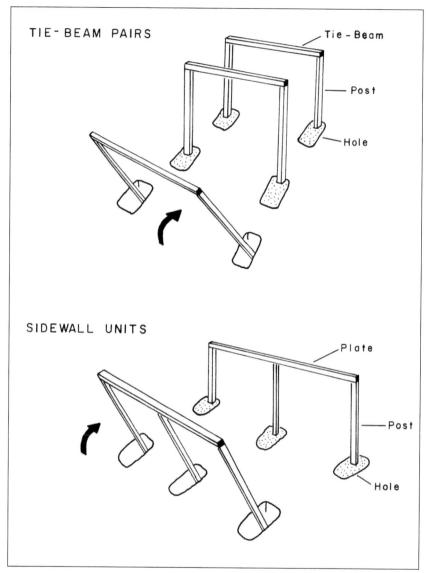

Figure 2.3. The two principal methods of raising preassembled frames of earthfast build-ings. (Drawings by Alexander H. Morrison II and Chinh Hoang, courtesy of HSMC.)

Research in seventeenth-century records revealed that small planters' dwellings and outbuildings were inexpensive. Starting with standing oak trees, three carpenters could complete a small dwelling in about three weeks. So as we designed a small farmer or tenant house of ca. 1670, we tried to sim-plify. The entire building would have only six mortise and tenon joints (post to plate) and no diagonal wall braces. All the other joints were lapped into notches and fastened with nails or wooden pins. As anticipated, carpenter Peter Rivers was able to frame and erect the building quickly. The wooden chimney, carefully copied from a surviving English chimney, took far too long to construct. We still had more to learn about seventeenth-century construction.

In early 1981, we did learn more. Crawling beneath the floors of St. Mary's County's oldest home, Sotterley, 1703–1704, we discovered that the oldest part of the house was post-in-the-ground (now encased in brick). The wall sills were lapped into notches in the cypress posts. When we wiggled into the narrow spaces behind the attic walls, we found similar lap joints connecting the horizontal timbers at the top of the walls (wall plates) to the posts. There were no time-consuming and thus expensive mortise and tenon joints in either the wall or roof frames (Stone 1982:266–271; John O'Rourke 2006, pers. comm.).

ARCHAEOLOGICAL CASE STUDIES

The following are four earthfast buildings excavated by HSMC. These case studies show a range of construction methods and how the careful reading of the post hole and mold evidence can reveal the ways that housewrights built these structures. These building plans are shown in figure 2.4.

Van Sweringen Council Chamber Inn (18 ST1-19)

The kitchen's footprint was defined by a fireplace foundation reused from the Phase 1 kitchen, a brick floor, and eight post molds and holes, as seen in figure 2.4A. The post molds were from unhewn, "club foot" posts, making it impossible to precisely dimension the structure, but it measured approximately 20'-8" long by 18'-6" wide (four 5-foot clapboards long by three boards and a door wide). Inspection of surviving clapboard shows that 5-foot clapboards are approximately 5'-6" long and the ends of the boards were beveled with a drawknife and overlapped during installation. Our experimental archaeology in reconstruction demonstrates that this minimizes rain penetration and allows overlapping boards to be well secured with one nail. The central post on the south wall of Van Sweringen's kitchen had been replaced during the life of the structure. As both north and south post holes are stepped in the same direction, we believe that both wall frames were preassembled prior to the carpenter recruiting extra men to push up the frames (the sloping one side of a set of post holes makes it easier to tip the posts into the holes). Both frames were reared north to south.

The Phase 2 kitchen presented only one real challenge: interpreting the

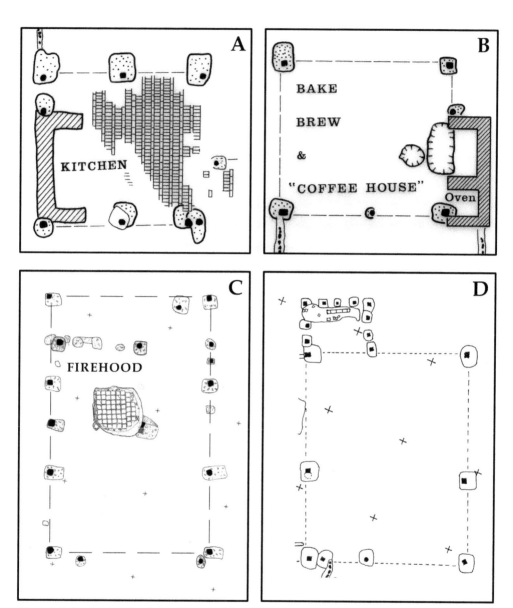

Figure 2.4. Comparing the plans of four earthfast buildings excavated at St. Mary's City: *A*, Van Sweringen Kitchen; *B*, Van Sweringen Coffee House; *C*, Smith's Ordinary; and *D*, The Print House. (Courtesy of HSMC.)

two post molds at the southeast corner. Based on colleagues' evidence of "propped" buildings, one possibility was that the kitchen corner post had begun to fail and was shored up by an adjacent "prop" post (King 1996). However, when we excavated the hole and its two molds, we found that the corner post had been installed last—evidence of a mistake. The carpenter had cut the plate of the south wall exactly 2 feet short. Apparently, he did not recognize his error until after rearing the walls. Then he had to install a new corner post and extend the rafter plate.

The kitchen was reconstructed with hand-hewn locust posts. Using Sotterley as a prototype, the wall plates and interrupted sills (short sills fitted between the posts) are notched and lapped to the posts and fastened with locust pins. Carpenter James Laws rove most of the 2×4-inch scantlings for the roof trusses from one high-quality white oak log in a short morning—a remarkable demonstration of what old-growth oak made possible for frontier carpenters.

Van Sweringen's Coffee House

Our 1977 test case, Garret van Sweringen's original bake and brew house, was a building made into a fashionable coffee house. The "Coffee House" was not a post-in-the-ground building. It was a building framed on continuous sills supported above the ground by short timber pilings, timbers known to colonial Chesapeake carpenters as "blocks" (figure 2.4B). We determined this from the variable orientation and depth of the block holes. Their basal elevations varied by 0.80 feet. We were familiar with the timber mold and hole signature of block-supported sills from Little and Israel's excavations at the John Hicks site (see chapter 12).

The coffee house was dimensioned for 6-foot clapboards. It was three boards and a door in length and three boards wide. The locations of the ante-hearth, subfloor pits showed that the ground floor joists were laid on approximate 3-foot centers (Stone 1983:12, figure 8a).

Smith's Ordinary (18 ST1-13B)

Captain William Smith had enclosed, but not finished this 30'-9" by 20'-2" "ordinary" when he became fatally ill late in 1667 (an ordinary provided price-regulated food, lodging, and stabling). Smith was a recent immigrant, a carpenter, and an entrepreneur. We believe that the archaeology of the building reveals that Smith or his journeyman was a reasonably competent carpenter. However, the carpenter had more to learn about clapboard carpentry, and, working in haste, he made one glaring error.

The evidence for the exterior wall frame of the ordinary consisted of eight post holes and molds and the shallow remnants of holes for three wall studs. Two of the holes retained rectangular molds (see figure 2.4C). The hole-set studs showed that the building's walls had been constructed without sills. The building was carefully excavated. Diagonal measurements revealed that the east and west walls were imperfectly aligned. Cross sections of the timber molds revealed that two had axe-cut ends. The molds were re-planned twice below the feature surfaces. The timber molds varied in dimension from 7" × 8" to 9" × 9½", and the northwest corner post had been hewn from a timber with enough curve so that the foot of the post had only three corners. The building was destroyed by fire in 1678. Charcoal from post molds revealed that the wall posts had been hewn from black locust while the posts of a later shed addition (not illustrated) were white oak. White oak is rot resistant, although not as durable as black locust. Red oak and yellow pine specimens were also identified and may be from interior elements (Alden 2005).

Our analysis of the site plan revealed that the ordinary was constructed with two preassembled sidewall frames. Both were raised east to west—the west frame first, then the east frame. Two different laborers dug the post holes. The laborer who dug the southern four holes was the more experienced; his holes were rectangles oriented to the direction of rearing, thus easing the descent of the post feet into the holes. Base elevations of the posts were very similar, varying by only 0.21 feet.

While the carpenter had learned much during his time in the Chesapeake, he had not fully absorbed the logic of building with clapboard. The ideal dimension for a building six boards long is 30'-0", thus allowing end-lapped boards 5'-6" long to extend slightly beyond the ends of the walls and roof. The ordinary, however, was framed 30'-9" long. Thus the carpenter had to saw several odd-length clapboard logs.

From a mistake, it is clear how the carpenter laid out the post locations. As the building had no sills, the dimensions were worked out on the plates for the tops of the walls. Starting at one end of a plate, the carpenter used his 2-foot rule to dimension a 9-inch post seat. With square and pricker or knife, he scribed (scratched) its location. A pricker was a period tool resembling an icepick that allowed a carpenter to mark lines on the wood. Then, with pricker and 10-foot rule, he measured 10 more feet, scribed a line, measured 10 more feet, scribed a line, and then measured a final 10 feet to mark the end of the plate. Thus, the ordinary is 30 feet and one post in length.

Having marked the bay locations, the carpenter reversed direction and scribed the locations of the post joints (mortises or notches). This is when he made his revealing mistake. At the first mark north of the south end, he scribed the joint on the wrong side of the 10-foot mark, thus shortening the south bay and lengthening the middle bay. When the second plate was laid against the first and scribed, this mistake was transferred to the second. While these mistakes caused no structural problems, they probably led to some cursing when the workers clapboarded the walls.

The ordinary's firehood and end passage suggest that Smith was from the north of England (Pearson 1985:128–130, 157; Harrison and Hutton 1984:42–73, 182–186). The Smith's Ordinary firehood was large, about 10 feet square, and served as a heated inner room (some English firehoods retain their original benches). With the exterior door opening into the passage behind the firehood, the occupants of the firehood were protected from drafts just as in North Yorkshire or Derbyshire. Within the firehood and almost in the center of the building was a small, 6-foot-deep cellar. The cellar's location kept its contents frost-free during the coldest winter.

The Print House (18 ST1-14)

If our interpretation of the Print Shop post molds is correct, it was an unusual structure—a story-and-a-half, bent-framed building constructed during a period in which one-story, sidewall-reared buildings were the norm. During the excavation, Timothy Riordan's crew planned the features at their surfaces, used a probe to establish the depth of the hole-set timbers, and, at half their depth, redrew the holes and molds and dimensioned the structure. Five wall-post molds survived in good condition. The surface plan of the features is rather uninformative (see figure 2.4D). The print house is an example of information from within the post holes being more important than their surface plan.

Three sets of information suggest that the Print House was bent-framed: the depths of the post holes, the post hole alignments, and the installation of the posts small end down. The critical information was that the depths of the post molds and their construction holes varied by bent pair to compensate for the slope of the site. The deepest posts were the gable posts at the east, downhill end of the structure. Next deepest were the bay posts between the hall and parlor, while the posts at the west, uphill gable were the shallowest. This would be unusual for a side-wall framed building (Riordan and Hurry 2015).

Having chosen the hypothesis that the building was bent-reared, we conjectured the rearing sequence from the post hole/post mold relationships. The east bent has posts centered in its construction holes, and thus appears to have been reared first. The west gable posts appear to have been reared next, as, to get the building almost square, the carpenters had to shove this bent frame to the south sides of its poorly located post holes. (A side-wall framed building would have one side centered in its post holes.) Then the central bent frame was reared. If this hypothesis is correct, the building's sills were lapped—not mortised and tenoned—to the posts. We are confident that the building was silled, as site preservation was excellent. Stud molds and holes would have survived—Riordan's crew found the stud molds of the wooden chimney.

Below surface disturbance, the post molds were square and relatively small, averaging 7 × 7 inches. Deeper in the holes, the molds of two posts became gradually less square. At the bottoms of the SE and SW post holes, the post molds were round and 7 inches in diameter. One north wall post mold contained several large pieces of carbonized black locust. From this we can deduce that the wall posts were hewn from small-diameter locust logs set with the tops of the logs in the bottoms of the post holes.

Old-field locust generally has little taper. Why would the carpenter place the waney end of the post in the ground? It is the end with the least area to bear on the subsoil and the most sapwood for termites. Our conclusion is that the carpenter wanted to have the largest amount of wood at the upper end of the posts to allow for strong mortise-and-tenon connections. We think that this is evidence of story-and-a-half construction with robust tenons connecting the tie-beams to the posts. At a 1½-story house of 1672 in Ipswich, Massachusetts, the tenons of the tie-beams are 2½ inches thick. Thus, in our reconstruction, we have posts that are 7-inch poles at the bottom transitioning at the top into square-cornered 8×8s.

EARTHFAST BUILDING EXCAVATION

From our excavations of these earthfast buildings, we learned that the best way to excavate timber molds is by following a specific series of steps (Morrison 1985:119–134):

1. Map the surface features of a building.
2. Determine the axis on which each timber mold and hole will be cross-sectioned and mark the ends of the line with nails. Record the nail locations on the plan.
3. Determine the depth of the post holes with an agronomist's core probe.
4. Determine the depth (or depths) at which to map the timber molds, with one 0.5 foot above the bottom. More if the shape changes higher up.

5. Excavate and section all the molds and holes to that depth.
6. Map the molds and holes.
7. Dimension the building with string lines, plumb bob or level, tape, and transit/total station.
8. Complete sectioning the molds and holes to the bottom of the features.
9. In one session, measure the basal depth of the timber molds and post holes (they may differ) with transit or total station.
10. Complete excavation of the molds and holes.
11. Map the excavated shapes of the holes.

We recommend cross-sectioning timber molds and holes along their long axes. Generally, this will produce the most information. However, always section at least one post at right angles to the ridge line of the building. Not all posts were set perpendicular. In Virginia, Nicholas Luccketti excavated post molds outside a building that sloped toward the building. These were props installed to keep a deteriorating building upright (Nicholas M. Luccketti 1980, pers. comm.). Someday, an archaeologist may become famous by excavating the curved timber molds of "crucks"—arched timbers that were both wall post and the principal rafters of the roof.

The five structures discussed above illustrate how Historic St. Mary's City staff researched buildings targeted for reconstruction, and how the information required for reconstruction continually challenges us to become better archaeologists. Three-dimensional reconstructions, however, are only one of the products of this research. As of 2018, Historic St. Mary's City staff have uncovered and recorded the architectural remnants of 21 colonial buildings on the park lands or the college campus. All these discoveries increase our knowledge of the past.

In 1981, our discoveries at the St. John's and Van Sweringen sites were combined with research on 23 other Chesapeake sites and published in "Impermanent Architecture in the Southern American Colonies." The project was the brainchild of Cary Carson, who had moved from being architectural historian and director of research for Historic St. Mary's City to being director of research for Colonial Williamsburg. With the help of four coauthors, Carson assembled an enormous amount of information on the transference of European traditions of impermanent architecture to the New World. In New England, the impermanent structures built by settlers were quickly replaced by well-framed dwellings equal to or better than those they had left. In contrast, in the Chesapeake impermanent structures continued to be built well into the eighteenth century—for so long that many details of late seventeenth-century impermanent construction were carried over into the well-built farmhouses of the mid and late eighteenth century (Carson et al. 1981).

Why did impermanent construction continue so long in the Chesapeake? Drawing on the work of Lois Carr and her colleagues, Carson explains the economic and demographic roots of impermanent architecture. The initial tobacco boom and prosperity of the first half of the seventeenth century was followed by a 45-year depression, 1666–1710 (Menard 1973; Clemens 1980:226; Carr and Walsh 1994:112–113). Equally important was the high death rate inflicted by Chesapeake diseases upon Europeans. During the seventeenth century, only a minority of Chesapeake-born children reached majority with both parents still alive. High mortality truncated wealth accumulation.

While Carson paints the big picture, he does not slight archaeological detail. The essay contains 10 mini-site reports and a gazetteer briefly describing all 25 sites. Beautiful renderings explain archaeology and architecture to the reader. The essay does not include the Historic St. Mary's City recipe for excavating timber molds. An earlier version of this research was published by Morrison in 1985.

In 1982, Stone completed a doctoral dissertation on Chesapeake farmstead architecture. While it parallels, in part, "Impermanent Architecture," Stone provides more detail from seventeenth-century Maryland documents. He also expands upon the influence of clapboard carpentry and tobacco. The 5-foot (5'-6") clapboard had as profound an influence on seventeenth-century Chesapeake architecture as today's 4×8-foot sheet of plywood or drywall does on modern architecture. In Virginia, by the mid-1620s, a 10-foot post spacing was becoming common and buildings sometimes were dimensioned in boards. Just as important as housing the planter and his servants, was housing his crop of air-cured tobacco. Initially, tobacco was hung on strings to cure. By the 1670s, tobacco was being hung from sticks resting on the scaffolding poles, beams, and roof collars of tobacco houses. As these "tobacco sticks" could be split from inferior portions of the 5'-6" logs being riven into boards, the tobacco stick reinforced the 5-foot clapboard in dimensioning Chesapeake farm buildings well into the eighteenth century. As carpenters constructed more tobacco houses than dwellings, tobacco house carpentry had a profound influence on dwelling construction (Stone 1982:230–339; Walsh 2010:95, 157; Glover 1676:635).

There is more to learn. Fortunately, research continues. Willie Graham and colleagues summarized Virginia excavations in a 2007 article published in *William and Mary Quarterly* (Graham et al. 2007). Extensive research on Virginia colonial architecture is available in Lounsbury's *Essays in Early American Architectural History: A View from the Chesapeake* (2011) and in Carson and Lounsbury's 2013 edited volume titled *The Chesapeake House: Architectural Investigations by Colonial Williamsburg.* At Historic St. Mary's City, a challenge facing the staff is locating the cottages within the 1634 St. Mary's Fort. How were these cottages constructed? Will they be early "Virginia" structures like those constructed along the James River in the mid-1620s, or like the 1619 buildings of Martin's Hundred, remain improvisations based on temporary British structures (Stone 1982:249–259; Noël Hume 1982:41, 138, 151, 192, 218–221; Carson 2011:86–103)? Only additional, meticulous excavations, informed by knowledge of earthfast architecture, can answer this and similar questions.

3

Soil Analysis at the St. John's Site

An Earthy View of Early Maryland Revisited

SILAS D. HURRY AND ROBERT WINSTON KEELER

Archaeologists excavate often vast quantities of soil to recover artifacts and reveal cultural features. Screening through varied sizes of mesh yields many small fragments that would otherwise be missed. What about the soil itself? Does it hold archaeological evidence invisible to the eye? This subject was first explored in historical archaeology in the early 1970s when HSMC archaeologist Garry Wheeler Stone talked with soil scientist John Foss, then at the University of Maryland. They hypothesized that human activities could alter the chemical concentrations in the soils and these chemical "artifacts" could give insights about the lives and activities of people in the past. In the 1970s, chemical analysis of soils was expensive and time consuming. Foss, as a soil agronomist, suggested that a standard agricultural assessment that includes calcium, phosphate, and potassium could serve as an inexpensive way of assessing soil chemistry, and by extension, human behavior. This research was undertaken when the Historic St. Mary's City Commission was beginning the process of unearthing the first major seventeenth-century building to be archaeologically examined in St. Mary's City: the St. John's site (18ST1-23). The St. John's site was the home plantation of John Lewger, the first secretary of the colony and Lord Baltimore's personal representative. He built his house in 1638 and it stood, under a number of owners, uses, and occupants, until the first decade of the eighteenth century.

Stone and Foss considered the types of human behavior that could be manifested by a variety of soil elements. The most obvious of these is the concentration of phosphate. Phosphate has its origin in the deposition of organic waste material. Food, animal, and human waste all contribute to the amount of phosphate in the soil. Potassium is mostly from potash which was a byproduct of the deposition of fireplace ash. In the seventeenth century, a fire would be constantly burning in the kitchen to facilitate cooking for the occupants. The amount of fireplace ash generated by maintaining a fire throughout the year would be staggering. A second source of potassium in the soil could be from lye. Lye was created by leaching wood ashes and then was used in converting corn into hominy and the making of soap. The final element that has a clear cultural manifestation is calcium. Most calcium is from the decay of oyster shell in the naturally acid soils of the Tidewater region. Calcium could also derive from lime made by calcining oyster shell. Like lye, lime can provide the alkali which is needed to make hominy. Calcium on a site may also derive from the architectural use of lime in mortar and plaster.

This trio of chemicals, phosphate, potassium, and calcium, can serve as "fingerprints" of human interaction resulting in chemical modification of the soil. What one is observing is not so much in terms of absolute numbers as variation from a mean. All things being equal, the distribution of any of these chemical "fingerprints" should be relatively consistent across a natural system. It is generally the intervention of human beings that is creating the variations, though some natural processes can also affect the concentrations. It was proposed that both deposition and the avoidance of deposition would create peaks and valleys in chemical values which reflect human behavior We will look at the soil chemical distortions in two distinct ways: large areal sampling to document land use across the site, and specific activities which affect the chemistry of the fill of individual cultural features within a site. We will first look at the broad, sitewide distribution.

SPATIAL DISTRIBUTION OF SOIL CHEMICALS: THE 1970S SAMPLES

Archaeologist Robert Keeler used soil samples collected from the plow-disturbed soils of the St. John's site by Garry Wheeler Stone and Alexander H. Morrison II to create distributional maps of the principal soil nutrients suggested by Foss. The soils were tested for the standard agricultural assessment offered to farmers by the Soils Agronomy Laboratory at the University of Maryland as part of the Cooperative Extension Service. Keeler produced these maps as part of his doctoral dissertation at the University of Oregon (1978). This dissertation examined the distribution of a variety of artifact types and soil chemistry in and around the St. John's site. Keeler demonstrated that human activities leave behind unmistakable, patterned modification of the soil chemistry on plowed archaeological sites. Otherwise unobservable evidence of human activity emerged in the form of major

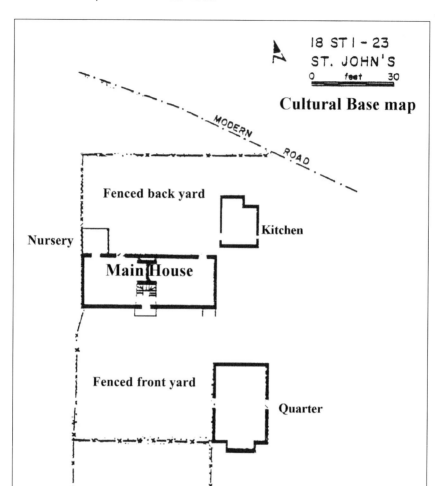

Figure 3.1. Site plan from 1970s excavations.

concentrations where deposition occurred and in "clean" areas where deposition was restricted.

Figure 3.1 shows the cultural features discovered in the first campaign of excavations in the 1970s. Because of the more intricate stratigraphy within the core architecture of the site, the area within the foundations of the main house was excluded from the analysis and an impermeable interpolation boundary was created around the architectural remains. Figure 3.2 depicts the distribution of soil phosphates in and around the St. John's home lot in Keeler's original analysis, while figure 3.3 shows potassium distributions and

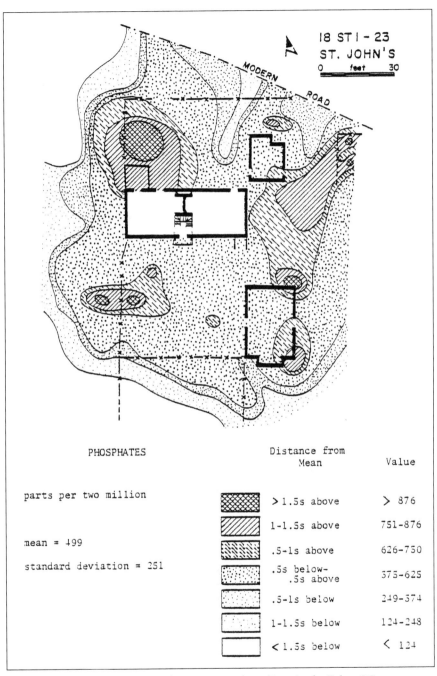

Figure 3.2. Phosphate distribution from 1976 sampling. (Drawing by Robert Winston Keeler.)

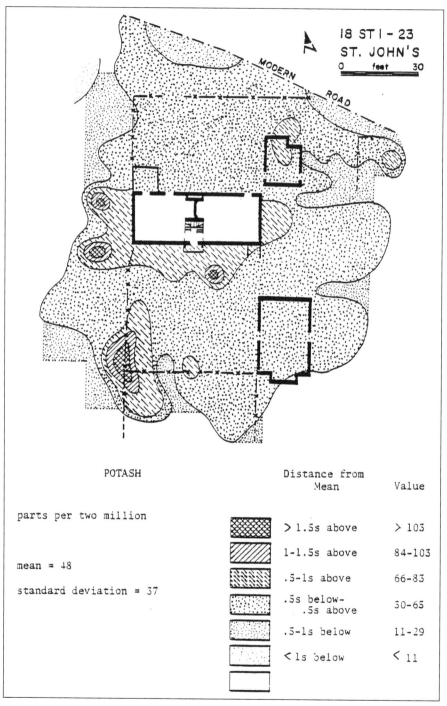

Figure 3.3. Potassium distribution from 1976 sampling. (Drawing by Robert Winston Keeler.)

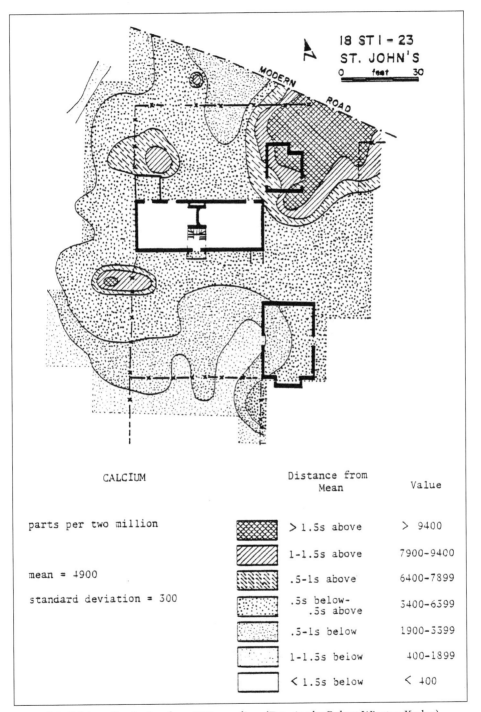

Figure 3.4. Calcium distribution from 1976 sampling. (Drawing by Robert Winston Keeler.)

figure 3.4 shows Keeler's original calcium distribution. These distributions were based on a total number of 112 samples and the contours were visually interpolated.

The most clear-cut relationship between human behavior and alteration to the soil chemistry is seen in the phosphate map (figure 3.2). Keeler showed a major backyard midden rich in organic material. The high phosphate levels were interpreted as the result of surface midden development from organic kitchen wastes and chamber pots. There is also a low area visible in the back-yard which Keeler interpreted as a pathway which was kept clean of organic deposition. The front yard shows relatively low levels of phosphate except in the middle of the western front yard fence gate area showing a concentration related to this gate. Additional peaks are obvious on the corners of the front yard outbuilding and to the north and east of the kitchen. Keeler found that potassium has a more discrete and less diffuse pattern than phosphate (see figure 3.3). A major concentration occurs in the southwest corner of the enclosed front yard, and lesser clusters occur immediately west of the main house within a larger spread of potassium likely deriving from the central hearth of the main house. Additional concentrations are related to the kitchen fireplace, which was rebuilt during the life of that building. Oddly, the front yard outbuilding's fireplace does not register in the maps. All the potassium distributions doubtlessly emanate from the fireplaces, or where their ashes were dumped.

The calcium distribution discovered by Keeler showed a concentration in the backyard behind the hall and a major spread of calcium associated with the freestanding kitchen (see figure 3.4). A discrete cluster in the location of a gate on the western side of the front yard fence probably marks the place where a basketful of oyster shell was deposited in the walkway, probably to fill a muddy hole.

SPATIAL DISTRIBUTION OF SOIL CHEMICALS: THE 2000S SAMPLES

Subsequently, as part of a major effort to develop the St. John's site into an archaeological museum, HSMC returned to the site early in the twenty-first century to undertake additional archaeology on elements of the site that would be impacted by the development of the museum and its exhibits. As part of this phase of research, additional samples of plowed soils were recovered in a more systematic method than the samples used by Keeler. This much larger sample, collected between 2002 and 2006, has been utilized in this current analysis. The 1970s soil chemical analysis was based on 112 soil samples, while the more recent campaign resulted in a total of 210 soil samples from plow zone. This collection of samples was designed to be as systematic as possible across the site and was intentionally extended beyond the geographical scope of the earlier tests. This second soil sampling campaign was hindered by the mechanical stripping of the far front and back yards as a part of the 1970s excavations.

The additional excavations undertaken in advance of the construction of the St. John's Museum yielded a more refined understanding of the site plan, as seen in figure 3.5. This is a necessarily generalized map depicting the persistent cultural features determined by the multiple campaigns investigating the St. John's Site. Figures 3.6, 3.7, and 3.8 depict, respectively, the distributions of phosphate, potassium, and calcium. All these distributions were generated using Surfer, a 3D-mapping program developed by Golden Software of Golden, Colorado. All these new distributions were created using the kriging option, where interpolated values are modeled by a Gaussian process governed by prior covariances (Goovaerts 1997; Deutsch and Journel 1998). Under suitable assumptions on the priors, kriging gives the best linear, unbiased prediction of the intermediate values. The kriging algorithm is the default in Surfer and seems to work best with archaeological data. All these maps, like Keeler's, utilize contour intervals based on statistical calculations. Specifically, the central contour represents one standard deviation centered on the sample mean. Subsequent contours were calculated based on this central contour, representing one standard deviation in each contour, resulting in five total contours. The assumption is that "average" phosphate deposition is represented by the central contour and variance from it is indicated by the higher and lower contours. Everything less than the value suggested for the lowest contour is included in that contour while everything above the highest contour interval is subsumed under this highest concentration. This allows for consistency between sites because it is the *relative* concentration we seek to illustrate rather than absolute numbers. Discussion with chemists who have studied repeatability stress that the soil numbers resulting from one analysis will be proportionately comparable to earlier studies, but absolute numbers tend to vary widely based on previous techniques (Ruth Ann Armitage 2019, pers. comm.). Modern, automated soil studies tend to be more repeatable than earlier analyses based on simple acid reduction.

COMPARING THE SAMPLES

Beginning with the distribution of phosphate, most of the major patterns visible in Keeler's hand-drawn maps are still apparent in the computer-generated maps created with the larger sample. The major concentration in

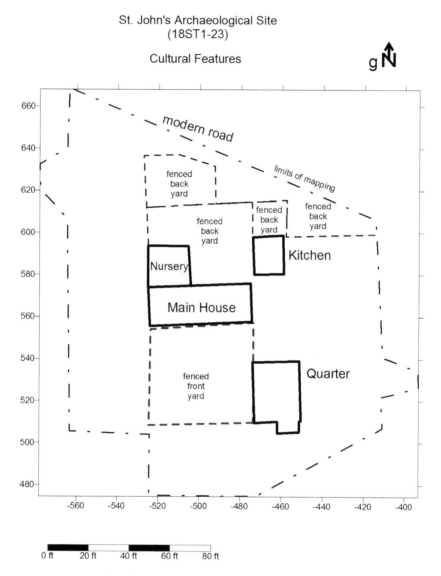

St. John's Archaeological Site
(18ST1-23)

Cultural Features

Figure 3.5. Site plan from the more intensive 2004 sampling. (Drawing by Silas D. Hurry, courtesy of HSMC.)

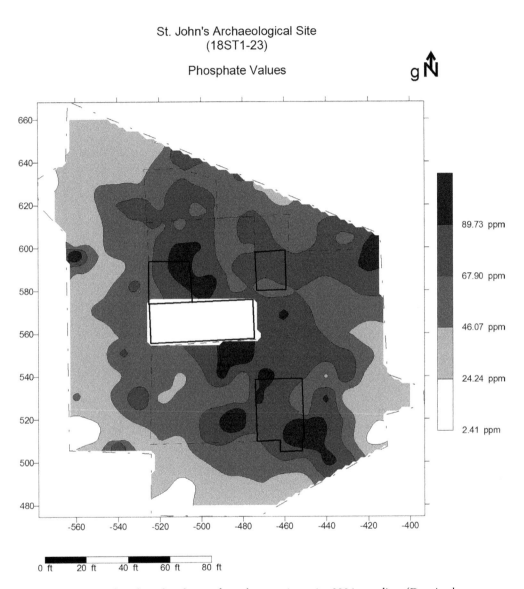

Figure 3.6. Phosphate distribution from the more intensive 2004 sampling. (Drawing by
Silas D. Hurry, courtesy of HSMC.)

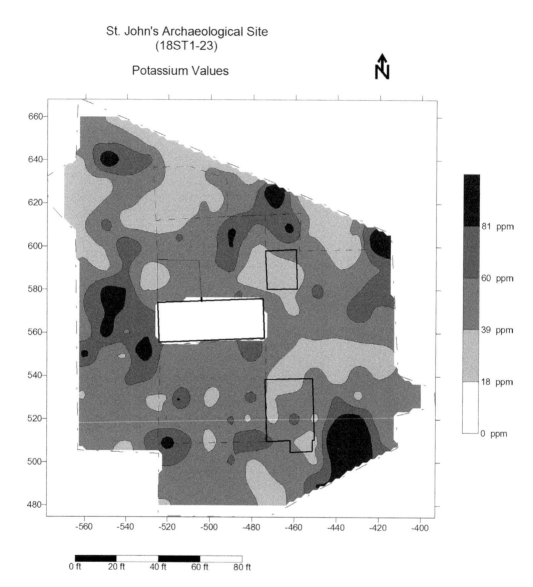

Figure 3.7. Potassium distribution from the more intensive 2004 sampling. (Drawing by Silas D. Hurry, courtesy of HSMC.)

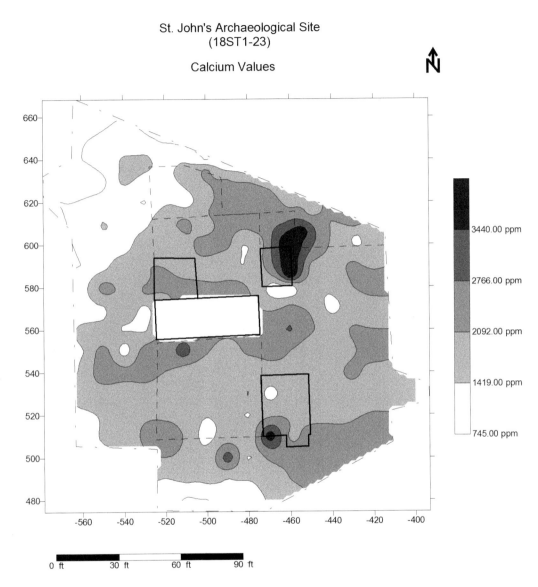

St. John's Archaeological Site
(18ST1-23)

Calcium Values

Figure 3.8. Calcium distribution from the more intensive 2004 sampling. (Drawing by Silas D. Hurry, courtesy of HSMC.)

the backyard is the result of a major garbage midden in the backyard service area north of the main house. This area of trash deposition was clearly visible based on the artifact densities observed during the excavations. This midden closely corresponds to the location of the backyard fences. The front yard western gate location highlighted by the original mapping is clearly visible on the new maps. The high concentration of phosphate off the southeastern corner of the quarter still remains, but the generally low phosphate quantities in the front yard are not as obvious because two additional concentrations, one near the bulkhead cellar entrance and another in the southeastern corner of the enclosed front yard stand out. These seeming differences are doubtlessly a result of the more intensive sampling. Phosphate "fallout" from the cellar entrance is not surprising. Since this cellar entrance is relatively late on the site, the associated phosphates are also most likely late and perhaps reflective of deposition into a cellar about to be abandoned. Numerous dumped artifacts were found covering the ramp leading down to the cellar during the excavations. Deposition in the southeast corner of the front yard probably comes from the quarter. Also less obvious than it appeared on earlier maps was the area of low phosphate deposition within the backyard which Keeler interpreted as a pathway emanating from the main house. While not as obvious, some hint of this is visible in the new maps. There are two additional phosphate "hotspots" not suggested by the earlier analysis, but these are both on the margin of the new maps and represent activity outside of the sampling scope on the earlier maps.

All of these concentrations are the result of the direct disposal of organic material. The backyard concentrations are the result of the deposition of quantities of organic refuse from food preparation and disposal of food scraps in the backyards. The concentration near the gateway in the western margin of the front yard while less intense and obvious than on the earlier maps is, as Keeler suggested, likely from the dumping of chamber pots just beyond the limits of the formal front yard, as is the high peak in the extreme southeast corner of the front yard and the area adjacent to the western wall of the quarter. The concentration on the western side of the quarter probably results from refuse coming out of the quarter itself. Likewise, the intense cluster in the southeast likely comes from the same source. The linear, somewhat lower concentration of phosphate emanating from the corner of the kitchen may represent a persistently used pathway to access the freshwater spring to the southeast, a route still evident on the landscape by a notch in the side of the ravine worn down by foot traffic.

Moving to the distribution of potassium at St. John's, the pattern recognized on the earlier map is somewhat reflected in the new mapping. The concentration in the southwestern corner of the front yard is still present, as is a concentration west of the main house which appeared as two distinct peaks in the original mapping. The entire area west of the house seems to have been a periodic location for the deposition of fireplace ash. This is one of the more accessible areas outside of the yards and nearest to the hearth in the hall where a fire would likely have been kept burning year-round while the parlor hearth likely had periods of disuse during the rather torrid Chesapeake summers. The major concentration in the extreme northwest of the sample area is not reflected in the original sample, but stands out in the new mapping. This area was beyond the original sample zone, as was the major concentration in the extreme southeast of the research universe. A concentration to the northeast of the yards is hinted at in the original sample, but it is more clearly defined by the larger sample. Indeed, this concentration and an adjacent concentration along the north central area of the study area is probably a function of the closer interval sampling better catching the variation. Most of these deposits are likely the result of the deposition of fireplace ash, though it is possible we are seeing evidence of hominy or soap making, particularly in the southeastern concentration. This southeastern concentration is relatively near the flow of the freshwater spring east of the home lot which supplied water to the inhabitants of St. John's. Hominy making is a water-intensive operation, and having the processing going on near or closer to the water source makes great sense. Transcripts of a court case involving an owner of St. John's in 1658 specifically mention hominy (Steiner 1922:205). The otherwise episodic nature of the potassium distribution fits well with fireplace ash deposition because this form of refuse is far less odiferous than phosphates. In general, the pattern we see in the new sampling is not unlike the pattern seen in the original sampling.

The calcium distribution depicted in figure 3.8 shows a major concentration associated with the detached kitchen, a peak in the southwest corner of the quarter, and a couple of small concentrations south of the hall in the front yard and south of the main front yard fence. It is possible that the major concentration related to the kitchen is the result of the architecturally derived calcium in the form of mortar associated with the chimney on the kitchen, while the high levels on the south end of the quarter may have a similar origin if mortar was used in the otherwise wattle and daub structure. Kitchen activity would have generated both shell and bone in this area, but the rebuilding of the kitchen chimney may have contributed some architectural lime. The extreme southern concentration and nearby lesser concentration beyond the main front yard fence seem most likely to have derived from oyster shell deposition in this area. The rest of the pattern is rather diffuse throughout the site and is probably a function of the ubiquitous utilization of oysters and their widespread deposition throughout the site. These patterns are not significantly different from the overall pattern identified in Keeler's original work with the exception of the quarter concentration, which was hinted at in Keeler's original mapping.

In general, the two distinct sets of sampling—and the distributions of phosphate, potassium, and calcium each document—are in agreement. The mapping supports the validity of the process and the long-term stability of the soil chemistry pattern as evidence of a wide range of human activities. The use of a computerized algorithm removes some of the "human factor" from the process. In his dissertation, Keeler describes these hand-drawn maps as "these gems of graphic alchemy" (1978:31). There is a degree of subjectivity in the mapping which Keeler sought to overcome by using descriptive statistics, especially standard deviations to corral these grossly "unnormally" distributed data into something resembling a normal distribution. The computer algorithm, based on the statistical model of kriging, removes any subjectivity and standardizes the process both across chemical elements and between sites so a degree of comparability can be achieved. However, sample spacing and frequency can produce differences.

Perhaps one of the greatest problems with the underlying assumptions is the continuity of activity within a cultural setting and the inherently non-temporal sensitivity of soil chemistry. It is not feasible in the plow zone to separate phosphate, potassium, or calcium deposition from 300 years ago from deposits of like material from 100 years ago. This creates an analytical problem for sites which were occupied, abandoned, and reoccupied, or even sites where occupation was continuous but not consistent in the use of space. A new land use regime will create a pattern which overlies and intermixes with any previous evidence of deposition and thereby masks the original utilization of the property. On archaeological sites occupied repeatedly over several hundred years, the occupants who happened to deposit the greatest amount of organic refuse, fireplace ash, and oyster shell create the pattern we can recover, or at least contribute the most significantly to the composite pattern resulting from all the occupations.

St. John's was an unusual case where three-quarters of a century of occupation seems to have honored a front yard–backyard utilization scheme. The built environment provided parameters for locations where activities and their concomitant soil chemistry modifications were manifested. In addition to soil chemical distributions, Keeler's dissertation includes extensive mapping of a range of temporally discrete materials. Ceramic types and styles of tobacco-smoking pipes showed major patterns of how people were utilizing the site areas during different time periods, but the general land use, as suggested by the distribution of various bulk, nontemporally distinctive materials such as oyster shell and architectural rubble, is amazingly consistent—the backyard was always treated as a backyard and the front yard was treated as a more well-kept front yard. In contrast, soil chemical pattern confusion was clearly demonstrated at St. Mary's City in the study of chemical distributions in the Town Center area near the Brome Slave Quarter. Here we had a major series of seventeenth-century sites which were subsequently occupied by a nineteenth- and twentieth-century plantation site, associated outbuildings, and gardens. It was not feasible to separate the human behaviors which created the chemical patterns since there were numerous patterns intermixed. On the other hand, it was feasible in both of these site areas to discern changing land use by mapping temporally discrete artifact classes. Datable ceramics, glass, and other artifact types in plow-disturbed soils reflect temporally discrete activities, while nontemporally discrete forms of distributional deposition may fail to clearly show this type of behavior.

SOILS AND FEATURE INTERPRETATION

The second set of examples used to explore variations in soil chemistry from the St. John's site includes cases where we examined the relative concentration of soil elements within features. The purpose of a large, rectangular feature in the western backyard was not immediately certain when uncovered in the 1970s. This feature serves as the first example of how soil chemistry can indicate function. The pit had multiple soil strata, as seen in figure 3.9A, and the excavated stratigraphic units are seen in figure 3.9B; the two top strata (53W, 53Y) were found to be later fill. Most of the upper strata were artifact-rich trash deposits containing quantities of food waste, oyster shell, charcoal, and ash. In contrast, the bottom layer was a dark brown soil that contained few artifacts and was mounded near the center of the feature. Soil analysis revealed that, despite the near absence of trash, this bottom layer had soil phosphate counts more than 10 times those found in the actual trash layers (figure 3.10). This was surprising because the trash layers were anticipated to have higher than normal organic residues due to food waste being a substantial part of the deposit. Calcium levels, in contrast, were more than twice as high in the upper trash layers as found in the soil from the bottom strata, likely related to the presence of quantities of bone and shell (figure 3.10). The very high phosphate content of the bottom layer confirmed the suspicions of the archaeologists: the feature originally served as a privy or toilet. This interpretation reached by Keeler in 1978 is the earliest use of soil chemistry

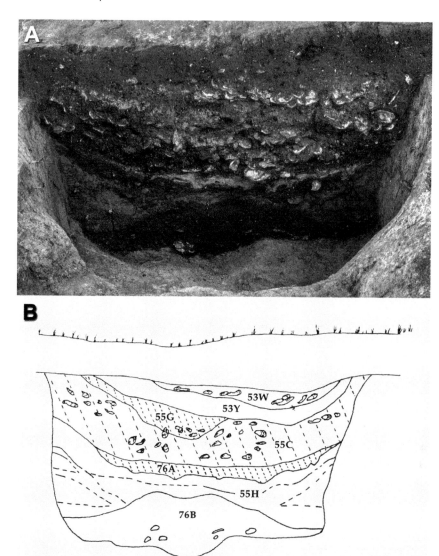

Figure 3.9. Stratified ca. 1650 feature identified as a privy: *A*, Photograph of the feature profile; *B*, the feature strata as excavated. (Courtesy of HSMC).

to resolve an archaeological question on a colonial site in the Chesapeake Bay region. It is also the first privy identified on a seventeenth-century site in St. Mary's City and remains today the only privy we have found. The high concentration of phosphate in the bottom of the privy should not come as a surprise. Henry Glassie has written that "the spoor of culture on the land

Phosphate and Calcium Measured in Privy Strata

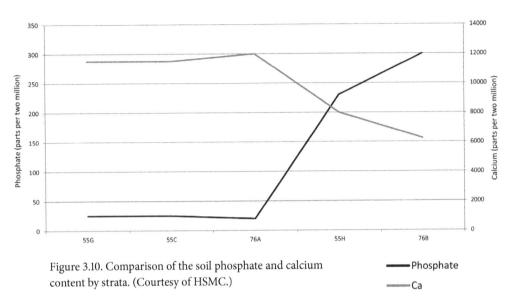

Figure 3.10. Comparison of the soil phosphate and calcium content by strata. (Courtesy of HSMC.)

━━━ Phosphate

━━━ Ca

is amazing and easily followed" (1972:30). The phosphate patterning is the "spoor of culture" in its most literal form.

The most recent archaeological work in the yards at the St. John's site further delineated a building that was initially interpreted as a sheep shed. The fieldwork demonstrated that it was actually an unusual aisled building of uncertain purpose. Measuring 20 × 17 feet, it had 3-foot-wide aisles along its long sides. Too small to serve as a stable or to be livestock stalls for cattle or even sheep, it was hypothesized that the structure might have been a chicken house (Miller 2006). This possibility was evaluated through the careful application of soil chemistry in the structural posts. Samples of soil from five of the building's posts were collected, along with comparative samples of 25 other post molds from around the site that were unrelated to the backyard building. Because chicken litter is known to be particularly high in phosphorus, the analysis tested for its concentration in the soils. The molds of the aisled building had a mean phosphorus level of 96.78 mg/kg while the other posts produced a mean phosphorus measure of 60.83 mg/kg. Hence the building post molds contained a considerably greater concentration than did the other site post molds. Applying soil analysis provides strong support for the hypothesis that this unidentified structure served as a chicken house.

Discussion

The delineation of areas of waste disposal and pathways helps to clarify the structure and function of the St. John's home lot by focusing on activity areas and patterns of traffic flow among them. At first glance, the St. John's home lot appears to have developed without rhyme or reason. Indeed it did not grow in the rigid, mechanistic fashion of many later Tidewater plantations with their strict organization separating work and "symbolic" space often characterized as parts of a "Georgian Landscape" (Deetz 1977:111). Development at St. John's occurred largely in an organic and functional way within the parameters of a folk cultural tradition and in response to the wants and needs of a maturing frontier society. St. John's is far more vernacular than formal. In order to understand the pattern in this process, it is necessary to perceive not only the obvious remains of buildings, fences, and pits, but also the more subtle remains of refuse scattered about the yard, nonarchitectural areas of activity, and the pathways which linked all these structural elements into a dynamic and patterned whole.

In the years since the original thesis that soil chemicals in plow zone could be predictive of human landscape use, much additional research into the significance of soil chemicals has occurred (e.g., Abrahams et al. 2010; Bair and Terry 2018; Hayes 2013; Oonk et al. 2009; Wilkins 2015). Most of this recent work has focused on feature fill and soil analysis, and the use of new and increasingly less expensive technologies such as hand-held x-ray fluorescence which lets the researcher test soils in the field. Reviewing these new methodologies and their applications is beyond the scope of the current study, but suffice it to say that the majority of these studies have focused on specific chemicals in features rather than on wide, areal sampling of the plow zone. Indeed, the war for the significance of plow zone itself and the need to at least sample before wholesale mechanical removal of the plow-disturbed soils seems to have been finally won. Rather than "the mist that separates us from the seventeenth century" (Garry Wheeler Stone 1975, pers. comm.), the utility of studying the plow-disturbed horizon is now widely recognized. Given the refuse disposal pattern of surface deposition into sheet middens which were subsequently homogenized by the plow, much of the material culture that was discarded is found in the plow-disturbed soils. Stripping away the plowed soils removes a majority of the artifacts from the site and clearly biases our ability to understand an archaeological site.

We do want to discuss some critiques and suggestions by archaeologists working with the soil chemistry patterns in plowed soils. Custer et al. (1986) attempted to apply the methodology to a nineteenth-century farmstead in northern Delaware. This site had extensive oral informant information and pictorial data which helped to identify activity areas within the site. The researchers found, however, that the predicted soil signatures which should be linked to the specific activities were not at all obvious. The soil chemical patterns did not match the activities, although some of the artifact patterning from plow zone did. We would argue that in the late nineteenth century an almost industrial level of activity was expressed in the recycling and redisposition of manure and other organic debris so that the pattern in question was more complex than in a simple agrarian setting like the early Chesapeake. The researchers did suggest that a correlation between soil pH and certain activities could be demonstrated. Soil pH is a complex issue since many different activities can collectively affect the acidity of the soil. However, as noted above, the multiple land uses within the site under analysis may well have masked and/or confused the pattern. Unless we have consistent land use and concomitant elemental deposition, soil chemistry can be a rather blunt activity area indicator.

Pogue (1988) applied a similar regime of soil chemical analysis to a terminal seventeenth-/early eighteenth-century site in Calvert County, Maryland, barely 16 miles from the St. John's site. This site, King's Reach, had been plowed like St. John's and also represents a primarily domestic occupation. Pogue found the analysis of "anthrosols" added meaning to the interpretation of colonial sites and clarification of land use patterning around the overall home lot. In reviewing the literature, Pogue states that "as with any spatial sampling program, the size of the interval between soil samples remains a crucial determinant of the validity of the results" (1988:13). Sampling density is essential to capture a true picture of what has occurred on a site. Pogue also attempted to ascertain the meaning of additional soil elements which are now routinely included in agricultural soil analysis, including magnesium, without great success. However, his research does support the general thesis that soil chemistry is in itself an artifact of human behavior and as such, is a significant set of data which should be routinely collected and analyzed.

Meyers et al. (2008) examined a late nineteenth-century hacienda in the Yucatán peninsula of Mexico to examine the changing land use on such sites as the economic system changed from debt-peonage to a more free labor setting. The testing showed a strong consistency in land use from before the economic system change to that which followed it. The researchers were able to use phosphate distribution to show continuity in human behavior and demonstrate activities which did not clearly manifest themselves in the artifact patterns. Specifically, they were examining sherd size as an indicator of land use with a basic model of a structural core (where the house is located) and swept patio area where numerous activities occurred, and an outer boundary of deposition demarked by phosphates. The researchers had proposed that the size of sherds within the swept patio should have been indicative of the edges of the patio. In practice, they found phosphate concentrations a better "edge" indicator (Meyers et al. 2008:379–385). Perhaps this example points to the reliability of the methodology on preindustrial sites. The researchers specifically describe the site as being relatively briefly occupied and having a clear abandonment date with the coming of the Mexican Revolution. The pattern is not overly muddied by reoccupation or diverging land use during the period of occupation.

To conclude, soil chemistry is an invisible artifact of human occupation which can be seen only through analytic intervention. While not as obvious as other artifacts, soil chemical patterning is a direct result of human habitation. It is not, however, temporally diagnostic, so its interpretive value needs to be "buffered" by an understanding of site formation processes and the general site land use history. Study of soil chemistry can be a deeply meaningful analytical tool to understanding site usage. The essential point is that soil samples need to be taken at the onset of the project. Just as with geophysical remote sensing, it can be difficult to apply to a site after the digging is well under way; in retrospect, we should have taken systematic soil samples at St. John's when the project began. It costs little to take the soil samples, and the opportunity for interpretive insight is outstanding. Human behavior can alter the chemistry of an archaeological site in ways not obvious to the human eye or detectable by the best excavator. Soil chemistry captures activity which does not necessarily leave visual clues, but does speak to human behavior and adds nuance to our interpretation. Ultimately, soil chemistry analysis can lead to an appreciation of activities which otherwise leave few traces for the archaeologist to discover.

4

Finding Ephemeral Homes of the Enslaved

A St. Mary's City Example

RUTH M. MITCHELL AND HENRY M. MILLER

For historical archaeologists, locating the homes of the wealthy and prominent is generally easy, but finding the dwellings of the poor is another matter. Wealthy sites are usually rich in material remains and accompanied by documentation that helps to identify them. In contrast, the dwellings of the impoverished and the enslaved are often undocumented and contain a sparse material record. This chapter is the story of an archaeological project that discovered several long forgotten and barely visible sites once occupied by enslaved field workers of a major eighteenth-century plantation at St. Mary's City. We describe the project, evaluate methods of site discovery, and present the investigation's unusual findings.

A Field along Mattapany Road

The oldest roadway still in use in Maryland is at St. Mary's City and dates before 1634. Called Mattapany Road, it began as a Maryland Indian path and became a dividing line between two early colonial land tracts. In 1990, Historic St. Mary's City (HSMC) archaeologists were asked by St. Mary's College of Maryland (SMCM) to conduct a survey of a field along Mattapany Road where the college wanted to build a parking lot. Historical records provided no evidence of past habitation on the tract and implied it had been used for agriculture since the seventeenth century. Furthermore, as it was a long distance from water, archaeological settlement models for southern Maryland gave it a low probability of containing any sites of significance. Nevertheless, an archaeological evaluation was still necessary to conclusively test this prediction. Because St. Mary's City is a National Historic Landmark, HSMC conducted a more intensive survey strategy than is typical using several methods. These were a controlled surface collection of the field, followed by formal excavations and supplemented by digging shovel test pits.

Site Identification Methods

Our experience has shown that the archaeological visibility of historic period sites varies widely depending upon the length of habitation, the type of occupation or activity that occurred there, the types of building materials used, the wealth of the occupants, land use since abandonment, and many other factors. To locate sites, archaeologists have developed a number of methods, depending upon the region, resources, and types of sites expected (see Banning 2002; White and King 2007). Remote sensing using metal detectors, magnetometers, and ground penetrating radar can be highly effective, but these methods are often expensive and do not produce reliable dating evidence. In the Eastern United States, two widely used survey methods are surface collection, especially controlled surface collection (CSC), and shovel test pits (STPs) excavated at regular intervals.

The simplest method of surface collection is to walk an area with soil exposure and collect any artifacts that are observed, marking their locations on a map. This is best conducted in a recently plowed field, which provides the greatest surface visibility. To conduct this type of survey systematically using CSC, a grid system is laid out in numbered squares of the same size and artifacts are retrieved by square number, thereby gaining more precise spatial control over their distributions (Riordan 1988). If a possible site is detected with these methods, the area is typically tested via excavation to better evaluate the potential cultural resource. The Mattapany Road project became a vivid example of the CSC method and provided an excellent opportunity to compare the results provided by CSC and STPs. Consequently, a deliberate methodology was developed to apply these two survey strategies and compare their results to the findings from subsequent intensive sampling via unit excavation.

Mattapany Controlled Surface Collection

Because the study area had been in agriculture for more than a century, the zone proposed for parking lot construction was replowed and disked to produce a generally level surface. Following two hard rains to wash the soil, the 600×475-foot plowed area was gridded in 10-foot squares. Each square was assigned a unique number and all exposed artifacts were collected and bagged by provenience. An aerial photo of the study area is seen in figure

4.1A. Larger collection units such as 25-foot or 50-foot squares have also been used by archaeologists, although the level of detail decreases as the unit size increases. A total of 2,633 10-foot squares were sampled with this method, which yielded nearly 4,000 artifacts. Subsequent identification and plotting of the artifacts by type allowed their distributions to be evaluated. The first mapped were the stone artifacts, nearly all of which are of prehistoric origin (figure 4.1B). Most are debitage fragments, but there are also some tools, including 14 projectile points spanning a broad range of time. These artifacts are distributed broadly throughout the study area, with some concentration evident in the northeast and southeast corners. While Maryland Indians may have occasionally used the area, there was not a major occupation here, perhaps because it was not close to freshwater.

In contrast, square shafted nails of either wrought or cut manufacture show clear patterning in the southeast part of the study zone (figure 4.1C). Far more abundant are brick fragments (figure 4.1D), which tend to cluster in three areas: the northeast corner, the southeast zone, and along the southwest edge of the collection survey area. Both artifacts imply the presence of some type of architecture.

Ceramics are one of the best indicators of domestic occupation, and archaeologists recovered both colonial and postcolonial sherds that generally span the ca. 1750 to ca. 1840 period. As can be seen in figure 4.1E, ceramics cluster in the eastern and especially the southeastern part of the survey area, and along the western edge. Also normally indicative of dwellings in the Tidewater region of the Chesapeake are fragments of oyster shell that were brought to a site as food (figure 4.1F). Their distribution tends to mirror that of the bricks and nails, strongly suggesting that these are locations where buildings stood. Oysters were used by both Maryland Indians and European immigrants, so it is hard to tell by the shells themselves who deposited them. At Mattapany, the spatial overlap of the shells with nails, brick, much of the European pottery and glass, as well as the presence of cattle and swine remains in the same area, makes it most likely that the oyster shells are related to the people who lived on the site during the historic period.

Visual inspection of artifact distributions is an essential step in the effort to identify sites. However, it can at times be difficult to determine if an artifact distribution is indicative of human behavior. Because of the uniform data that controlled surface collection provides, this can be evaluated using a statistical test called the Morisita Index (Morisita 1959). This test uses a quadrant method in which the number of specimens per quadrant forms the basis for the analysis. The index calculates the degree to which a distribution deviates from random. Artifacts may be distributed in three ways:

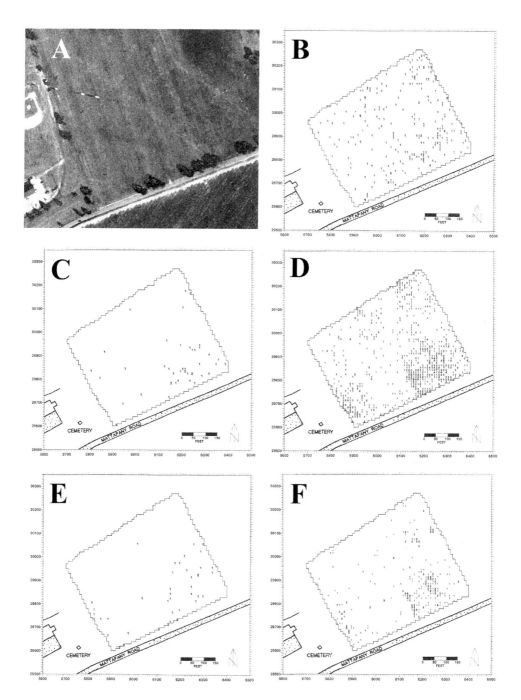

Figure 4.1. Comparison of the distributions of artifact groups recovered during the surface collection at Mattapany Road: *A*, Aerial showing the study area; *B*, Lithic distribution; *C*, Nail distribution; *D*, Brick distribution; *E*, Ceramics distribution; and *F*, Oyster shell distribution. (Figure by Ruth M. Mitchell and Henry M. Miller, courtesy of HSMC.)

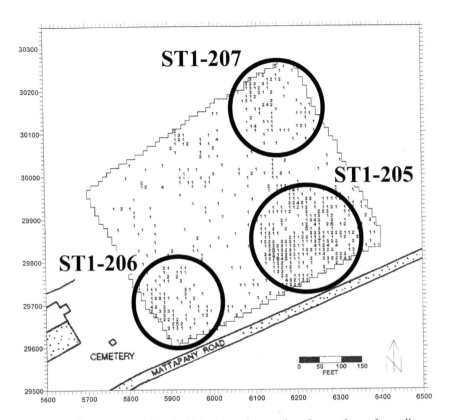

Figure 4.2. The three sites defined within the study zone, based upon the surface collection evidence and testing. (Figure by Ruth M. Mitchell and Henry M. Miller, courtesy of HSMC.)

randomly, uniformly, or in clusters. With this Index of Dispersion, 1 equals a random distribution, greater than 1 is more clustered, and less than 1 is more uniform. In archaeology, clustered distributions are generally indicative of human activity (Garratt and Steinhorst 1976 provides the means to test for significance).

For the Mattapany project, the field was divided into 24 quadrants containing 100 collection squares each. The prehistoric lithics have a dispersion of 1.22, or close to a random distribution. Square-shafted nails yield a figure of 1.89 while brick is 1.95, indicating both artifact types are strongly clustered. Colonial and postcolonial pottery has a similar dispersion figure of 1.94, but remarkably, oyster shell is even more concentrated with an index of 2.66. These patterns are clearly nonrandom. Hence, the historic period materials show a high degree of clustering, suggesting sites of human occupation.

At least three sites may be defined for the study zone (figure 4.2). They are designated sites 18ST1-205, 18ST1-206, and 18ST1-207 (Mitchell et al. 1999). While a few randomly scattered seventeenth-century artifacts were recovered, there is no evidence of domestic occupation in the 1600s, although the land was almost certainly used for agriculture during that time. Site 18ST1-207 at the far northeast corner of the study zone was only minimally tested, and most of site 18ST1-206 appears to lie outside the study zone in an area that became a cemetery for Slavonic immigrants in the early twentieth century. Extending the survey into the cemetery was not within the project scope nor would it have been considered appropriate. Site 18ST1-205 is the most thoroughly investigated of the three as it was discovered in the heart of the proposed construction area. Therefore, it is the focus of the rest of this chapter.

Comparison of Survey Methods with Excavation Results

The surface collection revealed the presence of site 18ST1-205 and it was further evaluated with test excavations. This provided an excellent opportunity to compare CSC and STPs as methods of survey. This evaluation is enhanced by more comprehensive artifact data derived from intensive excavation of the plowed deposits within the site. For this analysis, we took a 115 unit sample of the excavation units from the site. These are 5×5-foot squares, each a single quadrant of a larger 10×10-foot square that had been surface collected. An STP was excavated in the adjacent unexcavated portion of each of these 10-foot squares.

Table 4.1 shows the data recovered by each method of investigation. The most abundant artifact groups are brick, oyster shell, and later nineteenth- and twentieth-century glass. Most of these modern glass fragments are not related to the site occupation because of their date and distribution. They were recovered primarily from the units closest to Mattapany Road and represent bottles thrown into the field by passersby. In contrast, the ceramics, nails, brick, and shell clustered further out in the field, in the area determined to be the historic site. The 115 excavation squares yielded a total of 2,773 artifacts, for an average of 24.1 artifacts per 5×5-foot unit. Not included are recent plastic objects and coal. For comparison, the nearby St. John's site, occupied between 1638 and ca. 1715, yielded an average of 2,301 artifacts per 5×5-foot unit. Smith's Ordinary, inhabited for only 11 years before burning down in 1678, featured an average of 181.7 artifacts per unit. With only 24.1 artifacts per 5×5-foot square and an occupation span of about 50 years (see below), site 18ST1-205 is unquestionably a site with low artifact density.

Table 4.1. Comparison of the Artifacts Recovered by Three Different Methods from a 115-Square Sample at Site 18ST1-205

Artifact Group	Excavation Units		Surface Collection		Shovel Test Pits	
	#	%	#	%	#	%
Prehistoric Ceramics	6	0.21	-	-	-	-
Prehistoric Lithics	150	5.41	9	4.20	-	-
Fire-Cracked Rock	16	0.57	-	-	-	-
Colonial Ceramics	79	2.84	5	2.33	3	5.35
Colonial Glass	25	0.90	-	-	5	8.93
Tobacco Pipe	16	0.57	2	0.93	2	3.57
Postcolonial Ceramics	105	3.78	15	7.01	2	3.57
19th-/20th-century Glass	270	9.73	17	7.94	-	-
Wrought/Cut Nails	95	3.42	6	2.80	1	1.78
Handmade Brick	1,435	51.75	103	48.13	37	66.07
Daub	144	5.19	-	-	-	
Faunal Remains	9	0.33	1	0.46	-	
Oyster Shell	342	12.33	47	21.96	3	5.35
Miscellaneous Iron	28	1.00	6	2.80	-	
Other	53	1.91	3	1.40	3	5.35
TOTAL	2,773	99.94%	214	99.96%	56	99.97%

Since one of the project goals for this survey was to analyze artifact recovery methods, we needed to determine a way to make the data from each recovery method directly comparable. The main challenge was that the surface collection grid was divided into 10×10-foot grid squares, while our excavation units measured 5 × 5 feet. In order to compare these two data recovery methods, we extrapolated the total 5×5-foot unit assemblage (2,773 artifacts) into a 10×10-foot unit assemblage by multiplying the total artifact count by 4 (or 11,092 artifacts), and then dividing by the number of excavated squares (115 squares). This calculation yielded an average total number of artifacts per 10×10-foot square of 96.4. With this accomplished we could effectively compare the sample of artifacts recovered from the surface of a 10×10-foot area during the surface collection survey with the estimated total artifacts that would have been recovered had we excavated the entire 10×10-foot area.

In the 18ST1-205 area, the surface collection recovered 214 artifacts, for an average of 1.86 artifacts per 10-foot grid square. When expressed as a percentage of the average total number of artifacts per 10×10-foot square as calculated above, the surface collection yielded 1.92 percent of estimated artifacts. As we have shown, this was sufficient to recognize clustering of the artifacts and thus allow site identification. In contrast, STPs at a 10-foot interval recovered a total of only 56 artifacts, most of which were brick fragments, averaging 0.48 artifacts per STP. Comparing the STP artifacts with the total estimated from a 10×10-foot square, they comprise 0.49 percent of the total, or about one fourth that of the surface collection. These counts were too low to display recognizable clustering.

For artifact-rich sites, either method will likely lead to site discovery. But for short-term sites or those with fewer artifacts due to the poverty of inhabitants, there is a much higher probability that such sites will be discovered using CSC, and a much lower probability that they will be found if STPs are the only survey method used. Especially critical for this is the testing interval. The spatial distribution of STPs at 18ST1-205 was within 10 feet of every excavation unit. If the interval had been every 20 feet, we can estimate that an STP at this site would have yielded only 0.12 artifacts from that 400 square foot area on average. In contrast, a surface collection made in 20-foot squares would recover an estimated 7.41 artifacts. At wider STP intervals of 25, 30, or 50 feet, only rich sites will ever be identified, unless the excavator is fortunate enough to hit a feature or a major artifact concentration.

Dating the Site

Having identified the site, the next step was determining the time period when the site was inhabited. Specific artifacts recovered from the site, such as white clay tobacco pipes, ceramics, glass, and nails, helped in dating the occupation period. On this project only a few white clay tobacco pipe fragments were recovered; five bowl fragments have straight sides, which is suggestive of a terminal seventeenth- or eighteenth-century manufacture. Most of the measurable stems are 5/64 inch and 4/64 inch, implying a mid to late eighteenth-century date, although the number of measurable stems is too small to place much reliance on them.

Ceramics are far more abundant, with 291 sherds from 23 different ware types recovered (some of these are seen in figure 4.3). Of these, 134 sherds are likely of colonial or early postcolonial date. They include white salt-glazed stoneware, late Staffordshire combed slipware, Rhenish blue and gray stoneware, manganese mottled earthenware, Buckley ware, creamware, and several specimens of late eighteenth- to early nineteenth-century southeast Pennsylvania ware. Four creamware sherds display overglazed painted enamel decoration, a method used on creamware between ca. 1765 and ca. 1800 (Noël Hume 1970, 1978). Some tin-glazed earthenware, two sherds of

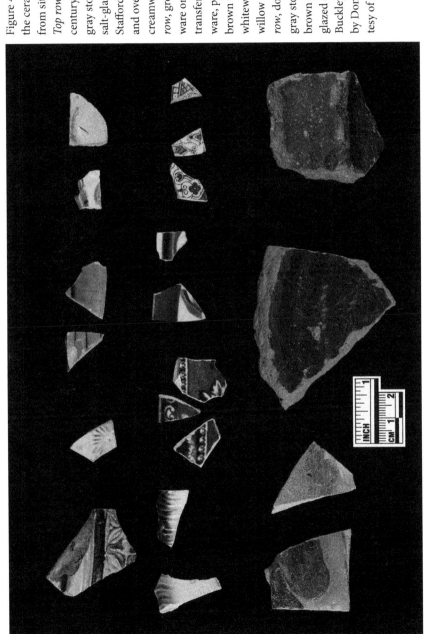

Figure 4.3. A selection of the ceramics recovered from site 18ST1-205. *Top row*, Eighteenth-century Rhenish blue and gray stoneware, white salt-glazed stoneware, Staffordshire slipware, and overglaze painted creamware in red. *Middle row*, green and blue edge-ware on pearlware, blue transfer-printed pearl-ware, painted wares, brown transfer-printed whiteware sherds, and a willow ware sherd. *Bottom row*, domestic blue and gray stoneware, domestic brown stoneware, brown glazed earthenware, and Buckley ware. (Photograph by Donald L. Winter, courtesy of HSMC.)

English soft-paste porcelain, and two fragments of Chinese porcelain, along with 21 specimens of colonial redware were also found.

There are 157 sherds of postcolonial pottery from this site. Most prominent among these are 73 fragments of pearlware, 55 sherds of whiteware, and 21 sherds of American brown or gray stoneware. Decoration provides the most accurate dating of pearlware and whiteware. While the majority of the pearlware sherds are plain, specimens of shell edged, underglaze painted, and underglaze transfer printed specimens are present, along with a few annular and sponge decorated sherds. Most of the whiteware sherds are plain, but shell edge decorated, underglaze hand-painted, and transfer printed specimens are present. The shell edge decorated sherds of both pearlware and whiteware appear in blue and green, and the style of the edge molding dates most to the ca. 1790–1840 period (Miller and Hunter 1990). The transfer printed vessels also provide good dating evidence. One group of sherds is from a Fruit and Flower border style made by Henshall & Company or Henshall, Williamson, and Company, which operated between ca. 1790 and 1828 (Larsen 1975:211–213; Snyder 1995:61). Transfer printed whiteware sherds include one vessel with a brown stipple print and another with a willow pattern print; both are probably post-1820 in date. Other specimens display a blue floral motif or a fine line green decoration that likely dates ca. 1820–1830.

Glassware from the occupation is represented by at least 17 vessels. There are 66 sherds of green blown round bottles and one sherd from a large case bottle. One base is from a ca. 1750s bottle, but the other green glass bases are from bottles dating to the ca. 1775–1820 period. Of particular note is one fragment of a blue-green colored bottle that is believed to be of French origin. These tend to be present on sites occupied during and immediately after the American Revolution, when France was an American ally (Noël Hume 1970:142–143). Additionally, there are seven thin, green blown glass sherds and one brown glass sherd from small case bottles, sometimes described as "snuff" bottles, typically dating to the early nineteenth century. A single sherd from a small aqua-tinted glass bottle was also recovered.

This range of artifacts points to an occupation that began in the later eighteenth century and continued into the first decades of the nineteenth century. Nails also support such an occupation period as the majority of the nails are handmade wrought specimens (71) or square-shafted nails (59). Since only 9 cut nails were recovered, it is likely most of the square-shaft specimens are also wrought. Four wire nails of post-ca. 1880 date were found scattered along Mattapany Road and are not related to the site. Overall, the recovered artifacts indicate that habitation at 18ST1-205 spanned a period of about 50 years, beginning ca. 1775–1785 and continuing into the early 1830s, based upon the latest decorated ceramics.

Discovering the Site's Occupants

With the date of the occupation established by the artifacts, the next question is: who lived there? Documentary evidence makes it certain that the owners of this land dwelled elsewhere. John Mackall acquired the land in 1774, although a dispute prevented him from effectively acquiring all the property until 1783 (Carr 1969). He owned it until his death in 1813, and the property passed to his son and daughter, who died in 1815 and 1816 respectively. The plantation was inherited by Mackall's son-in-law, James Brome, who lived in a house on the opposite side of Mattapany Road, not far from site 18ST1-205. He died in 1823 and the land was managed for the children by a caretaker until 1840, when son John Mackall Brome came of age and redeveloped the plantation, building a new house on the St. Mary's River that still survives. Hence this site was part of the Mackall and later Brome plantations, but neither owner lived there. The artifacts suggest occupation ceased around the time Dr. John Brome completely reconfigured the plantation landscape ca. 1840.

Potential occupants were tenants, an overseer, or enslaved African Americans. Documents indicate that there were tenants on the plantation, but the earliest detailed listing is from an 1825 tax assessment (Maryland State Archives 1826). In it, four tenements are listed, and these are again included on an 1834 assessment. These structures are the Benjamin Broome, Mrs. Price, Jeremey Rymer, and Wheatley tenements. Benjamin Broome had a brick house located on the river, and Mrs. Price's home was partially of brick construction; archaeology makes it clear that any structures at site 18ST1-205 were not brick buildings. The Rymer frame tenement house was located adjacent to the home of Mrs. Price. Wheatley's tenement is noted as having burned down and not been rebuilt; there is no evidence that site 18ST1-205 was destroyed by fire (Maryland State Archives 1841).

To determine the location of Mrs. Price's and Rymer's tenements, we consulted the 1820 Federal census. This lists the households in the St. Mary's City area as the census taker visited them and there is a pattern to the recording. By identifying known households using a detailed 1824 map, we could reasonably trace the route of the census taker. This clearly shows that the Broome, Price, and Rymer tenements were not in the Mattapany study area, but confirms that Price and Rymer were adjacent dwellings, being listed as households #33 and #34. Clearly, the sites found during this archaeological survey were not occupied by either the property owners or their tenants.

Another possibility is that the inhabitants could be an overseer and his family. However, the presence of three sites in close proximity here suggests the likelihood of multiple dwellings, and these sites may have been occupied by a larger group of people, rather than an overseer and his family. Also, there is no documentary evidence that overseers were used on the Mackall or Brome plantations. On the other hand, there is strong evidence that numerous enslaved people lived and labored on both plantations. While their homes are not documented in any surviving records, surviving tax assessments show that the number of enslaved people on Mackall's plantation varied from 22 to 40 individuals between 1795 and 1814 (Carr 1969). Based upon all available evidence, we concluded that these Mattapany Road sites were the dwellings of enslaved people.

The initial plan of the project was to fully excavate the entire 18ST1-205 site in preparation for construction. As this work was under way, HSMC and local citizens recognized the sites' significance to African American heritage and lobbied to have the construction plans altered. The parking lot was redesigned to avoid significantly impacting the identified sites so as to protect them from development. Today most of these three sites found during the survey are preserved in place.

CLUES TO ENSLAVED LIFE

The enslaved people who lived at this site used a wide variety of material items including ceramics. Analysis indicates the pottery sherds represent a minimum of 122 vessels. Fourteen of these are drinking vessels, while dining vessels are represented by 15 bowls, 13 plates and dishes, 5 saucers, a tureen, and 10 flatware vessels that are probably plates. Food preparation, dairying, or perhaps serving is indicated by two redware bowls, four pans, and five milkpans. Food storage vessels include 4 butter pots and 13 jars and crocks. There are also 25 hollow ware vessels for which a precise form could not be determined. Based on the ware, 9 of these are probably food processing or storage vessels and 15 were probably used in dining. No cooking vessels were found, but these were likely made of metal, meaning they are found less frequently archaeologically. Supplementing the ceramic beverage vessels were 10 glass wine bottles, a flask, 2 glass tumblers, and 1 wine glass. In addition, there were four small glass bottles for storing snuff, medicine, or other material. One sherd of a glass mirror was also recovered. Thus, the total assemblage of 140 ceramic and glass vessels from site 18ST1-205 consists of 41 that were beverage-related, 59 used for dining, 26 for food processing or storage, and 4 to store other substances like medicine or snuff.

Previous research by historical archaeologists has found that the homes of the enslaved tend to contain a greater quantity of hollow ceramic forms, such as bowls and drinking vessels, and fewer flatware forms, such as dishes and plates (Otto 1984; Adams and Boling 1989; Russell 1997; McIlvoy 2010). To evaluate this hypothesis, the tablewares from site 18ST1-205 were divided into hollow and flat forms with a total vessel count of 75. Of these, 47 (or 62.6%) are hollow forms and 29 (or 37.3%) are flat forms. This conforms to the pattern other archaeologists have recognized on sites of enslavement.

Among these vessels are specialized forms including two teapots, one of salt-glazed stoneware and another of creamware. Because teapots have a specific function, their presence suggests that this imported beverage or other herbal drinks were consumed by the site's residents. Chinese porcelain is present in the form of two vessels, one a saucer and the other a flatware, and there are two vessels of undetermined form made from English soft-paste porcelain from the second half of the eighteenth century.

The ceramic collection not only has a variety of wares, but also a diversity of decorations. This includes slipwares, overglaze and underglaze hand-painted wares, annular, sponged, stamped, molded, and transfer printed wares. Of particular note are pearlware sherds transfer printed in a "Diorama" series that dates to the ca. 1815–1830 period (Samford 1997:6) and whiteware vessels with brown transfer print and one with a green fine line decoration that date to ca. 1820–early 1830s (Snyder 1995).

While some of the older ceramics might represent hand-me-down items, this is unlikely to explain the most recent pottery. The presence of several quite fashionable transfer printed wares suggests that the enslaved people occasionally had some ability to acquire new items like ceramics and were not solely dependent upon the plantation owner for all domestic goods. It is notable that none of the vessel decorations match, implying piecemeal purchase instead of buying in sets (see chapter 13 for a further exploration of this topic). Indeed, it is important to acknowledge that despite the severe restrictions placed upon them, archaeology suggests that the enslaved had the agency to participate to a degree in the market economy, allowing them to express a sense of self through the purchasing of specific items of material culture.

ARCHAEOLOGICAL FEATURES

The artifacts demonstrate that the site was occupied by enslaved people during the late eighteenth and early nineteenth centuries. A variety of cultural features were found on the site, including post holes, pits containing charcoal, brick and daub, and several unidentified linear features. Definitive features of architectural origin, such as brick chimneys or hearths, building foundations, and large structural post holes, were absent from the site.

Given the agrarian setting, it is not surprising that most of the features observed at the base of the plow zone were plow scars. However, an intriguing set of linear features that were initially thought to be plow scars were discovered. Unlike plow scars, these ran some distance and then turned at right angles. This set of trench features forms an enclosure measuring 27 feet wide by 70+ feet long, creating a rectangular shape (figure 4.4). Inside the rectangle were a number of features of an undefined nature, including intrusions with brick, small post holes, and a large pit at the west end (Units 4373 A and B) that contained charcoal, daub, and brick. The trench varied in width from about 0.7 feet to 1.5 feet and was widest on the north and south sides. Close inspection of the trench in several places revealed the presence of post molds within it. These indicate that the trench was dug to hold closely spaced vertical timbers, and the shapes of the molds indicate that both small complete logs and split timbers were used in its construction. Such a feature is usually interpreted as a palisade, fences which are frequently found on seventeenth-century sites. But it was the fill around and under the molds at the bottom of the trench that was very strange. It was a distinctive brownish-yellow clay unlike any other soil found at the site. In every other palisade fence excavated at St. Mary's City, the fence trenches are backfilled with the soil excavated from the trench. We hypothesized that the clay may have been obtained from a deeper stratum. To test that hypothesis, we excavated unit 3750A down five feet into subsoil and cored four feet deeper. None of the distinctive yellow clay in the palisade trench was found. Subsequent searches around St. Mary's City have likewise failed to find any clay of this color, so its source remains unknown.

Equally confounding is the date of this feature to sometime in the late eighteenth or early nineteenth centuries. Palisade fences are extremely rare in the Chesapeake region during that period, with the main exceptions being military contexts, such as the siege lines built during the Revolutionary War at Yorktown, Virginia. Consultation with archaeologists throughout Virginia and Maryland, including Norman Barka, Ivor Noël Hume, William Kelso, Alain Outlaw, Nicholas Luccketti, Julia King, and Paul Shackel, indicated

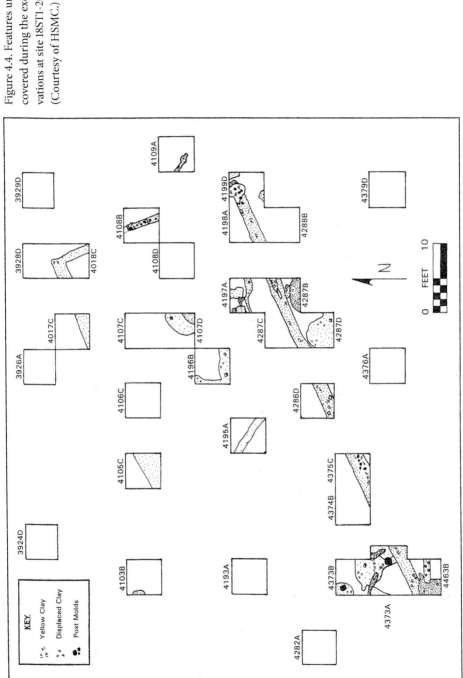

Figure 4.4. Features uncovered during the excavations at site 18ST1-205. (Courtesy of HSMC.)

that they have not found palisade fences on sites of this period either. And no one has previously found trenches in the Chesapeake backfilled with a soil foreign to the site.

Several examples of trench-built structures have been excavated in South Carolina. Thomas Wheaton found that slave quarters at the Yaughan and Curriboo sites consisted of trenches that held vertical timbers which supported the walls. It has been argued that these are African construction practices (Wheaton et al. 1983), although the case for a French origin has also been made by several authors (Steen 1999; Shlasko 2002). In these instances, the trenches define the wall lines, and are relatively deep, usually from 1.5 to 2.5 feet. Posts are often set at intervals of several feet, although a few cases are known of more closely set timbers. These buildings range in width from 11 to 25 feet and 20 to 40 feet in length.

While these dimensions are not a strong match for the feature found at the Mattapany Road site, the South Carolina and Maryland cases do share one similarity. At both Yaughan and Curriboo, the trenches were not backfilled with the soil excavated from them, as is typical and was found in the post holes at these sites. Instead the Yaughan structures had a fill of red clay different from the surrounding subsoil, and at Curriboo the trenches were filled with gray clay that is not native to the site (Wheaton et al. 1983:160–161). That clay had a swirled appearance, suggesting to Wheaton that it had been partially kneaded and he observed that it was identical to the clay used to make the colonoware ceramics at the site (Wheaton 1987:5). This is a very unusual practice not seen on French sites, where backfilled soil is used (for example, Stone 1974; Walthall 1991; Steen 1999). The discovery of such a practice on sites inhabited by enslaved Africans is curious.

So what does this feature represent? One hypothesis is that it served as a fenced enclosure for a livestock pen. However, chemical testing of the plow zone soils showed that phosphate concentrations occur mostly outside the fenced area, not within it, as would be expected with a livestock pen. Given the South Carolina examples, the possibility of its being a structure must also be considered. If it was a building, its dimensions were 27 to 29 feet wide, and more than 70 feet long, much larger than any other known examples. It is true that nails, brick fragments, and some daub do cluster along or within the feature area, strongly implying architecture. But a key piece of evidence comes from the excavation records. The trench extends only about 1.5 inches into subsoil. Even taking into account soil erosion in the field, this trench is unlikely to have ever been more than 14 or 15 inches deep. All excavated building trenches in South Carolina are much deeper than this because they needed to provide structural support. This makes it far more likely that the Mattapany site feature was a palisade fence rather than a building. The most feasible explanation is that it was a fence that formed an enclosure, perhaps something like a compound around the houses of the enslaved occupants. Perhaps such a fence provided the residents some limited privacy from travelers on the immediately adjacent road.

But if the trench represents a fence, where are the houses? Although the dwellings of the enslaved are seldom described in any detail and few survive, documents suggest that during the late eighteenth to early nineteenth centuries the vast majority of enslaved Africans in Maryland lived in log dwellings with chimneys made of wattle and daub (McDaniel 1982:43–44, 74–75). Today, of the hundreds of these structures that once existed, a single log quarter survives in southern Maryland at the Sotterley Plantation. And archaeologically, such structures leave relatively few clues. The logs may have been ground-laid or rested on shallow cobble or brick foundations, and the chimneys often consisted of hewn log sections stacked horizontally to form a flue that was plastered with clay daub (McDaniel 1982:74–75). Once the structures were demolished and the location converted to agriculture, few subsurface clues of these buildings or chimneys survive, because plowing to depths of 8 to 10 inches will destroy most physical evidence of log homes. All that would be left to suggest their presence would be clusters of nails, brick fragments, and the debris of domestic life. Given the archaeological features and distribution of artifacts at site 18ST1-205, we conclude that this investigation has discovered a fenced enclosure within which several log cabins inhabited by the enslaved people of the Mackall and early Brome Plantation once stood. Figure 4.5 shows an African American log home in Georgia that is similar to what we believe stood at the Mattapany site. Except for the palisade fence and perhaps an interior root cellar or two, few archaeological features of this house would survive plowing.

In 2016, St. Mary's College began development of the land on the opposite side of Mattapany Road from site 18ST1-205. Because of the known potential for more sites similar to it, an archaeological survey was conducted (McMillan et al. 2017). This survey employed STPs at 25-foot intervals, and a small number of artifacts were discovered. Because of the potential for low-density sites in the area as proven by our previous work, these artifacts were given special attention and the STP survey was followed with testing that suggests several more homes of the Mackall Plantation enslaved community may have stood in this area. Few cultural features were detected, and the occupations had artifact densities as low as those at 18ST1-205. This

Figure 4.5. An African American quarter thought to be similar to those that stood at site 18ST1-205, including a surrounding palisade fence. (Photograph is of a log slave cabin in Barbour County, Alabama, 1936. Source: Library of Congress, Manuscripts Division, Federal Writer's Project, United States Work Projects Administration. WPA Slave Narrative Project, A917, vol. 1, https://www.loc.gov/item/mesnp010000/.)

further demonstrates that the area along Mattapany Road was a previously unknown center of African American life during the late eighteenth and early nineteenth centuries.

CONCLUSION

The work conducted along Mattapany Road is a valuable case study about survey methodology in historical archaeology. History indicates that there are many low-density sites like these because of the many thousands of enslaved people who were once held on Chesapeake plantations. This is probably also the case for poor tenant farmers both black and white. In southern Maryland, the enslaved made up 45 percent of the population in the 1790 United States census. These homes are almost never documented, nearly all have vanished, and their traces can be very difficult for archaeologists to find. Indeed, our investigation demonstrates that such sites can have very low archaeological visibility and be easily missed. If a casual pedestrian survey or shovel test pit survey at wide intervals had been used, it is likely the sites discussed here would have been completely missed. And in that case, the area would have been declared free of archaeology, and the fragile traces of these enslaved lives destroyed forever by construction. Fortunately, the more time-consuming and costly controlled surface collection method was employed that yielded sufficient evidence for archaeologists to notice the clustering of materials which led to site discovery. This shows that the choice of archaeological survey methodology can be critical in determining the types of sites that are found. While shovel test pit excavation is faster and thus cheaper, it retrieves relatively few artifacts, and this is a critical factor for low-density sites, especially those of the enslaved and very poor. Thus, economics continues to disfavor the lowest status people, allowing their sites to be overlooked or dismissed as an insignificant scatter of artifacts. For these sites, controlled surface collection is a preferred method of archaeological reconnaissance. This project demonstrates how challenging yet important it is to locate such dwellings and preserve their stories.

The Mattapany Road project revealed a previously understudied community of enslaved Africans and African Americans. The archaeology not only yielded evidence about the material goods they possessed and even perhaps purchased, but also revealed an unusual construction method and type of enclosure that is very rare in this region during the late eighteenth and early nineteenth centuries. Whether this is an African practice remains a matter of debate and is a puzzle that only future research can ultimately solve. Perhaps most importantly, this work is a demonstration of how historical archaeology can produce important new perspectives on enslaved people long overlooked by history.

5

Ceramic Studies at Maryland's First Capital

SILAS D. HURRY

WHY POTTERY?

"The Creator Has an Inordinate Fondness for Beetles" is a quote often misattributed to Charles Darwin. One could equally say "archaeologists have an inordinate fondness for ceramics." Ceramics in their myriad of types and varieties so often dominate artifact discussions that one could assume that people awoke in the morning to contemplate what pot they were going to break that day and how it would affect their life. In reality, people in the past were far less concerned about ceramics than so many other details of their lives. It is indeed the archaeologists who are fixated on pottery. Why are we so focused on these burnt pieces of clay? Ceramics by their nature have two distinct traits: they are fragile in use and stable in the ground. Ceramics will persist in archaeological sites while most organics will rapidly decay away. In most of the past, organic materials were the most common and significant elements within material culture. In the colonial period, the greatest amount of wealth owned by most individuals was in the form of their clothing, bed linens, and other textiles. These nonpreserving materials were the way one advertised one's relative status and how people sought to differentiate themselves from others. Even durable materials like pewter do not necessarily end up in the archaeological record. While a broken ceramic pot has no inherent value, broken pewter vessels have considerable recycle value and are therefore seldom discarded (Martin 1989). An extremely high status item like an upholstered or "turkey work" chair would leave at most a handful of metal tacks for the archaeologist to recover. Ceramics were so insignificant in the day-to-day life of most colonists that in probate inventories, bureaucratic documents listing all of an individual's worldly possessions to ensure the proper division of estates often lumped them together, as in "a parcel of earthenware and other trumpery" (Maryland State Archives 1689).

Trumpery is defined in the *Oxford English Dictionary* as "worthless stuff, trash, rubbish" (1971:3421).

POTTERY AS ECONOMICS, GEOGRAPHY, AND POLITICS

All of this being said, ceramics and the study of ceramics are extremely important in the examination of the past through archaeological inquiry into material culture. Ceramics serve as time indicators, trade indicators, and symbols of cultural elitism. Their significance in understanding the archaeological record cannot be overemphasized. The strength of archaeology is in finding facts that were not written down. Ceramics are the very words and syntax of these facts.

Earthenware, stoneware, and porcelain, in addition to tobacco pipes, all made of ceramic, are the primary tool for dating historic deposits. In addition to being quite durable in the ground, ceramics are a product which reflects rapid change in technology and taste. Potters compete through novelty—something new always appeals to the consumer. As technology evolves, potters find cheaper or otherwise more efficient means of producing and decorating pots. Innovation means change, which allows us as archaeologists to calibrate time in cultural deposits.

Ceramics also point to trade patterns and distribution chains that were the result of larger economic and political changes. This can most clearly be seen in early Maryland in terms of the international nature of ceramics on first-generation sites in the colony. In addition to German stonewares, Dutch tin-glazed and other earthenware, Italian slip-decorated earthenware, French Martincamp stoneware from Normandy, Portuguese micaceous red earthenware, and Iberian "olive" jars were all well represented in the early assemblages. This extremely "international" range of ceramics stands in stark comparison to what comes subsequently. With the passage, and more importantly the enforcement, of England's Navigation Acts after about 1660, the ceramics in St. Mary's City begin to become almost universally British in origin. There are exceptions like the various stonewares from what eventually became Germany that continued in broad use because the English did not "invent" stoneware until the end of the seventeenth century. One can see the result of economic policy in the soil of early Maryland sites.

One can also see hints of political alliances in the pottery in use. From 1580 to 1640, Portugal was ruled by the monarchs of Spain during a period some historians have referred to as the "Babylonian Captivity" (Hanson 1981:5, 77). In 1640, the Braganza family led an uprising that wrested control of Portugal from their Spanish overlords. The old adage that "my friend's enemies are my enemies" and its corollary, "my enemy's enemies are my friends," held true, and the Braganza dynasty became close allies and trading partners with England. This culminated with the betrothal of Catherine of Braganza to Charles II in 1662. With the rise of the Braganzas, the Portuguese micaceous redwares and the more formal Portuguese tin-glazed earthenware flowed into England, and hence to sites in Maryland. The significance of the Braganza connection carries into an entire range of material culture and economic impacts from the adoption of the tea ceremony and Chinese porcelains through the establishment of a British presence in India. Bombay, now Mumbai, was part of Catherine's dowry (Thomas 1965).

One can also see hints of internal economic change and trade connections within the British economy in the presence of different types of ceramics. The earliest ceramic assemblages, in addition to being broadly international in scope, seem to have large quantities of London area–derived ceramics. Most notably, Border wares from the Surrey-Hampshire border region just southwest of London dominate the ceramic assemblages in terms of utilitarian earthenwares (Pearce 1992). When first recognized by Henry Miller at the St. John's site in the 1970s, what was then called Surrey ware or Surrey-Hampshire ware was a distinctive pottery with a whitish paste and a clear lead glaze that appeared yellowish on the pots. Mostly storage forms, dairy forms, and other food preparation shapes like pipkins, Border wares constituted the majority of utilitarian ceramics in the earliest phases at the St. John's site. Quantities of London Area Post-Medieval Redware are also present. Later in time, ceramics from the west of England, including Donyatt and most importantly Devon, become much more numerous in assemblages. North Devon sgraffito and gravel-tempered earthenware providing both dining shapes and utilitarian forms become increasingly common later in the seventeenth century with the rise of the outports, notably Bristol, Barnstaple, and Bideford. This same phenomenon can be seen in the ascendancy of Bristol-made pipes which dominate in the last quarter of the seventeenth century. All these trends relate not to a change in manufacturing, but rather to changes in distribution and trade within the tobacco economy. The London region continued to produce ceramics in a major way throughout the seventeenth century, but the distribution to the Chesapeake changed through time.

An interesting aspect of the trade and distribution of pottery in St. Mary's City is the quantities of locally produced pottery which find their way into the artifactual record of the seventeenth century. I am specifically speaking about the work of Morgan Jones. Jones arrived in Maryland in 1661 as an indentured servant owned by Robert Slye at Bushwood, approximately 25 miles north on the Potomac River. Slye was one of the wealthiest planters in Maryland in the third quarter of the seventeenth century. His probate inventory of 1671, while containing no assigned values, encompasses 56 pages in transcription. The inventory includes what appear to be mounted ostrich eggs, a cabinet of tortoise shell and ebony, numerous silver vessels, and debts deemed recoverable of nearly 300,000 pounds of tobacco. Notable in the inventory is a space referred to as the "pott house." Jones had passed his indenture by the time Slye died so that there is nothing in the "pott house" to reflect his handiwork, but in other places in the inventory are listed "431 earthenware porringers" (Maryland State Archives 1671).

After completing his indenture, Morgan Jones apparently relocated to the south shore of the Potomac in Westmoreland County, Virginia, not far from Machdoc Creek, by 1669. Here he operated a pottery in partnership with Dennis White on a plantation owned by John Quigley. Intriguingly, Quigley contracted to build the brick State House in St. Mary's City in 1675, suggesting that the Potomac River was not a barrier, but rather an avenue in the colonial period. Following his time operating the kiln with White on Quigley's plantation in Westmoreland County, Jones appears to have acquired a plantation on Maryland's Eastern Shore and settled into a life as a planter. He may have continued potting on his new plantation because his probate inventory includes "a parcel of earthenware" appraised at £2 which is a huge amount suggesting a great deal of earthenware.

It was the Jones's kiln in Westmoreland County where Morgan Jones pottery was first discovered and described by William Kelso and Edward Chappell (1974). They excavated the kiln site and recovered numerous waster vessels that documented the range of shapes and forms being produced. Notable among these was a handled pitcher with a distinctive thumbprint-impressed termination. Three relatively complete examples of this pitcher form were subsequently discovered in our excavations in St. Mary's City (see figure 5.1). The first of these were found in a salvage excavation in 1977. Examination of the distinctive paste and range of forms represented at the Westmoreland site allowed Henry Miller to identify numerous utilitarian earthenware cups, pans, milk pans, and bowls among the ceramics from the St. John's site. The paste has notable amounts of red ocher and mica inclusions characteristic of the clays of the Chesapeake coastal plain. Subsequently, Morgan Jones pottery has been recorded on numerous sites in both Virginia and Maryland (Straube 1995).

Figure 5.1. Earthenware pitchers made by Maryland's first European potter, Morgan Jones (1661–ca. 1680s). (Donald L. Winter, courtesy of HSMC.)

EXOTICA

While many of the ceramics recovered in St. Mary's City represent rather common pottery types seen on numerous sites in English North America, some of the material deserves further mention because it is simply unusual. Most notable in this regard is a collection of ceramic fragments from the Van Sweringen site. The most exotic of these are fragments of very carefully decorated earthenwares that had been manufactured in Turkey in the province of Kutahya, south of modern Istanbul. In the sixteenth through eighteenth centuries, Kutahya was the center of ceramic production in Turkey. Kutahya was the successor to Iznik, the modern name for Nicaea. Iznik is located between Kutahya and Istanbul and served as the principal production site for highly decorated ceramics in the preceding centuries. Both Iznik and Kutahya were well known for their decorative tiles in addition to their ceramic vessels. These brightly decorated ceramics using a range of rich colors were shipped throughout the Islamic world and imported into Europe from this specialized ceramic center. It would be more proper to call these Armenian ceramics rather than Turkish because the entire potting tradition was Armenian rather than Ottoman (Carroll 1999).

This type of ceramic has been found only on four other archaeological sites in North America. Two of these are located in Williamsburg, Virginia, while the other two are in Nova Scotia, Canada. The Williamsburg examples come from Raleigh Tavern and Weatherburn's Tavern while the Canadian examples are from Fortress Louisburg and Canso on Cape Breton. The Nova Scotia and Williamsburg examples clearly date to the eighteenth century while our example dates to either the late seventeenth or very early eighteenth century (Audrey Noël Hume 1978; Hansen 1986; Carroll 1999).

Also discovered at the Van Sweringen site is a type of red stoneware identified as Elers ware. Elers ware is described by Noël Hume as red-bodied, unglazed stoneware (Noël Hume 1970:120). Elers was a rather novel ceramic type when introduced late in the seventeenth century. It occurs almost solely in tea-related forms. Our specimen was initially identified as Elers, but further research seems to indicate that our specimens are actually Yixing. Yixing is the Chinese ceramic that the Elers brothers were imitating. Its usage goes back to around AD 1000, but it was exported in quantities beginning in the seventeenth century. Our specimen has a fragmentary reign mark indicating that it was made in the Qing dynasty and dates from 1662 to 1722 (Aaron Miller, pers. comm., 2018).

It is intriguing that both these ceramics were from the Van Sweringen site. Garrett Van Sweringen arrived in the Maryland colony in 1665 after the capture of the Dutch colony of New Amstel in Delaware by the English. While in St. Mary's City, Van Sweringen operated a successful ordinary and eventually a private inn. He was a creative entrepreneur who appears to have operated a brew house and a bakery and what appears to be one of the earliest coffee houses in English North America. Van Sweringen served variously as sheriff of St. Mary's County and alderman and mayor of St. Mary's City. It is possible the coffee cups are associated with his elegant inn and coffee house. Garrett Van Sweringen would have had the exposure to a range of ceramic types both in Holland and subsequently in the Dutch possessions in the New World.

It is also possible that these unusual ceramics were owned by William Deacon, a Royal customs collector who married Garrett's son's widow, Mary Neal, in the early eighteenth century. A third possibility is that Neal, who married four times and was a descendant of both the Calverts and James Neale (who served on the Governor's council and was Lord Baltimore's special representative to Amsterdam disputing Dutch claims to Delaware), may have owned such unusual pottery. Regardless of the owner, these are undoubtedly exotic ceramic vessels.

POTS NOT PIECES

One of the essential and significant contributions of ceramic studies from St. Mary's City is the use of ceramic vessel analysis. Some of the earliest vessel analyses by archaeologists were undertaken by prehistorians. Anna O. Shepard, in her seminal 1956 study *Ceramics for the Archaeologist,* promoted vessel analysis as a means of better understanding past lifeways. I quizzed a number of colleagues about the history of the use of vessel analysis by historical archaeologists and all agreed that it was something historical archaeologists have always done. While Noël Hume does not use the phrase vessel analysis in *Historical Archaeology* (1968), he discusses the many insights that can be drawn from cross-mending. When one examines published studies from the 1960s, '70s, and '80s, sherd counts are the main data. For example, Stanley South's pattern analysis is based on counts of fragments rather than vessels.

The process of undertaking a vessel analysis essentially boils down to sorting all the ceramic fragments into like types and then examining each of these piles of similar sherds for distinctions that make them individual vessels. With the more vernacular or folk type of pots manufactured in the seventeenth century, this is often relatively easy. There is considerable variation between pots of the same type because they are produced through a craft activity. One of the challenges is the amount of variation within a given pot. Sometimes two different sides of the same pot can look quite different. Post-depositional transforms are also a challenge. We have an example of Donyatt slipware from St. Mary's where one of the sherds was separated from the others and highly burned after breakage. Because the fragments mend, they are clearly the same pot, but at first glance, one may not think they belong together. Perhaps the greatest challenge in doing a ceramic vessel analysis is the uniformity of appearance among pots that emerged with the advent of industrial levels of production in the eighteenth and nineteenth centuries. Created in plaster of Paris molds, these pots were designed to look alike as elements of sets. Sorting plain refined white earthenwares can be difficult at best.

Generally, one undertakes a ceramic vessel analysis with the understanding that all pots have rims and bases. These are often the key sherds in defining a ceramic vessel. However, we do not always recover rim and base sherds for each vessel, so a unique sherd or set of similar sherds not represented by either a rim or a base still can constitute a ceramic vessel. A large degree of finesse and perception of the variation that occurs in a given pot are needed to complete a ceramic vessel analysis that actually captures the essence of an assemblage (the basics of performing a vessel analysis are outlined in Voss and Allen 2010).

Historic St. Mary's City has pursued ceramic vessel analysis for more than 40 years. The earliest such study was published by Garry Wheeler Stone, Stephen Israel, and Glenn Little working with material from the John Hicks site (Stone et al. 1973; a revised summary version of these studies can be found in chapter 12). When George Miller joined the staff of the St. Mary's City Commission in 1972, he undertook a ceramic vessel analysis of materials recovered from the Tolle-Tabbs site located on the outskirts of St. Mary's City which had been occupied from the mid-eighteenth century into the mid-nineteenth century (Miller 1974; see chapter 13 for an updated version of this study).

In 1972, the St. Mary's City Commission archaeology team, directed by Garry Wheeler Stone and Alexander H. Morrison II, began intensive investigation of the St. John's site in St. Mary's City. This site, occupied from 1638 through approximately 1720, had been the home of the colony's principal secretary, a planter/factor of Dutch extraction, and the colony's governor, and finally served as one of the larger inns or ordinaries in the capital (see chapter 7). Henry Miller analyzed the ceramics from the site, dividing the occupation into three phases. He achieved this by seriating the feature contexts and then relating these sequences to the ceramic fragments within the contexts and thereby dating the ceramic vessels. Miller's analysis of these ceramics was aided by a progression of students of whom I am fortunate to count myself a member.

Miller went on to analyze vessels from excavations at the Van Sweringen site, Chancellor's Point, and a sequence of sites within the Town Center complex, including the Leonard Calvert House and Smith's Ordinary. All these analyses incorporated usage of the POTS nomenclature developed by Beaudry, Long, Miller, Neiman, and Stone (Beaudry et al. 1983). POTS, or the Potomac Typological System, is an emic typology created following the terminology seen in contemporary documents, notably probate inventories from Maryland and Virginia in the seventeenth and early eighteenth centuries. By using the same emic categories of organization as the users of the ceramics, we can glean insights into what the pots we find may have meant to their users.

COMPARING BETWEEN SITES RATHER THAN WITHIN ONE SITE

The greatest strength of a collection like that of Historic St. Mary's City is the opportunity to compare the ceramic assemblages of numerous sites to see patterns of use rather than the idiosyncratic behaviors of one site's inhabitants. At the St. John's site we can see change through time on one site. By examining multiple sites occupied in the seventeenth century, we can see differences in site function, and attempt to access the economic and social differences between sites. The St. Mary's collection has the advantage of representing one place and a consistent approach to ceramic vesselization, which actually allows one to compare apples to apples rather than apples to a disparate recipe for fruit cocktail.

The sample used for this study incorporates a range of sites from St. Mary's City (see table 5.1). The sites, in mean chronological order, are the Chapel Field Phase I; St. John's Phase I; Smith's Ordinary; St. John's Phase II; the Print House; Chapel Field Phase III; and St. John's Phase III. Miller oversaw the analysis of the three phases of St. John's and Smith's Ordinary. The remaining St. Mary's components were analyzed by Ilene Frank working on the two Chapel components and Katie Cavallo analyzing the Print House assemblage under my direction.

While these assemblages were initially organized using the POTS nomenclature, to simplify comparisons the collections have been aggregated into seven functional groups: beverage storage (jars, jugs, bottles); beverage service (cups, mugs, drinking pot, flask); food preparation (pipkin, milk pan, large bowl); food storage (butter pots); food service (plates, dishes, saucers, porringers, small bowls); hygiene-related (galley pots, basins, chamber pot); and generic vessels, which includes some of the ambiguous multifunctional forms. It is understood that many of these vessels could be and probably were used for different functions; the goal is to focus on the main or principal functional classes.

Looking across the spectrum of sites we see a great deal of variation, with very few hygiene-related vessels and disparate ratios of beverage to food forms (see figure 5.2). Hygiene seems best represented at Smith's, but this could be a site formation issue because the building burned to the ground with its contents, a process that seems to have added an unusual number of galley pots to the assemblage. Alternatively, Van Sweringen is known to have had an indentured servant who provided medical services (Miller 2008). The general trend shows more drink-related vessels through time, though the pattern is not absolute. Chapel Phase I shows more drink-related vessels than subsequent assemblages, but this is probably a function of numerous beverage storage containers, primarily jugs. St. John's Phase I shows a higher ratio of food-related vessels while Smith's Ordinary, St. John's II, and the Print House demonstrate a decline on the food side. The Print House, St. John's III, and Chapel III all have ratios leaning toward the beverage-related

Table 5.1. Ceramic Vessel Assemblages from St. Mary's City

	Chapel Field I 1635–1645		St. John's I 1638–1665		Smith's Ordinary 1666–1677		St. John's II 1665–1685	
	#	%	#	%	#	%	#	%
Food Preparation	12	27.91%	31	37.35%	38	14.73%	38	44.19%
Food Storage	1	2.33%	7	8.43%	27	10.47%	7	8.14%
Food Consumption	3	6.98%	28	33.73%	79	30.62%	8	9.30%
Total Food		37.21%		79.52%		55.81%		61.63%
Drink Storage	25	58.14%	11	13.25%	46	17.83%	18	20.93%
Drink Consumption	0	0.00%	2	2.41%	32	12.40%	11	12.79%
Specialized Drink	0	0.00%	0	0.00%	4	1.55%	0	0.00%
Total Drink		58.14%		15.66%		31.78%		33.72%
Hygiene	2	4.65%	3	3.61%	32	12.40%	3	3.49%
Other	0	0.00%	1	1.20%	0	0.00%	1	1.16%
Total Vessels	43	100.00%	83	100.00%	258	100.00%	86	100.00%

	Print House 1670–1700		St. John's III 1685–1715		Chapel Field III 1680–1720	
	#	%	#	%	#	%
Food Preparation	14	11.67%	26	15.48%	35	21.08%
Food Storage	0	0.00%	19	11.31%	19	11.45%
Food Consumption	26	21.67%	16	9.52%	12	7.23%
Total Food		33.33%		36.31%		39.76%
Drink Storage	4	3.33%	21	12.50%	6	3.61%
Drink Consumption	71	59.17%	68	40.48%	83	50.00%
Specialized Drink	2	1.67%	7	4.17%	6	3.61%
Total Drink		64.17%		57.14%		57.23%
Hygiene	3	2.50%	10	5.95%	4	2.41%
Other	0	0.00%	1	0.60%	1	0.60%
Total Vessels	120	100.00%	168	100.00%	166	100.00%

vessels. This final group contains our most recent sites, so we are seeing a chronological trend. The low hygiene numbers mean what we are seeing are primarily the differences in food and drink vessels.

Looking at only the food-related vessels, we see little consistent patterning. Food preparation ranges for sites that served as ordinaries barely cluster at all, with Smith's Ordinary, the Print House, and St. John's Phase III all demonstrating variable distributions. Perhaps the availability of many alternatives to ceramics for food preparation explains the extreme variability. Cast iron, bell metal, and tin pans and pots were not uncommon items based on contemporary probate inventories. Part of the variability may stem from

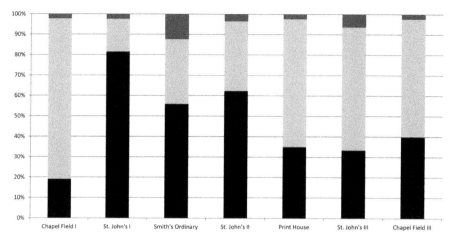

Figure 5.2. Comparison of ceramic vessels from St Mary's City sites by general functional categories. (Figure by Silas D. Hurry.)

■ Hygiene

▦ Drink

■ Food

the differing significance of dairying in the various households. Perhaps the categories are a bit too broad so that the strong dairying signature from the earliest phase at St. John's is not terribly distinct. Food storage also appears to range considerably. Our two earliest cases, St. John's Phase I and Chapel Field I, are not particularly comparable, while our two latest assemblages seem very similar. Food service is equally variable. Highlighting those assemblages related to ordinaries, we see some comparability among this subset, but not necessarily a clear pattern.

Looking at the comparison of all three food-related activities, very little in the way of pattern emerges (see figure 5.3). Perhaps we are again seeing the use of alternative materials. Probate inventories are awash with possibilities. Clearly pewter plates, which were a common food service material, may represent part of this variability, as could treen and silver (Martin 1989). None of these would end up in the archaeological record because plate and pewter have intrinsic value and treen would not survive to be recovered.

An important subset of food-related ceramics is those specifically attributable to dairying activities (see figure 5.4). As pointed out by Carr et al. (1991), part of establishing a successful plantation in the early Chesapeake involved developing the farm—improving fencing, planting orchards, developing dairying, etc. Looking at the most obvious dairy-related ceramic vessels—milk pans and butter pots—we see a rather consistent pattern with the exception of Smith's Ordinary, which seems to have an inordinate number of butter pots earlier than other sites. While urban, and not directly related

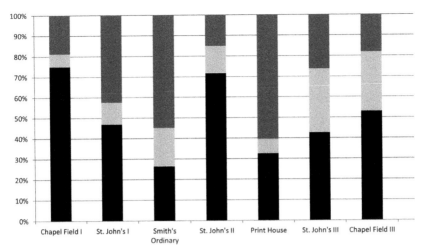

Figure 5.3. Comparison of food-related ceramic vessels from St. Mary's City sites. (Figure by Silas D. Hurry.)

■ Food Consumption
▨ Food Storage
■ Food Preparation

to a developing farm, Smith's has one of the highest raw counts of dairying ceramics. This seems somewhat anomalous, but it might relate to provisioning the ordinary. Milk pans are the vessel most clearly related to dairying, although they can have other functions. Butter pots can be used to store a wide variety of foodstuffs so their large percentage may be a function of this multiuse characteristic. The various additional assemblages seem to show the increasing significance of dairying through time, although the increase is not dramatic.

Looking specifically at the vessels related to drink, we see a major increase in the number of beverage service vessels over time and a comparable decline in beverage storage (see figure 5.5). This may relate to a general increase in individualized consumption as the period moved forward. While several of these assemblages were related to ordinaries, the trend is consistent over time. We see a decline in beverage storage in ceramics while we see a steady increase in beverage service. The decline in beverage storage probably relates to the introduction of the cheaper, free-blown round glass bottles replacing the ceramic vessels over time while there is a distinct increase in the number of individual drinking vessels. Specialized ceramic vessels for exotic beverages barely register in these collections as the craze for tea and coffee had not yet taken widespread hold.

The same set of trends can be seen looking at one site through time. As Miller has pointed out, the St. John's site shows a similar increase in individualized drinking vessels through time. While the late phase at St. John's

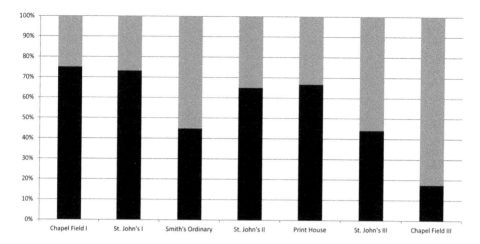

Figure 5.4. Comparison of dairy-related ceramic vessels from St. Mary's City sites. (Figure by Silas D. Hurry.)

■ Butter Pots
■ Milk Pans

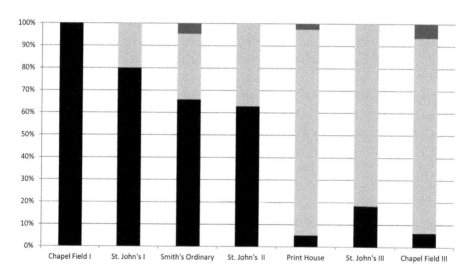

Figure 5.5. Comparison of beverage-related ceramic vessels from St. Mary's City sites. (Figure by Silas D. Hurry.)

■ Specialized Drinking
▨ Drink Service
■ Drink Storage

represents a period when the building served as an ordinary and home, similar trends can be seen elsewhere. This individualization of drinking vessels has been noted by a range of scholars working in the Chesapeake and elsewhere. Fraser Neiman working at the Clifts plantation in Westmoreland County, Virginia, saw a tripling of the number of individual drinking vessels in the first decades of the eighteenth century and a further tripling by the end of the third decade (1980a, 1980b). This proliferation of individualized drinking vessels was supplied by the increased production and distribution of the Staffordshire and Staffordshire-like slipwares, Rhenish blue and gray stoneware, and further enhanced by the development of English brown stoneware. Concepts such as a developing "Georgian-mindset" (Deetz 1977), a "consumer revolution" (Carson 1994, 2017), and a "rise in gentility" (Pogue 2005) have all been forwarded as explaining this phenomenon. Perhaps we are seeing an increase in gentility as an expression of a changing mindset abetted by a consumer revolution. Was the consumer revolution driven by cultural changes or propelled by the nascent industrial revolution? At this moment I do not think we know and in all probability it was all of the above and some other factors we have yet to recognize.

Another consideration in the very latest samples is the rise of the tea ceremony in the early eighteenth century (Roth 1961). The tea ceremony has its own set of very specific ceramic vessels. As a rule, tea vessels lead other forms in advances in decoration and concomitant cost and value. In their analysis of the John Hicks ceramics, Stone et al. (1973) found John Hicks to be ahead of the curve in adopting these specialized ceramics because of his rather direct connections to England as a merchant and mariner. Stone had seen a similar pattern in a study of New England probate inventories from the seventeenth century (1975). Ships' captains and mariners were the first to adopt tea equipage and this most fashionable of social activities. Lorinda Goodwin (1999) saw a similar process—upper status individuals using material culture to demonstrate their position and differentiate themselves from lesser people. This seems to present shades of Thorstein Veblen and his *Theory of the Leisure Class* (1899), which argued that the desire to obtain the trappings of the wealthy helps to keep the lower economic classes in check because they are attempting to acquire these trappings rather than overthrowing the entire system. The consumption of tea and ownership of the associated ceramics to consume it advertises one's position and to what one aspires.

WHY CERAMICS?

The study of ceramics throws a bright light on matters economic and political. International politics always has economic consequence. The rise of the Braganzas and their antipathy to the Spanish Hapsburgs led to friendly relations between Portugal and England. Friendly relations were lubricated by trade and profit so that we see material manifestations in the form of Portuguese ceramics on British colonial sites, while the rise of English mercantile policy can be seen in the disappearance of numerous European ceramic types as the grip of the Navigation Acts began to suppress all trade with ships not flagged in Britain. Internal changes in English ceramic trade also manifests themselves in terms of the availability of certain types as trade centers shift.

Economic isolation and depressed material availability led Robert Slye to indenture Morgan Jones to produce the mundane earthenware needed on the Chesapeake frontier. In bringing Jones to the colony, Slye was bucking the English mercantile policy. In a way he was foreshadowing the self-sufficient plantations which eventually grew in the eighteenth century where enslaved specialists created the very stuff of the plantation. Plantation owners would have among their enslaved carpenters, coopers, sawyers, blacksmiths, etc. (Morgan 1952:53).

Ceramic vessel analysis allows us to look beyond how things are broken to how they were used. People tend not to think deeply about the pottery they use, which is one reason it serves as an excellent surrogate to the sometimes unconscious human actions which speak to deeply held, if not always articulated, beliefs. A desire for order, a hope for economic advancement, and a belief in possibility can all be manifested in the way we use ceramics and how we discard them. The materials people use and discard are of great interest to archaeologists because the "stuff" encompasses technological innovation, changing tastes, and shifting worldview. As one of the most numerous and durable parts of the detritus of the past, ceramics help us date our sites and can inform our understanding of how people make a living from the landscapes we study. By looking at the pots rather than the pieces, we can hope to glean insights into the changing nature of culture and calibrate it to time.

PART 2

STUDIES OF SEVENTEENTH-CENTURY ST. MARY'S CITY

6

The Archaeology of Maryland Indians at St. Mary's City and the Interactions of Cultures

HENRY M. MILLER AND SILAS D. HURRY

Although St. Mary's City is well known for its seventeenth-century English colonial archaeology, excavations have demonstrated that the St. Mary's City National Historical Landmark also holds an abundance of sites inhabited by the native peoples of the Chesapeake Bay region over millennia. Only one of these many occupations is documented in historic records: an early 1600s village of a people known as the Yaocomaco. This chapter presents an overview of the Native American occupations at St. Mary's City with an emphasis on the contact period and Native-English colonial interactions. The first section summarizes the long history of Native American habitation prior to ca. AD 1600, the cultural complexity evidenced in the sixteenth and seventeenth centuries, and the first Native-English contacts in Maryland. The second section explores the archaeological evidence of Native-English interaction in seventeenth-century Maryland.

TEN MILLENNIA OF HABITATION

The earliest human presence known thus far at St. Mary's City consists of occasional stone artifacts called Palmer points, dated between ca. 11,000 and 10,000 years ago (note all projectile point dates are taken from a synthesis study by Hall [2013]). Even older Clovis points of the Paleo-Indians have been found within a few miles, but none yet at St. Mary's City. As part of museum excavations, archaeologists have retrieved a few St. Albans and Kirk Seriated points dating from 10,000 to 9,000 years ago during a time named the Early Archaic. The first indication of more intense habitation comes from a cluster of LeCroy Points that date to around 8,500 to 7,800 years ago (Miller et al. 2006). At that time, sea level was 75 feet below its current level, and the St. Mary's River did not exist; it was then only a small freshwater creek flowing toward the Potomac River (Kraft and Brush 1981). This was a time of rapid environmental change, with the forest shifting from boreal spruce and fir with populations of caribou, elk, and deer to an oak, hemlock, and birch forest with white-tailed deer being the only large mammal (Brush 2001:51). People at this time lived in small mobile, egalitarian bands. Only scattered evidence is found during the subsequent Middle Archaic period dating between ca. 7000 BC and ca. 3750 BC at St. Mary's City. The climate during this period was warmer and drier with the settlement more focused on inland swamps and major rivers (Brush 2001:51; Miller 2001:111–113). New tools such as atlatl weights, celts, and adzes were introduced during this time, but only a few points are found at St. Mary's, implying the area was used mostly for sporadic hunting encampments. Indeed, the paucity of evidence for human activity during this period is the case throughout Southern Maryland (Steponaitis 1980; Wanser 1982).

Things changed greatly in the following Late Archaic period. The forest became dominated by oak, chestnut, hickory, and pine, with nuts and acorns becoming widely available as a significant source of food (Brush 2001; Miller 2001). Hundreds of projectile points dating between ca. 3500 BC and 1800 BC have been recovered by St. Mary's archaeologists, with a particular concentration of Bare Island points, along with Piscataway, Savannah River, and LeHigh/Koens Crispin point types. These tend to cluster on high ground along the St. Mary's River, particularly in the area that later became the town center (Miller et al. 2006). The much greater quantities of artifacts from this period suggest there was a larger human population and more sustained use of the land that would become the colony's first capital. A significant factor here may be the presence of a major freshwater spring that still flows powerfully, although now it is about 50 feet offshore under 3 feet of water due to sea level rise and erosion. Along with these well-dated points, archaeologists have recovered more material culture, including ground stone axes and celts, atlatl weights, fire-cracked rocks, and a few fragments of steatite stone bowls, likely imported from quarries along the Fall Line in Central Maryland. This evidence suggests there was a larger population that was more sedentary and probably practiced a well-developed seasonal pattern of resource usage. Settlement focused on freshwater streams and the emerging estuary waters, while continuing around inland swamps. There is some suggestion that spring fish runs began being exploited at this time (Miller 2001:112–113).

Valuable environmental insights come from a partially inundated stream at the center of St. Mary's City called Mill Creek. From a pond at its junction with the St. Mary's River, geologist John Kraft took core samples in 1979

(Kraft and Brush 1981). Pollen analysis of the core by Grace Brush indicates that by about 4000 BC the land was covered by an oak, hickory, and pine forest, the composition that would not alter significantly for nearly 6,000 years afterward. Geological analysis of the core discovered that salty estuarine waters did not reach the St. Mary's City area until 3000–2500 BC, bringing oysters, crabs, and varied fish species to the area for the first time. Only when European colonists began cutting the forest to allow wide-scale plow agriculture in the eighteenth century did the forests undergo significant change, with oak and hickory greatly reduced, and a major increase in pine, accompanied by a huge jump in ragweed pollen (Kraft and Brush 1981; Brush 2001).

In the Early Woodland period, habitation continued, represented by the introduction of pottery. While the first Early Woodland ware (Marcey Creek and Seldon Island) have not been found in St. Mary's City, Accokeek ware (ca. 1250 BC to AD 50) and several point types are present. Accokeek ware is a sand or crushed quartz tempered ceramic with a cord-marked exterior (Egloff and Potter 1982). The archaeology suggests that St. Mary's was a location of more regular settlement, and this continued through the subsequent Middle Woodland period (ca. AD 50–900). It is likely that tribal units had developed out of the earlier bands by this time, if not earlier, and these had both larger population and stronger territorial connections with more sedentary lifeways. People lived in villages along the waterways with some summer camps and dispersed collecting and inland hunting sites (Potter 1993:138–143). Evidence suggest that nuts, acorns, and some seeds like amaranth and chenopodium were significant in the diet and oysters were being harvested (Miller 2001:113–115). Sites at St. Mary's have yielded numerous points and several pottery types of Middle Woodland date, including concentrations of Pope's Creek, Prince George, and Mockley ware, indicating increased use of St. Mary's City as a dwelling place and again implying a rising population (Miller et al. 2006).

The most intensive native occupation occurred in the Late Woodland period (ca. AD 900–1600). Maize and related crops reached the region between about AD 650 and 900, but it was not until the 1300s that agriculture became a key element of subsistence (Potter 1993:142–143). Accompanying this was another significant increase in population and a trend toward more permanent settlement. Environmental data show that the period from AD 1000 to about 1300 was a considerably warmer and dryer time, with cooler and moister weather predominating after AD 1300; this transitioned into the "Little Ice Age" about 300 years later (Brush 2001:53).

Settlement during the Late Woodland consisted of towns, smaller outlying agriculture hamlets, and seasonal procurement locations. Even with the

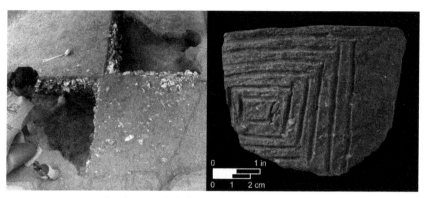

Figure 6.1. Late Woodland oyster shell feature during excavation and Rappahannock Incised pottery from it. Carbon 14 analysis gives a date around AD 1250 for this feature. (Courtesy of HSMC.)

practice of agriculture, native groups tended to disperse seasonally to take advantage of spring fish runs and oysters, or later autumn foraging and hunting. Another significant technological innovation during this period is the bow and arrow, indicated by many small triangular points. Shell-tempered pottery (Townsend ware and its variant Rappahannock Ware) predominates, continuing a ceramic tradition using shell that began in the Middle Woodland (Miller et al. 2006; Egloff and Potter 1982). Archaeologists at St. Mary's City have found a number of subsurface features from this time. They contain oyster shell and range from small individual cooking or roasting pits to large deposits containing thousands of shells and other artifacts (see figure 6.1). It is clear that estuarine resources such as oysters were a significant element of Late Woodland foodways, although white-tailed deer remained the single most important source of meat, hides, tallow, and sinew (Miller 2001:118–119). Several of the large shell features have been excavated, and in addition to oysters, they yielded bones of white-tailed deer; gray squirrel; raccoon; cooter, box, and painted turtle; a large bird (probably turkey); and sturgeon. Analysis of the oyster shells indicates they were harvested in the spring.

In the Late Woodland period, cultural complexity in the Chesapeake region increased with the rise of a sociopolitical unit called a chiefdom. In this system, peoples of multiple tribes were linked under a chief. In Virginia, there arose the larger paramount Powhatan chiefdom, on Maryland's Eastern Shore the Nanticoke chiefdom, and in Southern Maryland the Piscataway-Conoy chiefdom (Potter 1993). At the time of European contact, it is estimated that the native population in Southern Maryland had increased to about 8,500 people (Feest 1978). There is also evidence in the form of palisaded villages that conflict had arisen in the Late Woodland, especially after ca. AD 1400 (Potter 1993:147). It is into this complex cultural and political setting of agrarian peoples that the Maryland colonists entered in the spring of 1634.

The Yaocomaco and English Contact

Although Captain John Smith in his 1608 voyages around the Chesapeake did not enter what is now called the St. Mary's River, it is likely that a people known as the Yaocomaco were living there at the time. The first English to contact the Yaocomaco were probably from Jamestown seeking corn in the first quarter of the seventeenth century, but sustained interaction with English traders for corn and furs began in the later 1620s. Henry Fleet is the best documented Potomac River trader during this time. He was held prisoner for five years by an unnamed native group along the Potomac who spoke an Algonquian language, perhaps the Anacostans, during which time Fleet became fluent in Algonquian and learned about indigenous customs. He used this knowledge to become a major fur trader in the Potomac by 1630. Fleet is the first to record the name of the Yaocomaco in a 1631 account (Seib and Rountree 2014:64, 183, 213). It must be noted that our written knowledge of the native people in St. Mary's comes only through English eyes and voices, as there was no indigenous written language; only occasional Native American statements are recorded by English translators in records such as the *Archives of Maryland*. There were at least 12 different tribal groups in Southern Maryland, and most but not all were part of the Piscataway-Conoy paramount chiefdom (Potter 1993:10, 194). These varied peoples all spoke Algonquian languages and seem to have shared generally similar lifeways but were distinctive tribal or chiefdom groups. The documented peoples include the Anacostians, Acquintanacsuck, Choptank, Mattawoman, Mattapanient, Nanjemoy, Pangayo, Patuxent, Piscataway, Potapaco, Wiccocomicos, and the Yaocomaco. Unfortunately, there is very little ethnographic or archaeological evidence about some of these groups. In this chapter, names of individual groups are used where there is documentation and appropriate, but the different indigenous people who lived in Southern Maryland are otherwise collectively referenced by the more inclusive term Maryland Indians so as to not exclude any group.

In late March of 1634, the Maryland expedition arrived in the Potomac River, temporarily landing on an island they named St. Clements. The first major action of expedition leader Leonard Calvert was to sail up the Potomac to meet with the leader of the Piscataway. At the main village of Piscataway,

Henry Fleet served as interpreter and interceded with the "Tayak" or "Emperor" of the Piscataway people (White 1910:41, 72). It was recognized that the Piscataway-Conoy was the paramount chiefdom that ruled much of Maryland's western shore, primarily along the Potomac River (Potter 1993:174–178; Seib and Rountree 2014). Calvert sought permission to settle from the Tayak who answered "that he would not bid him goe, neither would hee bid him stay, but that he might use his owne discretion" (Hawley and Lewger 1910:72). After receiving this ambivalent response, Calvert sought a place to found the colony. Fleet was already familiar with the village of Yaocomaco and directed Calvert to it, where negotiations began with the Yaocomaco "werowance" or leader and the "wisoes" or chief advisors (White 1910:73). Note that the same name is used for the Yaocomaco people and their village at St. Mary's and they were Algonquian speakers. The village had many good features, including high ground, good soil, cleared fields, excellent springs, abundant timber, safe anchorage, and direct access to the Potomac and Chesapeake Bay. Because of frequent attacks by the Susquehannock Indians of what is today Pennsylvania, the Yaocomaco were in the process of consolidating their settlements for better protection. They perceived that the newly arrived English bearing firearms and cannon could be a useful buffer against the Susquehannock, as well as offering the opportunity to establish direct trade relations with the English.

An agreement was reached that the English would acquire the village and a surrounding 30 square mile area in which to found Maryland. In exchange, the Yaocomaco received bolts of cloth, axes, hoes, and other metal tools (White 1910:73). Both groups made pledges of mutual friendship. The one caveat was that because the annual corn crop was being planted, the Yaocomaco wished to leave people to tend the crop until harvest. A substantial portion of the village was therefore immediately vacated, with people moving across the St. Mary's River to the main Yaocomaco settlement located on the opposite shore, and some Yaocomaco remaining at St. Mary's. The English moved into the empty Yaocomaco houses, creating a unique situation where people from two very different cultures lived side by side for about six months.

English records note that these early interactions were friendly, and some of them are described in the 1635 *Relation of Maryland* (Hawley and Lewger 1910). For example, the newly arrived English had no familiarity with "Indian corn" (maize) and "the Indian women seeing [the English] servants to be unacquainted with the manner of dressing it, would make bread thereof for them, and teach them how to doe the like." The Yaocomaco men went hunting for deer and turkey with the English daily, and brought fish to the English "in great store" (Hawley and Lewger 1910:75). The English also learned slash and burn agriculture and the cultivation of corn from the Yaocomaco. Writings by Father Andrew White (1910) and Hawley and Lewger (1910) provide the only specific ethnographic information about the Yaocomaco people. This friendly cultural interaction was essential for the successful beginnings of Maryland, and its peaceful nature is exemplified by the statement that the Yaocomaco "women and children came very frequently amongst [the colonists]" (White 1910:75). Nevertheless, tensions arose.

In 1642, a colonist named John Elkin killed the werowance of the Yaocomaco. Although he admitted his crime, when he was brought to trial, the jury found Elkin not guilty because they did not think English law applied to pagans. Governor Calvert and Secretary John Lewger found this a miscarriage of justice, ruled that the same law applied to Indians, and ordered the jury to reconsider. A guilty verdict was finally reached but later changed to manslaughter (Browne 1887a:177, 180, 183). This is the first hint of a division between Lord Baltimore's intended policy regarding Maryland Indians and the perspective of many of the colonists. With the loss of their leader and another killing in 1643, the Yaocomaco moved directly across the Potomac River from St. Mary's to live along a Virginia stream still called Yeocomico River (Potter 1993:48). In 1652, they were dwelling with a neighboring group called the Matchotics along the Virginia shore, and around 1660 they moved further up the Potomac River. The last reference to the Yaocomaco as a distinct group is in 1676 and they probably merged with other Algonquian speaking peoples thereafter (Seib and Rountree 2014:76).

A COMPLEX SETTING

The Maryland settlers entered a landscape that was already politically quite complicated. The Powhatan chiefdom in Virginia was expanding northward and coming into conflict with the Piscataway-Conoy chiefdom (Potter 1993:174–180). Rivalries between different native groups along the Potomac also sparked unrest. Even greater problems were the frequent raids by Susquehannocks from Pennsylvania and by other Iroquoian-speaking people from the New York area. These raids resulted in many deaths and the taking of captives. Henry Fleet estimated in 1631 that over the previous decade, as many as 1,000 Piscataway had been killed during these attacks (Seib and Rountree 2014:188). Contact with the Virginia English had been a mix of friendliness and violence. There was early trading for corn, but following the murder of English traders in the Potomac in 1623, the Virginians launched a reprisal on the Piscataway, who were likely innocent of the crime, and "put many to the swoorde" and burned houses and cornfields (Potter 1993:187). Thus, the Piscataway had good reason to be cautious when more English arrived a decade later. Maryland authorities sought peaceful relations, and unlike the Virginians, they saw the Piscataway and related groups as diplomatic allies. However, the expanding process of English immigration and associated quest for land caused conflict, and roaming cattle and hogs soon began damaging Indian cornfields. The first request to resolve land issues was made by "six nations" including the Choptico Indians in 1651, when they asked that territory be formally set aside for them along the Wicomico River. Lord Baltimore agreed to this out of "Honour and Conscience" and established Choptico Manor (Browne 1883:329–331).

In the mid-seventeenth century, Maryland was something of a battleground. Raids by the Susquehannock and other Iroquoian tribes on both Maryland Indian and English colonists caused destruction and fear. In 1666, following powerful attacks by Iroquoian Indians and increasing friction with the colonists, a major treaty was agreed to by 12 Maryland tribal groups and colonial officials. At the meeting, Werowance Mattagund is recorded saying "Your hogs and Cattle injure us, You come too near us to live & drive us from place to place. We can fly no farther let us know where to live & how to secure from the Hogs and Cattle" (Browne 1884:15). Signed on 20 April 1666 at St. Mary's City, this treaty had a number of provisions detailing mutual responsibilities, specified that penalties for murder or the killing or stealing of livestock applied equally to the English and Indian, required Indians to fence their crops, and declared that the Maryland Indians had the right to freely hunt, crab, fish, and fowl. It also required Maryland Indians to lay down their arms and call out when approaching a colonial settlement, gave Lord Baltimore's government the right to select the Tayak, and provided for aid and protection during times of attack (Browne 1884:25–27). Nevertheless, continuing English settlement on native lands prompted Lord Baltimore to establish more manors in 1668 that would serve as reservations for Maryland Indians. To the existing Choptico Manor were added Piscataway Manor, Panquia Manor, Zekiah Manor, and Mt. Calvert Manor (Browne 1887b: 34–35). Control of the manors, however, was placed in the hands of English stewards who became the liaisons between the native peoples and provincial government and usually played an essential role as interpreters (Seib and Rountree 2014:93–95). Manors had been a feature of Maryland from the beginning, but this was a novel application of this traditional medieval English method of land control in the complicated cultural setting of early America. Lord Baltimore's government and leaders of the Maryland Indians made serious efforts to honor the treaty, and each side rendered assistance when requested. Despite Lord Baltimore's instructions, the colonists' desire for land only increased as more immigrants arrived, and their encroachment was unrelenting. English settlement in former hunting areas seriously reduced the ability of native peoples to practice their traditional lifeways.

Continuing attacks by Iroquois in the 1670s and 1680s prompted the Piscataway to relocate to a location called Zekiah Fort by 1681 (Strickland 2019). After Lord Baltimore's control was overthrown in a 1689 rebellion, the Royal government which was then established had less interest in diplomatic relations with Maryland Indians. The Piscataway Tayak and many of the Piscataway people decided to move to Virginia in the mid-1690s and then to Heater's Island in the Potomac River in Frederick County, Maryland. After 1704, the Tayak and many of the Piscataway moved to Pennsylvania, where they lived for the next 50 years, and migrated into New York after 1754 (McKnight 2019:174–178). However, research by Seib and Rountree (2014) demonstrates that many of the Southern Maryland Indian peoples remained on the manors that had been established for them, or returned from Pennsylvania to again live on their ancestral lands. In 2012 the Piscataway Indian Nation and the Piscataway-Conoy tribes were formally recognized by the State of Maryland.

ARCHAEOLOGICAL EVIDENCE OF YAOCOMACO

Because the Yaocomaco village is well documented, it is appropriate to ask about its archaeological signature and material clues to the interaction between these cultural groups. Archaeological evidence for the village consists primarily of a shell-tempered, smooth-surfaced ceramic named Yeocomico ware thought to date to between ca. 1510 and ca. 1690 (Egloff and Potter 1982; Potter 1993:87). Analysis of the distribution of this ceramic does not show an intense concentration, as might be expected with a palisaded village site. Instead, sherds are found in smaller, widely scattered clusters, and located on high ground in the vicinity of freshwater sources. A few small arrow points, stone scrapers, and lithic debitage have also been recovered. Such evidence matches the interpretation of Yaocomaco as an agricultural hamlet instead of the main village of the Yaocomaco people. Houses were scattered or loosely grouped among the agricultural fields, gardens, and remaining stands of forest, a general pattern John Smith had observed during his exploration of the Chesapeake in 1608 (Smith 1624:31). Although traces of house post holes and some fire pits have been found, no complete house pattern of post holes has yet been uncovered archaeologically. However, recent intensive

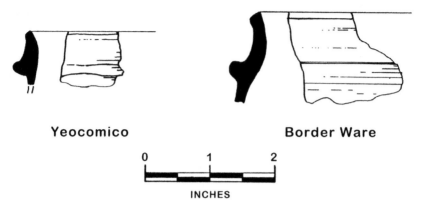

Figure 6.2. Yeocomico ware rim sherd and Border ware pipkin rim. (Drawing by Henry M. Miller, courtesy of HSMC.)

ground-penetrating radar survey has identified several locations where such buildings may have once stood, and they will be tested in coming years.

Among the sherds of Yeocomico pottery is one unusual specimen found near the 1635 home of Governor Leonard Calvert. It is a rim sherd that flares outward at the lip and has a ridge or band of clay on the exterior (see figure 6.2). Examination of the paste suggests it was made by folding over the original rim to create the ridge. Such a form is not typically found on Late Woodland Townsend or Yeocomico wares, although applied or folded strips are used on early precontact Potomac Creek ware, which has distinct crushed stone or sand temper (Egloff and Potter 1982). During analysis, it was recognized that the rim shape bears a strong resemblance to English Border ware pipkins found in early contexts at St. Mary's City, as shown in figure 6.2. This appears to be a Yaocomaco vessel whose shape was influenced by the ceramics being used by the Maryland colonists during the time they lived together (Miller 1983:33–35). While this cannot be proven, such a rim is not normal on Yeocomico ceramics, and the form similarity is striking, despite one being wheel thrown and the other handmade. If this interpretation is correct, this is direct physical evidence for the interchange between the two cultures at St. Mary's City during the year 1634 or soon afterward.

EVIDENCE OF INTERACTION

Seventeenth-century native pottery is rare in later colonial contexts at St. Mary's City, but evidence of Native-English interaction comes from other materials. Among these are small shell beads that were part of wampum or roanoke. These native-produced shell beads comprised a type of currency and were adopted to some extent by the colonists in the fur trade and for other exchanges. For the native peoples, the shells had both ritual and sacred significance, were placed in burials, and used in gift giving during negotiations with distant tribes (Rountree 1989:71–73; Curry 1999:84–88).

Evidence for the colonial use of shell currency and other native goods can also be found in the documentary record. Especially useful are probate inventories taken of colonial homes for the purpose of settling estates. One notable early example is the 1639 inventory of merchant Justinian Snow, who lived near St. Mary's City. It lists several colonists owing him payments in native currency ranging between 5 and 20 "arms length of Roanoke." There was also a charge for "Delivery to the Indian Emperor [of the Piscataway] a great Knife" (Browne 1887a:88, 110). Shell beads appear in other early inventories, and a 1642 probate of Richard Lusthead includes "3 Indian baskets," showing the acquisition of other native-produced goods (Browne 1887a:94). "Indian corn" (maize) and "Indian beans" are listed in a number of these early inventories, with pumpkins sometimes also noted, documenting the adoption of local crops. Examination of 1,004 probate inventories from St. Mary's County, Maryland, dating between 1665 and 1720 identified 20 households possessing Indian wooden bowls, mats, trays, and baskets. The listing of these items in the late seventeenth century and into the first quarter of the eighteenth century inventories demonstrates the continued presence of native peoples in the region, and the ongoing exchange of material goods.

Tobacco Pipes

By far the most common surviving material evidence for interaction between the Maryland Indians and settlers found on colonial sites are tobacco pipes. These pipes are produced from local brown clay and are typically called terra-cotta or red clay pipes, although one researcher has used the term Chesapeake pipes (Emerson 1988). Archaeologists have recovered thousands of these pipe fragments at St. Mary's City, and the first collection to be studied in depth was from the St. John's site (Henry 1979). This topic remains one of strong archaeological interest (cf. Agbe-Davies 2010, 2015; Emerson 1988, 1994; McMillan 2015; Mouer et al. 1999; Rafferty and Mann 2004; Sikes 2008). The vast majority of these pipes were handmade, but some were produced using European pipe molds. These molded specimens are believed to have been made by colonial artisans. One major example of such establishments is the Swan Cove site operated by Emanuel Drue in the

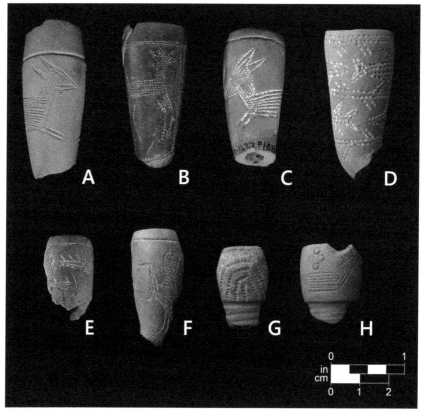

Figure 6.3. Terra-cotta pipes from St. Mary's City: *A–C*, Running Deer pipes; *D*, Striped Bass; *E*, Sturgeon and Catfish; *F*, Human and Large Bird; *G*, Susquehannock Cord Impressed; *H*, Susquehannock Pipe with Running Deer. (Photograph by Donald L. Winter, courtesy of HSMC.)

1660s. Located in Anne Arundel County, Maryland, this site was excavated by Luckenbach and Cox (2002).

In most cases, the hand-formed variety represents the overwhelming majority of the pipes. Among the hand-formed specimens in Maryland, there are two basic types. The most common have a relatively straight-sided bowl that has smooth surfaces except where impressed for decoration (figure 6.3A–F). These were likely made by Algonquian-speaking Indians. The other type (figure 6.3G–H) is called the Susquehannock style and features a collared bowl with the lower bowl and stems frequently grooved with shallow lines.

Terra-cotta pipes have a bowl that is usually decorated and a stem of varying length, but seldom more than 6 or 7 inches long. Decoration on the bowls usually consists of impressed lines forming geometric or animal images; these shallow impressions were often filled with white clay prior to firing to highlight the decoration. This style of decoration is referred to as *pointillé*. Experiments by T. Dale Stewart in the mid-1950s found that one tool frequently used to impress these dotted lines were fossil shark teeth. Stephen Potter later reached the same conclusion, while Hurry and Miller also confirmed it and added the possibility of combs and other tools (Potter 1993:226–228, Hurry and Miller 1992). Shark teeth are commonly found in the Chesapeake region, eroded out from exposed Miocene fossil beds. These pipes also typically have an impressed line just below the rim of the bowl on the exterior, reflecting an Algonquian pipe tradition that was copied by Dutch and English pipe makers. Indeed, it has been proposed that these terra-cotta pipes provided the model used by Dutch pipemaker Edward Bird to make a heel-less elbow pipe for sale in America (Huey 2008). English pipe makers in Bristol later copied this "export" form for the American market in the 1660s. Thus, pipes from the Chesapeake had a direct influence on the forms of white clay pipes being produced in Europe for sale in the American colonies. Support for this comes from the recent discovery of the first Chesapeake "Running Deer" pipe in the Netherlands, found in Schermer, north of Amsterdam (Van Der Lingen 2013).

Decoration appears in the forms of impressed panels and geometric shapes, including triangles and stars and the images of animals. Especially common are "Running Deer" pipes, although in some cases the short legs might indicate a dog or other mammal (figure 6.3A–C). Several fish have also been found on the pipes, including those that appear to be sturgeon, striped bass, and catfish (figure 6.3D–E). Unique thus far among the terra-cotta pipes found in the region is one showing a human figure standing on the back of a long-legged bird, probably a great blue heron (figure 6.3F). Recovered from the moat of Pope's Fort (Miller 1983, see chapter 8), it likely dates ca. 1650. Given the significance of birds to American Indians, this might represent a shaman (Pritchard 2013), or perhaps the trickster figure believed to ride birds (Ricketts 1966:337–338). Animal motifs seem to be primarily a phenomenon of the seventeenth century, because pipes recovered in prehistoric ossuaries generally display geometric forms if they are decorated (Curry 1999).

These hand-formed pipes are thought to be the products of peoples native to the the Chesapeake Bay region and are a continuation of a native tradition of pipes found in Chesapeake/Carolina region. Such pipes with the bowl at an oblique angle to the stem are found in precontact ossuaries in Maryland (Curry 1999). There has been a controversy as to the makers of the handmade pipes. Matthew Emerson suggested that Africans, enslaved or free, were the makers (1988). This idea was countered by Mouer et al. (1999), who argued that they are a continuation of the local pipe making tradition by native peoples. Given bowl form, decorative motifs, and similarity to precontact specimens, the argument for regional Native American production seems to best fit the evidence. However, this does not preclude the possibility that enslaved or free Africans produced some pipes.

Which native group made the pipes is uncertain. There are stylistic differences between pipes found on the James River and those on the Potomac, although the "Running Deer" pipes are present in both areas. However, star pipes are far more common on the James (Sikes 2008) while the Running Deer motif is most common on sites along the Potomac (Hurry and Miller 1992), implying they had an upper Chesapeake origin. There is also some difference in bowl forms of pipes found along the James and Potomac Rivers. One Native pipe production site has been excavated along the Virginia shore of the Potomac at Nominy Plantation (Mitchell 1976; Luckenbach and Kiser 2006). There is also evidence that terra-cotta pipes were made at St. Mary's City. During the investigation of Pope's Fort, excavators found pipe making waste, including clay lumps with fingerprints, clay roughly formed into a pipe bowl shape, and unfinished pipe bowls. Much of this material was found in the moat fill and likely dates ca. 1645–1650. It indicates the presence of at least one native person at the site during that period. Of particular note is one pipe that is a Susquehannock collared bowl type but decorated with a "Running Deer" motif (figure 6.3H). Such a merging of two different pipe making traditions is intriguing and may be indicative of the cultural complexity and instability that characterized the mid-seventeenth-century Chesapeake.

The most remarkable terra-cotta pipes found at St. Mary's City are two displaying human faces. These are larger, well made, and elaborately decorated pipes recovered from the late 1640s fill of the Pope's Fort moat (figure 6.4). Unlike the decoration on most other terra-cotta pipes, these effigy pipes have impressed lines composed of small, square, precisely spaced dots, not the serrated edges found on sharks' teeth. These lines are comparable to the rouletting seen around the rim of white clay pipes, implying that the tool used was a fine-tooth bone comb, a manufactured gearwheel, or some similar tool. As with the other pipes, the impressions were filled with white clay to highlight the lines. Thus far, no comparable specimens have been identified in the Eastern United States. They are unlike Iroquoian pipes from New York, Huron pipes from the Great Lakes, Susquehannock pipes from Pennsylvania, or Algonquian pipes from Virginia or North Carolina (Miller

SIDE   **FRONT**   **TOP**

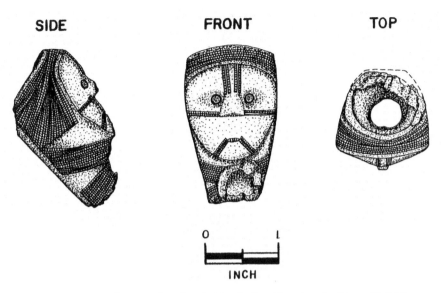

0   1
INCH

Figure 6.4. Human effigy pipe found at St. Mary's City. (Drawings by Henry M. Miller and James O'Connor, courtesy of HSMC.)

1983:37–39). One possible observation may have relevance here. In 1634, Andrew White reported that English traders had seen a ceremony among the Maryland Indians at their council house where they "brought forth a bagge of Poate, which is their tobacco, with a great tobacco pipe and carried about the fire . . . they filled the pipe, and gave to every one a draught of smoake from it which they breathed out on all parts of their bodies, as it were to sanctife them" (White 1910:45). However, the origin and specific purpose of these rare effigy pipes are unknown.

Terra-cotta pipes are the strongest archaeological evidence for the ongoing interaction between the Maryland Indians and the English. It is therefore appropriate to ask how long this exchange endured. To answer that question, the percentages of white clay and terra-cotta pipes from 26 well-dated contexts in the upper Chesapeake region from ca. 1640 to ca. 1730 have been assembled and are presented in table 6.1. Terra-cotta pipes predominate on pre-1660 sites, making up from half to two-thirds of the total pipe assemblage. There are some molded pipes made by colonists in these samples, but the majority of the specimens are of native origin. The pipe trade seems to have begun not long after Maryland was established and flourished from ca. 1640 to the 1670s. Henry (1979) suggested that this was due in part to shortages of supplies that the colonies suffered during the disruptions of the English Civil Wars and their aftermath. These shortages may have had a role, but the production and use of terra-cotta pipes continued well after trans-Atlantic commerce had been restored. Table 6.1 shows their early prevalence and then significant decline during the 1670s. By the 1680s, terra-cotta pipes are rare and in a number of cases, the few specimens present may be due to the admixture of materials from earlier in a site occupation. This suggests a terminus around 1675. The 1670s were a time of great instability in the region. A 1675 Virginia attack on a Susquehannock fort in Maryland helped precipitate Bacon's Rebellion, and intensifying raids by the Iroquois took a toll. It is possible that this unrest and legitimate fear of raids in the 1670s and 1680s may have reduced interaction and brought about a decline of pipe exchange. But as the occasional appearance of Indian baskets and mats in late seventeenth- and early eighteenth-century inventories demonstrates, not all exchange ended. But for terra-cotta pipes, archaeology indicates their exchange had ceased by ca. 1680.

OTHER NATIVE SITES

The archaeology of seventeenth-century Maryland Indians began with the excavations in the late nineteenth century. This work focused on a number of ossuaries that were part of a burial practice of periodic mass interments of the deceased known as the Feast of the Dead. Numerous ossuaries have been found along the Potomac River dating between the late 1400s and ca. 1680, most of which seem to be associated with the Piscataway-Conoy chiefdom (Curry 1999). Those created after the English settlement of Maryland contain a variety of European goods including glass beads, hawk bells, iron and brass artifacts, and in one case, 18 copper medals originally intended as admission tokens to the Ceremony of the Kings Touch during the reign of Charles I (Curry 1999:35). To date no ossuaries or individual Native American burials have been found at St. Mary's City.

Excavation on the Piscataway site complex in the 1930s and 1940s was not conducted in what we would consider a professional manner, but the recovered data are reported by Stephenson et al. (1963), and Potter (1993) provides a good summary of the findings. Recent work on Piscataway-related sites is providing important new insights (King and Strickland 2016; Strickland 2019). Particularly notable are excavations led by King and Strickland at Zekiah Fort, the main Piscataway dwelling site between 1680 and ca. 1695. These reveal that the Piscataway continued a strong preference for their traditional ceramics, with 80 percent being Potomac Creek pottery and European ceramics accounting for 19.5 percent. In terms of pipes, however, white clay pipes comprise 73 percent of the assemblage, with terra-cotta pipes only

Table 6.1. Frequencies of White Clay and Terra-Cotta Clay Pipes Found on Sites in the Upper Chesapeake Bay Region, 1638–1730

Site	Date	White Clay Pipes	Terra-Cotta Pipes	Reference
Privy, St. John's 18ST1-23	1638–ca. 1655	45 (37.8%)	74 (62.1%)	HSMC
Dairy, St. John's 18ST1-23	ca. 1640–ca. 1655	73 (41.9%)	101 (58.0%)	HSMC
Old Chapel Field 18ST233	1637–1660	204 (36.8%)	350 (63.17%)	Sperling & Galke 2001
Pope's Fort 18ST1-13	1645–ca. 1650	112 (32.1%)	236 (67.9%)	HSMC
Wm. Stone Occupation 18ST1-13	1650–ca. 1660	77 (37.7%)	127 (62.2%)	HSMC
Broadneck 18AN818	1649–ca. 1660	105 (37.1%)	178 (62.9%)	Luckenbach & Cox 2002:12–17
Chancellor's Point 18ST1-62	ca. 1640–ca. 1680	318 (67.6%)	152 (32.4%)	HSMC
John Hallows 44WM6	1647–1681	883 (86.4%)	139 (13.6%)	McMillan 2015
Early Henry Coursey 18QU30	1658–ca. 1675	217 (49.8%)	218 (50.0%)	Custer 2019
Compton 18CV279	1651–ca. 1685	940 (85.8%)	155 (14.1%)	Gibb 1994
Patuxent Point 18CV271	ca. 1658–ca. 1695	584 (83.2%)	118 (16.8%)	Gibb 1994
Homewood 18AN871	ca. 1660–ca. 1670	663 (87.4%)	95 (12.5%)	Gadsby & Callage 2002:18–27
Skipworth Addition 18AN795	1664–ca. 1682	294 (99.6%)	1 (0.3%)	Cox 2002:66–71
Mattapany-Sewall 18ST390	1663–ca. 1700	540 (97.4%)	14 (2.5%)	Pogue 1987:16–18
Clifts Phase I 44WM33	ca. 1670–ca. 1685	319 (90.3%)	34 (9.6%)	Neiman 1980a:165
Feature 12 18ST704	ca. 1675–ca. 1695	368 (99.7%)	1 (0.3%)	Polglase et al. 2001:64–157
Large Circular Trash Pit, St. John's 18ST1-23	ca. 1680–ca. 1700	290 (91.3%)	11 (3.6%)	HSMC
Pit 925, Calvert House 18ST1-13	ca. 1680–ca. 1700	420 (97.6%)	10 (2.3%)	HSMC
Clifts Phase II 44WM33	ca. 1685–ca. 1705	98 (96.0%)	4 (3.9%)	Neiman 1980a:168
Later Henry Coursey 18QU30	1680–ca. 1745	1364 (98.5%)	20 (1.4%)	Custer 2019
King's Reach 18CV83	ca. 1690–ca. 1715	2706 (99.7%)	8 (0.3%)	Pogue 1991
Harmony Hall 18PG305	1692–1718	314 (100%)	0	Sonderman et al. 1993
Kitchen Pit, St. Johns 18ST1-23	ca. 1700–ca. 1715	158 (96.9%)	5 (3.0%)	HSMC
Clifts Phase III 44WM33	ca. 1705–ca. 1720	1933 (99.3%)	12 (0.6%)	Neiman 1980a:171
Rumney Tavern 18AN48	ca. 1700–ca. 1730	872 (100%)	0	Gryczkowski 2002:92–99

27 percent (Strickland 2019:170–171). This suggests that terra-cotta pipe use had also declined markedly by this time among Maryland Indians. But as Strickland observes (2019:170), the terra-cotta pipes are mostly associated with the elite habitation area of the fort, perhaps indicating they retained a status and ritual significance. Other materials at Zekiah include glass beads, glass bottle fragments, copper alloy objects, iron nails, and other iron artifacts. In 1699, the Piscataway moved to Heater's Island, and archaeology was conducted there in the 1970s. McKnight (2019:177) reports that it yielded glass beads, gun parts, European flint, lead shot, bottle glass, and iron nails. Significantly, white clay pipes and European ceramics predominate in that assemblage. The archaeological data from these sites attest to the dramatic changes that occurred in Piscataway material culture over a span of less than a century.

CONCLUSION

St. Mary's City contains a wealth of Maryland Indian archaeology that can illuminate the human experience in this location over nearly 11,000 years of time. It is also a place where some of the first sustained interaction between native people and the English occurred. The Yaocomaco were key allies in the successful beginnings of the Maryland colony, not only providing shelter and cleared land but also conveying knowledge of nature, culture, and cuisine to the newly arrived immigrants. Lord Baltimore sought to maintain good relations, established manors for the native groups, and provided some protection of the "Friend" Indians from attacks by "Foreign" Indians. Both the native groups and provincial government tried to honor the provisions of the 1666 treaty. While Maryland officials made some effort to control encroachment of English migrants onto native lands, this ultimately failed as immigration continued and the pressure for land increased. Inadequate enforcement of treaty provisions took its toll, along with disease and persistent raiding by Iroquoian groups. These greatly reduced the numbers of Maryland Indians in Southern Maryland. And yet the people remained on their ancestral lands and the old manors, persisting despite oppression, limited resources, and neglect. As they were when the first English immigrants arrived, Maryland's Indian peoples remain a vibrant element of the state's culture today.

7

St. John's Freehold

The Archaeology of One of Maryland's Earliest Plantations

RUTH M. MITCHELL, HENRY M. MILLER,
AND GARRY WHEELER STONE

Built by John Lewger in 1638, St. John's Freehold is one of Maryland's earliest plantations. Lewger had arrived in Maryland in late 1637, sent by Cecil Calvert, the Lord Baltimore, to serve as the colony's Secretary. Calvert and Lewger had been students together at Trinity College, Oxford, where Lewger received a B.A., M.A., and Doctorate of Divinity degrees (Middleton and Miller 2008). He was ordained as an Anglican minister and served the parish of Laverton in Somerset, England, for a few years. He converted to Catholicism in 1635 and thereby lost his ministry (Stone 1982). Afterward, renewing his acquaintance with Calvert that year, Lewger was sent to Maryland by Lord Baltimore to help administer the government and report back on colonial affairs.

Upon his arrival in the colony, Lewger selected a prime piece of land immediately adjacent to the settlement of St. Mary's and named it St. John's Freehold in honor of his patron saint. Work began soon after to erect a large farmhouse and establish a plantation (Stone 1982:90). Lewger took an active role in the new government, hosting meetings of the Assembly on several occasions and serving as chief administrator of the fledgling society under Governor Leonard Calvert. Captured by Parliamentary troops in a 1645 attack, he was taken back to England in chains and placed on trial. The court found him not guilty, and after regaining his freedom Lewger returned to his family in Maryland. Once he arrived, he learned of the death of his wife and decided to leave Maryland. After his return to England in 1648, he became a Catholic priest and served for the rest of his life as chaplain to Lord Baltimore. John Lewger died in 1665 while aiding plague victims in London (Wood 1813 4:696–697).

Lewger's son, John Jr., stayed at St. John's for a few years but sold the property in 1650 (Browne 1883:70). In 1654, the house was acquired by Simon Overzee, a Dutch merchant who made a number of improvements to the property, but died suddenly in 1660. The next owner was Governor Charles Calvert, who lived there between 1661 and 1667. Afterward, he leased the plantation to a series of innkeepers. St. John's main house stood until ca. 1715, when it was demolished and the site was converted to agriculture for the next two centuries.

ARCHITECTURE OF THE HOUSE

The historical record provides scant information about the appearance of the structures at St. John's. Gleanings from the documents provide clues to the site, including the names of residents and the fact that there were additional buildings and features present, but their character, size, building arrangements, and interior usage of space is undocumented. When archaeology began at St. John's in the summer of 1972, excavators had no idea of what they might find. What kind of house did Lewger build and how did he shape the landscape around the house with the addition of outbuildings, fences, and other features? Only archaeological excavation could provide answers to these questions. After the initial excavations, archaeological work continued for four more seasons. A second campaign of investigation occurred between 2001 and 2005 to clear areas for the construction of an exhibit building at the site, which opened in 2008.

The most conspicuous feature of the site is the stone foundations of the main house encountered soon after the excavations began (figure 7.1). The cobbles were collected from the shores of the St. Mary's River; many of them still have oyster shells adhered to their surface. The foundation is rather remarkable by virtue of the fact that the Tidewater region is underlain by sand, clay, and gravel; stone is very rare. The cobbles were laid in a shallow construction trench, and when the stones were fully uncovered, they told excavators that the St. John's house had measured 20.6 feet wide and 52 feet long. The main entrance was into a small lobby against an H-shaped, central chimney. To the left was the hall, which originally served as a kitchen, work space, and living room. The larger space to the right was likely intended as a parlor suite of master bedroom and two small inner rooms, but Secretary Lewger decided not to partition the space so that he could host meetings of the courts and Assembly (see figure 7.2). The site was exceptionally well preserved, to such an extent that beneath a thin remnant of destruction rubble, the molds of floor joists remained undisturbed with the vertical flooring nails

Figure 7.1. The main house at the St. John's site as revealed by the archaeological excavations between 1972 and 1976. (Photograph by Garry Wheeler Stone, courtesy of HSMC.)

still in place. In the center of the building, a complex arrangement of brick-work proved to be the brick foundations of two superimposed chimneys. The earlier 1638 brick and wattle and daub chimney had been dismantled to make room for a fully bricked chimney dating to 1678. A 1678 lease to an innkeeper named Henry Exon required the rebuilding of the chimney and replacing the roof (G. W. Stone 1974:168). Archaeology demonstrated that Exon did in fact build a larger chimney constructed entirely of brick. Probably at the direction of Charles Calvert, instead of using common clapboard or shingles, Exon covered St. John's with a roof of imported Dutch pantile, a distinctive and very rare architectural feature in early Maryland.

Once the plan of St. John's was revealed through the archaeological work, research began to determine the type of house Lewger had built. Fieldwork in England and consultation with architectural historians found that Lewger had built an East Anglian style, center-chimney, lobby-entry farmhouse. Historical research suggests that Lewger's family did come from that area of England (Middleton and Miller 2008). Although small by contemporary British standards, St. John's was one of the most impressive homes in early Maryland. It was box-framed and assembled with many mortise and tenon joints that added to the time and cost of construction, but was fully in keeping with the British architecture of East Anglia (Barley 1961:67–77, 139–145; Hewett 1970). St. John's was also exceptionally well finished for the time and

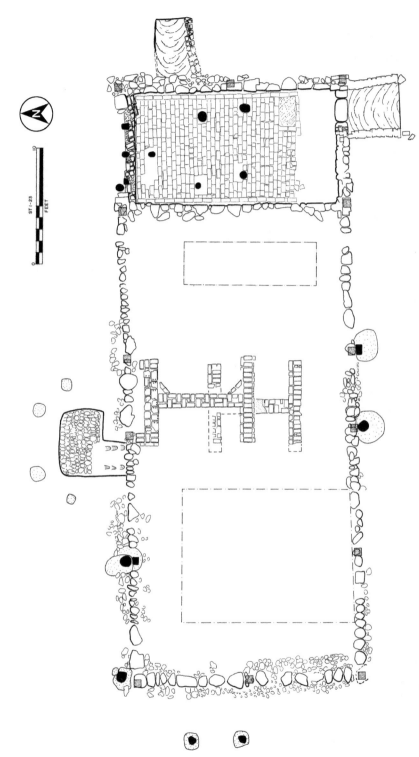

Figure 7.2. Plan view of the main house at St. John's showing the archaeological evidence for the foundations, chimneys and exterior additions, and porches. (Courtesy of HSMC.)

place, featuring wood floors, brick fireboxes, plastered walls, and windows glazed with glass panes cut in unusual geometric shapes including triangles and pentagons (Miller 1978). For the roof and exterior wall coverings, Lewger apparently had the workers use oak clapboards rived into 5-foot lengths. Historical evidence suggests that merchant Simon Overzee upgraded the house with large expenditures for carpentry of 5,000 pounds of tobacco and £55 sterling in the mid-1650s (G. W. Stone 1974:152). This may have included lining the cellar with locally quarried sandstone. It is the only stone-lined cellar from the early Chesapeake yet discovered.

The main house also featured several additions with hole-set timber foundations (see figure 7.2). These included door shades on the east and west gables. Along the north wall, a stone-floored dairy was erected with access from the hall room that initially served as the kitchen. This was a Lewger period addition associated with the effort to reestablish traditional English dairying practices in Maryland. It was demolished and the cellar filled during the Overzee period. Excavators also located an addition to the northwest corner of the building. It is thought to be a room called "the nursery" that was built for Governor Charles Calvert in the early 1660s. Additional evidence uncovered three outbuildings in the yards surrounding the house and these are discussed below.

THE STORAGE BUILDING/KITCHEN

The earliest support building erected in the yards of St. John's was a small structure off the northeast corner of the main house. It is represented by eight post holes, a brick chimney base, an earlier wattle and daub chimney, and a small storage pit. This structure began as an unheated storage building with a wattle and daub chimney later added to make it into a living space for servants. Finally, it became the kitchen. The original was a 15×20-foot building, although it was not precisely laid out. Measurements show that the west wall is 19.55 feet long while the east wall is 20.10 feet, making it more of a trapezoid than a rectangle (see figure 7.3). It had two bays approximately 10 feet wide. The west wall bays, measuring from exterior gable to center of the middle post, are 10.0 feet on the north and 9.55 feet on the south. In contrast, the east wall bays are 10.90 feet and 9.30 feet, respectively. Much of this variation is due to the northeast corner post being set too far north. In terms of width, there is more consistency. The north, center, and south post pairs are 15.1 feet, 15.3 feet, and 14.8 feet, measuring outside to outside.

The post holes were relatively small and do not display consistent shapes or mold placements within the holes. Bottom elevations for the molds vary

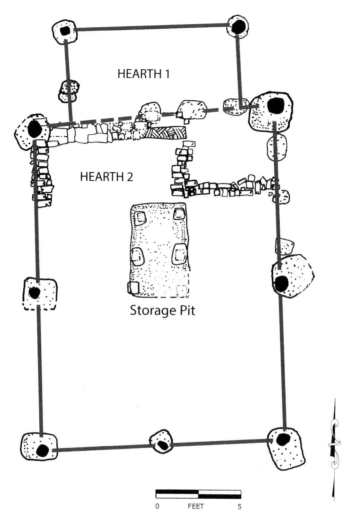

Figure 7.3. Archaeological plan view of the kitchen building found adjacent to the main house at St. John's. (Courtesy of HSMC.)

by almost 0.4 foot. In the cross-sections, the post molds in half of these holes extend below the bottom of the original holes by 0.1 foot or more. There is no evidence of soil having been scooped out from under them. Molds lower than the hole may indicate that considerable weight was pressing down on these timbers, perhaps from a building higher than a single story.

The most distinctive aspect about these posts is their shallow depths. They only extend 1.40 feet to 1.60 feet into subsoil. This is far shallower than any of the other main structural posts excavated at the St. John's site. For example, the posts of the building in the front yard went 2.50 feet into subsoil. This is a vital clue and it strongly supports the hypothesis that this was a box-framed building set on shallow wooden blocks. Blocks would not need to be as deeply set as those of a post-in-the-ground structure because they do not carry the same loads. Repair would also be easier, and block-supported, box-frame structures would likely experience less decay, thereby allowing the building to survive longer (Carson et al. 1981:153). If it was a box-frame structure on blocks, precise placement of the piers would not be as crucial as in a fully earthfast-supported structure, perhaps accounting for the variations seen in these posts' positions. In the center of the north and south gables are additional posts. They are much smaller, set about 0.7 foot more shallow than the other posts, and likely helped support the long 15-foot span of the gable sills. There are other smaller holes found along the wall lines and some of these may have held later reinforcement timbers to support decaying sections of sill.

Based on the artifact assemblage, this structure was occupied for a long period of time, perhaps as many as 70 years. Inspection of the surface plans of the kitchen posts does not yield any evidence of repairs. Repaired post holes are often rather obvious on the surface of the hole, as is the case at Clifts Plantation (Neiman 1980a). For this building, it is only by examining the post cross-sections that evidence of repair becomes obvious. This is probably because the original posts were set at shallow depths in small holes and the larger repair holes obscured or obliterated much of the surface evidence of the earlier hole. Identification of these repair phases is important because they support the idea derived from artifact data that this structure stood for a long time.

Initially, the building was unheated and probably erected as a storage building. Although the term kitchen is associated with a place of cooking, in the seventeenth century it also frequently referred to an unheated service space for the storage of food, beverages, and other materials (Giles 1985:142–143). This latter sense of "kitchen" may have been the original purpose of this building, because the hall originally served as the main location for cooking. Later, there is good evidence that a chimney was added, represented by several post holes off the north gable. Two large posts are 5 feet out from the gable, and set precisely 2 feet inward from each corner (see figure 7.3). These posts define a wattle and daub (also known as mud and stick) chimney that was 11 feet wide and 5 feet deep, centered on the north gable of the building. Simon Overzee may have had the chimney added in the mid-1650s so it could be used for servant and/or slave housing.

The only documentation for the structure is found in a 1678 lease, by which time it was called the kitchen. A major episode of repair and alteration occurred that year by order of Lord Baltimore: "repair the Room called the Kitchen and the Store & chamber over them and to brick the Chimneys up to the Wall plate and daub and lath it up to the Top and Brick the Floor" (G. W. Stone 1974:168). This document suggests that the kitchen building consisted of a ground floor room and a chamber or perhaps a second floor space with a store and chamber. It may have been a story and a half building. Exon was to build a brick chimney to replace the wattle and daub stack, and archaeologists confirmed that he did so when they found the brick chimney base. Located at the north gable of the structure, the chimney base measured 9.8 feet wide and 5 feet deep. From the southeast corner of this chimney is a line of brick 6 feet long and 1.2 feet wide that extends to the east wall of the building. The purpose of this line of brick is a matter of debate. It might have buttressed the chimney but in doing so would have cut off the north-east corner of the room. Perhaps it was intended to do so, thereby creating a small secure storage area, or alternatively, perhaps it was a space to hold a stairway. While these are possibilities, we think the best explanation is that Exon reduced the building's length by 5 feet and created a new, fully bricked north gable. The old wattle and daub chimney had required removal of most of the studs on the north wall, and may have created leaks that caused decay of the timbers. Rather than repairing them, Exon removed the original gable timbers and used the joist and rafter pair that was 5 feet to the south as a new gable. These timbers were tied directly into the brickwork. Exon's efforts created an improved 15 feet by 15 feet kitchen and extended its useful life for several decades.

This kitchen is a very early example of a block-supported structure in early Maryland. As with the main house, it used box framing and may have been one and a half stories high. Unlike the house, it rested on wood instead of durable stone. Almost certainly John Lewger had this building constructed, still employing an English carpentry approach but showing the first signs of adaptation and a move toward earthfast construction on St. John's Freehold.

OVERZEE'S STOREHOUSE

Southeast of the main house, excavators discovered a 20-foot by 30-foot earthfast structure. Except for an undisturbed block in the center of the structure that was retained for preservation purposes, all of the plow zone was excavated over the building. All features were mapped, but only two were excavated so as to maintain maximum preservation at this publicly owned site (a photograph of the features of this structure can be seen in chapter 2, figure 2.1).

The building is defined by eight large structural posts (figure 7.4). Based on field measurements, the entire structure was 30.47 feet long and 20.47 feet wide. The posts formed three bays laid at 10-foot intervals. These post holes are large (2.1 × 2.7 feet to 3.0 × 3.8 feet) and deep, with the two excavated structural post holes extending more than 3 feet below the original land surface. Post hole shapes are mostly rectangular, with the long axis of the holes parallel to the building's east and west walls. The two excavated holes were stepped on their north sides, and in both cases, the posts did not rest on the bottom of their holes but were 0.20 and 0.37 feet above it. This is significant because it indicates that the builders made an effort to level the building to a specific elevation. Analysis of the mold-hole relationships and post hole shapes demonstrates that the building was erected with bent assembly (see chapter 2, figure 2.3).

In addition to the large structural posts, the building had smaller central support posts on each gable, and pairs of post molds near the center of the building on each facade. These were likely door posts, framing doorways 3 feet in width. One of the unexpected findings is the presence of stud molds along the wall lines, spaced at 2.5 foot intervals. These studs would have been lapped into the plates from the exterior after the frame was erected. This is the clearest evidence yet found of earthfast stud wall construction in early Maryland. Later, a chimney was added on the south gable of the building, the evidence for which is two large posts that framed a 5 foot deep and 10 foot wide wattle and daub chimney. Instead of being centered on the gable, however, the chimney was offset to the east side. Additionally, a patch of orange, fire-altered subsoil confirmed the hearth location. Much brick was found in the vicinity but no intact masonry footing is evident; these bricks were probably used to line the firebox. Significantly, stud molds were found along the entire south gable, strong evidence that the chimney was not original to the structure, but a later addition. Therefore, this structure was initially unheated.

Based on the artifacts, this structure was probably erected in the 1650s and it stood for several decades. Pipes, ceramics, and glass attest to an occupation between ca. 1660 and ca. 1690 that was largely domestic in nature. Further evidence of the structure's longevity comes from fences, with three or more generations of fence ditches extending from its northeast, northwest, and southwest corners. Having multiple generations of fences is strong evidence that this building was an integral part of the St. John's landscape for a long period.

We propose that this building began as a storehouse for merchant Simon Overzee, who likely built it a year or two before his sudden death in 1660. St.

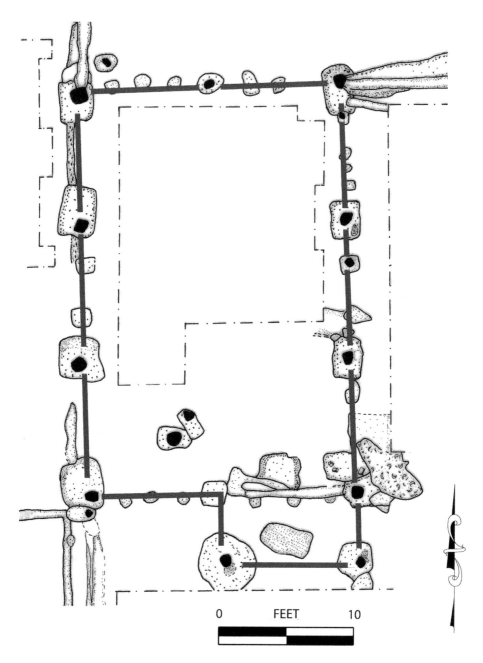

0   FEET   10

Figure 7.4. The archaeological plan of the post hole evidence for the 1650s building in the front yard of St. John's. It was originally constructed as a storehouse and later converted into a quarter. (Courtesy of HSMC.)

John's next occupant, Governor Charles Calvert, probably added the chimney to use the structure as a quarter. He had many persons to provide shelter for, and because this building is less than 40 feet from the door of his dwelling house, it was well suited to serve as a lodging space. Later innkeepers at St. John's continued to use the building for domestic purposes.

The Aisled Building

In the opposite corner of the St. John's landscape, northwest of the main house, is the last building to be discussed here. First identified in the 1970s, it was thought to have been a small animal shed open on the south side. However, recent excavations revealed that the original archaeology had only uncovered two thirds of the building. Instead of a shed, it was a structure that measured 20 feet long and 17.3 feet wide (figure 7.5). Of earthfast construction, it was formed by 12 posts arrayed in four parallel lines of three posts each. The two center lines of posts are more substantial than the outer posts and appear to form a core structure 10 feet wide and 20 feet long, divided into two bays. The outer posts are approximately 3 feet from the core posts, and the molds indicate they were set 6 to 8 inches more shallowly than the center posts. In the center of each gable are small post holes. Because these are only 5 feet from major posts, they are unlikely to have been sill supports and were more likely door posts. All the structural post holes have shallow steps or shelves on one side. These stepped holes, the position of the molds in the holes, and the undercutting of the hole walls strongly suggest that this building was erected using sidewall assembly (see chapter 2, figure 2.3). We know it was made of durable black locust because wood fragments of this species survived in four of the molds.

In plan, the structure consisted of narrow sheds or aisles installed along each side of a 10×20-foot core. These sheds created narrow interior spaces about 3 feet wide and 20 feet long along the outer walls. After construction, this building was enclosed by a paling fence, an action suggesting that it was intended to keep animals in or out. The 3-foot widths of the aisles, however, are too small for horses or cattle, so it could not have been a stable. Several buried sheep were found nearby, but even for sheep, 3 feet seems narrow. Another possibility is that the structure was intended for poultry and the aisles held roosts. To test this theory, soil samples were taken from the post molds (Miller 2006). If it was a chicken house, soil in the molds would have likely received some of the chicken litter. Potassium and nitrogen are major components of chicken litter, but these chemicals are more readily absorbed by biological activity and thus less likely to be retained in soils. Phosphorus,

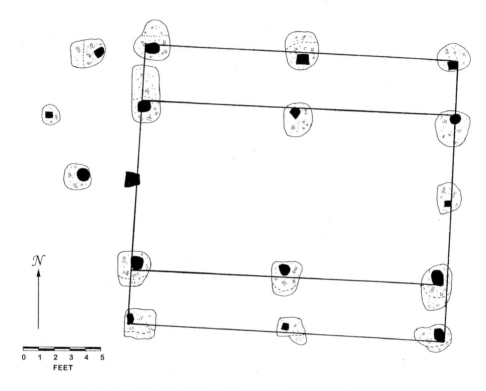

N

0 1 2 3 4 5
FEET

Figure 7.5. Archaeological evidence of the aisled building uncovered in the backyard of St. John's. Built in the 1650s, it was apparently used as a poultry house. (Drawing by Henry M. Miller, courtesy of HSMC.)

on the other hand, is also very prominent in chicken litter and survives much longer archaeologically as phosphate (Ritz and Merka 2004; Keeler 1978). Therefore it was the target chemical. While almost all post molds are rich organic soil, given the nature of their formation process, those of a chicken house would be expected to have higher phosphate values. Therefore, soil samples were taken from 30 post molds excavated around the site, five of which came from the aisled building. The aisled building post molds had a mean phosphate count higher than that of the others (97 parts per million [ppm] vs. 61 ppm), supporting the hypothesis that it served as a chicken house.

An aisled structure like this is rare in the Chesapeake. It bears a close similarity in plan to Dutch aisled structures, most notably the Dutch barn, although its scale is much smaller. Artifacts and other evidence suggest that it was built after ca. 1650. It may have been erected by Simon Overzee, the Dutch merchant who lived at St. John's from ca. 1654 until his death in early

1660. However, while the plan might be Dutch, construction in 10-foot dimensions with sidewall assembly suggests it was actually built by an English-trained carpenter (see chapter 2). Without question, this is a curious structure in the context of early Maryland architectural history. It probably stood into the 1680s.

EARLY FOODWAYS

The St. John's excavations produced close to 1 million artifacts of many types, and they provide insights about many aspects of seventeenth-century life. One of these is foodways. St. John's yielded the first samples of seventeenth-century animal remains from Maryland to be analyzed (Miller 1984, 1988b). Bones and shells spanning the 75-year occupation were assembled to learn about the diet of the inhabitants and how it changed, as well as the types of animals they consumed from both domestic and wild sources. The bones were divided into two phases for analytic purposes. Phase 1 includes remains from the 1638–ca. 1665 period, while Phase 2 spans the ca. 1665–ca. 1715 period. A total of 598 identifiable bones make up the early samples, while 739 bones came from Phase 2 features.

From the early contexts, a total of 18 different species were identified (4 domestic and 14 wild). Based on bone counts, wild animals were extremely important, with almost 70 percent of the specimens from nondomestic species. Most abundant were the remains of the sheepshead fish, which make up one-third of the total bones; today it is largely extinct in the Chesapeake Bay. Second were bones of white-tailed deer, accounting for 24 percent of the sample. Other fish include red drum and white perch. Among the other wild animals were raccoon, box turtle, and a variety of birds such as mourning dove, passenger pigeon, goose, and duck (mallard, canvasback, and scaup). Abundant oyster shell indicates that this species was also widely consumed.

Domestic animals in Phase 1 include cattle, swine, sheep or goat, and chicken. Cattle are the most common with 93 bones (15.5%) and swine second with 79 (13.2%). Sheep or goat are represented by only five identified elements and there are four chicken bones. However, eggshells were frequently found in the deposits, suggesting this was an important contribution of the chicken. Cattle, swine, and chicken thrived in the new environment of Maryland, but such was not the case with sheep. Lack of grass in the largely tree covered environment was one factor, but perhaps more important were predators, especially wolves. While mature cattle and swine could defend themselves, sheep were largely defenseless. Direct evidence of this is found in the St. John's archaeology and history. Excavators discovered two buried sheep in the backyard of St. John's. One was a pregnant ewe who died two weeks before she would have given birth to two lambs. Her hind quarters were mostly missing and no knife cuts are found on the bones, likely a result of being killed and partially eaten by predators. In 1643, Lewger wrote to Lord Baltimore telling him that in the past year, four of the sheep being kept at St. John's had been "Killed by wolves" (Browne 1887a:277). Based upon the early date of the burial, this may be one of the sheep Lewger referenced in his letter. The second sheep burial was also early, but it is a largely intact skeleton. During this period, maintaining and protecting a herd of sheep would require the constant care of a shepherd, and in the labor-short economy of early Maryland, growing tobacco was a far more effective use of human labor.

While bone counts are useful, they do not allow accurate evaluation of the diet. To address this subject, the minimum number of animals represented for each species is calculated and their meat contributions estimated. A key assumption here is that most of an animal killed at the site would have been consumed by the household. When this procedure is performed, domestic species account for 62 percent of the available meat while wild animals make up more than one-third of the total (37.4%). In terms of importance, beef is first with 42 percent and venison second with 31.4 percent, followed by pork with 18 percent. The only other significant contributor is sheepshead fish, which contributed 4.3 percent of the meat. Seasonally, fish were probably even more important. It is significant to note that in 1643 a hunting license was granted for "an Indian called Peter to carry a gonne for use of John Lewger," perhaps accounting for some of the venison at St. John's (Browne 1885:143). St. John's was an elite household, and the consumption of quantities of both beef and venison during this early period may be a reflection of that status.

How did the diet change over time? The Phase 2 sample of 739 bones contained 23 identified species. A number of these were not considered food items: dog, horse, rat, mice, and woodpecker. Thus, the same number of edible species is present. Five are domestic and thirteen wild. Among the new wild animals are opossum, rabbit, gray squirrel, turkey, blue crab, and snapping turtle. Although the wild species are more diverse, they were dramatically less significant to the colonial diet in the late seventeenth century. In this sample, domestic species contributed 93.5 percent of the estimated meat while all wild sources account for only 5.5 percent. Deer remained the most important wild animal but its contribution fell from 31 percent to 3.9 percent. Sheepshead declined from 4.36 percent to only 0.29 percent. Beef was the most prominent meat, making up almost 66 percent of the total, and pork rose to 25.5 percent. Sheep/goat accounted for only 2.75 percent of the meat.

The animal bones from St. John's indicate that the human diet underwent a radical change during the seventeenth century. In the early decades of settlement, domestic animals were already important, but wild animals contributed more than one-third of the meat. Of these, deer was the most significant followed by fish, mostly the sheepshead. The focus of the meat diet changed to one emphasizing domestic animals, primarily cattle with swine second. This transition reflected the success of domestic livestock in the Chesapeake environment and the availability of domestic meats. After wolves were reduced and pasture established, sheep also became a small but notable element in the colonial diet. However, they were never as significant in Maryland as they were in Britain. It is also possible that overharvesting had reduced the deer population, but that cannot explain the drop-off of fish and wildfowl consumption because both are migratory. The small scale of colonial fishing or fowling could not have significantly reduced these large populations. It seems colonists took fewer wild animals over time and concentrated on readily available domestic species. People still ate fish and oysters and they may have had some seasonal importance, but wild species provided more variety than comprising core elements of the diet. Utilizing a wide variety of sources provides greater food security in an unfamiliar environment such as early Maryland. As the society stabilized and matured, the dietary focus shifted to species found to be both reliable and having economic value, either as barreled meats or as livestock. This striking transformation is not indicated in the documentary record, but is clearly demonstrated by the archaeology.

Conclusions

The archaeological data regarding housing and diet from the St. John's Freehold provide valuable insight into change and adaptation in early Maryland. John Lewger invested heavily in the construction of his great house. Bringing English carpentry concepts and methods resulted in a structure that was a direct transplant from East Anglia. It is significant that soon afterward, even Lewger moved toward using a more cost effective type of architecture. A storage building erected next to the main house rested not on stone foundations, but on wood blocks set in shallow holes. This is the earliest example of earth-fast architecture found on the site. St. John's next occupant, Simon Overzee, built two more structures and both were post-in-the-ground buildings. The first may have been a chicken house and the second was a stout 20×30-foot storehouse in the front yard. Notably, this storage building featured not only substantial posts, but also wall studs set in shallow holes. Well framed, it was later converted into a quarter and stood for at least 30 years. At the same time, Overzee made a substantial investment in the main house with improvements, including quarrying and installing a sandstone lining for the cellar under the building. Why he went to this expense for the cellar remains unexplained, but both the new storehouse and cellar improvements were probably related to his ambitious efforts to expand his merchant activities. St. John's next occupant was Governor Charles Calvert and a future Lord Baltimore. He moved into the recently repaired and upgraded house, and due to his wife's pregnancy, had a room added to the structure intended to be a nursery. Although newly arrived, Calvert did not choose English architecture, but had workers construct an earthfast addition with raised, interrupted sills. After 1638 at St. John's, it is clear that the residents abandoned traditional English architecture for a newly revived medieval form of construction based upon earthfast timbers. This was a realistic adjustment to the frontier environment they found in early Maryland—a labor-short and timber-rich setting. This architectural evolution led to the development of the "Virginia House" that came to predominate in the Chesapeake region and was also common in other early English colonies.

On the other hand, faunal analysis indicates that diet was very different from that of England during the first decades of settlement. In addition to corn, Marylanders' diet depended on a variety of wild animals, with a significant reliance on deer and fish, especially seasonally. The original scarcity of livestock and the fact that the colony featured a tree-covered landscape with little open land made using traditional British practices difficult. Perhaps the most profound and long-lasting dietary shift was from wheat and barley to maize, a new crop grown using Native American agrarian practices. As the colony became more settled, labor more available, and land more cleared, noticeable changes in diet occurred. In the last quarter of the seventeenth century, the colonists' diet became more similar to consumption patterns in England in terms of meat, although meat was probably more abundant in the colony than in England. More wheat was grown, but corn remained the primary food grain. Beef and pork predominated while lamb and mutton never became as prominent in the Maryland diet as it was in most of Britain. During this later period and continuing through the eighteenth century, the dietary emphasis was upon cattle and swine with wild food providing mostly variety.

The St. John's site provided the first evidence about how immigrant culture changed in the planting of Maryland. Indeed, the pioneering archaeology at St. John's opened the first material window into the nature of seventeenth-century life in the early colony, with evidence about subjects ranging from architecture, food, and ceramics to surprisingly elegant glassware, changing cultural landscapes, and interactions with Native Americans. St. John's is one of the key sites in seventeenth-century Maryland and Chesapeake archaeology, and we are confident that the vast collection of artifacts and data from the site will provide even more insights through future studies.

8

"Master Pope's Fort"

Archaeological Investigations of a Fortification of the English Civil Wars in St. Mary's City

CHARLES H. FITHIAN

During the seventeenth century, conflicts within Britain and between Britain and European powers would have repercussions among the American colonies established along the eastern seaboard. Military and naval actions can be directly linked to these nationalist and imperial struggles. The period of the English Civil Wars was no different. Beginning in 1642, this "war without an enemy" would pit king against Parliament, and would last until Royalist forces were finally defeated at the Battle of Worcester in 1651 (Tucker and Winstock 1972:8–13). This series of civil wars resonated in the American colonies in different ways. For example, we know that many New Englanders served on the side of Parliament (Fairbanks and Trent 1983:54, 60). What happened in the Chesapeake colonies would be quite different. Virginia, and especially Maryland, would be unique in that they would be directly militarily affected by this civil war. In the decade after initial settlement, the Maryland colony was prospering and experiencing steady growth. In February 1645, this growth would be disrupted and Maryland entered what was termed the "Plundering Time."

THE ENGLISH CIVIL WARS COME TO MARYLAND

Mariner Richard Ingle, a controversial figure in early Maryland economic and maritime affairs and one who had earlier run afoul of the Proprietary government, arrived aboard the ship *Reformation* with Parliamentary letters of marque in hand. Claiming Maryland leaders were in league with enemies of the Parliament, although Lord Baltimore had actually been able to remain neutral, Ingle attacked the young colony. His first act was the capture of a

Dutch trading ship then lying in the St. Mary's River. From this first action, the capitol at St. Mary's City was seized, surrounding plantations plundered, livestock stolen, prisoners taken, and the Catholic chapel burned. Governor Leonard Calvert, unable to effectively raise the militia to counter the rebellion, was forced to flee to Virginia along with some Proprietary loyalists.

By the following spring, Ingle had departed for England. In his wake, he left the Maryland colony in the hands of Protestant supporters, but his actions triggered a long period of instability within the colony. The Calverts, however, were not idle. In December 1646, Leonard Calvert returned with a military force and reestablished Proprietary authority. Calvert's return was not an end to the unrest in the colony, for Maryland's troubles continued through the ongoing phases of the war in Britain and into the period of the Protectorate (1653–1660). More military action occurred when in 1655 the Battle of the Severn, a pitched battle between Puritan and Proprietary forces fought near present-day Annapolis, ended in the defeat of the forces loyal to the Calverts. The restoration of the Maryland colony to Proprietary control finally occurred in 1658 as a result of an agreement between Lord Baltimore and the government of Oliver Cromwell.

The above description is but a brief outline of a very complex series of events. Timothy Riordan's (2004b) analysis of the rebellion demonstrated that the political, economic, and social disruption it triggered was far more extensive than previously thought, and would impact the colony's subsequent development in many significant ways. More than a parochial squabble with a disgruntled mariner, his fine-grained research revealed that the scale and nature of the events of the Maryland rebellion closely resembled those that occurred in many parts of Britain throughout the period of the Civil Wars.

Historical documentation for this important period of Maryland history is fragmentary. However, records indicate the Protestant rebels seated themselves in several fortified strongholds, the most prominent of which was called "Master Pope's Fort" (Miller 2000). The records are silent as to the identity of this fort's builder, although Nathaniel Pope, a Maryland planter known to have been in active rebellion against Lord Baltimore, was placed in charge after Ingle's departure for England and may be a likely candidate. Another source refers to it simply as a "fortified citadel" (Riordan 2004b:232). Other references are court proceedings in which various individuals were seeking restitution for their losses during the rebellion. None of these records provide any information regarding the fort's location or its physical dimensions or layout, and they record only brief references to any activities that occurred around or within its walls. It would be through a multiyear, intensive archaeological research program undertaken by the Historic St. Mary's City Commission that the location of this important site would come to light.

THE ARCHAEOLOGY AND MATERIALITY OF POPE'S FORT

In 1981, Village Center Project excavations were the first to identify key structures and areas that composed the core of St. Mary's City. Among these was the Leonard Calvert House. Built in 1635, this building served as the early seat of government as well as the governor's personal residence. It was during investigations around this structure that Pope's Fort unexpectedly came to light (Miller 1983, 1986). Through the serendipitous failure of a septic tank connected to a nearby nineteenth-century structure that overlaid the seventeenth-century Village Center, and subsequent excavations preparatory to its replacement, the first archaeological evidence of the fort would emerge (figure 8.1). The septic tank was discovered to have intruded into an artifact-laden early seventeenth-century feature. Initially thought by researchers to have been a midden feature associated with the early occupation of the Calvert House, the excavation of undisturbed portions of this feature and nearby units revealed it to be a portion of a small bastion and a section of an associated fortification ditch. Further investigations revealed a very complex set of seventeenth-century military remains surrounding this structure.

Approximately 150 feet to the east of the septic tank area, a second, much larger semicircular bastion, ditch, and associated palisade section were uncovered (figure 8.2). To the north of the Calvert House, test units also found sections of a fort ditch that clearly connected to the first bastion and ditch (in the septic tank area), but that extended further eastward beyond the larger second bastion, and then curved southward and then turned west, forming a ditch line parallel to one to the north and probably connecting to another small bastion on the fort's southwest corner. A gate that opened to a path leading down to the spring and river was suggested on the south palisade wall, and a possible second gate was suggested by post holes that formed an opening on the north palisade wall east of the northwest bastion. In the midst of this tangle of fort ditches and other archaeological features was the Calvert House. It was later discovered that this structure had a direct relation to the surrounding military features and would be key to their interpretation. While the basic plan of Pope's Fort is established, some aspects of its construction are unclear, notably its west wall and southwest bastion areas (Timothy B. Riordan 2020, pers. comm.). In 2019, excavations in the southwest bastion area revealed complex mid-seventeenth-century archaeological

Figure 8.1. Discovery of Pope's Fort due to the failure and replacement of a septic tank, 1981. The fort ditch with the curving section and adjacent palisade fence ditch form a corner of the northwest bastion. Excavators are (*left to right*) Steve Fadley, Edie Wallace, and Charles Fithian. (Photograph by Alexander H. Morrison II, courtesy of HSMC.)

deposits that were clearly fort-related. However, it was unclear as to what specific structures/construction they represented and this must await further analysis and investigations (Travis G. Parno 2019, pers. comm.).

The initial interpretation seemed to indicate the presence of two separate fortifications. The large bastion was believed at first to be the archaeological remains of St. Mary's Fort. This 120-yard-square fort, built by the Maryland colonists upon their arrival in 1634, was thought to have been in the Village Center area. The features of the smaller Pope's Fort were initially interpreted as representing a separate fortification intruding onto the earlier St. Mary's Fort. Post-excavation analysis of plan and cross section drawings, stratigraphic associations, and artifact distribution data, however, presented a very different interpretation. The sections of ditch that were extending northwest and southwest from the large bastion were found to actually turn and connect with the parallel ditch sections to the north and south. Of particular importance was the discovery that the dimensions of the interior of the large bastion matched the dimensions of the width of the Calvert House (see figure 8.2). The dimensional similarity between these architectural features firmly established the contemporaneity of the two structures, that they were spatially related, and that the width of the Calvert House gable end

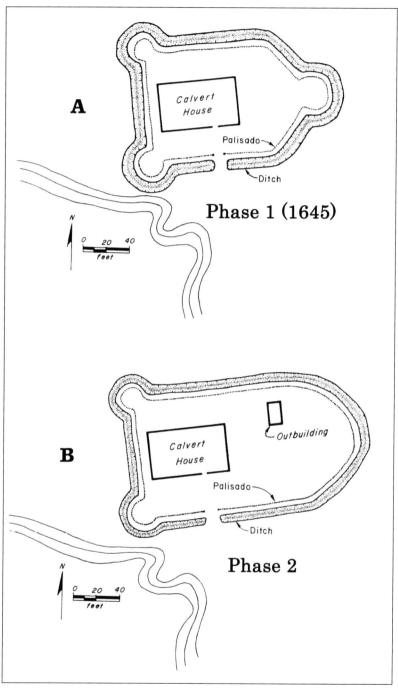

Figure 8.2. The archaeological plan of Pope's Fort in relation to the Leonard Calvert House, showing the two phases of construction: A, Phase 1, 1645; B, Phase 2, ca. 1647–1650. (Drawing by James O'Connor, courtesy of HSMC.)

guided the placement of the larger bastion to its east. Without question, the large bastion was not a part of the earlier St. Mary's Fort and was instead of a later date. The sections of the ditch that extended eastward beyond the large bastion were found to cut through its ditch fill and connected with the fort's north and south walls. The analysis showed that archaeologists had discovered not two separate forts, but instead a single fortification that underwent a later expansion. Excavations conducted in 1986 and in the years that followed confirmed the findings of the laboratory analysis and research. The earlier 1634 St. Mary's Fort continues to be elusive.

The first phase of Pope's Fort was a fortification approximately 180 feet in length and 120 feet in width, enclosing 21,600 square feet. Surrounding the Calvert House, this fort consisted of smaller bastions on the northwest and southwest corners on the west or river side, and the single large bastion located on the east end. Phase II of the fort was still 120 feet wide, but was enlarged to approximately 210 feet in length, enclosing 25,200 square feet. In the second phase, the two west end bastions remained, but the large east bastion was torn down, its ditch filled in, and the palisade extended further eastward. The palisade trench in both phases was between 1 and 2 feet wide; however, the height of the palisade cannot be determined based on evidence so far recovered. The post holes of an earthfast building were also found intruding into the fill of the larger Phase I bastion ditch. The purpose of the structure is unknown; however, artifacts associated with it indicate a contemporaneity with the Pope's Fort occupation, and were likely related to factors prompting the fort's enlargement. The gates probably remained in the same locations as before. The date of the expansion is unknown, but it may have happened after Leonard Calvert's capture of the fort in 1647, or possibly when Governor William Stone took possession of the property in 1649.

Both phases of Pope's Fort consist of a wooden palisade surrounded by a ditch. The palisade is usually 5 feet from the interior ditch edge with the ditches varying from 5 to as much as 10 feet wide in areas. Stratigraphic profiles of the fort's ditch revealed an additional construction feature. A thick layer of displaced subsoil was consistently found on the interior side of the ditch bottom of both phases, indicating that significant erosion was coming consistently from the fort wall side of the ditch. These soil deposits suggest that earth excavated from the ditch was being packed against the wooden palisade, thus strengthening it and in effect creating a type of earthen rampart (figure 8.3). Over time this soil, not secured by any additional structure, eroded back into the ditch, thus creating the stratigraphy encountered. Above these lower wash strata and early artifact-bearing soil deposits, the ditch fill was composed of a relatively simple stratigraphy, suggestive of a

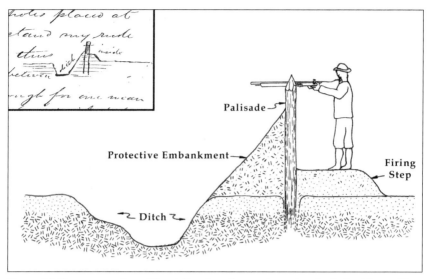

Figure 8.3. The construction of Pope's Fort based upon the archaeological evidence. The inset is an 1864 sketch of a Union Army fortification in Virginia that shows the same construction method still being used more than two centuries later. (Drawing by James O'Connor, courtesy of HSMC; inset by Charles E. LaMotte, May 8, 1864, LaMotte Papers: RG 9200-L02-000. Delaware Public Archives, Dover.)

rapid dismantling at the end of the fort's life. A chronology of approximately a decade, or less, for the fort's use is suggested by the presence of post-1660 artifacts, such as Morgan Jones ceramics, later tobacco pipes, and round bottle glass being found in only the later, uppermost levels in and over the ditch fill.

Thousands of artifacts associated with the fort were recovered. The diversity of the material, which includes both domestic and military objects, represents the occupation of the site by the fort's garrison, their prisoners, and subsequent reoccupation after Leonard Calvert's return from Virginia. Included in the artifact assemblage are white clay tobacco pipes of English and Dutch manufacture, terra-cotta pipes, including one with an elaborately decorated human face, ceramics from England, the Netherlands, France, and Germany, and hundreds of fragments of flat-sided case bottles. Several thousand animal bones represent the utilization of both wild and domestic species. Cow bones from as many as five individuals came from a single area at the bottom of a section of fort ditch. Such a high percentage of cow bones correlates well with references in the court records to Blanch Oliver's "Cow . . . killed att his Master Popes ffort" or to Thomas Sturman's "pyed calf that came unto Popes ffort" (Browne 1887a:383, 423).

Figure 8.4. Sword hilt, cannon ball, and exploded cannon barrel fragment recovered from the ditch of Pope's Fort. (Photograph by Donald L. Winter, courtesy of HSMC.)

The armaments-related artifacts found associated with the fort form a highly significant assemblage of military material culture. Some of these items are the first recovered from Maryland sites. Unlike other aspects of early Chesapeake society, the military developments in the region remain poorly understood. The Pope's Fort artifacts offer valuable information not only for understanding the events that took place in Maryland during the Civil Wars, but also for providing insights into the military material culture and evolution of English military practices on the early Chesapeake frontier.

The garrison of Pope's Fort was successful in acquiring two types of large ordnance. From the fill of the fort ditch, two iron round shot and a section of an exploded iron cannon barrel were recovered. One of the cannon balls is of a size and weight used with a gun known as a saker. The second, and larger, iron shot and the cannon barrel section were from a larger artillery piece known as a demi-culverin (figure 8.4). Comparative measurements of the barrel fragment indicate its dimensions were very similar to one of several seventeenth-century demi-culverins recovered from the St. Mary's River in the late 1820s. Peterson provides the best information on the dimensions of these artillery pieces (1969:14). Both types could be cast in iron or bronze. Sakers were 9½ feet in length and weighed approximately 2,500 pounds, whereas demi-culverins were approximately 10 feet in length and weighed approximately 3,600 pounds. Both cannons were likely mounted on field carriages. Sakers and demi-culverins were prominent among the different types of English artillery of the period, and strengthened the fort's defensive capabilities.

Small arms are represented in the artifact assemblage by a gunspring, a nearly complete "bellied" gunlock, gunflints and flintworking debitage, and lead ball and shot. The iron spring, known as a feather spring, is part of the lock of a snaphaunce or doglock weapon, and functioned to put tension on the battery, keeping it positioned or closed while protecting the priming powder in the pan. The "bellied" gunlock, also from a flint ignition firearm, was recovered in the 2019 excavations, and is a type consistent with the site's mid-seventeenth-century date (Puype 1985:20–21). Evidence for the presence of other types of firearm ignition systems was not recovered.

Gunflints and flintworking debitage clearly demonstrate the presence of flint ignition firearms at the fort. The increased reliance on flint ignition arms in effect revitalized the production of stone tools in England. The introduction of flint ignition weapons in the late sixteenth century had not created an English gunflint industry on any scale by early in the seventeenth century. Instead, the manufacture of a suitable flint was on an individual level, and excavations revealed considerable evidence of the garrison producing their own gunflints. Recovered in the plow zone around the Calvert House and in the fort ditch fill were locally produced gunflints and quantities of production waste. Flakes or spalls were driven off imported English cobbles and were then shaped and trimmed to a workable size that fit the cock of the gun. The gunflints from Pope's Fort are generally irregular in shape and exhibit a range in skill levels used in their production. Similar gunflints and debitage have been identified at other sites in St. Mary's City (Miller and Keeler 1986).

Munitions in the form of lead ball and shot represent a number of firearm calibers. They range from large caliber balls used in large bore military style muskets to smaller round ball and goose shot usually associated with hunting and food procurement. One of these pieces of shot is of particular note as it is flattened due to having been fired and impacting a target. This lead musket shot was recovered from the fort's ditch and its surface contained embedded sand and animal bone fragments that were absorbed on impact. The shot's location suggests it was fired at the fort and impacted the soil piled up along the exterior of the fort's wall (Stacy et al. 1990:758).

Edged weapons are represented by the presence of the part of a hilt from a sword (see figure 8.4). This plain iron counterguard displays a forward curving quillion, the remains of a broken-off knuckle bow, and one surviving lateral branch that would have connected to the sword's pommel. A sword

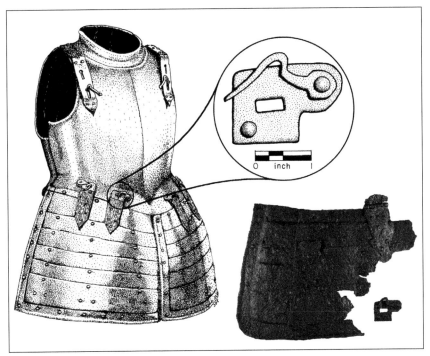

Figure 8.5. Drawing of seventeenth-century pikeman's armor showing the use of the fastener from one set of armor found at Pope's Fort and the complete tasset from another set of armor recovered from the ditch. These are the first specimens of body armor found in Maryland. (Drawing by James O'Connor and photograph by Donald L. Winter, courtesy of HSMC.)

with a hilt such as this would have been considered a standard munitions grade weapon.

Within the military artifact assemblage was the first archaeological evidence of the use of body armor in Maryland. Three individual artifacts represent at least two, but possibly three, separate components of a type of plate body armor known generally as "pikeman's armor" (figure 8.5). This group consists of one nearly complete right tasset, a corner of another right tasset, and the distinctive latch with an articulating keeper or hook. Tassets, or taces, were metal plates that attached to the bottom front of the breastplate and were intended to protect the wearer's upper legs and groin. The nearly complete tasset is composed of two different construction methods. Individually wrought iron lames riveted together composed the right side; the left was composed of a single piece of metal on which the lames were stamped and simulated. The combination of these two methods is indicative of a well-executed repair. This tasset was attached and articulated from the breastplate by metal hinges. The second tasset fragment is the lower right corner of another right tasset, also a section with a simulated lame. The third artifact is a metal latch that helped secure a tasset to the lower front of a breastplate. Unlike the first tasset with its metal hinge, this latch was riveted to a leather strap that acted as the hinge.

INTERPRETATIONS AND INFERENCES

In a manner similar to their domestic architecture, colonists to the Chesapeake brought and used a variety of types of military architecture. From archaeology and documents, at least five basic types of military architecture that ranged from large, enclosed settlements to fortified houses to simple barricades composed of palisades can be identified (Fithian 1991). Pope's Fort is a form of earthwork fortification that converted the Calvert House into a fortified garrison house. While small by Anglo-European military standards, in a colonial Maryland context this fortification would have presented an imposing presence on the landscape. This fort should not be considered an example of a military vernacular architecture. Its three-angled plan, wooden palisade with earthen reinforcement, well-sited bastions, and integrated heavy ordnance suggest its builders had some knowledge regarding the application of elements of formal military architecture and the concepts of defense. Additionally, they employed a fort design apparently well known in English colonization. A preliminary search of period military literature has failed to locate any direct references to this style of fort construction. However, an examination of a series of maps drawn by military cartographer Richard Bartlett of the late sixteenth–early seventeenth-century military campaigns in Northern Ireland has found illustrations of fortifications very similar to Pope's Fort (Hayes-McCoy 1964). In a *Plan of Armagh City and Mountjoy Fort on the Blackwater Valley,* and another such as "the castel of coole more" constructed during the Lough Foyle Expedition, are two examples of fortifications composed of a three-bastion or three-angle arrangement with an interior structure, and which bear a strong similarity to the Maryland fort (Hayes-McCoy 1964:5 and Map III; 26 and Map XVI; see figure 8.6). Also of significance is that all these forts were English-built, and although appearing as masonry construction they were actually built of earth and timber (Hayes-McCoy 1964:xiii, 2). Of architectural note, the drawing of the "Mountjoy Fort" mentioned above shows gates immediately adjacent to the smaller bastions. This pictorial evidence supports the interpretation

Figure 8.6. Mountjoy Fort in Ireland, 1602 (*left*), and Pope's Fort in Maryland, 1645 (*right*). The fort on the left is one of the few known examples of an English three-angled fort similar in plan and construction to Pope's Fort. While the illustrator drew it as a masonry construction, it was actually constructed of timber and earth. (Mountjoy Fort: detail from *Plan of Armagh City and Mountjoy Fort on the Blackwater River*, ca. 1602, MS 2656 (3), image courtesy of the National Library of Ireland; Pope's Fort: courtesy of HSMC.)

of palisade and post hole features on the Pope's Fort north wall near the northwest bastion as a gate.

The similarity between the Irish and Maryland fort plans suggests a design utilized by the English in their colonial settlements. Evidence for the association of this plan of fortification with the English comes from an unexpected source—a description of a fort on the Delaware River. A Swedish fortification, Nya Elfsborg, constructed in early 1643 by Governor Printz, was described in 1645 as an "earthwork" (Hudde 1877:28–29). On October 13, 1643, David De Vries, a Dutch patroon involved with the Dutch settlements on the Delaware River, visited Nya Elfsborg and described it as "with three angles," and a week later he further wrote that it was "made after the English plan, with three angles close by the river" (De Vries 1643:27–28). Clearly, a three-angled plan fortification had become recognizably "English" by European observers prior to the middle of the seventeenth century.

The earthen reinforcement of the palisade is an important feature of the fort's architecture. The addition of soil placed against the wooden palisade in this fashion in effect created a rampart that strengthened the fort's defensive capabilities. This practice is well documented during the English Civil Wars when earth excavated from surrounding fortification ditches was added to older masonry fortifications (Harrington 2003:28). These modifications made them more resistant to battering by artillery and more difficult for assault by infantry. The ditch with earth and wood rampart at Pope's Fort indicates its builders anticipated potential adversaries were going to be trained in European-style warfare, and that they would need more substantial protection than that afforded by an unsupported wooden palisade. Furthermore, this construction method should not be viewed as an anomaly, and archaeologists should be alert to this feature being present at other forts and earthworks with ditches from other time periods. For example, dating from the American Civil War, three companies of the Fourth Delaware Volunteer Infantry occupied a fort near Cedar Run, Virginia. While the plan of the fort is different, writing in May 1864, Lieutenant-Colonel Charles E. LaMotte, the post's commander, described and illustrated a construction method that is identical to that seen in the Pope's Fort archaeology (see figure 8.3). He stated that "This stockade is built of heavy oak logs placed on end & planted firmly in the ground & dirt thrown up against them from a ditch on the out side 6 ft wide & 6ft deep" (LaMotte 1864).

The excavated military material culture reveals important changes and adaptations that had been taking place in the Chesapeake region prior to midcentury. The archaeological data in the form of only flint ignition weapons suggest the garrison was armed only with that ignition system. Data from Chesapeake sites and historical documentation indicate that flint ignition weapons rapidly replaced the matchlock as a combat weapon in this region, and that by the early 1640s matchlocks had largely disappeared. For example, a 1624/1625 military muster reveals flint ignition arms to be the dominant shoulder arm of Virginia colonists, with matchlocks being present but in much smaller numbers (Peterson 1956:43, 323). In Maryland, the 1638/39 militia legislation allowed the use of "matchlocks" or "firelocks" (Browne 1883:77–78). However, by 1641, the colony's requirements included only a "musket . . . with a snaphance lock" (Browne 1885:101). In this instance, the term "snaphance" was used as a generic term that denoted a flint ignition firearm and not the specific lock type that is associated with that name. Clearly, both lines of evidence indicate Chesapeake colonists were selecting firearms that were more reliable and efficient to handle in military activities in wilderness environments regardless of adversary. This comparatively rapid technological selection seen in Chesapeake military practice stands in sharp contrast to the persistence of the use of matchlock firearms by British and European armies until the early decades of the eighteenth century. Contracts for the manufacture of firearms for the New Model Army in the 1640s and 1650s show the continued preference for matchlock over flint ignition muskets by the sizeable numbers of the former being produced by various gunsmiths (Mungeam 1968:93–96). The two ignition systems would continue to be used together in the British service until matchlock weapons were withdrawn during the reign of Queen Anne, and flintlock weapons became the sole weapons system produced by the creation of the Ordnance System of Manufacture in 1714–1715 (Blackmore 1961:38–39; Goldstein and Mowbray 2010:6). The preference for flint ignition systems is further evidenced by the presence of locally made gunflints and the debitage from their manufacture. Found at early seventeenth-century sites, and now at a site with a clear mid-century date, these artifacts are evidence for the preferential selection and increased use of flint ignition arms. They indicate that a "do it yourself" stage of gunflint production discussed by de Lotbiniere was still the means by which these technologically critical items were produced in the Chesapeake (1980:154).

The iron counterguard could have formed part of a hilt of a short cutting sword or possibly a broadsword (figure 8.4). Its shape is very similar to a counterguard on a cutlass carried by Benjamin Church during King Philip's War, 1675–1678 (Peterson 1956:81), and one on a midcentury English broadsword in the collection of the Royal Armouries in Leeds, England (Lavin 2000:33, figure 45). While it is difficult to determine precisely which sword type the counterguard belonged to, both types of swords would have been useful for colonial forces operating in a frontier environment.

The armor components recovered from Pope's Fort raise interesting questions about the use of these defensive armaments in the Chesapeake region. From the perspective of the Chesapeake region's humid climate, varied and complex wilderness environments, and mobile and efficient American Indian warriors, archaeologists initially viewed the presence of body armor as an anachronism, or as a technology out of place in New World conditions and therefore quickly abandoned (Noël Hume 1979:757; Outlaw 1990:58). However, the archaeological record has in recent decades provided more information on how long this equipment was used, and has permitted the development of a different perspective on its usage.

Most archaeologically recovered armor dates to the initial period of settlement, such as the material from Jamestown, or to the 1620s. Examples of sites with armor assemblages dating to the latter period would include the Main Site (Outlaw 1990:28), and Martin's Hundred (Noël Hume and Noël Hume 2001). By contrast, the Pope's Fort armor was recovered from the latest dated archaeological context excavated in the Chesapeake region to date, and demonstrates body armor's much longer and continued role within Chesapeake military equipage and practice well into the middle of the seventeenth century. Harold Peterson was the first to posit that the use of armor in the Chesapeake continued until then (1956:14). His assessment at that time was not based on direct physical evidence; however, the Maryland armor confirms that he was correct. Additionally, the Pope's Fort armor is the first archaeological evidence of armor usage from Maryland, and as such it expands the known geographic range for the use of these defensive armaments in the region. An evaluation of the construction methods represented by the armor components indicates that these armaments were not simply obsolete equipment emptied out of English armories, nor are they exactly exemplars of the armorer's craft. Instead, they are an example of good munition grade armor that would have seen widespread usage among rank and file soldiers.

What then can be said of armor's use and how did the soldiers employ it? Rather than a process of wholesale abandonment, the argument advanced here is that armor usage went through a selective retention caused by the same adaptive processes as seen in other aspects of Chesapeake life (Graham et al. 2007). The hypothesis maintained here is that breast and backplates were retained while the various attachments and appendages were discarded. That the Maryland armor consists entirely of tasset components, and that a preliminary review of data from several sites finds attachments or attachment parts to be common in body armor assemblages, supports this argument. This lightened armor could be worn by itself, or in conjunction with soft armors such as quilted coats or leather buff coats. A reduction in weight and the increasing of mobility were likely the objectives of these changes.

The archaeological and documentary records appear to be in agreement. This process appears to have started early in Virginia. In 1611, Thomas Dale in his military reforms for the colony wanted the "shot," or men armed with muskets, to use a "light armor," composed of back and breastplates only. He also mentioned the use of soft armors in conjunction with the plate armor (Kelso and Straube 2004:144). A similar process can be seen in Maryland, when in 1639, Marylanders sought "20 corslets," again a term used to designate back and breastplates only, for an expedition against American Indians (Browne 1885:85–86). It is important to note that the men on this expedition were to be armed only with firearms.

A reduction in weight and the facilitating of movement were not the only parts of this adaptive process. Three breastplates recovered from two Virginia sites exhibit a modification in the form of a small plate attached to the edge of the upper front of the right armhole of the breastplate (Kelso and Straube 2004:143–144). This alteration is thought to provide a rest for the butt of a shoulder arm to help steady the weapon when the soldier was taking aim. Its presence reveals a further Chesapeake adaptation for musketeers wearing armor.

Just as Chesapeake colonists were opting for more efficient firearms and modifying defensive armors, so too were they altering their military tactics and formations. Armor altered in the manners described above could be integrated effectively into new tactics that were being developed and deployed. In 1608, Smith described how he trained his men to "march, fight and skirmish in the woods," and later George Percy reorganized his "fyles" for his raids against Indian towns (Arber and Bradley 1910:34; Percy 1922:271). Both references show the development of more flexible, open order formations as a response to the conditions of wilderness warfare. These developments served as a foundation for the later development of light infantry formations and tactics in New World Anglo-American warfare, and would have been effective regardless of adversary. The changes present within Chesapeake military material culture and practices created a sharp contrast between colonists armed for New World combat and their counterparts on British and European battlefields.

It should be noted that procurement records for the New Model Army dating to the 1640s and 1650s indicate that the large amounts of armor being produced consisted only of the breast and backplates and a helmet. For example, in 1650 Edward Anslow produced "1500 backs, breasts and potts" for the army (Green 1875:599). The use of scaled-down armor may also have been a product of broader changes in the application of military technology at midcentury. Nevertheless, body armor was clearly still considered to be a part of the colonist's military equipage at midcentury, with environmental factors probably hastening the modification of armor usage in the region.

Was Pope's Fort the site of a military action? Did the rebels and forces loyal to the Calverts engage one another there when Governor Calvert returned? The historical record does not record references or descriptions of pitched battles of any scale in the St. Mary's City area. However, some records make references to events such as the "taking of St. Thomases ffort," a Catholic stronghold captured by Ingle's men (Browne 1887a:381). The use of the term "taking" in this context suggests military force was required to capture this post. But is the archaeological record revealing an unrecorded episode of this disruptive period in Maryland history? Some Pope's Fort artifacts, such as the flattened bullet and a section of burst cannon barrel, may be providing the physical evidence that Pope's Fort was also taken by force. A lead shot that impacted the earth placed against the palisade indicates a firearm was deliberately fired at the fort, and the burst cannon indicates a piece of artillery in the fort was discharged while loaded with a projectile. A piece of artillery such as this would not have exploded unless charged and shotted. The low number of supporting artifacts makes this interpretation tentative; however, their presence suggests the fort's defenders did not give up their post without some level of resistance or at the least maintained an honorable defense. Furthermore, they raise the possibility that the area around the fort and Calvert House should be considered a potential early battlefield in future archaeological research at St. Mary's City.

CONCLUSIONS

While many questions await further investigation, the discovery of and excavations at Pope's Fort have brought to light the first archaeological site associated with the English Civil Wars in North America, and has provided a broader perspective on this series of conflicts. This small colonial fort has revealed early Maryland's connections to the wider Atlantic World, and serves as a reminder that those avenues also brought war and the radical ideas of the English Revolution. As a well-preserved and intact site, Pope's Fort forms a significant part of the physical record of the contested landscape that Maryland became in 1645. Its builders, well aware of a type of military architecture known in the expanding English world, had the knowledge and ability to construct a fortification that consisted of formal elements of military architecture in a frontier environment. They created a fortification that provided for strong defense and occupied a commanding position along the St. Mary's River. Perhaps they had gained this knowledge through involvements in earlier English colonial ventures, or perhaps they were veterans of Anglo-European conflicts and saw similar structures on other landscapes. The various types of military artifacts recovered were part of the materiality of English military practice, but also reflect broad changes occurring in military technology as well as adaptations to New World conditions. This fort and its artifact assemblage demonstrate that military affairs of the seventeenth-century Chesapeake, often viewed as static and culturally uninformative, were more complex and dynamic than previously thought, were influenced by the regional environment as well as broad patterns of technological change, and experienced evolutionary changes and adaptations similar to those identified in other aspects of English culture in the region.

9

Community, Identity, and Public Spaces

The Calvert House as the First State House of Maryland

WESLEY R. WILLOUGHBY

In March of 1634, 150 or so British settlers landed on the shores of Maryland to initiate a novel social experiment: to establish a new community based on the ideals of freedom of conscience and conviction. Cecil Calvert, the second Lord Baltimore, inherited this charge from his father George, first Lord Baltimore, who died shortly before receiving the Maryland Charter from Charles I in 1632. Devout Catholics in a country where "Popery" was officially outlawed, both Calverts had developed distaste for the injustices that manifest when religion is fused with politics (Jackson 2008:5). While Maryland was certainly a commercial venture for the Lord Proprietor, it was also intended to be a more open society where religion and government would comprise separate institutions. Religion was to be no business of the government, and it would not warrant any restrictions with regard to public life. With this principle in hand, Cecil Calvert sent his agents, along with volunteers seeking new life and opportunity, to North America to form a new community. This community was to be one where individuals could worship freely, hold public office, vote, and otherwise participate in the civil governing of the colony regardless of religious affiliation (Jordan 1987; Miller 1988a; Jackson 2008).

The seventeenth-century Chesapeake has often been characterized as politically unstable, disordered, socially weak, chaotic, and demographically disrupted (Horn 1994; Jordan 1979; Walsh 1988:200). It is often contrasted with trends seen in the New England colonies, where closed, corporate, homogenous, and cohesive communities prevailed (Walsh 1988:200), and mature and stable governing institutions were attained rather rapidly (Jordan 1979:243). Scholars have explored some of the ways immigrants adapted to novel conditions associated with the colonization of the Chesapeake (Carr et al. 1991; Horn 1988, 1994). But how was social order established in new settlements such as Maryland? How did individuals of diverse origins find ways of cooperating and producing workable, stable, and long-lasting institutions (Carr 1978:72)? These are poignant questions considering the many difficulties settlers to the region faced during the seventeenth century. Maryland throughout the seventeenth century was an overwhelmingly rural, agrarian colony organized around the tobacco plantation economy. It was plagued by a number of challenges: extremely high mortality; no uniform, binding religion; striking social inequality; unbalanced sex ratios; lack of a well-developed institutional and economic infrastructure; the virtual absence of towns or even clustered settlements; and no organized standing military or police force (Walsh 1988; Carr et al. 1991). Yet despite these many obstacles, Maryland offered social and economic opportunities, was able to grow, and eventually flourished.

Scholars have long remarked on the connection between community and social order. Gloria Main has argued that in seventeenth-century Maryland, the lack of well-developed, settled communities was indeed a hindrance to the proper governance of the people (1982:42). This reflects long-standing beliefs that a society lacking community or developed settlements would necessarily lack order, social discipline, and good government (Horn 1994:235). From this perspective, community and sociopolitical order are invariably linked and codependent. Thus how was a sense of community, and by extension, sociopolitical order, constructed in a newly established settlement such as colonial Maryland? What roles did public sites play in this process? How did public sites structure spheres of communal interaction and promote social intercourse? Using Maryland's first statehouse (ca. 1662–1676) as a case study, this chapter examines the role social usage of early public sites may have played in mediating processes of community formation in the emergent cultural setting of the seventeenth-century Chesapeake. Specifically, archaeology is used to examine the development of this important site and analyze some of the ways public interactions within the built environment helped establish order and community in seventeenth-century Maryland.

This work builds on growing archaeological discourses which recognize that the study of communities must address their processes of construction and perpetuation in mutual action (e.g., Canuto and Yaeger 2000; Owoc 2005). These approaches view communities as socially constituted institutions contingent on human interaction for their creation and continued existence. Such an institution is dependent on physical venues for repeated, meaningful, suprahousehold interactions (Canuto and Yaeger 2000:5–6). Public sites thus constitute vital elements of human interaction and are crucial for understanding past communities. It is this interaction approach to community that I have adopted for this particular study. This perspective borrows heavily from practice theory (Bourdieu 1977; Giddens 1979), which, minimally defined, seeks to examine and understand human action in relation to social and material structures (Ortner 1989:12). As a working hypothesis, I suggest that early government sites provided two important functions: they established a formal environment to represent and display government authority, and they provided important venues for large-scale community interactions. Interactions within these venues helped form and sustain a cohesive community and functioning society.

GOVERNMENT SITES AND COMMUNITY IN COLONIAL AMERICA

The potential relevance of government space as a center for community and social interaction may not be obvious to those of us in contemporary society. Today there seems to be little social dimension to these sites apart from that which takes place in the context of government business. Overall, little has been published on the social history of government space, particularly during the colonial period. Scholarship has often focused on their significant roles in the birth of American democracy and governing institutions. In some of these sites, significant historical events took place that set precedents that later shaped and defined our nation and identity. Such events include: the first meeting of the House of Burgesses in Virginia, 1619, establishing representative government in the American colonies; the passage of Maryland's Toleration Act in 1649, establishing freedom of religion and conscience; the Halifax Resolves, April 1776, constituting the first official government action calling for American Independence. David Jordan has criticized historians for focusing too narrowly on such constitutional precedents and not giving attention to the broader social dynamics of politics (1979:245). Besides historical significance, government sites occupied central roles in representing government authority and maintaining social order, and they were key components in the establishment and maintenance of colonial and early American society.

Some historians, however, have begun addressing important social aspects of early government sites and have painted a very different picture from how we view these sites in the present. Carl Lounsbury, in particular, remarks on how monthly court day in eighteenth-century Virginia brought citizens of all social classes together to transact a variety of business (2005). This one-, two-, or three-day event transformed the courthouse grounds into a marketplace, playing field, and social center. Court days provided opportunities for members of local society to conduct business, sell goods, renew ties of friendship, or participate in other amusements (Lounsbury 2005). Lee Shepard further notes that court day in Virginia counties drew not only individuals who had official business in the courthouse, "but also those who wished to attend elections, to buy, sell, or trade crops, horses, dry goods, and other items, or to be entertained by speeches, races, games of chance, or similar pastimes" (1995:459). He goes on to indicate that on Virginian court days the major portion of a county's free white male population came together through a variety of activities to renew or refine a collective sense of belonging (Shepard 1995:459). Gloria Main argues that court days, in addition to bringing the citizenry together, provided the most important social and political entertainment of the annual calendar in the tobacco colonies (1982:46).

Archaeological research on these government sites, however, has been relatively rare, and with the exception of some earlier work conducted at Historic St. Mary's City and Jamestown, little has focused specifically on America's seventeenth-century beginnings (e.g., Miller 1994; Horning 1995). Yet from the above references, it is clear that public sites were essential venues for communal interaction. The research presented here seeks to better illuminate the social use of these sites and develop a more complete and nuanced understanding of the diverse role they played in the colonial process. Certainly Lord Baltimore's New World community was at least in part "imagined" in principle by himself, but it was also one that came to fruition, albeit in a different form than originally intended or envisioned. While early Maryland was fraught with challenges and met with variable success, the fact that the colony's original guiding principles of representative government and freedom of worship are part of our national constitution more than 300 years later bears testament to the merit of its ideals. It is clear that public sites in the colonial Chesapeake provided important foci for collective and communal, ritual interaction among early settlers (e.g., Main 1982; Shepard 1995; Lounsbury 2005).

BACKGROUND: THE CALVERT HOUSE SITE

The Calvert House Site (18ST1-13) has been the subject of intensive archaeological research since the early 1980s. Though some of the details regarding the site are still being worked out, much of what is known concerning its history and architecture comes from the first major excavations carried out at the site between 1981 and 1984, coupled with the sparse documentary record. This work has been summarized extensively elsewhere and will be only briefly summarized here (see Stone 1982; H. Miller 1983, 1986, 1994).

The building was constructed sometime following the initial months of settlement of the colony for Lord Baltimore's brother and first governor of Maryland, Leonard Calvert. By the time the structure was completed, ca. 1640, it consisted of a twin-gabled, framed building with two parallel banks of rooms measuring 40 by 67.5 feet (figure 9.1). In 1645, amidst a brief rebellion associated with the English Civil War, Governor Calvert fled the colony and his house was occupied by the rebel Nathaniel Pope. During this time a palisade and ditch was constructed around the house, which became known as Pope's Fort (see chapter 8). Governor Calvert regained control of the colony and reoccupied the house until his death in 1647. Governor William Stone then occupied the house until his death in 1659, after which time Leonard Calvert's heir, William, reacquired the property. William immediately sold the tract to an innkeeper.

During the early decades of settlement, the colonial Assembly periodically met at the site, often rotating meetings between the governor's house and the provincial secretary's house at St. John's. By 1661 the provincial government had been looking for more permanent accommodation and formally purchased the house and surrounding lot in 1662 for use as the first official State House of Maryland (Carr 1994; Miller 1994). The site was then renamed the Country's House in reference to its new public function (Miller 1994:66). Since the Assembly met for only short periods each year, in order to help defray maintenance costs, the legislature leased the building to innkeepers who were made responsible for its upkeep (H. Miller 1986:13, 1994:66). When St. Mary's was incorporated as the first official city within the colony in 1667, the Country's House was the authoritative center of the colony and the focal center for the city's Baroque town plan (Miller 1988a, 1994). Figure 9.2 gives a conjectural view of the structure as it may have appeared in the later seventeenth century.

In 1676, no doubt due in part to the awkwardness created by the site's concurrent function as both government meeting house and public ordinary, a new brick State House was constructed on the north end of town. Though committees still occasionally met at the site, most of the government functions were removed from the Country's House and the building reverted back to being a full-time inn (Miller 1994:66). It continued to operate as a public ordinary until its abandonment sometime around the turn of the eighteenth century.

Figure 9.1. Photograph of the eastern end of the Calvert House foundation. (Photograph by Garry Wheeler Stone, courtesy of HSMC.)

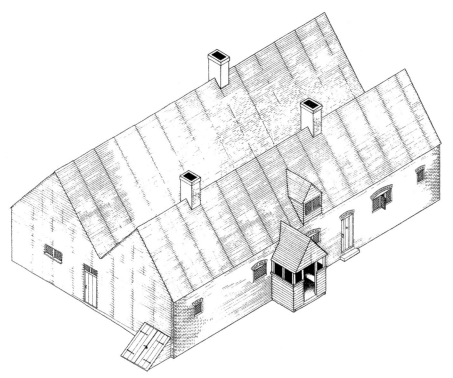

Figure 9.2. Conjectural drawing of the Calvert House as it may have appeared in the later seventeenth century. (Drawing by Garry Wheeler Stone and Chinh Hoang, courtesy of HSMC.)

PUBLIC INTERACTIONS AT THE COUNTRY'S HOUSE

Two types of government meetings occurred with some frequency at the Country's House between 1662 and 1676 that likely drew significant crowds to the fledgling capital: (1) meetings of the Provincial Court; and (2) meetings of the Lower House of the Assembly. David Jordan (1987) provides a fairly detailed and balanced account chronicling the rise and development of the provincial Assembly. However, this essay is particularly focused on the social use of Maryland's first statehouse and thus focuses discussion on the public gatherings that likely developed in association with the government meetings that occurred at the site. While the documentary history of the legislative proceedings is relatively rich, what these public events looked like and how the associated public gatherings articulated within the site have been almost completely left out of the historical record. Despite this, there are a few references that allude to the busy times and vibrant interactions these gatherings entailed, no doubt facilitated by the site's alternate function as a public ordinary.

A "Complaint from Heaven with a Huy and crye," issued in 1676, indicates the burgesses "are called Deligates, but the Country calls then Delicats, for thy gladly com to such Christenings at St. Mary's where there is good cheere made, and the poore Country payes every time, one two or more hundred thousand pounds of tobacco for it" (as quoted in Jordan 1987:95). The document further complains that the upper house dictated what actions the lower house was to take, and if there were any protests "then perswadinge spirits goe forth" (as quoted in Jordan 1987:95). This suggests that spirits and likely other victuals were significant features of Assembly meetings and that alcohol was apparently used in attempts to mediate tensions among members and between both houses. There is also some indication that tavern activity among burgesses during periods of adjournment also occurred with some frequency. A number of payments to the innkeepers who leased the structure are recorded in the archives for lodging and feeding burgesses (Browne 1884). Given the site's concurrent function and status as the largest ordinary in the colony, it is likely the majority of burgesses were some of the site's primary patrons during these meetings. Alcohol was apparently no unusual feature of these tavern interactions. On May 1, 1666, merchant Edward Erberry was prosecuted by the Upper House for verbally insulting a number of burgesses from the General Assembly the previous evening. According to testimony from a number of burgesses, Erberry "did call the whole howse Papists, Rogues, Turdy rogues, &c" and "sayed wee are a Company of Turdy fellows and were ashamed of the place from whence wee came," among other insults (Browne 1884:55–56). Erberry's response to the charges was that apparently "he Remembered none of those words as is alledged only he Confesseth that he was in drinke" (Browne 1884:56). Being drunk was apparently not an adequate defense and Erberry was sentenced to 39 lashes in public.

A few other references indicate Assembly meetings were busy times at the Country's House and the developing town of St. Mary's City. On April 11, 1666, Marmaduke Snowe petitioned the Upper House to hear him dispute "Errors" assigned against him by Thomas Gerard that day "forasmuch as your Petitioner being lame and sickly & the Ordinary at this present so full of People that Accommodations are wanting to your Petitioners Condition in reference to a Continuance" (Browne 1884:11). This reference clearly indicates Mr. Snowe had hoped for an immediate audience rather than a continuance since no suitable accommodations were left available to him. No doubt the "Ordinary" in the reference is the Country's House since it was the only official one in operation at the time.

Just one week and a day following the above petition (on April 19, 1666), references indicate both houses were reconsidering a contract made previously with William Smith to build a new State House, which he apparently had failed to do despite receiving some payment for it. Both houses agreed to repeal the Act for the contract as long as Smith repaid the tobacco "he hath already received towards the building of the Great Stadt House" but that "further both houses do think of some way to provide an House merely to hold Courts of Assembly apart from any victualling House whatsoever" (Browne 1884:28–29). This reference alludes to the awkwardness caused by the concurrent function of the site as Assembly meeting place and public ordinary and that both houses saw the need for a more exclusive, dedicated space for government business.

One final reference from the 1666 proceedings of the upper house regards a lease granted to William Smith by the Assembly for an additional three acres of the "Country's Land." In the response to the request given to the Upper House, the Lower House indicated that it "doe Consent that Wm Smith may haue three acres of the Countrys land for one and thirty yeares to him & his Executors to be layd out by the Governor, provided the sd Smith & his Executers be obliged to build a new howse thereon at his owne Costs & charges & keep ordinary therein for the Countrys service & for the entertaynment of all psons whatsoever attending Pro^{all} Courts & Assemblys or vpon their other necessary occasions at other tymes" (Browne 1884:51). This clearly illustrates the recognized need for public accommodations for individuals attending meetings of the government. Although it mentions "other necessary occasions at other times," the specific mention of the necessity for the "country's service" and for the "entertainment of all persons attending Provincial Courts and Assemblys" provides some indication that meetings of the government were especially busy times in St. Mary's.

Though these few passing archival references suggest that meetings of Provincial Courts and Assemblies were certainly among the busiest, most widely attended events within the early capital, details concerning the extent and nature of the larger associated public interactions and how they articulated within the built environment have been left almost completely out of the documentary record. The earliest description of such public activity in early Maryland comes from a satirical poem published by Ebenezer Cooke in 1708 titled "*The sot-weed factor: or A Voyage to Maryland. A Satyr. In which is describ'd the laws, government, courts and constitutions of the country, and also the buildings, feasts, frolicks, entertainments and drunken humours of the inhabitants of that part of America.*" Cooke was a London-born lawyer and land agent who came to Maryland in 1694 and resided in St. Mary's City for a short time. He was apparently so appalled by the conditions he encountered that he thought it fitting to record his experience there in satirical verse. Though his observations must be regarded with a healthy level of skepticism, several passages describe the public scene at government meetings at the turn of the eighteenth century. Upon his initial arrival to a Maryland town on court day, he describes "roaring Planters on the ground . . . Carousing Punch in open Air" and that no quarters were to be found. After court adjourned he found "A Herd of Planters on the ground, O'er-whelmed with Punch, dead drunk." He was finally able to find a place to sleep in a "Cornloft" (Cooke 1708:15–17). This certainly leaves the reader the impression of a crowded, drunken scene with accommodations left wanting.

While no doubt exaggerated for publication, it is precisely this type of scene or impression one gets from the above passing archival references. Although Cooke's account takes place some 30-plus years following the government use of the Country's House, it perhaps serves as a useful analogue for the types of social gatherings and interactions that characterized the site during meetings of the courts and assemblies in the 1660s and 1670s. It certainly falls in line with descriptions of these events in Virginia later in the eighteenth century. Referring to Virginia, which was culturally very similar to Maryland given their shared tobacco economy, Carl Lounsbury notes how monthly court days brought citizens of all social classes together to transact a variety of business (2005:5). He notes that country vendors often set up temporary booths to cater to the hunger, thirst, or other material wants of the crowd, giving the courthouse grounds the appearance of a bazaar. Horseraces, games of fives or other ball games, games of chance, cockfighting, brawls, and other pastimes were also regular features of the gathering (Lounsbury 2005:5–8; Shepard 1995:459–465). As Lounsbury puts it, "punctuating the isolated routine of rural life, court day was a great social event, providing the opportunity for members of local society to renew ties of friendship over a drink in the tavern or participate in harmless amusements" (2005:38). These community gatherings associated with court day remained prominent regular social events into the twentieth century (Lounsbury 2005; Shepard 1995). But what does archaeology tell us about these activities and how they may have been structured at the Country's House during the seventeenth century?

AN ARCHAEOLOGY OF PUBLIC SPACE IN A SEVENTEENTH-CENTURY COMMUNITY

In order to examine the connection between public space, interaction, and community formation/integration, this research focused on two broad goals: (1) reconstruct the lot surrounding the Calvert Site through time; and (2) examine the distribution of artifacts across the site through time. The goal was to contextualize the site during the period it served as the State House and examine whether there is any evidence that a formal environment was established and associated with its function and status as statehouse, as well as whether there is any evidence indicating its significance as a major social center during its government period. This research uses data collected over 30-plus years of excavation on the site. Preliminary excavations were conducted between 1981 and 1984. Since then additional excavations have been conducted in 1995 and every summer since 2008, resulting in more than 400 5×5-foot excavation units dug within the site boundary. This analysis drew on materials sampled from approximately 151 excavation units, which represented approximately 36 percent of the excavation units completed as of the time of the analysis (2011–2012).

The analysis first entailed reconstructing the Country's House lot over time by sequencing various landscape features excavated on the site (primarily fence lines and outbuildings) using superposition and temporally diagnostic artifacts. Second, temporally diagnostic artifacts (primarily ceramics and pipe stems) from middens across the site (largely retrieved from plow zone contexts) were divided into three distinct phases:

Phase I, ca. 1640–1660 (Pre State House), represented by Border ware, Portuguese Micaceous Red Earthenware, Dutch Coarse/Flemish ware, early Tin glaze, and 3.2 to 3.8 mm tobacco pipes.
Phase II, ca. 1660–1680 (State House), represented by Morgan Jones pottery and 2.8 mm pipes.
Phase III, ca. 1680–1700 (Post State House), represented by Staffordshire-like Slipware, Manganese Mottled ware, English Brown Stoneware, and 2.0 to 2.4 mm pipes.

The distributions of these materials were then mapped using the Surfer computer program. Once mapped, the sequenced distribution patterns were then overlaid on the sequenced landscape reconstructions in order to correlate changes in material distributions and disposal behavior with changes in the lot configuration. This expands preliminary analysis conducted by Miller (1986, 1994) that first examined changes in disposal behavior across

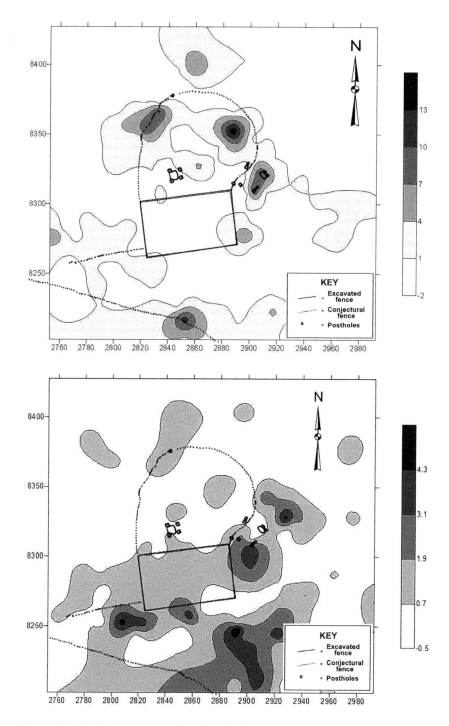

Figure 9.3. Phase I (1635–ca. 1650s) artifact distribution of ceramics (*top*) and white clay tobacco pipes (*bottom*). (Figure by Wesley R. Willoughby.)

the site using materials collected from the initial excavations recovered in the early 1980s. This analysis includes a much broader sample of materials and then integrates the material distributions with more recent landscape reconstructions. The results of this analysis demonstrate a number of interesting changes in how the site was organized and utilized at different periods.

The earliest lot structure and distribution sequence (ca. 1640s) shows a somewhat haphazard, randomly oriented fence arrangement (figure 9.3). Artifact concentrations occur to the northeast, inside the fence, as well as outside where an early outbuilding oriented with the fence is located. Tobacco pipes are distributed primarily in the front, east, west, and southeast yard areas.

By the 1660s there are a number of changes evident in the lot (figure 9.4). The fence takes on a more ordered layout directly oriented with the structure. A cross-fence partition enclosed the rear yard and segregated a small, cellared outbuilding (probably a dairy) away from the immediate yard area. The enclosed portion of the rear yard is largely clear of refuse apart from a low-density scatter of tobacco pipes. Likewise, a large portion of the immediate front yard is also largely free of refuse. Disposal is mostly concentrated to the sides of the main building with a cluster also located to the southeast. A small post arrangement is located in front of the structure which could possibly represent a stocks-and-pillory.

Once the government function was removed from the site ca. 1676, there appear to be a number of changes in the lot and in disposal behavior (figure 9.5). The fence is expanded to enclose the front and side yards, making the main building less publicly visible. The fence is oriented somewhat with the Baroque town plan, though it is not very precisely laid out. Disposal clearly continues to the east and west of the main building. However, of particular note is a concentration of ceramics directly in front of the main structure, as well as a concentration of tobacco pipes in the immediate rear yard. There appears to have been less of a concern for keeping these areas clean once the government function was removed and it converted to a full-time inn. One other interesting feature dating to this phase is the oval trench feature in the rear yard, which is consistent with a cockfighting/animal baiting ring. This indicates an area of specialized recreational use and may represent a shift in what was thought appropriate behavior on the site once the government function was removed (see chapter 10).

Comparative analysis also revealed insights regarding the importance of the Country's House as a social center. A number of middens were identified by the distribution analysis, some of which appear to be somewhat temporally isolated, others not. Table 9.1 compares the temporally diagnostic

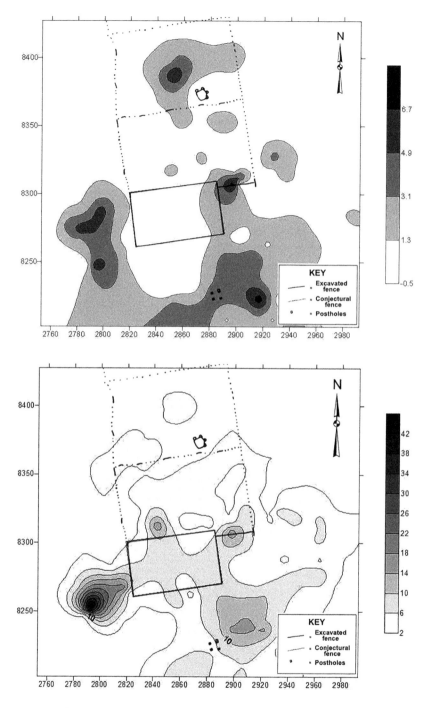

Figure 9.4. Phase II (ca. 1660–ca. 1680) artifact distribution of ceramics (*top*) and white clay tobacco pipes (*bottom*). (Figure by Wesley R. Willoughby.)

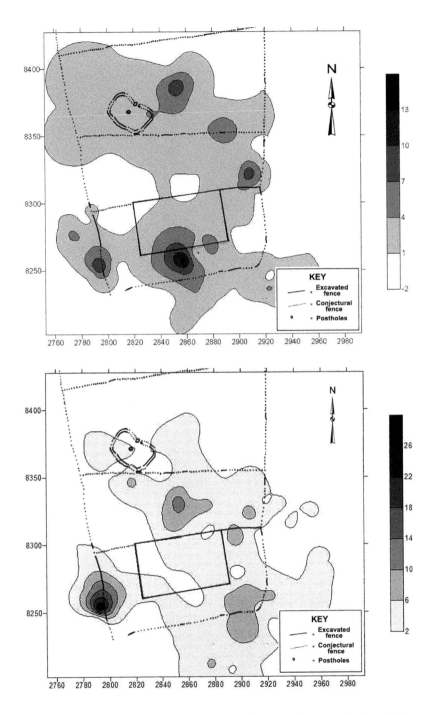

Figure 9.5. Phase III (ca. 1680–ca. 1700) artifact distribution of ceramics (*top*) and white clay tobacco pipes (*bottom*). (Figure by Wesley R. Willoughby.)

Table 9.1. Proportions of Temporally Diagnostic Ceramics from Comparative Contexts

Context		Ph. I	Ph. II	Ph. III	Total
West Midden	N	42	78	52	172
	%	24.42	45.35	30.23	100
Northeast Midden	N	21	34	29	84
	%	25.0	40.5	34.5	100
Statehouse Midden	N	14	64	40	118
	%	11.86	54.24	33.9	100
Inn Midden	N	4	0	28	32
	%	12.5	0	87.5	100
North Cluster	N	44	11	49	104
	%	42.3	10.58	47.12	100

ceramics from the middens. The north cluster displays early and late periods of deposition, the west and east middens show continuous deposition, the front midden shows primarily Phase III material, and the southeast midden shows deposition primarily during the State House phase. Of note is the larger proportion of Phase II material in the west and northeast middens given that they span all three phases of occupation. The distributions of tobacco pipes by bore diameter show a similar trend, displaying peaks at 2.8 mm (which tend to date predominantly to the ca. 1660–1680 period). Together these quantitative differences suggest the government phase was the period of most intense activity at the site. Despite remaining the largest public ordinary in the colony after the government function was removed, activity seems to have declined during the last decades of occupation, perhaps as the center of activity shifted closer to where the new State House was located, and more ordinaries were operating.

Overall the data indicate that there were conscious efforts to maintain a more formal and potentially higher status environment during the site's tenure as the official State House. This also appears to be the period of most intense activity at the site despite it remaining the largest public ordinary in the colony through the end of the seventeenth century. Thus even though the site served as a major political center during the 1660s and 1670s, the site also appears to have been a major social center as well, suggesting government meetings indeed served as a catalyst for large-scale public gatherings at the site.

CONCLUSIONS

The formal environment that appears to have characterized the Country's House has important implications for structuring interactions and facilitating the negotiation of community and political order during periodic government meetings. The formality evident at the site is perhaps best understood in the context of larger developments taking place beginning during the Restoration of the English monarchy in the 1660s. This period saw the rule of law becoming central to people's understanding of the distinctiveness of the English political system (Graham 2003:60). In England, market and guild halls that were once used to hold courts were being replaced by purpose-built courthouses as an effort to create more dignified settings for the administration of the law (Graham 2003:60). Formality at the Country's House may reflect this trend. It may also reflect trends occurring at the time to reorganize public space for purposes of consolidating political authority. Some note that beginning with the Restoration, there is evidence that there was great reform, "a re-territorialization of places and bodies, a re-alignment of domains, discourses, manners and states of mind" (Stallybrass and White 1986:90). Part of this manifested with the creation of new sites of assembly and a more refined public sphere that is viewed as an attempt to regulate body and crowd behavior (Stallybrass and White 1986:83–84). The formality that archaeology reveals at the Country's House was part of this larger trend to structure human interactions and influence behavior subconsciously through sensory cues in the social and physical environment (Bourdieu 1977; Stallybrass and White 1986:90). This environment helped define and communicate social order to the public and affect perceptions of government authority and legitimacy (McNamara 2004). This eventually culminated in the development of the Baroque town plan and the new brick State House in 1676 (e.g., Miller 1988a; Leone and Hurry 1998).

These public sites also, in effect, served as a stage where political authority was exercised and displayed during the public performances of the Provincial Court and Assembly. While no doubt important for influencing perceptions of authority and order, such events also served as a significant mechanism for integrating individuals from an overwhelmingly rural population into a cohesive community. The archaeological and archival data suggest the Country's House was also the scene of large-scale public interactions that developed in association with the meetings of provincial government. These public events were some of the few times each year that large numbers of individuals from the scattered plantations came together to connect outside of the normal structure of daily life. Such events helped make a community by creating what Inomata and Coben call "objectifications of experience" and making them accessible to others by transcending the limitations of individual experience (2006:24). The tavern, market, and other activities associated with these events provided opportunities for individuals to participate in large-scale social interactions and exchange, establish and renew social bonds, and connect as part of a larger community in a place of both social and political significance. In short, these public events and associated gatherings materially evidenced at the Country's House helped forge a sense of community and common identity while simultaneously orienting individuals to a developing landscape and society of order and authority.

10

"The most bewitching Game"

Games and Entertainment in Seventeenth-Century St. Mary's City

TRAVIS G. PARNO AND TIMOTHY B. RIORDAN

Certainly there is no Man so severe to deny the Lawfulness of Recreation.
Charles Cotton, 1674

In the early summer of 1674, Maryland's General Assembly passed the "Act against the Prophaning of the Sabbath day." The law dictated that ordinary keepers were not to sell hard liquor or allow "any tipling or gaming att Cards, Dice, ninepin playing or other such unlawfull exercises" on Sundays (Browne 1884:414). Those who did permit such activities in their establishments on the day in question would be subject to fines of 2,000 pounds of tobacco and forfeiture of their ordinary licenses, a penalty aimed at preventing "the great dishonor of Allmighty God the Discredit of Christianity and the debauching of youth and the increase and encouragem^t of vice and Profanesse amongst all sorts" (Browne 1884:414–415). Four years later, in the fall of 1678, the Assembly doubled down on the earlier law by passing "An Act for keeping holy the Lords day." In addition to reaffirming the previous statute, this legislation forbade colonists from forcing their servants and slaves to labor on Sundays. It also expanded the previous act's list of prohibited Sunday activities to include "Drunkeness Swearing gaming at Cards Dice Billiards Shuffell boards bowles Nynepins horserace fowling or hunting or any other vnlawfull Sportes or recreations" (Browne 1889:52). Both pieces of legislation reveal that even if Maryland's seventeenth-century colonists followed the letter of law on Sundays, on the six remaining days of the week, they had a voracious appetite for a variety of games and entertainment.

As archaeologists, it can be challenging to locate material evidence of seventeenth-century entertainment. When we do, we typically focus on the record of alcohol consumption recorded in fragments of glasswares and ceramic vessels recovered at public establishments such as inns or ordinaries.

Other sorts of entertainment, such as games or gambling, leave little behind in terms of material culture. Here historical archaeology is at an advantage: by examining the combination of historical and material records, we can better understand the nature of entertainment in the colonial period.

At Historic St. Mary's City, we are uniquely situated to explore these questions because of the sheer number of ordinaries that operated in the colonial capital. When the courts were in session or when the General Assembly convened, the capital's modest population swelled as colonists and representatives from area tribes traveled in from the hinterlands to be heard by colonial authorities, participate in the commerce that the gatherings would bring, or to simply take in the spectacle (see chapter 7). With so many people traveling to St. Mary's City, ordinaries were a natural solution. The need was particularly acute in the latter half of the seventeenth century as the colony's population increased dramatically from an estimated 701 in 1650 to 4,018 in 1660 and then to 11,440 in 1670 (it would go on to triple that figure by 1700; Menard 1984:72). In 1662, members of the General Assembly formally recognized the need for ordinaries with the passage of "An Act for the Encouragem' of Ordinary Keepers," which offered assistance in settling debts to those who held licenses to manage ordinaries (Browne 1883:447–448). The act was renewed two years later (Browne 1883:537). The legislation appeared to have been successful. In the second half of the seventeenth century, at least 40 different individuals operated inns or ordinaries in St. Mary's county (Historic St. Mary's City 1975).

As some of the only public buildings in early Maryland, ordinaries served a variety of crucial social functions. At their most basic, ordinaries were mandated to offer food, drink, and accommodations at set prices to visitors and their horses. As out-of-town guests passed through, they read publicly posted official proclamations and brought news from abroad. During periods in which the provincial government or courts were in session, ordinaries provided lodging to travelers in huge numbers, while also often providing space for members of the Assembly to convene. Provincial affairs were discussed during the day before giving way to more casual socialization in the evening, sometimes all under the roof of the same building. Court records also tell us that merchants occasionally stored goods in ordinaries and, in many cases, keepers ran their own stores out of their ordinaries. Prior to the establishment of an official postal system in 1695, ordinaries were logical places to distribute mail. They were also often used to temporarily house prisoners following their arrests.

Ordinaries were busy places and as centers of activity, they were natural venues for socializing. With socializing came drinking, games, and entertainment. However, despite strict regulations promising services at established prices, ordinaries were not always open to all. For example, beginning in 1658, acts awarding ordinary licenses included verbiage declaring that indentured servants and apprentices were not permitted to "remain tipling, or drinking" in ordinaries without their master's permission (the law did not explicitly extend this ban to enslaved people, but they were almost certainly included in the prohibition; Steiner 1922:48). By 1674, ordinary keepers were forbidden from extending more than 400 pounds of tobacco in credit per year to nonfreeholders (Browne 1884:407). When a related law was renewed in 1695, the General Assembly extended the stated credit limit to sailors (Steiner 1918:48). Four years later, in 1699, further restrictions were placed on ordinary keepers serving poor freemen to prevent "their own Ruine" (Browne 1902:522). The intent of these decrees was twofold: (1) to prevent conflict between ordinary keepers and servant- or slave-owners who bore responsibility for their laborers' ordinary bills and (2) to protect, in a paternalistic manner, those members of the population who could not or should not have been trusted to care for themselves. The regulations also served to draw clearer boundaries around these groups, effectively Othering them while denying them full participation in the social benefits ordinaries offered.

ENTERTAINMENT IN ORDINARIES

It is difficult to separate activities associated with ordinaries from alcohol consumption. Indeed, it is critical to understand the role of alcohol as a social lubricant, the beverage that was more trustworthy than water and, in the words of a seventeenth-century Virginian, possessed the power to "unbend the Mind from severer Applications, promote a social Temper, and diffuse a general Satisfaction through the Ranks of Life" (as quoted in Salinger 2002:119; Cotton credits games with a similar ability to "unbend the Mind," 1674:ii; see also Smith 2008). Alcohol could also amplify the emotions experienced while gaming, which Charles Cotton outlined in his 1674 treatise on games, titled *Compleat Gamester* (see figure 10.1). Cotton recounts witnessing the player who "is transported with Joy when he wins; so losing, he is tost upon the Billows of a high swelling Passion, till he hath lost sight both of Sense and Reason" (1674:2). Within the confines of seventeenth-century ordinaries, gaming and drinking went hand in hand.

Forms of entertainment in ordinaries can be divided into two general categories: those that tended to take place inside the ordinary, and those that more commonly occurred on the grounds surrounding the ordinary. Within

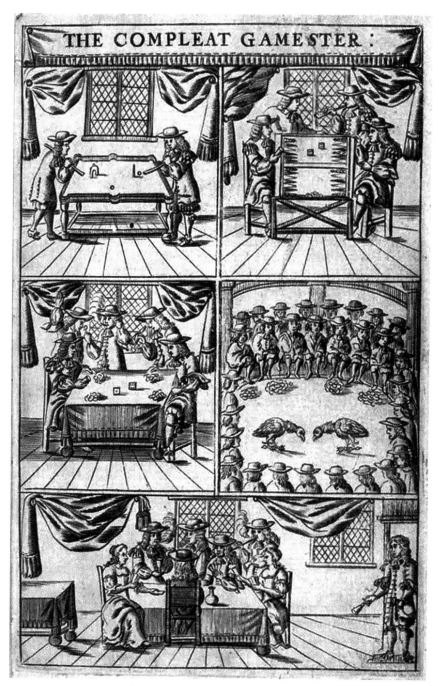

Figure 10.1. Frontispiece of Charles Cotton's *Compleat Gamester,* published in 1674. (No. 129898, The Huntington Library, San Marino, California.)

the first category, we have games involving dice, cards, and tables. Within the second category, we see activities such as lawn bowling, horse racing, cockfighting, and other forms of animal baiting.

Dice games were among the simplest and most common seventeenth-century amusements. Cotton outlines the rules for three types of dice games (Inn and Inn, Passage, and Hazard). These games were not without controversy, however, as moral observers tended to draw a distinction between games of skill ("wise play") and games of chance (Walsham 1989). The former allowed the player to exercise the mind and demonstrate dominance, whereas the latter exposed one to the whims of fate. Cotton refers to Hazard as "the most bewitching Game," because once one starts to play, "he knows not when to leave off" (1674:123). Cotton may have been on to something: the documentary record suggests that disputes which began at the dicing table often ended in court. In 1674, John Quigley appeared in court to accuse Isaac Foxcroft of withholding 5,552 pounds of tobacco earned during what must have been a lengthy game of Passage (Merritt 1952:445–446). Despite Quigley's protestations, the Provincial Court could not determine whether any bets to that amount had actually been made and so found in favor of Foxcroft, declaring that Quigley must cover the accused's court fees as a penalty for Quigley's "false clamour" (Merritt 1952:446). In a 1661 case, Daniel Johnson begged the court's assistance in calling in a debt of 5,550 pounds of tobacco owed to him by Thomas Gerrard (Steiner 1922:584–585). Johnson presented the court with a bill signed by Gerrard stating that he owed Johnson the sum, but Gerrard testified that the bill was "unjustly gotten at dice" (Steiner 1922:585). Witness testimony quickly proved that the bill was rightfully earned and Gerrard was ordered to pay what was owed. Although he was ultimately unsuccessful, the fact that Gerrard hinged his defense on the dubious legality of gambling winnings suggests that Maryland colonial society could be skeptical of agreements forged at the dicing table.

Despite these concerns, dice games remained popular throughout the colonial period. At St. Mary's City, six-sided dice have been found during excavations at the Country's House, Garrett Van Sweringen's home, and St. John's. All three properties functioned as ordinaries in the second half of the seventeenth century. The dice that have been found were made almost exclusively of bone, with the exception of one small lead die found at the Country's House. That site also yielded another unique specimen: a bone die featuring one pip each on three of its faces and four pips each on its three other faces. We are not aware of any period games that require equal probability outcomes of 1s or 4s. It seems that the numbers (1 and 4) were significant somehow; if they were not, a coin or similarly weighted disc could be used instead of a nonstandard die. While not likely, it is also possible that this die was used for nefarious purposes. The pages of *Compleat Gamester* are replete with warnings against "Rooks" and "pretended Gentlemen" out to cheat the casual game player through illicit means (Cotton 1674:4). In some cases, these involved so-called Fulham dice, or bone dice loaded with a drop of mercury added to the side opposite the one the user wished to be rolled (the Fulham name comes from the London neighborhood that was home to dicers during the medieval period; a set of loaded dice was found on the Thames foreshore and is currently archived at the Museum of London; see Museum of London n.d.). Also common were dispatchers, or dice that were made with two sets of three numbers, either highs (2, 4, and 6) or lows (1, 3, and 5). These were used by fraudsters under the pretext that one can see only three sides of a six-sided die at any given time, so by switching a dispatcher into the game at a convenient time, they can swing the roll in their favor more predictably. The die found at the Country's House, however, bore only two different numbers, rather than three, so any fraud could be discovered with ease. For this reason, it seems likely that the curious die was produced for an honest, but as yet undetermined, game.

Card games were another type of common seventeenth-century diversion. Because playing cards do not survive in the archaeological record, we must rely on historical records. Cotton's *Compleat Gamester* provides the rules for 23 different card games. Although they do not feature in period court records with the frequency of dice, cards appear occasionally in probate inventories. For example, the 1679 inventory of wealthy merchant-planter (and one-time Deputy Governor) Thomas Notley includes an entry for "3 packs of Cards" valued at one shilling and sixpence (Maryland State Archives 1679). Irish Catholic planter Michael Rochford's 1678 probate inventory lists "a Packe of Cards" valued at 16 pounds of tobacco (Maryland State Archives 1678a). Other probate inventories that included playing cards were those of Royal Governor Lionel Copley, ordinary keeper John Baker, and planter James Pattison (Maryland State Archives 1693, 1687, 1698). In general, it appears that the popularity of card playing crossed lines of religion, class, and occupation.

Another collection of games that were popular in seventeenth-century Maryland were those requiring some combination of tables, boards, playing pieces, cards, and dice. Included in this category are billiards, chess, and various forms of backgammon (e.g., verquere, trictrac, doublets). Backgammon and its variants were quite popular and, despite involving dice, were elevated to a status of acceptability above games that only utilized dice (Walsham 1989). They often feature in the tavern scenes of seventeenth-century Dutch genre paintings, such as *The Trictrac Players* by Willem Duyster and *Playing Backgammon* by Adriaen van Ostade. They also appear in the probate inventories of some of St. Mary's City's ordinary keepers. Richard Chilman operated an ordinary not far from the colony's brick State House. When he died in 1678, his probate inventory included a "[pair] of Playing Tables" valued at 300 pounds of tobacco (Maryland State Archives 1678b). After innkeeper Garrett Van Sweringen died, his 1701 probate inventory listed a "paire of playing Tables" worth 15 shillings (Maryland State Archives 1701). Although no known archaeological evidence of backgammon has been found at St. Mary's City, a turned bone chess piece was recovered from the St. John's site.

Clearly residents of and visitors to seventeenth-century St. Mary's City were no strangers to tabletop games. Yet so-called gaming pieces—modified ceramic disks recovered from many historic sites—remain absent from St. Mary's City's archaeological record. Gaming pieces have been found on colonial and postcolonial sites throughout eastern North America and the Caribbean (e.g., Klingelhofer 1987; Armstrong 1990; Russell 1997; Smith and Watson 2009; Parno 2011; Streibel MacLean 2015). They are typically interpreted as components of a variety of games which often included other elements such as boards, dice, or ceramic sherds modified into other shapes (see Panich et al. 2018). Either the population of St. Mary's City opted not to use gaming pieces in their recreation, or we simply have not discovered any yet.

Cockfighting and Animal Baiting

Outside the confines of ordinaries, entertainment occupied more space and, occasionally, more substantial materials. The various forms of lawn bowling needed only an available space and a set of bowls. Horse racing required little more than the animals involved and an open road or path. James I was a patron of the sport, and it became particularly popular in England during the reign of Charles II (Culver 1922). Its popularity spread to the colonies; by 1665, the first recorded track (New Market) was built in what is today Long Island, New York, and records of races can be found in Virginia beginning in the 1670s (W.G.S. 1895).

Perhaps the most raucous and, to our modern eyes, brutal forms of seventeenth-century entertainment were cockfighting, bull baiting, dog fighting, and other forms of animal blood sport. Animal blood sport, loosely defined as one animal fighting another for the purpose of spectacle, was an important part of the social experience of residents of England and English settlers coming to the New World in the seventeenth century. Paris Garden, the London bear-baiting and bull-baiting center, attracted large crowds after these activities became commercialized in the sixteenth century (Brownstein 1963). Such entertainments were not restricted to London but were common all over England (Scott-Warren 2003). Cockfighting, another example of blood sport, was an ancient pastime in England (Smith and Daniel 2000:75–82). It is said to have reached its most elaborate development in the sixteenth century and from then to the eighteenth century, it enjoyed considerable royal patronage.

Given its popularity in early modern England, it is no surprise that English colonists brought animal blood sport across the Atlantic during the colonial period. There are numerous references to cockfighting in colonial North America and it continued to be a popular diversion for all classes (Gems et al. 2008:17). Newspapers advertised so-called mains in major cities while many matches along the frontier went unheralded. As settlers moved westward, the practice traveled with them. While cockfighting is relatively well documented, other blood sports are less frequently described. Only bull-baiting receives any significant mention and that relatively late. A series of newspaper ads published in 1774 report bull-baiting on Long Island, New York, as if it were a regular occurrence, adding that it would occur "every Thursday during the season" (*Rivington's New York Gazetteer*). A 1796 advertisement in a Baltimore newspaper states: "The Citizens of Baltimore are informed, that the young butchers of Centre Market having purchased a BULL, there will be a BULL-BAITING on Monday next, at 1 o'clock . . . Only one dog to run at a time" (*Federal Gazette and Baltimore Daily Advertiser*). Not only does this show the commonplace nature of blood sport in America at the time, but it hints at the function bull-baiting served historically, beyond merely the promise of entertainment. Throughout the Middle Ages it was a common conception that meat from a bull, because of the nature of the animal, was nearly indigestible. To make it edible, the bull had to be excited to a hot or fearful state by being baited (Farman 2006:10–12). In parts of England, butchers were legally required to have bulls baited before they could sell the meat (Brownstein 1963:254). While there was no longer a legal requirement in Baltimore, it is likely that the butchers were responding to traditional ideas.

Although blood sport had a popular following, there was opposition to it, both in England and in English colonies, from an early period. This had less to do with concerns about animal cruelty and more to do with the activities of the human participants. Puritans of the sixteenth and seventeenth centuries railed against theatrical performances and bear-baiting, particularly when they occurred on Sundays (Dickey 1991:262). Cockfighting was decried because it fostered the unrestrained mixing of classes and upset the natural order of society (Baker 1988:86–97; Nicholson 2005:113–114; see also Powell 1993). All the blood sports were inseparably linked to rowdy behavior, drinking, swearing, and gambling. In the minds of the Godly, blood sport was associated with such unsavory activities as card playing, bowling, and stage plays. As early as 1700, Pennsylvania passed an "Act against riotous sports, plays and games" which specified a wide variety of blood sports (Mitchell and Flanders 1896:5). Virginia outlawed cockfighting in 1740 (Gems et al. 2008:17). Despite these early attempts, both cockfighting and animal baiting continued. By the early nineteenth century, public opinion was starting to shift against cruelty toward animals; it was on these grounds, for example, that the General Assembly of Maryland passed legislation outlawing animal blood sport within the Baltimore city limits in 1818 (22 years after the aforementioned advertisement for weekly bull-baiting was published in the local newspaper) (Baltimore City 1828:198). In Joseph Strutt's 1801 volume *The Sports and Pastimes of the People of England,* Strutt writes that "bull and bear-baiting is not encouraged by persons of rank and opulence in the present day; and when practiced, which rarely happens, it is attended only by the lowest and most despicable part of the people" (205).

Blood Sport Architecture

In the seventeenth and eighteenth centuries, most people, including the "lowest and most despicable," could find publicly advertised blood sport at a central location which could attract a large audience. In urban areas, this frequently involved a well-built, permanent structure (e.g., Mackinder et al. 2013). London baiting rings often had multiple tiers for spectators. In more rural areas, events were commonly set in the backyard of the local tavern or ordinary (Smith and Daniel 2000:98–99; Kelly 2014:166). The arenas constructed at these venues were usually much more ephemeral structures than those found in urban areas.

In its simplest form, cockfighting needed only a flat, open surface. Many rural cockfights were conducted within an area marked only by a rope laid on the ground. In more permanent establishments, the cockpit, or fighting area, varied from 8 to 24 ft. wide, with 20 ft. being the most often mentioned size (Gilbey 1912:41; Ruport 2006:110–111; Collins et al. 2005:70). The ideal shape was circular, but square, rectangular, and oval examples have been reported. It was enclosed by a board fence, 1–2 ft. high, which angled outward. The trench created for the board fence is often the most obvious archaeological feature associated with this activity (Brown et al. 1990:59–60; Nicholson 2005:103–117). Cockpits could often have one or more hinged gates (Dinwiddie 1899:175–176). In its online typology of Monument Class Descriptions, Historic England lists cockpit types for circular, square, rect-angular, and polygonal forms. One example of an archaeologically excavated English cockpit was located in St. Ives, Cambridgeshire (Nicholson 2005). While heavily impacted by later development, the feature consisted of a cir-cular trench 21 ft. across, with a fighting area approximately 18 ft. wide. The trench itself averaged 2.3 ft. wide and there was a 3-ft. gap on the south side. There was a small pit located on one side of this gap, but it was not preserved well enough to determine whether it was a gate. Artifactual evidence sug-gested a seventeenth-century or early eighteenth-century date of use.

Across the Atlantic, Gregory Brown and colleagues working at the Shields Tavern back lot in Colonial Williamsburg uncovered a circular trench roughly 20 ft. south of the tavern's eastern end (1990). The feature measured 12 ft. in diameter, 2 ft. wide, and 1 ft. deep. The presence of white salt-glazed stoneware in the top two layers of the trench led Brown and his team to date the feature to the early eighteenth century. They also cited a February 1751 announcement in the *Virginia Gazette* that advertised a cockfight at the George and Dragon in Williamsburg. In 2003, excavations behind the Peyton-Randolph House led by Mark Kostro resulted in the discovery of a chicken metatarsus that had been modified by removal of its spur (Kostro 2005:54–58). The trimming or removal of a rooster's natural spur allowed for its replacement by a more lethal silver, iron, or steel spur. A similarly modified metatarsus was found at the Rich Neck slave quarter site (Kostro 2005:57). This confluence of evidence suggests that cockfighting was a popu-lar pastime in colonial Williamsburg.

Other forms of animal blood sport, such as bull- or bear-baiting, also occurred in designated areas, but these have generally received less descrip-tion in historical literature. Visual recordings of bull-baiting and bull-baiting areas range from the massive, multitiered arenas of London's Paris Garden to designated spaces with a distinct lack of dedicated architecture beyond a sturdy post or iron ring attached to a spike driven into the ground. For ex-ample, in the Birmingham neighborhood known as the Shambles, an open area surrounded by butcher shops was maintained for the purposes of bull-baiting. A sketch by Birmingham artist Samuel Lines Senior shows a large ring at the center of the space (the sketch is undated, but bull-baiting and other forms of blood sport were outlawed in England by the 1835 Cruelty to Animals Act, so the sketch likely predates this legislation). William Secord also notes that in the case of bull-baiting, because the objective was for a dog to bite and latch onto a bull's sensitive nose, "a circular low ditch was provided for additional sport—so that the bull could hide his nose from the dog" (1992:95; see also Kalof 2007). A similar practice was recorded by an eighteenth-century English commentator, who noted that in most cases "a hole is made in the ground for the creature to put his nose into" (quoted in Kelly 2014:222). Whether for cockfighting, bull-baiting, or other types of animal blood sport, colonial period arenas came in a wide range of forms and functions.

ANIMAL BLOOD SPORT AT ST. MARY'S CITY

During an intensive investigation of the Town Center in the early 1980s, archaeologists testing the north yard of the Leonard Calvert House (18ST1-13), also called the Country's House, encountered segments of a curious feature in a few of their 5×5-ft. excavation units (for an overview of the history of Country's House, see chapter 7). The feature in question appeared to be a wide, gently curving trench. Nearly 30 years later, over the course of multiple field school seasons, HSMC archaeologists explored more of the strange feature and revealed what appears to have been a semicircular trench enclosing an area roughly 28 ft. wide and 18 ft. across, or nearly 500 sq. ft. in area (see figure 10.2). Based on the feature's general form, its temporal links to use of the Country's House as an ordinary in the third quarter of the seventeenth century, and the preponderance of artifacts related to smoking and drinking found in its vicinity, initial interpretation identified this feature as the archaeological remnant of a seventeenth-century animal baiting pit.

The trench discovered at Historic St. Mary's City is similar in form to the archaeological examples of cockpits seen in St. Ives and Williamsburg. All three trenches measured between 2 and 3 ft. wide and each trench was originally excavated to an approximate depth of 1 to 1.5 ft. That these trenches were dug to a relatively shallow depth is not necessarily surprising; the construction of fences surrounding cockpits and baiting rings, particularly in rural areas, was often rudimentary. Kym Rice cites a 1700 probate inventory that describes a cockpit as built of "only old boards" (1983:112). A shallow trench with a wattle fence or row of low boards would be enough to temporarily pen small animals without the need for the construction of a more substantial paling fence or palisade. One excavated segment of the Country's House trench contained what appears to be a thin post mold angled slightly outward that was identified in profile. This may be the best evidence for a light fence built with an outward angle, similar to those described in cockfighting handbooks (see above).

The clearest difference between the example found at the Country's House and the others is one of shape (oval, rather than circular). The three features

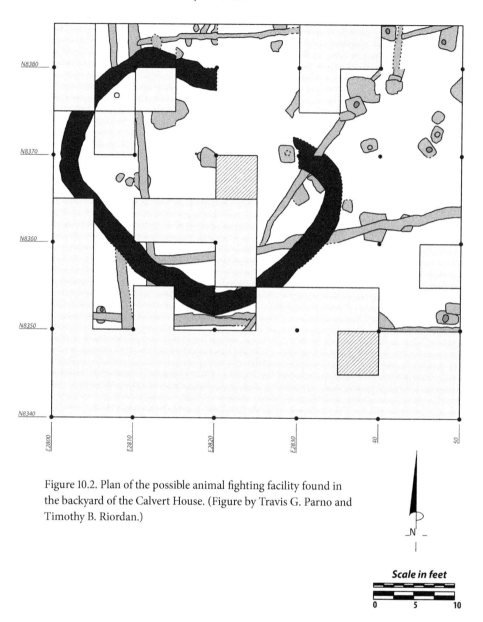

Figure 10.2. Plan of the possible animal fighting facility found in the backyard of the Calvert House. (Figure by Travis G. Parno and Timothy B. Riordan.)

also vary in area, with the Country's House example being the largest at nearly 500 sq. ft. and the Shields Tavern example being the smallest at 113 sq. ft. In addition, assuming that each trench is evidence of a space enclosed by a fence of some sort (as opposed to a trench intentionally left unfilled), there remains the question of entrance into and egress from the feature. The trench excavated at Shields Tavern did not include an obvious gate or other method of entry, although the southeastern quadrant of the trench ran under a reconstructed dairy so any means of entry may have been hidden by the reconstruction. The cockpit at St. Ives featured a 3-ft. gap on the southwest side of the trench which could have afforded entrance via a gate or movable barrier. The Country's House feature was constructed with a gap on the northeast side. Post holes found near the gap may indicate that a gate was built to bridge the span, although the relationships between these post holes, the trench feature, and other post holes in the vicinity are still being examined. If no gate was present, it is possible that a movable barrier, such as a wattle hurdle, could have been used to provide or deny access to the feature's interior.

An examination of the artifacts found in the plow zone layer above the Country's House trench and in the feature itself suggests that the area was one in which individuals or groups gathered to smoke tobacco and consume alcohol in the third or fourth quarter of the seventeenth century. The trench cuts fences associated with the 1650s layout of the property and the artifacts support a late seventeenth-century date of use. White clay pipe fragments, round bottle glass, and table glass were found in higher quantities in units excavated in proximity to the trench feature when compared with those excavated in other parts of the yard (see figures 10.3 and 10.4). While concentrations of refuse are often associated with outbuildings such as kitchens or domestic work spaces, no outbuildings have been located in the areas adjacent to the trench feature, and although the artifact assemblage suggests congregating to smoke and drink, no other distinct activities or functions (such as food preparation, agricultural storage, or other domestic enterprises) are indicated by the material culture. Significantly, little bone or oyster shell was found in this area, suggesting that this was not a location used for general garbage disposal, but was instead an area of more specialized activity.

When we consider the archaeological evidence against the backdrop of the Country's House's occupational history, a picture begins to emerge. The artifact assemblage tells us that the area around the trench was a gathering place for smoking and drinking, social activities often associated with spectators at performance-based events. A use-date of the late seventeenth century places the feature in a time during which the Country's House was operated as an ordinary. During this period, the longest-tenured keepers of the Country's House ordinary were John and Elizabeth Baker, who managed the establishment from 1678 to 1693 (with the exception of a brief period in 1686 during which the Bakers' son-in-law, Thomas Beale, ran the ordinary). The Bakers spent thousands of pounds of tobacco altering the architecture of the Country's House through a series of internal modifications, including

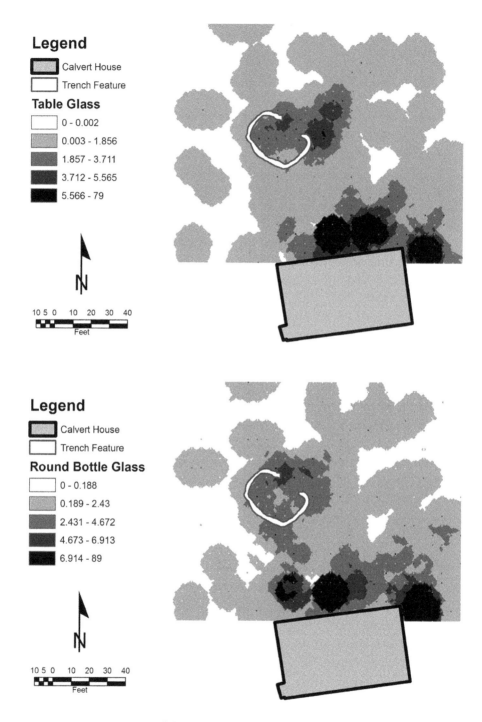

Figure 10.3. Comparison of the distributions of table glass and round-bottle glass in relation to the circular feature. (Figure by Travis G. Parno and Timothy B. Riordan.)

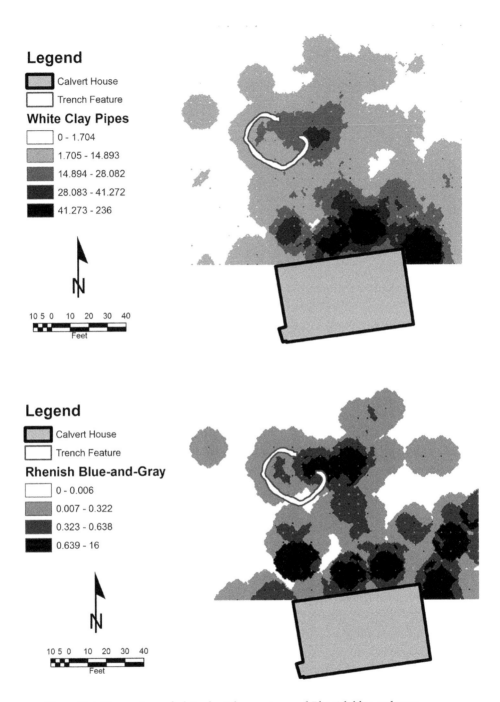

Figure 10.4. Comparison of white clay tobacco pipes and Rhenish blue and gray stoneware in relation to the circular feature. (Figure by Travis G. Parno and Timothy B. Riordan.)

the addition of a central passageway and brick-lined cellar (see H. Miller 1986, 1994). The Bakers' tenure at the Country's House began two years after the construction of the brick State House, which supplanted the Country's House as the colony's primary governmental meeting space. The updates the Bakers made to the Country's House were likely designed to improve the property and attract customers following the establishment's decline in political use. Given the popularity of animal blood sport during this period and the prevalence of cockpits and animal baiting rings in the yards of taverns and inns in both urban and rural colonial contexts, it seems no stretch to imagine that the Bakers could have installed such an attraction in the north yard of the property to entertain clientele for whom animal blood sport would be a normal part of life. The relatively shallow depth of portions of the Country's House trench, like those at the Shields Tavern and St. Ives cockpits, suggests that any fencing in place was likely low and insubstantial and this, together with the overall size of the trench, suggests that the feature would have been used for cockfighting or small animal baiting, rather than bull-baiting, bear-baiting, or other large animal blood sport.

However, a closer examination of the trench's stratigraphy, aided by recent excavations conducted at the site in the summer of 2017, may suggest that the feature was not meant to contain a fence. The recently excavated trench segment, located on the south side of the feature, measured roughly 2.75 ft. across and was originally dug to a depth of approximately 1.25 ft. Much like the other portions of the feature that have been excavated previously, this segment was almost completely flat-bottomed. In addition to a small pocket of plow zone slumped into the trench from the layer above, there were two identifiable fill deposits in the feature. The upper fill consisted of a combination of yellowish brown silt loam and displaced clayey material, likely mixed in from the surrounding subsoil, along with gravel and brick fragments. The lower fill was almost entirely silty loam, with very little other soils or inclusions. The deposit was distributed evenly along the floor of the trench and partway up its steep sides. This stratigraphic profile suggests that the trench may have been dug and then left open for enough time to allow 3 to 4 inches of humic material to wash into it. The upper strata would then represent a later fill event, one that involved soils from mixed contexts (although the origin of those soils remains unclear).

If the Country's House feature was not a fenced-in arena, but instead a flat-bottomed trench intended to be used unfilled for some time, this naturally affects our understanding of it. While the data seem to run counter to the interpretation of the feature as a cockfighting ring, the data do suggest a possible alternative along the same lines. Perhaps the north yard of the Country's House was not the staging ground for cockfighting, but for bull-baiting. Recall the words of William Secord (1992:95), who noted the practice of providing "a circular low ditch" for "additional sport—so that the bull could hide his nose from the dog." Certainly the Country's House ditch would fit that description; it also would explain the lack of an obvious gate for entrance and egress. However, if bulls were chained in the vicinity of this trench and set upon by dogs, we would expect that the ditch would not survive in pristine form. And indeed, there are signs that are suggestive of a partial collapse in at least one section of the trench's interior wall, where subsoil seems to have been pushed from the rim of the interior wall and deposited on the floor of the trench below. The caved-in rim was subsequently filled with the same silty material seen in the lowest level of the feature. Although we typically associate bull-baiting during the colonial period with the butchering and processing of animals, the fact was that these events were popular spectacles, and what better location for such a spectacle than the backyard of the largest ordinary in town?

LOOKING TO THE FUTURE

Evidence of seventeenth-century entertaining can often be elusive; however, the archaeological and historical records of St. Mary's City suggest that games, gambling, and other diversions were common features of the town's inns and ordinaries. Games utilizing dice, cards, and tabletop components were played throughout the city and, at least in ordinaries, were typically paired with alcohol consumption. Some ordinary keepers, such as John and Elizabeth Baker, used recreation to attract guests to their establishments. They knew what their customers expected when they entered an ordinary's confines. At their best, games encouraged communal interactions and the reinforcement of social bonds that were critical in areas where people often lived on remote plantations scattered across great distances. At their worst, games (and the alcohol often served along with them) coaxed "Rooks" and "pretended Gentlemen" into riotous behavior that landed them at the mercy of the courts (Cotton 1674:4).

This work comes at an interesting time as Historic St. Mary's City is about to launch a new phase of investigation at the Country's House. The project will include a fine-grained analysis of the building's architecture and history in preparation to reconstruct the house and appoint it with exhibits showcasing archaeological materials that highlight important moments from the site's history. Naturally the property's period as an ordinary will feature prominently in this new interpretation and we expect that drinking, gambling, and gaming will be topics of discussion. It is unclear what role, if any, the animal baiting trench will play in this new exhibit. There is little doubt that such features tend to evoke revulsion in modern audiences, but they also offer important touchstones for discussing topics such as violence, entertainment, and human-animal relationships during the colonial period. Given the ubiquity of these sorts of features and the unique position occupied by animal blood sport in both historical and contemporary society, it is unlikely that Historic St. Mary's City will be the last institution to grapple with these sorts of questions.

11

The Lead Coffins of St. Mary's

Burials of the Elite in the Early Chesapeake

KARIN S. BRUWELHEIDE, HENRY M. MILLER,
DOUGLAS W. OWSLEY, AND TIMOTHY B. RIORDAN

Among the many archaeological discoveries made at Historic St. Mary's City (HSMC), five rare seventeenth-century lead coffins stand out. Two of these burial containers were discovered at the end of the eighteenth century, and three more were uncovered in 1990. These are the only lead coffin burials from the 1600s yet found in North America. Who were these people, and why were they buried in a manner so different from thousands of other English settlers who died in early America? What can these burials tell us about life in seventeenth-century Maryland? This chapter summarizes the findings of a unique bioarchaeological investigation seeking to answer these questions.

On July 27, 1799, medical students conducted one of the earliest burial investigations in American history. Breaking into an early subterranean crypt in the graveyard of Trinity Episcopal Church, they encountered two lead coffins. One contained the bones of an adult male. The second was sealed and could not be opened, so it was removed from the brick vault. Cutting through the lead, the students found a wooden coffin inside and then a burial shroud. Student Alexander Williams described what they saw then: "When the face of the corpse was uncovered, it was ghastly indeed, it was the woman . . . Her face was perfect . . . eyes were sunk deep in her head, every other part retained its perfect shape . . . Her hair was short, platted and trimmed on the top . . . her dress was a white muslin gown . . . with short sleeves and high gloves . . . Her cap was with long ears and pinned under the chin . . . She was a small woman and appeared delicate" (Thomas 1913:322).

Local legend and historical research suggested these were the remains of Sir Lionel Copley, Maryland's first royal governor, and his wife, Lady Anne Copley, both interred in 1694. Within hours of exposure, Lady Copley's well-preserved body reportedly crumbled to dust, leaving only bones (Stanley 1853:16).

The second discovery came during a purposeful archaeological excavation of the first major brick building in Maryland, the Jesuit Chapel. Built in the 1660s, the cross-plan chapel was used until the early 1700s when public Catholic worship was forbidden by the government. Archaeologists explored the remains of this church to retrieve evidence to guide its eventual reconstruction. In one arm, or transept, of the cross-shaped structure, ground-penetrating radar and later excavations detected a large rectangular soil anomaly. A test unit revealed three lead coffins lying side by side: one large, one medium, and one small. Considering the significance of this discovery, principal investigators Timothy Riordan and Henry Miller reburied them in place until a coordinated research plan was formulated. Two years of discussion, research, and preparation ensued. Smithsonian forensic anthropologists, NASA scientists, nuclear physicists, engineers, conservators, a geologist, and experts in pollen and wood identification were contacted for assistance and advice. Historians assembled biographical details on a list of potential individuals who might be buried in such an unusual manner in the chapel. This initiative was named "Project Lead Coffins."

Before anything could be done with the earth-covered coffins, detailed information on lead coffin construction during the 1600s was essential for planning. To assist, Trinity Church's vestry permitted entry into the seventeenth-century vault first opened nearly 200 years earlier.

THE COPLEY VAULT

The original entry hole was located and reopened in April 1992. The disheveled burial containers were found lying side by side and remnants of wooden outer coffins or perhaps shipping cases were scattered about them (figure 11.1). After Governor Copley's death, it was anticipated that his body and that of his wife would be returned to England for burial. No such request came, so they were interred adjacent to the colony's State House in October 1694 (Browne 1900:120–121, 146). The woman's coffin, made from several sheets of lead cut to shape around the wooden inner coffin and soldered together, had once formed a tight seal that accounted for the high degree of preservation described in 1799. The man's coffin was less well made, with lead sheets soldered in some places and nailed in others. Identification as Sir Lionel Copley (b.1648–d.1693) and his wife, Lady Anne (b.1660–d.1692), was based on historical references (Papenfuse et al. 1979:234) as well as the close fit

Figure 11.1. The 1694 burial vault and lead coffins of Royal governor Sir Lionel Copley and his wife, Lady Anne Copley, as found by archaeologists in 1992. (Reproduced by permission from Chip Clark, Smithsonian Institution.)

between their recorded ages at death and the osteological ages of the examined skeletons.

After the project's technical director Mark Moore recorded the coffins' construction and measured the lead thicknesses, Smithsonian and National Museum of Health and Medicine scientists studied the skeletal remains. The Copley skeletons were well preserved, with hair and small amounts of desiccated soft tissue (dried periosteum) still present. The skulls, ribs, and vertebrae were dark in color due to preservation conditions inside the burial vault. A possible color effect from embalming was also considered because the eighteenth-century medical students had stated that Anne's "body was opened and the entrails removed and filled with gums and spice, and the coffin filled with the same" (Thomas 1913:322). The crania had been sectioned transversely through the vault, and the sternum of Anne was cut longitudinally. While autopsy can yield similar cuts, this procedure would likely not have been needed for the Copleys, who were known to have died from illness.

In addition to observations related to preservation, features indicative of age, sex, size, and robusticity were noted. Bone and tooth pathology were recorded, and samples were collected for tests of stable isotopes. Diets based on northern European staples produce different carbon isotope signals in tissues from the American diet in the Mid Atlantic, which emphasized dependence on maize. The Copleys, short-term English immigrants to the colony, provided baseline reference data, which at the time had not been reported for Colonial Americans.

No skeletal evidence for cause of death was noted for either Sir Lionel, aged 45 years, or Lady Anne, aged 32 years. His bones were normal, with the exception of right ribs four and five, and the left pubic bone, which had healed fractures. Not unexpectedly, his vertebrae displayed the onset of arthritis, characterized by lower vertebral compression and degeneration. One middle vertebra had fused with the articulating rib head, likely a result of trauma. Also noted were minor arthritic changes to the left knee joint. Anne Copley's remains showed beginning stage, age-related spinal degeneration. Her pelvis was marked with parturition pits, sometimes referred to as "birthing scars" (Mann and Murphy 1990:77), consistent with historical evidence. Documents indicate she and Sir Lionel had three children that survived past infancy, two boys and a girl (Papenfuse et al. 1979:234).

Dental observations provided information about the Copleys' health and foods they consumed. Sir Lionel had lost three teeth in life, and one tooth showed decay with an active abscess at the time of death. His anterior teeth were heavily worn, with the heights of their crowns reduced by more than half. Although more than a decade younger, Lady Anne had lost eight teeth in life and four showed decay. Dental calculus, calcified plaque-like deposits of tartar, was heavy, but tooth wear slight, a reflection of her age and a diet free of abrasive contaminants. The diets of both Lionel and Anne Copley included high levels of dietary protein, indicating an emphasis on meat, as expressed by elevated stable nitrogen isotope values. European cereal grains (i.e., wheat, barley, and rye) and animals foddered on these grains were likewise reflected in the Copleys' stable carbon isotope values. These values were consistent with high-status, seventeenth-century European diets lacking maize. Both Copleys lived in Maryland for less than two years before they died. That brief period of time did not result in detectable bone remodeling indicative of a transition to a New World diet.

Project Lead Coffins

With the evidence and insights gained from the Copley coffins, efforts turned to the unidentified Chapel burials. Before fully unearthing them, the grave was examined for clues. Soil layers told archaeologists that the large and medium-sized coffins had been buried at or about the same time, but that the small coffin was a later interment. A technique used to inspect nuclear reactors was adapted by Mark Moore to give a preliminary look inside the coffins. Using high-energy gamma rays, radiographs were taken through the lead and showed the interior of the coffin, burial container construction, the structure of the wood liner, an intact skull in the medium coffin, and the shadowy outline of a cranium in the large coffin. Each individual had been placed in a supine position with their bodies oriented east–west with head at the west end. This traditional form of Christian burial and the grave location inside a Jesuit church identified these individuals as Roman Catholics.

Because more precise identification of the three individuals would require multiple lines of evidence, a detailed study sequence was established so that each scientist could obtain data without compromising that of other specialists. Given their prestigious burial location near the sanctuary on the right side of the church, as viewed from the altar, and interment in lead, they must have been individuals of especially high status and social prominence. Because the Chapel was locked in 1704 and no longer used for religious purposes, the burials dated between completion of the Chapel in the late 1660s and 1704. Based on these facts, HSMC historian Lois Green Carr compiled a list of candidates who might have been buried in the chapel during this period. Because of the bias inherent in seventeenth-century records, it was primarily men for whom detailed information could be assembled. Specialized equipment was designed to sample the air in the coffins, and also to gently lift each container from the burial pit. The U.S. Army provided a field hospital tent so that the coffins could be opened in a clean and controlled laboratory environment.

In November 1992, the coffins were lifted one by one (figure 11.2). The small coffin was raised first, followed by the medium one and finally the largest coffin. Working from the smallest to the heaviest allowed the team to refine the lifting procedure and prevent damage. Each coffin was then gently transported into the medical tent, where they were carefully opened and immediately photographed. As with the Copley interments, each burial container was constructed from an internal wooden coffin wrapped in sheets of lead. Pollen and other samples were taken from inside the coffins, and the human remains were inspected and described prior to their removal.

Skeletal Analysis

As one might expect, the human remains themselves provided critical information. In addition to basic demographic data (age, sex, and ancestry) collected by the forensic anthropologists, markers of activity and dental and

Figure 11.2. The lead coffins at the Chapel site in St. Mary's City as uncovered by archaeologists in 1992. (Photograph by Henry M. Miller, courtesy of HSMC.)

bone pathology were recorded, along with standard radiography, computed tomography, and DXA (Dual Energy X-ray Absorptiometry) scan technology. Measurements of bone density aided in determining chronological age, disruptions in growth, and incidences of pathology, including osteoporosis. Chemical tests of bones and teeth initially involved carbon and nitrogen stable isotopes and were later expanded to include stable oxygen isotopes. As new methods developed, DNA analysis was conducted to confirm a familial

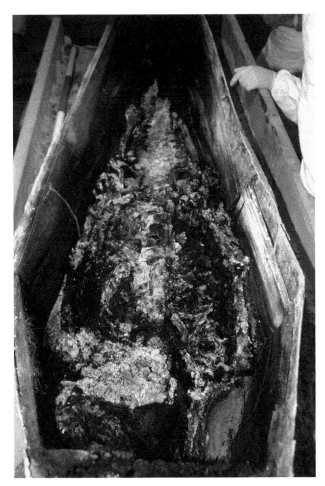

Figure 11.3. The remains of Chancellor Philip Calvert as observed when his lead coffin was opened. The upper body had largely transformed into white crystals of brushite, although the bones of the legs and feet were more intact. Ribbons from a burial garment were found at the neck and wrists and his head hair was fully preserved. (Reproduced by permission from Chip Clark, Smithsonian Institution.)

relationship between the infant and two adults. Ingestion of potential medicines incorporating heavy metals was tracked through mass spectrometry analysis of preserved hair.

No postmortem dissection was apparent on the individuals in the Chapel coffins, although the bodies had been carefully prepared. Preservation was less complete and more unusual than that encountered in the Copley vault, despite surprisingly well-preserved head hair in the adult coffins. Brushite, a colorless-to-white crystalline phosphate mineral that forms from the breakdown of calcium phosphate in the presence of water, had almost entirely replaced the skull and torso bones of the large adult (figure 11.3). The leg bones and feet of the skeleton (HSMC 1) were better preserved. The remains in the smaller adult coffin (HSMC 2) were more complete, although some ribs and vertebrae were also highly degraded by brushite formation.

The infant skeleton in the smallest lead coffin (HSMC 3) was missing bones of the legs below the thigh. For some reason, the infant's upper body was elevated on a layer of soil intentionally placed inside the coffin, and distinct from the surrounding grave fill. In contrast, the lower limbs rested directly on the wooden floor of the coffin and as a consequence, were subjected to greater acidity from the wood and varying degrees of dampness. Ultimately this led to their deterioration. In addition, a gray clay loam was found on top of the child's upper body. It too differs from the grave fill and must have been intentionally placed over the body before the lead covering was fixed in place. Its presence is also unexplained. Perhaps the infant was buried elsewhere, exhumed, and reinterred in the lead coffin inside the chapel. Green, copper-oxide stains from shroud pins that once secured burial wrappings were present on the infant's skull, right clavicle, and a left rib, where a small fragment of linen was also present. The cranial vault and left tibia and fibula of the smaller adult showed similar green stains from pins.

The large coffin (HSMC 1) contained the remains of a male with an estimated stature of 5 feet 6 inches based on femur and tibia lengths. The large coffin size suggests he was corpulent, especially in comparison with the compact smaller adult coffin. Features of the limb bones and teeth indicate an age of more than 50 years at death. This age corresponds with minor arthritic changes in the limb joints and lower spine. The 17 recovered teeth for this male show virtually no wear or calculus, and only two small cavities at the time of death. Due to brushite deterioration of the skull, tooth data are somewhat inadequate to strongly support assumptions about his dental health, other than the wear of the represented teeth was slight, particularly in view of his estimated age. Remnants of silk ribbon were found partially preserved at the neck and wrists suggesting he had been buried in a funerary garment, but none of this fabric survived.

The smaller adult lead coffin (HSMC 2) contained the remains of a female with a stature of about 5 feet 3 inches and an estimated age of more than 60 years. This woman had lost 20 teeth in life and the crowns of her remaining front lower teeth were worn down to the root stubs. Concave facial surfaces of the incisor roots reflected excessive wear from her attempts at oral hygiene. To clean their teeth, some colonists used recipes containing acidic, abrasive ingredients such as vinegar and tobacco ash. A cloth soaked in this solution was used to vigorously scrub the teeth. Cleaning polished the teeth, but over time, removed the enamel and inflamed the gums, leading to periodontal disease and alveolar bone resorption of the tooth sockets.

The woman's skeleton was gracile. Markers indicative of childbirth were not apparent due to bone deterioration. However, injuries in life were evident

Figure 11.4. The remains of Anne Calvert in her coffin *(left)* and her femurs, showing the poorly healed fractured right femur. (Reproduced by permission from Chip Clark, Smithsonian Institution.)

in her right femur, which had fractured in a spiral pattern (figure 11.4). It healed with the leg shortened, causing her to walk with a pronounced limp. A chronic bone infection (osteomyelitis) persisted for the remainder of her life. Spinal arthritis and back trauma in the form of fused vertebrae and a fused rib were also noted. Heavy metal testing of her hair by the Center for Applied Isotope Studies, University of Georgia, showed episodic spikes of arsenic, with higher concentrations closer to the scalp suggesting periodic ingestion of a "medicine" containing this element with a dose given near the time of death.

Isotope testing of the man and woman to determine diet revealed that both individuals had grown up in England but had resided in Maryland for many years prior to death. The woman's nitrogen isotope value reflects less consumption of meat, at least partially a result of poor dental health and painful chewing. Reduced food consumption due to loss of teeth, her postmenopausal age, and impaired mobility caused by the leg fracture all contributed to this woman's marked loss of bone density (osteoporosis). The severe leg fracture resulted in infection that periodically flared up, caused leg swelling and bone necrosis, and resulted in draining fistulae that carried pus to the skin. Extreme discomfort with no effective medical treatment would have necessitated bed rest and the sustained inactivity led to further bone loss.

The infant in the smallest lead coffin (HSMC 3) was 5 to 6 months old at the time of its death based on dental development (Moorrees et al. 1963; Smith 1991) and bone growth. The lower deciduous first incisors had just begun to erupt. The humerus measures 75 mm in length, which is consistent with an age of about six months (Ubelaker 1989). The skull, ribs, and long bones of this infant show multiple pathological changes. The bones of the cranial vault had 5–6 mm wide openings from abnormal mineralization during growth (figure 11.5). The spongy bone of the cranium also shows expansion and increased macroporosity (porotic hyperostosis), a condition indicative of anemia. The sternal ends of the infant's ribs are expanded and flared (figure 11.5). These rib changes, together with the cranial lesions, are indicative of rickets, which is often earliest and most clearly seen in the osteo-cartilaginous junctions of the ribs, long bones, and skull (Ortner and Putschar 1981). Causes of rickets include Vitamin D deficiency, insufficient intake of calcium and phosphorus, and chronic intestinal disorders (Zimmerman and Kelley 1982). In its most common etiology, rickets can be prevented by sufficient exposure of the skin to sunlight, which internally enables synthesis of Vitamin D. The colonial practice of swaddling infants kept babies warm during cool temperatures, but likely culminated in severe Vitamin D deficiency. The additional colonial practice of bleeding patients to effect cures may have exacerbated this infant's poor health.

IDENTIFICATION AND INSIGHTS

To conclusively identify these individuals, other information was needed. Palynologist Gerald Kelso predicted that pollen frequencies would indicate season of death and/or placement in the coffin. Pollen swabs were taken from around the skeletons, and from the sides and lids of the wood and lead coffins. The swabs from the woman's coffin showed high levels of ragweed pollen, indicating a late summer or autumn burial. Evidence from the woman's chest and hand area revealed a concentration of aster and vetch pollen, indicating she was buried holding a bouquet of autumn blooming flowers.

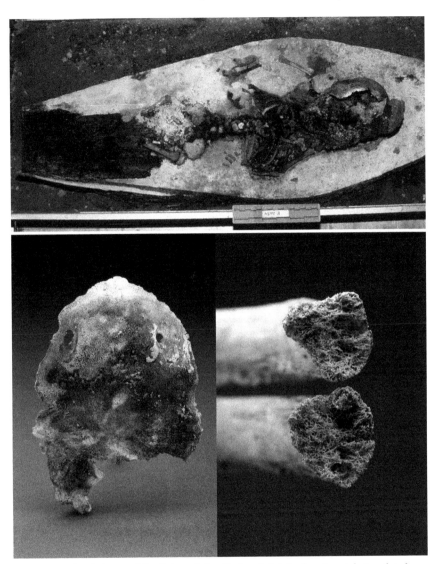

Figure 11.5. The skeleton of the Calvert baby (*top*) and details showing rickets-related cranial lesions (*bottom left*) and flared ribs (*bottom right*). (Reproduced by permission from Chip Clark, Smithsonian Institution.)

The child's coffin held numerous exceptionally well-preserved grains of oak and pine pollen, reflecting a spring interment. The man's coffin yielded no predominance of any specific type, but a mix of pollen from all seasons suggested burial at a time when no species was actively pollinating—the winter (Kelso and Miller 2016).

The pollen signal from the male's coffin is a significant clue. Only one person identified by historians matches the assembled evidence: Chancellor Philip Calvert, youngest son of the first Lord Baltimore. Philip was about 57 years old when he died on January 14, 1683. He was one of the most prominent individuals in Maryland, serving as governor, chancellor, and chief justice for the colony (Carr 1992). Muscle markings on the skeleton indicate that the man did not engage in strenuous physical labor and his coffin size suggests he had considerable body mass, both signs of high social status during the seventeenth century. Burial in a lead coffin, originally reserved for royalty and nobility (Litten 1991), is also highly suggestive of wealth and prestige during the Early Modern period. Consistent with the isotope evidence, Philip is known to have been raised in England, but lived in America for a considerable time before he died.

The female remains are believed to be those of Philip's first wife, Anne Wolseley Calvert, who may have been 68 or 69 years old at her death. A church record in England lists an Anne Wolseley who was baptized in 1610 (Carr 1992:2). Philip came with Anne to Maryland from England in 1657 and they lived in the colony for about 25 years. The infirmed Anne Calvert, after a long life for the times, died in the autumn of 1678 or 1679, three to four years before Philip. There is no evidence they had children. Although they represented the elite of the colony, virtually nothing was recorded about their health, lifestyle, or cause of death, and even the existence of the baby buried alongside them is undocumented.

We now know that the child is the biological son of Philip Calvert. A 2016 DNA extraction from the adult male and child by the Reich Laboratory of Medical and Population Genetics at Harvard University determined that the infant was a boy and a first-degree relative of the man. They were not full siblings, as they do not share the same mitochondrial DNA sequence inherited from the mother. Rather, they have a father-son relationship with matching Y chromosome haplogroups (Reich et al. 2016). Attempts to extract DNA from the female identified as Anne have failed, but because Anne Wolseley Calvert was in her late forties when she came to America, and more than 60 years old at death, the infant could not have been hers. It was more likely to have been the son of Philip and his second wife, Jane Sewell.

After Anne's death, Philip married 16-year-old Jane Sewell. Although there is no written record of it, she and Philip apparently had a child. Before Philip suddenly died in January 1683, he would have known he had an heir. The boy was about 6 months old at death and, as the pollen shows, was buried in April or May. Therefore, he would have been born in November or December of 1682. Three to four months after Philip's death, his child was also dead. It was obviously thought that the infant merited a burial similar to his father, including a coffin encased in lead. Lead, however, was in short supply, and sheathing for the baby's coffin was cobbled together from six pieces of scrap lead, perhaps remnants from Anne's and Philip's coffins. A year later, Jane sailed to England with her stepfather Charles Calvert, 3rd Lord Baltimore, and her mother, also named Jane Sewell. Young Jane never remarried and was buried as "Mrs. Jane Calvert" at St. Giles in the Fields in London on May 17, 1692 (Carr 1992; Burial Registry St. Giles in the Fields, London, 1660–1691). Thus ended the Philip Calvert family.

DISCUSSION

With this unique group of remains from high-status Maryland colonists, some important observations can be made. Regarding the skeletal analysis, of particular importance are the stable carbon and nitrogen isotope values (table 11.1) obtained from four adults—two known, elite, recent immigrants (Lionel and Anne Copley) and two elite, long-term Maryland residents (Philip and Anne Calvert). These values clearly demonstrate that even the wealthy, who likely had much more access to imported goods, still transitioned from a European, wheat-based diet to one incorporating regional American foods. Biochemical data from these known individuals provide baseline values essential for evaluating both residency and status in the Chesapeake for remains that are not identified.

More extensive data on the health and lifestyles of the Chesapeake colonists will be published in the future, but here, females show poor oral health relative to the males. Anne Calvert, the oldest adult, had lost 20 teeth in life. Anne Copley, about 30 years younger, had lost 8 teeth. Lionel Copley had less dental pathology, and the dentition of Philip Calvert, although incomplete, shows little decay and minimal tooth wear. The diets of wealthier colonists likely promoted dental decay, perhaps more so for females because of easier household access to larger amounts of sugar that the affluent could afford. Evidence from non-elite burials at the Chapel of this same time period tends to display less severe dental disease (Owsley and Bruwelheide n.d.). Dental health related to both social and gender status requires further exploration through more detailed examination of data and documentation of additional colonial period remains.

Examples of traumatic injury and disease indicate Maryland's elite were not immune to these conditions. Lionel Copley sustained several fractures in life, but none that caused his death. Years before she died, Anne Calvert severely fractured her right leg. She lived with a debilitating condition

Table 11.1. Demographic Data on Five Lead Coffins from Historic St. Mary's City

Burial	Sex	Osteological Age	Birth Date	Death Date	Estimated Stature (cm)	$\delta^{13}C_{Collagen}$ ‰ [a]	$\delta^{15}N_{Collagen}$ ‰ [a]
Sir Lionel Copley	Male	45–49 years	1648	1693	175.2±3.27	-19.4	13.1
Lady Anne Boteler Copley	Female	30–34 years	1660	1692	164.2±3.72	-19.5	13.3
Philip Calvert (HSMC1)	Male	50–59 years	1626	1683	171.4±3.27	-17.6	12.3
Anne Wolseley Calvert (HSMC2)	Female	60+ years	1610?	1678/1679	161.7±3.72	-17.32	10.5
Infant Calvert (HSMC3)	Male	5–6 months	1682?	1683?	NA	NA	NA

Note: a. Generated from Delta values [$\delta R = [(R_{sample} - R_{reference})/R_{reference}]*1000$] where R is the ratio ($^{13}C/^{12}C$ or $^{15}N/^{14}N$) compared with the V-PDB and atmospheric air C and N reference.

exacerbated by a chronic bone infection. Most surprising was the Calvert infant. Neither wealth nor access to "state of the art" medical care could save this baby who suffered from conditions that physicians of the time did not understand nor know how to treat.

After death, these prominent colonists were treated with high-end burial customs that had increased in formality as the colony matured. This is evident in the remains themselves, as the Copley skeletons had postmortem modifications consistent with elaborate embalming practices, likely enhanced by the expectation that their remains would be shipped to England. The two Calvert adults who died earlier were treated in a different manner. Anne Calvert was laid out, "dressed and trimmed," as was the period expression (Litten 1991:72), by having her feet, knees, and wrists tied together with silk ribbon, some of which survived. Her burial clothing is unknown, but she was wrapped in a linen shroud with numerous fresh sprigs of rosemary strewn over her midsection. Sweet-smelling herbs were often placed under the shroud to mask the odor of death in England (Litten 1991:72). At the same time, rosemary had a long traditional use in English rituals including weddings and funerals because it symbolized remembrance, as William Shakespeare wrote in *Hamlet*, "There's rosemary, that's for remembrance" (Shakespeare 1992, Act 4, Scene 5:199). Anne's treatment followed period practice and shows that English traditions regarding burial had been successfully transplanted to colonial America. A few years later, Philip Calvert was interred wearing a newly fashionable long-sleeved shift tied with silk ribbons at the neck and wrists. His arms were at his side with clenched fists. There is no evidence of a shroud, suggesting his burial program followed what was considered the latest fashion for interment in England (Litten 1991). Such findings are important because there is little historical evidence about funerary practices in early America.

The Calvert and Copley burials show that British customs and fashion were followed in seventeenth-century Maryland, although lead coffins were the exception, even in Europe. Burial of the Copleys in lead coffins, much like their embalming, may partially be explained by the expectation of returning their bodies to England for burial. Encasing in lead was one of the few means for long-distance transport without decomposition becoming an unpleasant problem. At the same time, Lionel Copley was a knight and the first formal representative of the English crown in Maryland. Previous officers had been appointed by Lord Baltimore. Copley personally directed the placement of his wife in a lead coffin, so this burial form was his intention. The elite nature of their mortuary treatment is further emphasized by the location of their burial vault within a few feet of the powerful symbol of Maryland's government: the State House. This had not been a burial site previously, so this was apparently selected as the most dignified location for a person who was both a knight and the colony's First Royal Governor.

For the Calverts, it is unlikely that transporting their bodies back to England was seriously considered. Few relatives remained there, and there was no church or graveyard closely associated with the Calvert family. Their interment in lead must have another explanation. Philip's choice of having his first wife and later himself buried in lead was a conscious decision. Indeed, the range of pollen and insects present in the coffin suggests that Philip had his lead coffin premade and stored for its eventual use (Kelso and Miller 2016). Burial in wood coffins was standard by the late 1600s in Maryland, as excavations of other graves in the Chapel field site indicate (Riordan 2000), but the use of lead coffins was unprecedented. It was a choice, not a necessity, and that decision may relate to how Philip Calvert viewed himself and his family.

As the child of a baron, Philip was of noble birth, but as the youngest son had no claim to the title. Philip probably would have been considered landed gentry in England. But in Maryland, with Lord Baltimore having near regal powers over the colony, the Calvert family was at the pinnacle of society. Holding the powerful posts of Chancellor and Chief Justice enhanced Philip's prestige. At the time of his death, only his nephew Charles Calvert, the 3rd Lord Baltimore, was of higher status. Philip's choice of an elite form of funerary treatment may have been meant as a final statement of rank as Maryland's aristocracy. The interment of his six-month-old son in the same way strengthens this interpretation: it was meant to express Calvert family status. Thus, the lead coffins are an enduring statement that family members of the ruling proprietor perceived themselves as the nobility of the colony.

Summary

Discovery of lead coffins at St. Mary's City has led to unique investigations into seventeenth-century life and death in America. By integrating the skills and methods of diverse scholars and specialists in many fields, it has been possible to not only identify people, but also to learn about their lives and mortuary customs during a formative century of colonial Chesapeake society. These individuals were the aristocracy of early Maryland, and yet their skeletons reveal that they suffered a range of maladies, including serious dental disease, broken bones, nutritional problems, and other afflictions that now could be cured by modern medicines. This provides striking insight into the realities of health and medical and dental treatments in 1600s

America. Compiling this evidence from individuals at the top end of the social spectrum allows for more precise evaluations of the lives of the majority of people who made up early Maryland society. Such comparisons are under way using the dozens of other graves excavated at the chapel site that hold the remains of non-elite individuals from the seventeenth-century colony (Douglas W. Owsley 2019, pers. comm.).

This investigation demonstrates the diversity of evidence that may be obtained from the study of human burials. How the deceased were treated, their body arrangement, the nature and type of coffin used, and where they were interred all offer important cultural clues to status, rituals, beliefs, and the society of which they were a part. As with Philip Calvert, it can even give insight as to how a person viewed their place in society. Analysis of the bones, hair, and burial artifacts enabled identification and yielded data not otherwise available. Indeed, measuring isotope values of these skeletons helped develop a new tool by which immigrant status could be evaluated and distinguished from native-born persons. This study, and the synthesis of the evidence that emerged from it, provides a deeper understanding of life in America and the challenges of building a new society.

PART 3

AFTER THE CAPITAL

The Archaeology of St. Mary's City in the Eighteenth,
Nineteenth, and Twentieth Centuries

12

The Captain John Hicks House Site and the Eighteenth-Century Townlands Community

GARRY WHEELER STONE AND STEPHEN S. ISRAEL

In 1969, archaeologists working for the Historic St. Mary's City museum excavated a house site on the campus of St. Mary's College of Maryland. The site dated approximately 1725–1750 and it had been the home of an English mariner turned tobacco planter. The excavation of Captain John Hicks's house produced a number of "firsts." This was the first Maryland excavation of an earthfast building, the first Maryland report on a second quarter of the eighteenth-century historic site, and perhaps the first North American archaeological site for which the ceramics and glass finds were reported as numbers of vessels rather than numbers of sherds (Carr et al. 1971; Yentsch 1990:25).

How do you interpret an archaeological site when it is the first of its kind to be excavated? This was the challenge confronting Historic St. Mary's City and Contract Archaeology, Inc., in 1969. Because there were no other second-quarter eighteenth-century sites excavated in Maryland, there were no sites to directly compare with Hicks. This prompted the research team to turn to documents to provide context. Through leases, deeds, and court proceedings, the museum's historian, Dr. Lois Green Carr, identified Captain John Hicks and four neighbors whose estates were probated between 1733 and 1766. The inventories of these households provided details of these families' possessions—clothing, cash, credits and debts, household furnishings, slaves and indentured servants, tools, livestock, and crops. In total value, the inventoried movables varied from small planter's assets of £65 to those of the Royal Customs Collector for north Potomac, William Deacon, valued at £2,025. Comparing John Hicks's wealth with an economic study of Maryland's Chesapeake counties showed Carr that Hicks ranked in the top 10 percent of the population (Land 1965; Carr et al. 1971: 2:90). But Carr wanted to know more. How did John Hicks's tobacco-focused plantation compare with those of his neighbors? What were the economic structures of households and neighborhoods? In 1973, Lois Carr published her research in *Ceramics in America*. By then, she had analyzed an additional 345 St. Mary's County probate inventories. She found that about 30 percent of decedents owned no land and only the wealthiest half of the population owned slaves and generally only a few. Captain Hicks's 19 slaves and the large crops of tobacco that they grew, made him one of the county's largest tobacco producers (Carr 1973:75–81).

Carr's analysis of Captain Hicks's neighborhood was the beginning of a lifelong study of the social and economic structure of the Chesapeake. From her position as Historic St. Mary's City Historian, Carr extended her studies to include Anne Arundel and Somerset counties, Maryland, and York County, Virginia. By comparing Captain Hicks's excavated trash and the items listed in his inventory with the possessions of many other Chesapeake planters, it became clear that Hicks deliberately used artifacts to signal to his neighbors that he was a gentleman (Carson 2017). It is also clear that without *both* documents and artifacts, we would understand much less about the Hicks family.

THE TOWNLANDS

When Captain Hicks first sailed up the St. Mary's River, he observed the remnants of Maryland's first city (see figure 12.1). Conspicuous on "Church Point" was the 1676 State House, now the Anglican church. Behind the church were the ruins of the brick jail. To the east, along the riverbank, Joseph and Mary Van Sweringen lived in his father's former inn. At the old town center, the decaying ruins of the colony's first statehouse called the "Country's House" were obvious. Further east, on the Jesuits' land, only brick bats marked the site of the 1660s brick chapel, but the priest's house was still occupied. Other traces of the seventeenth-century community were rapidly disappearing as the land was turned to agriculture. During the period in which Captain John Hicks and his family occupied their new home on St. John's, roughly 1725–1745, Lois Carr was able to identify six families then living on the former town lands. It was an atypical neighborhood. Two families—Hicks's and William Deacon's—were headed by transplanted English gentlemen, two were craftsmen—a blacksmith and a joiner—and two were successive generations of a family that appear to have combined tobacco planting and crafts.

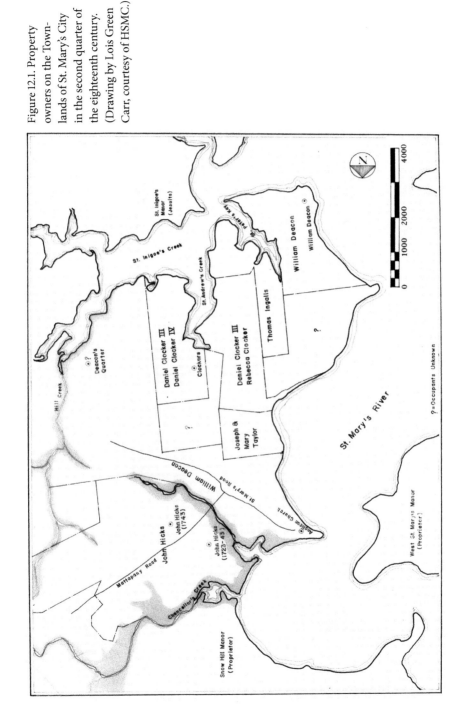

Figure 12.1. Property owners on the Town-lands of St. Mary's City in the second quarter of the eighteenth century. (Drawing by Lois Green Carr, courtesy of HSMC.)

William Deacon, Esquire, was the grandee of the area—Royal customs collector for the North Potomac and a justice of the peace. He had come to Maryland about 1722 and married Joseph van Sweringen's widow. For a decade or so they continued living in the former van Sweringen inn while Deacon invested his substantial income in townland property and mills, eventually owning more than 600 acres at St. Mary's (King and Miller 1987:40). He also acquired a half interest in the "Great Mill" at the head of the St. Mary's River. The latter produced flour for export and ship's biscuit (Carr et al. 1971: 1:16–19; Hammett 1973:248–249).

Probably in the late 1730s, Deacon built a new home at the southern edge of the former townlands at the confluence of the St. Mary's River and St. Inigoes Creek. Now called Rosecroft Point, this location was ideal for the customs collector. There he constructed a large, gambrel-roofed house, four rooms on a floor, with a kitchen and office wing and a rare stone quay on the shore.

In 1754, Deacon sold the land where the original city had stood to Captain Hicks's son, William, an agent for Captain Hicks's older brother, a Whitehaven, England, merchant. However, at his death in 1759, Deacon still maintained a quarter on St. Mary's Hill Freehold. There and at Rosecroft Point, Deacon grew wheat, corn, and a little tobacco. Of the five inventoried townland farms, only Deacon's had the plows and harrows needed to grow small grain and the reap hooks (sickles) to harvest it. Doing this work were 29 enslaved Africans and African Americans, including "Toney, Blacksmith," as listed in the 1759 inventory. Deacon's livestock was numerous: 21 horses, 25 cattle, 165 sheep, plus hogs, geese, and duck. Nothing is known about free employees. He probably had an overseer, perhaps neighbor Daniel Clocker (Carr et al. 1971: 1:26–29; 2:493–497, 513–523).

Near Deacon lived another immigrant, this one from New England. Thomas Ingalls was a "joiner"—a skilled woodworker who may have come to St. Mary's to help build Deacon's house. When Ingalls and his wife died in 1752, the appraisers of his estate found a shop filled with desks and tables under construction plus two unfinished violins. Besides Ingalls and his wife, the household consisted of two minor children and a servant boy. Ingalls did not grow tobacco, farming his 94 acres only to provide food for his family. The inventory lists corn, wheat, and rye, three old horses, four cows and calves, and hogs (Carr et al. 1971: 1:33–34; 2:497–498, 529–535).

The other craftsman known to have lived on the townlands was Joseph Taylor, blacksmith. Taylor, his wife, Mary, and their four children lived on 63 acres on the St. Mary's River north of Deacon. Mary Taylor spun wool, linen, and cotton. She or her husband was a weaver, as the house contained two looms. For weaving, they may have purchased or bartered thread and yarn from their neighbors. Their livestock consisted of six horses, five cows with calves, and ten sheep. The Taylors seemingly only engaged in subsistence agriculture as their equipment consisted of a "parcel of planters old working tools." Taylor died in early 1733, but his wife and children continued to live on their farm until at least 1738 (Carr et al. 1971: 1:31–32; 2:502–504, 536–539).

Daniel Clocker IV was the fourth of his family to live off of St. Inigoes Creek at the head of a cove. His great-grandfather, an indentured servant imported by the Jesuits, had been modestly successful in the New World by combining tobacco planting and carpentry. When his father died in 1747, the 190-acre plantation was divided between his sister Elizabeth and Daniel IV.

As with the Taylors, most of what we know about the Clockers comes from the probate inventory made after Daniel Clocker's death. His tools and equipment were limited to an old cart, some planter's tools, and a few carpenter's and cooper's tools. His wife's and daughters' spinning wheels, flax hackles, cotton cards, and knitting needles were worth about as much. His tobacco crop was small. Even if Daniel had been ill for an extended period, his three sons could have raised a larger crop. Clocker was solvent when he died with only minor debts. What was his source of income? We suggest Clocker served as William Deacon's overseer (Carr et al. 1971: 1:29–31, 2:501–502, 540–544). The livestock the appraisers found on Daniel Clocker's farm indicate subsistence agriculture and perhaps a modest dairy: 2 horses, 14 sheep, some hogs, geese, and 4 cows and 4 yearlings.

Were we comparing Captain Hicks's artifacts and inventoried possessions with only those of his townland neighbors, we would get a very distorted understanding of rural St. Mary's County, 1725–1750. In much of St. Mary's City, tobacco played a minor role in the economy. Deacon appears to have focused on growing wheat for his mill, a focus that allowed him to farm like a European (although with black laborers). The Taylors and Ingalls farmed only to provide food for themselves and their animals. Daniel Clocker IV grew only a limited amount of tobacco, gaining much of his income from some other activity. Elsewhere, the exact opposite prevailed. Lois Carr's initial sample of 345 St. Mary's County inventories found that every male-headed household had the axes and hoes needed to grow corn and tobacco, but few owned the reap hooks needed to harvest wheat. Among the 126 decedents that could be fully evaluated, only 19 were craftsmen. And most of these grew tobacco (Carr 1973:80–81). Four more decades of research by Carr, Lorena Walsh, and their colleagues only confirmed the 1973 analysis. In 2010, Lorena Walsh wrote that St. Mary's County was the "jurisdiction where commitment to tobacco was perhaps the most complete of any locality in the Chesapeake" (Walsh 2010:541).

Who Was Captain John Hicks (1695–1753)?

It was not difficult for Lois Carr to identify that Captain John Hicks had owned the land. Seven bottle seals—glass monograms added to wine bottles—were excavated from the site. Two seals were marked "John Hicks *1723*" (see figure 12.2). The proprietary rent rolls listed Hicks as the owner of St. John's as did his will in which he bequeathed St. John's to his son William and the adjacent St. Barbara's tract to his son George (Carr et al. 1971: 1:483–492). But who was John Hicks before he purchased land at St. Mary's? Answering this required searching further afield, in records of ships trading to New England and Virginia (Carr et al. 1971: 1:49; 2:483–493, 505) and, ultimately, a trip to western England to the Cumberland County archives. Recently, thanks to the digitalization of records, more details have come to light.

John Hicks was baptized February 2, 1695, in the town of Carlisle, the county seat of Cumberland, the son of John Hicks, Gentleman. In early eighteenth-century Cumberland, the locus of economic opportunity was the rapidly growing seaport of Whitehaven. By 1712, John Hicks's older brother, William, was working there as an employee of Thomas Lutwidge, a merchant trading with Ireland and the Chesapeake. On February 10, 1715, Father Hicks apprenticed his son John to Lutwidge. By 1718, John Hicks was one of Lutwidge's agents, captaining the ship *Prince Frederick* in transatlantic voyages. By January 1726, Hicks owned the *Prince Frederick,* but he was no longer its captain. Hicks had married and settled at St. Mary's.

While buying tobacco along the Potomac, Hicks had met Anne, about whom nothing is known except that she was Catholic. A son, William, was born in 1726, by which time Hicks was a St. Mary's townland tobacco planter. Did he continue acting as an agent for Lutwidge or John's brother William, now established as a Whitehaven tobacco importer? There is no documentary or archaeological evidence that he continued as a merchant, but it is probably relevant that immediately upon his death, his son William became an agent for his uncle William.

In sharp contrast to his neighbors, there is a great deal of evidence that Captain Hicks became one of St. Mary's County's larger tobacco producers. After his death in early 1753, the probate court inventory of his Maryland goods included 19 slaves, eight of whom may have been field hands. In 1753 and 1754, his son William produced nine and ten hogsheads of tobacco on the "St. John's with Addition" plantation. Captain Hicks's inventory lists a

Figure 12.2. Bottle seal of John Hicks found at the site and dated 1723. Recovery of the named seal was a significant clue in linking the archaeology with the documentary record. Diameter is 1.33 inches, or 34 millimeters. (Drawing by Donald L. Winter, courtesy of HSMC.)

cart worth 15 shillings and "a parcel of old planter's tools" worth £4.10.3. Seven fragmentary hoes, both grubbing and hilling (cultivating), were excavated from the cellar fill. Other excavated finds included a corn cob, parts from a sailboat, and horse harness fragments. The inventory enumerates 6 horses, 33 cattle, and 27 hogs, pigs, and piglets. While Hicks's plantation was dwarfed by the operations of Virginia's great planters or those of the Galloways or Carrolls of Maryland, it was the second largest in the neighborhood and one of the largest in St. Mary's County (Walsh 2010:433–448, 487–507, 541–554; Carr et al. 1971: 1:113–114, 119–121, 126–127; 2:489, 524–528).

Captain Hicks arrived in Maryland with money, business skills, and the manners of a gentleman. His household furnishings symbolized his status— the silver listed in his inventory and the fine ceramics and glassware found at the site of his house. He quickly became a justice of the peace, county sheriff 1732–1735, and a justice of the Provincial Court, 1738–1742. However, Captain Hicks infrequently attended meetings of the court. Beginning in 1734, tobacco prices improved, almost doubling by 1739. Perhaps Hicks decided to stay close to home and concentrate on earning money (Carr et al. 1971: 1:22; Clemens 1980:226–227).

By the late 1740s, seemingly, life was progressing well for Captain Hicks. He, wife, Anne, and youngest son, George, were living in a new house, on rich farmland from which, with his enslaved workers, he could produce large tobacco crops. Son William was in Whitehaven apprenticed to Uncle

William, Whitehaven's second largest tobacco merchant, and his daughters had both made good marriages, Elizabeth in England and Mary across the Potomac in Northumberland County, Virginia. Then Captain Hicks became concerned about his health, wrote his will, and returned to England, probably to Whitehaven, where he died in 1753, age 58 (Carr et al. 1971: 1:20–23, 485–489; Beckett 1981:112–113; Lewis and Booker 1967:9A).

While we have some knowledge of the Hicks family, we know almost nothing about the other families living on St. John's Freehold, for they were African American slaves. Information about them comes from Hicks's probate inventory, which is provided in the appendix at the end of this chapter. The appraisers of Captain Hicks's estate recorded only the enslaved people's names, ages, and values. Listed were four men, four women, and eleven children, but no indication of familial relations was provided, not even which woman was nursing eight-month-old "Doll." To the appraisers, the slaves were just stock, stock like the horses listed next.

EXCAVATION AND LABORATORY ANALYSIS

In 1968, the members of the St. Mary's City Commission became concerned that construction at St. Mary's College might impact a seventeenth-century archaeological site. They asked Orin M. Bullock, restoration architect, to test the area. Employing an early strategy used at Colonial Williamsburg, where closely spaced, hand-dug trenches were used to locate foundations, Bullock directed a mechanical trencher to dig 40 parallel trenches. While we do not recommend either technique today, the trenching was effective. It churned up oyster shell, brick rubble, and colonial artifacts. A hand-dug probe uncovered a brick foundation. To learn more, the Commission engaged J. Glenn Little, president of Contract Archaeology, Inc., to conduct 25 days of fieldwork. Little, assisted by Stephen Israel and a college student crew, started work on June 23, 1969 (see figure 12.3). Their charge was to locate, identify, and date the building (Carr et al. 1971: 1:2–4, 58–92).

The archaeologists began by hand excavating two trenches parallel and perpendicular to the foundation discovered in 1968. The plowed soil over the site was screened through ¼-inch wire mesh for artifacts. When the humus-stained surface of the subsoil was reached, it was shovel skimmed to expose the bright yellowish-brown subsoil against which soil disturbed by digging post holes and pits was clearly visible. They found a second brick foundation, both proving to be the footings of massive fireplaces the backs of which were 40 feet apart. Post holes and timber molds appeared to outline a building 16 feet wide. Between the chimneys the excavators found the outline of a filled

Figure 12.3. Rescue excavation of the John Hicks site in 1969 with co-director Stephen Israel (*right*) and excavator Steve Fadley. The parlor brick-chimney base can be seen in the foreground. (Courtesy of HSMC.)

cellar. Elsewhere on the site they found a number of landscape features, including refuse pits, depressions, and post holes. Five wine bottle seals were found with three dates: John Hicks 1723, William Deacon 1724, and William Deacon 1741. Preliminary examination of the artifacts suggested a date range of 1680–1750 and a clear association with Hicks. With the rich site facing imminent destruction, Glenn Little had no difficulty convincing Commission chairman Robert E. Hogaboom that more archaeology was needed.

Beginning September 2, 1969, the archaeologists started a disciplined race to uncover as much as possible before winter. By the time that field work ended on November 22, the field crew had uncovered 46 post molds from buildings, construction scaffolding, fences, and yard features, 16 pits and 12 shallow pits and lenses. One of the pits was a small outbuilding cellar. Another was a storage pit in front of the dwelling's kitchen fireplace. Most informative were the six layers found in the dwelling cellar. Below the agricultural plow zone the archaeologists found a layer of brick rubble, plaster, and mortar. This was followed by a layer of plaster and mortar, a third layer of plaster and brick fragments, then oyster shell and artifacts, followed by more oyster shell, and then a thin layer of gray-brown soil with shell, plaster, and charcoal. This deepest layer was the cellar floor (Carr et al. 1971: 1: figure 7, section C–D).

The cellar evidence showed that the demolition of the building had been carefully planned. The easiest way to have cleared the site would have been to burn the building, collect nails from the ashes, and salvage the chimney bricks. This Hicks's crew did not do. Nor did they tear down the building and then fill in the cellar (building rubble was on top of layers of oyster shell fill). The following is our hypothesis on how the Hicks's first house was dismantled.

John Hicks wanted to reuse the old house as an outbuilding at another location. So while some of his slaves took apart the additions to the house, others pried up the floor plank. Then, to fill up the chasm below the parlor floor joists, slaves began loading the kitchen midden—oyster shells and trash—into baskets, and emptying them into the cellar. When the additions were down, the crew stripped the interior walls and dumped the heavy plaster into the cellar. The chimneys were taken apart, the whole bricks cleaned for reuse, and the mortar and broken brick shoveled into the cellar. With the chimneys out of the way, the lightened house could be moved. On log rollers pulled by horses or oxen the building was dragged to a new location. Can we prove this? No, but it explains the evidence from the cellar stratigraphy.

The archaeologists and their student helpers were in the field for four months. It would take them more than a year to process the artifacts and prepare the 556-page report. The college loaned a science laboratory for the work, and students helped clean, count, measure, and draw the specimens. Richard Muzzrole from the Smithsonian assisted in setting up an iron conservation lab, and Glenn Little and Stephen Israel began corresponding about artifacts with other archaeologists and artifact and plant specialists (Carr et al. 1971: 1:ii).

The analysis of the Hicks site artifacts may be the first in which American historical archaeologists reported a complete collection of ceramic and glass objects by minimal vessel counts. Previously, archaeologists reported ceramic styles by sherd counts. As Little and Israel organized the Hicks site artifacts, they decided to emphasize function. Artifacts were sorted into broad categories such as architecture, agriculture, and travel, and then broken down into subcategories. Building hardware includes counts of hinges, keys, and locks; ceramic categories include dairy, storage, cooking, and dining vessels. Subsequently, Garry Stone—helped by George Miller and St. Mary's College students—refined the ceramic vessel descriptions (Stone et al. 1973). Other Chesapeake archaeologists began reporting ceramics by minimal vessel counts (Neiman 1980b; Kelso 1984; King and Miller 1987). Now, reporting ceramic and glass finds by vessel counts is widespread (see chapter 5).

The laboratory crew cleaned, sorted, and typed 2,753 pieces of dark wine bottle glass. These fragments came from more than 150 bottles; two whole bottles also were recovered. All identifiable bottle shapes are dated 1700–1740. Forty-six percent of the bottles are short and onion-shaped (ca. 1700–1720) and 54 percent are short but more cylindrical (ca. 1720–1740). Wine bottle seals provided dates (1723, 1724, and 1741). One of the biggest surprises was the excavation of Pit 14, into which at least 81 old wine bottles had been thrown and then deliberately smashed.

More helpful in dating the site were the fragments of white clay tobacco pipes. Almost 2,000 fragments were recovered. Using drill bits, the stem bore diameters were measured and found to vary from 7/64-inch to 4/64-inch. The Hicks site pipe distributions were compared to J. C. Harrington's chart of pipe stem diameters from well-dated sites and confirmed an occupation of ca. 1710–1750. When they used Lewis Binford's regression formula to estimate a mean occupation date for the site, the result from the stem fragments was 1734.82. Using just the stems from the cellar, the calculated mean occupation date was 1739.98 (Carr et al. 1971: 1:283–290; 2:411; Noël Hume 1970:296–308).

The Dwelling

For about 20 years, Captain Hicks lived in a dwelling that began as a 16×40-foot house with a dirt-walled cellar under one end (see figure 12.4). Initially, it probably had a kitchen and parlor downstairs and chambers in the attic. The structure was built to face southwest toward the boat landing. The cellar entrance, an outbuilding, and work areas indicate that the east side was the rear of the building. At some point an addition (storeroom, bed chamber?) was added to the river side of the parlor. This was a relatively modest house for an English merchant turned tobacco planter and influential community member. Sometime after about 1745, Captain Hicks constructed a new house on the adjacent St. Barbara's tract. Little is known of the new house except that it was considered large and constructed above a brick-walled cellar. Still, by English standards, it would have been unexceptional. When Hicks returned to Whitehaven about 1749, he found his brother living in "Tangier House," a stone dwelling five bays (windows) wide and three stories and attic high. Constructed 1686–1687 in a countrified Anglo-Dutch Palladian style, the front was elegantly finished with pediments above the entrance and windows (Jackson 1878).

Although John Hicks's first house was modest, it left important archaeological evidence, including the foundations of two fireplaces, the cellar, an ante-hearth pit, and excellent evidence of hole-set timber foundations. The

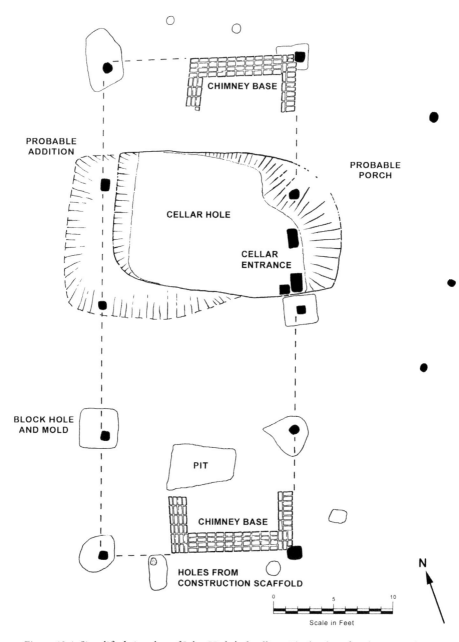

CHIMNEY BASE

PROBABLE
ADDITION

PROBABLE
PORCH

CELLAR HOLE

CELLAR
ENTRANCE

BLOCK HOLE
AND MOLD

PIT

CHIMNEY BASE

HOLES FROM
CONSTRUCTION SCAFFOLD

N

0   5   10

Scale in Feet

Figure 12.4. Simplified site plan of John Hicks's dwelling. The kitchen fireplace was obvious—it was larger than the parlor fireplace, the earth beneath the firebox was extensively
heat discolored, and in front of the hearth was a subfloor pit for protecting vegetables
from frost. When the house was first constructed, rainwater pouring off the roof eroded
the east and west cellar walls. After additions were added to the house, the cellar walls
stopped eroding. (Drawing by Garry Wheeler Stone, courtesy of HSMC.)

Hicks's house was an "earthfast" building—its foundations were short timbers set vertically in the ground like fence posts. This was the first earthfast building excavated in Maryland, and the type-site for defining "block"-supported framed structures. Late seventeenth- and eighteenth-century Chesapeake carpenters used "blocks"—short, hole-set pilings—to support the sills of framed structures above the ground (see chapter 2). The post holes and timber molds of the Hicks's house blocks varied in size and orientation, and their depths varied by 2.3 feet (see figure 12.4). Several of the block molds at Hicks contained remnants of rot-resistant black locust timbers (Stone 1982:323–326).

Block locations show that the building was framed of four 10-foot bays—a two-bay parlor at the north end and a two-bay kitchen at the south end. The cellar under the parlor and the storage pit in front of the kitchen fireplace show that the kitchen and parlor were floored with planks nailed to joists resting on the wall sills. The archaeologists recovered numerous pieces of plaster from the wall interiors. The backs of some fragments were impressed with the marks of brick (from the chimneys) or with wood grain impressions from horizontal, riven (split) wood lath that had been nailed to the wall studs. Most fragments have two coats of whitewash, and along the edges of some fragments are traces of paint—light pink and red/brown ocher. This paint suggests that exposed timbers (posts, joists) were painted for contrast with the whitewashed walls. Brick mortar examination showed that the exterior joints of the chimneys had been competently finished with "ruled" joints (Carr et al. 1971: 1:296–303). Many pieces (820) of window glass were recovered, especially from the cellar. None have triangular or polygonal corners and no window lead was recovered—more evidence that this was an eighteenth-century dwelling displaying sash windows (Carr et al. 1971: 1:247–250).

Excavators recovered 4,300 nails and nail fragments, of which 1,517 were complete. Surprisingly, there were very few short, plaster lath nails (172 or 5 percent) and even fewer of the clinch nails used to assemble doors and shutters (57 or 2 percent). We think Hicks's crew had salvaged the lath nails and dwelling doors (Carr et al. 1971: 1:105–106, 247–248). Likewise, very few T- or L-headed finish nails (32) were found. Such low frequencies suggest that the board and batten doors were salvaged for use elsewhere. Most of the nails were the sizes used for attaching siding, roofing, and flooring.

While John Hicks's first house was modest by English or urban American gentry standards, its size was well above average for St. Mary's County. When the nearby freeholds of Snow Hill Manor were surveyed in 1765, no house was as large as that of Captain Hicks's (Stone 1988:68–77). Although

Hicks was English born and of high status, he chose to build a Chesapeake home with earthfast foundations. Adopting the local architectural tradition for his first house followed an older seventeenth-century practice of planters erecting "impermanent architecture" as a starter so they could first invest in plantation development and later build a more permanent home. Hicks seems to have followed this same strategy.

Dairy and Kitchen

In the realms of the dairy maid and the cook, archaeology plays a large role. Lois Carr located five townland probate inventories between 1733 and 1766. There is not a single listing of a bucket, churn, or butter pot. Nevertheless, the cattle listed in all the inventories appear to be dairy herds with many cows and heifers and few steers and bulls. Captain Hicks's inventory enumerates 28 cows and yearlings and only 3 large and 2 small steers (see appendix below; Carr et al. 1971: 2:513–544).

While Hicks's inventory was silent, his trash was eloquent. By sorting the sherds from the site by color, texture, thickness, form, and projected rim diameter, the archaeologists were able to identify 18 of the large earthenware pans primarily used to cool milk and separate cream. There were even more "butter pots." These large containers could be used to store a variety of foods but were designed to store salted butter. Most were black-glazed, but the edges of the sherds show that they came from several sources including Buckley in Flintshire, Wales, and Staffordshire, England (Carr et al. 1971: 1:143–148; Stone et al. 1973:105–107). Captain Hicks's inventory lists 113 pounds of "pot iron," the total of his pots, frying pans, and other cast iron cooking vessels. From the cellar fill, the archaeologists excavated fragments of two medium-sized iron cooking pots and one small pot, the interior still partially covered with grease. They also excavated sherds from one earthen cooking pot, a pipkin (small handled cooking pot/sauce pan), and 12 "patty pans" (baking dishes) (Carr et al. 1971: 1:147–149; Stone et al. 1973:107).

Dining and Entertaining

Together, the archaeological and documentary evidence provides a great deal of information on how the Hicks household dined and entertained. The probate inventory lists 56 ounces of silver, 146¾ pounds of pewter, and the archaeologists recovered fragments from 235 ceramic and glass dining and drinking vessels (see table 12.1; see Stone et al. 1973 for a more detailed listing of the ceramic finds). This information is both specific and ambiguous.

Table 12.1. Ceramic and Glass Vessels from the Site of John Hicks's First House

Function Form	Dark Glass	Iron	Earthenware	Stoneware	Delft	Porcelain	Clear Glass	TOTAL
DAIRY/KITCHEN								
Butter Pots			23					23
Milk Pans			18					18
KITCHEN								
Cooking Pots		4	1					5
Pipkins			1					1
Patty Pans			12					12
CELLAR/KITCHEN/DINING								
Bottles/Jugs	150+		3	3				156
Serving Pans			6					6
DINING								
Platters					2			2
Plates				1	14			15
Dishes			13		2		2	17
Bowls			8		4		1	13
DRINKING (TRADITIONAL BEVERAGES)								
Cups			38	4				42
Mugs[a]			25	24	2			51
Glasses							27	27
Drinking Pots/ Jugs			2	3				5
Pitchers/Jugs			1	1	1			3
Decanters							2	2
Flask							1	1
DRINKING (NEW BEVERAGES)								
Large Bowls					2			2
Small Bowls				3	14	5		22
PUNCH								
Punch Glasses							2	2
TEA								
Teapots				3	1			4
Teacups				3	3	9		15
Saucers				2	3	6		11
Spoon Trays						1		1
MEDICAL/HYGIENE								
Drug Jars					1			1
Ointment Pots/ Eggcups			2		3			5
Bleeding Bowls					2			2
Chamber Pots				1				1
TOTAL	150+	4	153	48	54	21	35	465

Note: a. One pewter mug was recovered from a trash pit.

Which vessels were used for breakfasts, suppers, and work-a-day dinners versus when Captain and Mrs. Hicks dined with guests? Were some predominantly used by their children or the slaves?

Pewter may have provided a majority of the plates, dishes, and platters used throughout the occupation of the site as well as some hollow wares—a small pewter mug was found in a trash pit (Carr et al. 1971: 1:179, 2:409–410). Much of the time, pewter plates and dishes appear to have been paired with ceramic cups and mugs—so many were found (93) that at one time Little and Israel conjectured that they were excavating a tavern. Most of the cups were traditional earthenware forms, but the mugs were almost evenly split between earthen and stonewares. In size they varied from approximately a pint to one that may have held two quarts. The most common type was Rhenish blue and gray, but there were also English white stoneware mugs and a lovely brown stoneware mug probably from Nottingham (Oswald 1982:109, plate 65, 70, 115; for a parallel mug in white salt glaze dating ca. 1740, see Mountford 1971:43, plate 81). For wine, Captain Hicks had purchased glasses; fragments of 27 were excavated.

Some of Captain Hicks's tablewares probably came with him from England in the 1720s. Among the later vessels was a mid-1740s dinner service of English Delftware (see figure 12.5). Excavators recovered fragments from three plates, two dishes, and two platters. The service was painted in medium blue on white tin glaze in close imitation of contemporary Chinese porcelain. An identical surviving plate is dated 1746 (Lipski and Archer 1984: no. 500). Also, Chinese porcelain plates with the peony and pomegranate decoration were recovered from a 1752 shipwreck (Christie's 1986:162).

Mrs. Hicks had the vessels necessary to conduct a proper tea ceremony. The archaeologists excavated fragments of 4 teapots, 11 saucers, 15 teacups (9 of them blue and white Chinese porcelain), and numerous small bowls that could have served as slop bowls or sugar containers. The most highly decorated finds were fragments of a spoon tray with polychrome painting and gilding. For more robust entertaining, Captain Hicks had large Delftware bowls for mixing punch and glasses for serving it.

ARTIFACTS AND STATUS

From the evidence of probate inventories and archaeology, it was easy for Lois Carr to evaluate the social standing of the Townland inhabitants. At the top were the Deacons. With the income from farms, mills, blacksmith's shops, and the fees from his office as customs collector (estimated at £150 a year), and no children to provide for, Esquire Deacon was able to afford a

Figure 12.5. Blue and white English Delftware dinner service ca. 1740 from the Hicks site. The centers of the pieces have an adaptation of the Chinese peony and pomegranate pattern and the brown-edged rims are decorated with diaperwork shapes alternating with peony sprays. (Photograph by Donald L. Winter, courtesy of HSMC.)

lavish lifestyle. His probate inventory lists expensive clothing and a large collection of silver. He had more and better furnishings than Hicks, and instead of dining on Delftware, he had an enormous service of Chinese porcelain. While Mr. and Mrs. Deacon's dwelling was no mansion, it was the best in the area and they could have comfortably entertained a governor (Carr et al. 1971: 2:513–523).

The Hicks's home was much more modest, but Captain Hicks had the artifacts needed to signal that he was a gentleman: respectable furnishings, a decent table service, punch bowls and cups, and tea equipage. More importantly, in growing up in a gentry household, in clerking under a successful merchant, and in mingling with men of business in ports around the Atlantic, he had acquired gentility. The two Deacon bottle seals found at the Hicks site indicate friendship and social interaction with that prominent royal official.

Earlier in England and in Maryland, men's social standing depended not upon their clothes or their manners, but upon their reputations. Men's neighbors knew if they came from good families, if they were prosperous, and if they were honest. But reputation, except for the aristocracy, was not portable. As European populations, economies, and trade increased, the gentry needed new ways to signal their worth to strangers. Manners, clothing, and artifacts replaced, at least partially, reputation. While letters of introduction might be needed for serious business, when strangers met in a coffee house or at a boat landing, manners and clothing sufficed. Thus when Captain John Hicks began trading along the Potomac, he was recognized as a gentleman, and when he settled at St. Mary's, he quickly became a county leader (Carson 2017).

Carr's and Walsh's study reveals that the other Townland families—despite their modest land holdings—were more prosperous and lived more comfortably than the average St. Mary's County family. When blacksmith and weaver Joseph Taylor died in 1733, his goods were valued at £86, more than three times the county average, and the furnishings of the Taylors' home were above average. To measure rising literacy and living standards, 1636–1777, Carr and Walsh developed an "amenities index" (Carr and Walsh 1994:69–82). Probate inventories were scored for the presence or absence of 12 items ranging from bed linens to silver. When Taylor died in 1733, the mean St. Mary's County amenities score was about 2.6, while the Taylors scored 5, possessing bed linens, fine ceramics, spices, books, and a clock. The same holds true for farmer-carpenter Daniel Clocker IV. His 1766 estate, £65, was more than twice the county average and his amenities index score was 6: 50 percent higher than the county 1755–1767 average of 4. The mid-eighteenth-century St. Mary's County Townlands were a Southern Maryland oddity, crowded with gentlemen and with an above average standard of living (Carr et al. 1971: 2:536–544).

Conclusion

The excavation of Captain John Hicks's 1720s dwelling was the first of its kind in Maryland. Lacking comparative archaeological materials, Little and Israel turned to historian Lois Carr to provide context. She identified the site occupant and his neighbors, wrote minibiographies, created an economic context, and placed Captain John Hicks in it. His probate listing of artifacts substituted, in part, for comparative artifact collections. Such a comparison of an inventory with excavated finds, however, reveals that archaeology can greatly refine our knowledge of many aspects of material culture, trade networks, and household economies.

Carr's, Little's, and Israel's integration of archaeological and documentary research is both a success story and a warning. Historical archaeologists can make contributions to archaeology by publishing archaeological findings, but if we are to make a contribution to anthropology and history, we must use *all* relevant information. We may find this information in governmental records, maps, newspapers, diaries, literature, paintings, photographs, or surviving buildings. Cherish your archaeological friends but get to know economists, demographers, and historians (Carson et al. 1994; Carson 2017).

APPENDIX: JOHN HICKS PROBATE INVENTORY

The probate inventory of John Hicks provides context for interpreting the artifacts found on the archaeological site. The original spelling and syntax of the inventory in the archives are maintained as much as possible.

Maryland State Archives, PREROGATIVE COURT (Inventories) Book 55, pp. 27–30 [MSA S534-55; 01/11/05/044]

Inventory of Sundry Goods and chattels the right of M^r. John Hicks Late S^t. Marys County appraised by us the subscribers this 21 Day of August 1753 being first duly sworn (Vizt)

		Age	Currency
Negro Men	Jett	41 y$^{rs.}$	46-0-0
	Bumper	43	28- -
	Henry	40	28-0-0
	Ben	27	46- -
Boys	Jo	6	16- -
	Jacob	3	12-0-0
	Isaac	2	8-0-0
	Luke	2	8-0-0
	Michall	10	35-0-0
Women	Beck	42	25- -
	Luce	33	40- -
	Madge	40	20-0-0
	Clare	17	43- -
Girls	Agness	9	26- -
	Dinah	6	16- -
	Jane	8	21- -
	Bett	11	28- -
	Stace	5	14- -
	Doll	8 months	-5-
Horses	1 Horse Rantin	13	4- -
	1 D^o. Smoaker	8	6- -
	1 D^o. Poney	5	5- -
	1 D^o. Plummer	14	4- -
	1 D^o. Black	20	-6-
	1 Young Mair	4	1-10-

		Age	Currency
Sheep	63 Head	@6/	18-18-0
Cattell	7 Cows & Calves	@ 35/	12-5-
	3 Large Steers	@ 44/	6-12-
	2 Small Do.	@ 25/	2-10-
	6 yearlings	@ 13/	3-18-
	15 Cows	@ 30/	22-10-
Hoggs	14 Barrows	18 Mon.ˢ old at 10/	7-0-0
	2 Sows	Dᵒ.	1-2-6
	6 Small Shoats	6 Dᵒ. @ 4/	1-4-
	1 Sow & 4 Piggs		1-4-

1 Case of Drawers	3-13
1 Old Ovall Table	1-5-
1 Smaller Dᵒ.	1-5-
1 Desk and Book Case	4-0-0
1 Old Small Desk	1-0-0
1 Do. Large Do.	1-15-
1 Duch [Dutch] Cubbard	-12-5
1 Large Looking Glass	2-0-0
1 Smaller Dᵒ.	1-0-0
1 Dᵒ_Dᵒ_	0-5-
1 Old Clock	1-0-0
6 Old Chairs	-12-
4 Bedsteds	1-8-

oun-d*

Parcell of Old Silver 56:5			[not valued]
1 Bed Bolster Pillows 50ˡⁱ with a pʳ Sheets			
—3 old Blankets 1 silk Rugg old Quilt			5-5-6
1 Bed 2 Bolsters Pillows 75ˡⁱ wᵗʰ. 1pʳ. Sheets			
1 pʳ. Blankets 1 Counterpin Curtains & Vallins—			6-14-0
113ˡⁱ old pot Iron		@ 4d.	1-17-8
4 pʳ. Pot hooks	@	2/	-8-
2 pʳ. Pot Racks	@	8/	-6-
1 Box Iron Heaters			-7-6
1 Warming Pan With other Trifells			2-0-0
1 pʳ. Old Hand Irons			-5-
144ˡⁱ Pewter	at	1/6	10-16-0
2 ¾ Dᵒ.	at	1/6	-4-12
2 Earthen Dishes 1 Dᵒ. plate 1 Punch Bowl			-6-6
1 old Case With 5 Bottles			-6/6
1 Large Cubbard			1-10-
2 old Chests and other Trifles			1-1-
1 pʳ. Cast Hand Irons			-18-
1 old Tea Chest no cannisters			-6-
1 qᵗ. glass Decanter			-1-6
1 Old Cart & Wheels			-15-
1 old Cubbard Small			-9
& not any thing more—			617-9-3 ½

Bro^t from the other Side

<table>
<tr><td></td><td></td><td>oz-dwt</td></tr>
<tr><td></td><td></td><td>56-5 Old Silver—</td></tr>
<tr><td></td><td>his</td><td></td></tr>
<tr><td></td><td>Henry R Raley</td><td>Seal</td></tr>
<tr><td></td><td>mark</td><td></td></tr>
<tr><td></td><td>Jo. Leigh—</td><td>Seal</td></tr>
<tr><td>Kindred</td><td></td><td></td></tr>
<tr><td>George Hicks</td><td>Credr.</td><td></td></tr>
<tr><td></td><td>W: Hicks—</td><td></td></tr>
</table>

Additional Inventory

1 Bed & Covering, Bed Sted	3-4-0
4 Case knives & forks	-3-
Parcell of old Planters Tools	4-10-3
D°. of D°. Carpenter D°.	-8-
1 Small Law Book	-5-0
	£ 8-10-3

Maryland State Archives, PREROGATIVE COURT (Inventories) Book 57, p. 59 [MSA S534-57; 01/12/01/001]

A Second Additional Inventory of the sundry Goods belonging to John Hicks late of St. Mary's County deceased appraised by us the Subscribers this 31st. of August 1753

1 Iron Chain	22^{li}	@ 5^d	£ 0-9-2
2 ^{pr}. Iron Traces	7 ¾	@ 7 ^d	0-4-6 ¼
1 Brass Kettle	8	10 ^d	0-6-8
1 D° old D°	4 ¼	6 ^d	0-2-1 ½
5 Bridle Bitts		6 ^d	0-2-6
			£ 1-4-11 ¼
			Currency

<table>
<tr><td>Kindred</td><td>his</td><td></td></tr>
<tr><td>Geo. Hicks</td><td>Henry HR Railey</td><td>Seal</td></tr>
<tr><td></td><td>mark</td><td></td></tr>
<tr><td></td><td>Jo. Leigh</td><td>Seal</td></tr>
<tr><td>Creditor</td><td></td><td></td></tr>
<tr><td>W. Hicks</td><td></td><td></td></tr>
</table>

Note: * Ounces and pennyweights: a pennyweight is 1/20th of an ounce.

13

A Second Look at the Nineteenth-Century Ceramics from Tabbs Purchase and the Tenants Who Used Them

GEORGE L. MILLER

Early in my career I had the good fortune to be hired as the laboratory curator for the St. Mary's City Commission in 1972. This was my first full-time position after several years on seasonal archaeological projects. Learning about Maryland's first capital was our mission. In 1971 our field school began the excavation of what was believed to be a seventeenth-century site. Historical records indicated this area had been occupied from the seventeenth century. The depression of a filled cellar indicating the remains of a house led to the assumption that this site was from the early period. However, archaeology does not always go as planned, and this excavation was a good example.

Documentary research established that the house was on a 208-acre tract of land owned by the Anglican rector Moses Tabbs from 1765 until his death in 1779 (Maryland State Archives 1779). In Moses Tabbs's 1779 will he gave to his son, George Clarke Tabbs, "a tract of Land Lying in St. Mary's County called Tabbs Purchase" with instructions: "and I order my executors . . . to keep him constantly at a good school till he shall have learning enough, either for a Protestant Minister, Physician or Lawyer." George Clarke Tabbs was a minor at the time; this is also shown by a 1780 appraisal of the Tabbs estate entered in the orphans' court (Maryland State Archives 1780). His status as a minor suggests that 1780 began a long period of occupation of Tabbs Purchase by tenant farmers that lasted well into the mid-nineteenth century.

While not what was expected, this assemblage provided an opportunity for research on a ceramic assemblage from tenants of that period. My research led to the 1974 article, "A Tenant Farmer's Tableware" (Miller 1974). Back then, our knowledge of who occupied the site was limited. We knew that Moses Tabbs's son, George Clarke Tabbs, owned Tabbs Purchase until his death in 1799, when he left it to his wife, Lucretia (Maryland State Archives 1799). In 1821 Tabbs Purchase was sold to Daniel Campbell, a wealthy planter who lived at nearby Rosecroft (Maryland State Archives 1830). When the 1974 article was published the only identified tenant was William Kirby Sr., who occupied the property in 1798 and presumably still lived there at his death in 1803 (Federal Assessment List 1798; Maryland State Archives 1803).

There were other advantages to working in St. Mary's County that I came to appreciate. One was the quality of the county's court records. County probate inventories continued to list household items in great detail well into the late nineteenth century. In many other places the level of detail in probate inventories declined during the nineteenth century. The St. Mary's County economy remained tied to agriculture and watermen with a small stable population that was almost equally split between white and black residents until World War II.

Owners and Tenants of Tabbs Purchase

Subsequent research enhanced our knowledge of the tenants who most likely occupied the Tabbs Purchase house. A couple of guardian accounts from 1830 and 1851 describe the Tabbs Purchase house and its condition and list the land associated with it as being "208 acres more or less." Table 13.1 provides a summary of the various documents describing the transitions of ownership and occupants related to Tabbs Purchase from 1765 to 1866. This documentation is important for determining who acquired, used, and discarded the artifacts recovered from the site. Tracking down less visible members of society can be difficult. For the tenants occupying Tabbs Purchase, the Probate Court guardian accounts provided essential clues.

Subsequent research suggests that the Kirby family continued to occupy Tabbs Purchase into the 1840s. The 1810 census records list a James Kirby in St. Mary's County, but it is difficult to place him geographically (Bureau of the Census 1810). William Kirby's eldest son was James Mills Kirby, so the one listed in the 1810 census could be William's son. The 1820 census lists a Mary Kirby as the head of a family, so they may have been the tenants of Daniel Campbell (Bureau of the Census 1820). William Kirby's will does not list any women's names, suggesting he was a widower when he died, so it is difficult to know the relationship of Mary Kirby to William or possibly James Mills Kirby. Unfortunately, the 1830 census records for St. Mary's County are not extant. The 1840 census lists "Maret" Kirby as the head of a family (Bureau of the Census 1840). In different documents his name is spelled Merritt, Meril, and Maret. I use Merritt for this chapter. The 1840 Census lists

Table 13.1. Summary of Records of Ownership and Occupancy of Tabbs Purchase

Year	Owner	Occupier	Description
1765	Moses Tabbs	Moses Tabbs	Purchased the land that became known as Tabbs Purchase
1779	Moses Tabbs	Moses Tabbs	Moses Tabbs died in 1779
1779	George Clarke Tabbs, a minor	unnamed tenant	Son of Moses inherited Tabbs Purchase
1798	George Clarke Tabbs	William Kirby, Sr., tenant	1798 Federal Assessment list for St. Mary's County
1799	George Clarke Tabbs		Last will Nov. 29, 1799, leaves 1/3 of property to his wife, Lucretia
1803	Tabbs Family	William Kirby, Sr., tenant	William Kirby died in 1803
1821	Daniel Campbell		Tabbs family sold Tabbs Purchase to Daniel Campbell
1830	Daniel Campbell		Daniel Campbell died
1830	Sarah A.J. Campbell, a minor		Caleb M. Jones, guardian of Sarah Campbell, makes guardian accounts
1830	Sarah A.J. Campbell, a minor	Merritt Kirby family?	Caleb M. Jones in his guardian accounts lists money paid to them for work
1839	Sarah A.J. Campbell, a minor	Merritt Kirby	Listed as tenant in Caleb M. Jones guardian accounts
1840	Sarah A.J. Campbell, a minor	Merritt Kirby	Listed as tenant in Caleb M. Jones guardian accounts
1841	Sarah A.J. Campbell, a minor	Merritt Kirby	Listed as tenant in Caleb M. Jones guardian accounts
1851	Sarah Ann Golly Burch, (*nee* Campbell)	William Crawly, "mulatto"	Sarah's mother signs over her widow's dower right to Tabbs Purchase
1853	John and Sarah Campbell Burch		Sold Tabbs Purchase, then known as East St. Mary's, to Jane Biscoe for $1,200
1856	Wm. & Jane Biscoe		Sold Tabbs Purchase, then known as East St. Mary's, to Edward Joy for $2,000
1858	Edward Joy	Edward Joy family	Edward Joy died
1858	Emily C. Joy, James Ignatius Joy & Margaret Joy	Joy family	John M. Brome & John C. Ashcom evaluation of the Joy lands and slaves
1866	E. Marrion Joy	Joy family	John M. Brome appointed executor of the Joy estate

the number of "White Persons over 20 who cannot Read or Write" including all three adults of the Kirby family (Bureau of the Census 1840). It is not until the 1850 census that records list the names of all household members (Bureau of the Census 1850a).

After Daniel Campbell died in 1830, there were annual guardian account assessments of the value of the land by Caleb M. Jones, the guardian of Sarah A. J. Campbell, a minor (Maryland State Archives 1839). Most of the annual Guardian Accounts did not list the names of the tenants occupying Tabbs Purchase. However, the accounts for 1839, 1840, and 1841 list Merritt Kirby as the tenant. This suggests that the Kirby family continued to be the tenants of Tabbs Purchase (Maryland State Archives 1839). The 1830 guardian accounts list $1.87½ paid to Jane Kirby for making clothing "for the deceased's people." Merritt Kirby married Jane Price on December 24, 1821. It also lists $8.87 paid to Merritt M. Kirby for work performed (Maryland State Archives 1833). The 1850 census lists "Merit [sic] Kirby" in St. Mary's County and seven members of his household (Bureau of the Census 1850a).

Merritt Kirby, the grandson of William Kirby, is listed as born in 1797 in the 1850 census, so he would have been around six years old when his grandfather died in 1803. The only Jane Kirby in this family was identified as Jane R. Kirby, who was recorded as being 16 years old. Perhaps she was named after Jane Kirby listed in the 1830 guardian accounts. The elder Jane Kirby may have become the head of the family after the death of William Kirby Sr. Jane Kirby is listed in the Merritts' family in the 1850 census as being 43 years old. Among the neighbors to Merritt Kirby in the 1850 census are John M. Brome and the St. Mary's Female Seminary, indicating that Merritt and his family were still living near Tabbs Purchase.

Sometime after 1841, when Merritt was listed as a tenant, but shortly after the 1850 census, the Kirby family left Tabbs Purchase. Tabbs Purchase was part of the estate left to Sarah Ann Golly Burch (née Campbell) by her father. Sarah's mother signed over her dower's right to the land in February of 1851. In the indenture from that transaction the land is described as "that tract or parcel of land called 'Tabbs Purchase' containing two hundred and eight acres more or less situated lying and being in St. Mary's County on St. Mary's river now in the occupancy of William Crawly" (Maryland State Archives 1851). William Crawly is listed in the 1850 census as a 44-year-old with a 28-year-old wife and two young girls; all family members are listed as mixed race ("mulatto"). His family is number 874 on the census list while Merritt Kirby's family is identified as the 864th family.

The last description of Tabbs Purchase was in 1858. In 1853 John and Sarah Campbell Burch sold Tabbs Purchase, which by then was called "East St.

Mary's" to Jane Biscoe for $1,200 (Maryland State Archives 1853). In 1856 William and Jane Biscoe sold East St. Mary's to Edward Joy for $2,000 (Maryland State Archives 1856). Edward Joy died in 1858, which led to another evaluation of the estate for a minor. It reads: "We, John M. Broom and John C. Ashcom by virtue of the annexed commission to value the lands & Negroes of Emily C. Joy, James Ignatius Joy & Margaret Joy, deed [did] enter upon the lands of the aforesaid minor the larger proportion of which is woods, then a large old dwelling house on same, unfit to be repaired, and perfectly unfit for any white person to live in. Two small log quarters for Negroes in good order. 1 small log corn house, and small barn nearly new, we did value the land at sixty dollars per annum" (Maryland State Archives 1858). In addition to the land, Edward Joy owned seven enslaved African Americans of whom four were children. Mary Joy was still occupying Tabbs Purchase when the 1860 agricultural census was taken (Bureau of the Census 1860a). Garry Wheeler Stone has speculated that the comment "old dwelling house on same, unfit to be repaired, and perfectly unfit for any white person to live in" may have been a commentary on the Joy family's continued occupation of the house (Garry Wheeler Stone 1974, pers. comm.). Mary Joy appears to have lived there until her death in 1866, although the house was perhaps gone by then. John M. Broom, a neighbor, was appointed executor to the Joy estate (Maryland State Archives 1866). Exactly when the building was demolished is unknown.

In summary, tenants occupied the Tabbs Purchase house after the death of Moses Tabbs in 1779. From then until sometime after 1841 various generations of the Kirby family were listed as tenants. Sometime before 1850 William Crawly's mixed race family occupied the house, and after 1856 it appears to have been owned and occupied by the Edward Joy family. It may have been occupied into the 1860s. Almost all the ceramics from the basement excavations postdate the period of Moses Tabbs's occupation of the site and appear to have been produced during the late 1790s into the 1850s during the occupation of the site by the Kirby family.

THE SITE

The primary feature of the site was a large brick-lined cellar that was entirely excavated by students during the 1971–1972 field seasons under the direction of Garry Wheeler Stone and Sandy Morrison. The cellar had a dirt floor that appears to have been cleaned out at some point because almost no eighteenth-century artifacts were recovered from the excavations. The cellar entrance had timber steps, the molds of which were exposed by the

Figure 13.1. The Tabbs Purchase cellar during excavation in 1972 showing the stratified fill deposits with the cellar entry ramp at the lower right. (Photograph by Garry Wheeler Stone, courtesy of HSMC.)

excavators. When the steps were weakened by rot, fill dirt was covered over them to form a ramp. Figure 13.1 shows the Tabbs Purchase house site under excavation in 1972 with the bulkhead entrance to the cellar to the lower right. The ramp fill covered and thus sealed an early nineteenth-century deposit of artifacts that had accumulated on the cellar floor. Artifacts above this fill indicate that deposits continued into the 1850s. Hence, the artifacts dated to two periods of occupation, and the records presented in table 13.1 indicate the tenants who deposited them.

CERAMICS FROM THE OCCUPATION LEVELS

My 1974 article focused on the distribution differences between creamware, pearlware, and whiteware because that was thought to be significant at the time. Now is the time to correct that misleading exercise. The assemblage of the tenant farmer's tableware has almost no plain creamware. This suggests that most of these ceramics from the Tabbs cellar had accumulated after the end of the Napoleonic Wars. Prior to 1815 creamware tableware was the most common type imported into America. Deflation following the Napoleonic Wars caused falling prices for ceramics and other imported goods. The decrease in ceramic prices led to a greater consumption of decorated wares that generally replaced plain creamware (Miller and Earls 2008). The great majority of ceramics from Tabbs Purchase are decorated wares, mainly shell-edge plates, painted teas, and dipt bowls. These were the cheapest wares available with color decoration from the Staffordshire potteries.

Archaeologists and collectors have classified these wares as pearlware or whitewares that have been seen as the successors to creamware. In reality creamware was not replaced by pearlware, but by decorated wares. Potters and merchants classified the wares by how they were decorated, not by a ware type. Archaeologists have focused too much attention on the blue tint of wares that we call pearlware. Pearlware has become a pigment of our imagination, diverting our attention from the changes that were taking place. Pearlware and whiteware are terms that are close to nonexistent in the Staffordshire potters' price fixing lists, invoices, and account books. What archaeologists have called pearlware is almost never undecorated, and the potters, merchants, and consumers referred to it by the types of decoration of these vessels. To put it in other terms, the consumers of ceramics did not go to the country store and say, "give me a pearlware plate"; they ordered the wares by how they were decorated, that is, blue shell-edge plates, painted teas, colored bowls, printed vessels, etc. That is how they were recorded in account books and in probate inventories (Miller and Hunter 2001). Terms such as chrome colors and rim styles of shell edge do not occur in these documents and have been generated by chronology research. It is the decoration type that holds the interpretive value, not the ware type. That is why the ceramics from Tabbs Purchase were used to generate a minimal vessel count sorted by functional and decorative type for comparison with historical documents.

Two documentary sources were used in understanding our excavated assemblages. In 1973 three students from the field school extracted ceramics listed in a number of St. Mary's County probate inventories from the 1840s (Herman et al. 1973). In addition to the county records, Karin D. Boring compiled a study of ceramics advertised in the Washington, D.C., newspaper the *National Daily Intelligencer* for the period 1827 to 1837 (1975). Ceramics listed in the probate inventories and those advertised in the Washington newspaper frequently listed ceramics in sets. These records do not reflect the consumption pattern of tenant farmers who were of limited means. The tenants of Tabbs Purchase appear to purchase ceramics to replace individual broken vessels, as there is no evidence of the purchase of sets.

The Tabbs Purchase tenants appear to be influenced by the matched sets in the homes of their more affluent neighbors. The tenants tried to match patterns over time, but the number of potters producing these common types, such as the molded shell-edge wares, changed rapidly, causing a great variety in what was available (Miller and Hunter 1990). One could match at the level of green or blue shell-edge plates, but the molded rim pattern would not be the same, thus unlike a set of plates all purchased at one point in time.

Table Plates

The table plates from the occupation levels show that the earliest attempted set was of green shell-edged plates followed by a period of blue shell edge, and then by blue willow plates. These wares were produced by many Staffordshire potters and were very commonly listed in potters' and merchants' invoices during the first half of the nineteenth century (Miller and Earls 2008). Figure 13.2 illustrates some of the shell-edged plate rims from the occupation levels. Invoices from New York importers show that shell-edged plates were the most common tableware being sold during the first half of the nineteenth century (Miller and Earls 2008:86–87). We now have better chronological information for these various molded patterns, provided in table 13.2A. The beginning and end dates for the different molded types of shell edge were generated from a number of plates with maker's marks (Miller and Hunter 1990). Given the production dates for the types in table 13.2A, it is clear that shell-edged plates were in use for much of the first half of the nineteenth century. They were the cheapest available tableware with color decoration for this period.

Very few transfer printed vessels were recovered from the excavations. They would have been the most expensive types commonly found in nineteenth-century assemblages. Figure 13.3 illustrates some of the printed plates and saucers from the occupation levels. The information on the production dates for these wares has greatly improved and is presented in table 13.2B. All the printed wares in table 13.2B are from the upper occupation levels. They illustrate the movement from shell-edged and painted wares to printed wares, a shift that probably began in the 1830s. The introduction of chrome colors, particularly reds, around 1830 provided an insight into the changes that were taking place in the consumption patterns of the Tabbs Purchase assemblage. The Caledonia pattern saucer by F. Morley & Company is the *terminus post quem* ("date after which") for the occupation of Tabbs Purchase by tenants. The pattern was registered in 1846 by F. Morley & Company, which was in

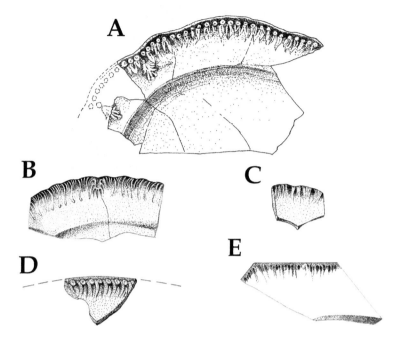

Figure 13.2. Five shell-edged plate rims from the occupation levels. *A*, Blue-edged ironstone plate with a raised rim motif, upper occupation level. *B*, Blue-edged pearlware plate with an impressed rim motif, from ramp fill. *C*, Green-edged pearlware dessert plate with an impressed rim motif, from occupation level. *D*, Blue-edged whiteware or ironstone plate with an impressed rim motif, upper occupation level. *E*, Octagonal blue-edged pearlware dessert or bread plate with impressed rim motif, upper and lower occupation levels. (Drawings by Gretchen Nolley, courtesy of HSMC.)

business until 1858. The transition from shell-edged and painted wares prob-ably is related to falling prices for printed wares, which greatly reduced the cost difference between printed wares and shell-edged and painted wares (Miller and Earls 2008:97). There is a possibility that some of the printed wares are from the Joy family after 1858.

Cups and Saucers

Painted teas (cups and saucers) were the dominant types being sold in the period from 1800 to ca. 1850, when they began to be replaced by printed teas and later by white granite (Miller and Earls 2008:86–87). Introduction of the chrome colors red and green led to a greater range of underglaze colors for painted and printed wares beginning by around 1830. These changes are better documented today than they were in 1974. Blue painted patterns in imitation of Chinese porcelain were introduced in Staffordshire around 1775

Table 13.2. Ceramic Vessel Descriptions with Updated Analysis and Dating

2A Vessel	SHELL-EDGED PLATES 1974 Description	Seen in figure 13.2 Revised Description	Date Range
C	Green shell-edge pearlware dessert or bread plate with an impressed rim motif. From occupation level of a unit.	Rococo pearlware shell-edged muffin plate	1784–1812
E	Octagonal blue-edged pearlware dessert or bread plate. From upper and lower occupation levels.	Octagonal pearlware shell-edged muffin plate	1790–1830
B	Blue-edged pearlware plate with an impressed rim motif. From ramp fill.	Even scalloped pearlware shell-edged plate with curved lines and bud	1802–1832
A	Blue-edged ironstone plate with a raised rim motif. From upper occupation level.	Embossed whiteware shell-edged plate	1823–1835
D	Blue-edged whiteware or ironstone plate with an impressed rim motif. From upper occupation level.	Shell-edged plate, unscalloped with a repetitive impressed pattern, whiteware	1841–1857

2B Vessel	PRINTED PLATES AND SAUCERS 1974 Description	Seen in figure 13.3 Revised Description	Date Range
D	Blue transfer-printed pearlware saucer. From upper occupation level.	Blue printed pearlware deep saucer with a landscape pattern	1800–1830
C	Blue transfer-printed pearlware saucer. From upper and lower occupation levels.	Dark blue printed saucer in a negative pattern	1820–1830
A	Green transfer-printed whiteware or ironstone saucer. From upper occupation level.	Chrome green printed whiteware saucer	1830–1850
B	Brown transfer-printed whiteware plate on whiteware or ironstone. From upper occupation level.	Brown printed whiteware saucer, Caledonia pattern, registered by F. Morley & Co. (Godden 1964:449)	Registered July 21, 1846, in business until 1858
E	Blue willow transfer-printed pearlware plate. From upper occupation level.	Blue printed whiteware willow plate	1820–1860

(continued)

Table 13.2—*Continued*

2C	PAINTED AND SPONGED CUPS/SAUCERS	Seen in figure 13.4	
Vessel	1974 Description	Revised Description	Date Range
B	Hand-painted blue-on-white pearlware saucer with an oriental motif. From lower occupation level.	China Glaze blue painted cup	1780–1815
A	Hand-painted pearlware blue-on-white saucer with a floral motif. From lower and upper occupation levels.	Blue painted pearlware deep saucer with broad floral motif	1820–1830
C	Hand-painted blue- and red-on-white ironstone or whiteware cup. From upper occupation level.	Blue and red (a chrome color) painted whiteware cup	1830–1840
D	Hand-painted sprig motif saucer (red, green, and black) on whiteware or ironstone.	Sprig painted whiteware saucer in red (a chrome color), green, and black	1830–1860
E	Pink sponge-decorated whiteware or ironstone saucer. From upper occupation level.	Pink (a chrome color) sponge-decorated whiteware saucer	1830–1880

2D	DIPT WARES	Seen in figure 13.5	
Vessel	1974 Description	Revised Description	Date Range
A	Mocha pearlware bowl with a strubbled worm motif (blue, brown, and white on yellow-drab-brown band). Sherds from lower and upper occupation levels.	Dipt ware common cable pearlware on a London shape bowl, decorated using a three-chamber slip cup	1811–1835
B	Mocha whiteware bowl with strubbled worm motif (brown, blue, and white on a tan band). From occupation levels of a unit.	Dipt ware common cable whiteware on a London shape bowl	1820–1840
C	Blue-and-brown banded pearlware bowl. From upper occupation level.	Blue-banded London shape whiteware bowl	1820–1840
D	Yellowware banded bowl with dark brown and blue bands. From upper occupation level.	Yellowware London shape bowl with banded decoration	1835–1860

Note: Individual vessel numbers are on file at Department of Research and Collections, Historic St. Mary's City, St. Mary's City, MD.

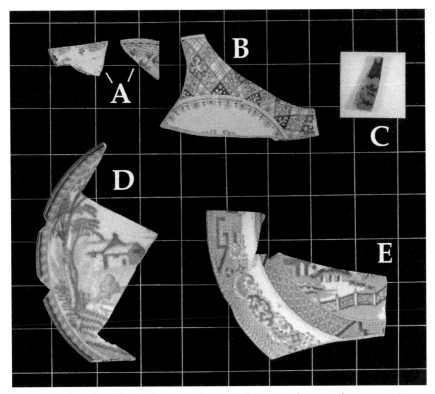

Figure 13.3. Sample of sherds from transfer-printed plates and saucers from occupation levels. *A*, Green transfer-printed whiteware or ironstone saucer, from upper occupation level. *B*, Brown transfer-printed saucer on whiteware or ironstone, from upper occupation level. *C*, Blue transfer-printed pearlware saucer, sherds found in both upper and lower occupation levels. *D*, Blue transfer-printed pearlware saucer, from upper occupation level. *E*, Blue Willow transfer-printed pearlware plate, from upper occupation level. Note the sherds are photographed on a grid of 1-inch squares. (Courtesy of HSMC.)

under the name China Glaze. China Glaze wares probably ceased production during the Napoleonic Wars that limited the availability of cobalt from Saxony following Napoleon's 1806 Berlin Decree. After the Napoleonic Wars, cobalt again became readily available, which led to broad blue painted floral patterns and dark blue printed wares that became much more common for the period ca. 1820 into the 1830s (Miller and Hunter 2001).

Figure 13.4 shows some of the painted and sponge decorated cups and saucers from the occupation levels. Table 13.2C gives the descriptions and updated information on the painted and sponged cups and saucers illustrated in figure 13.4. With the exception of the China Glaze cup, the painted teas from Tabbs Purchase postdate the end of the Napoleon Wars, and many

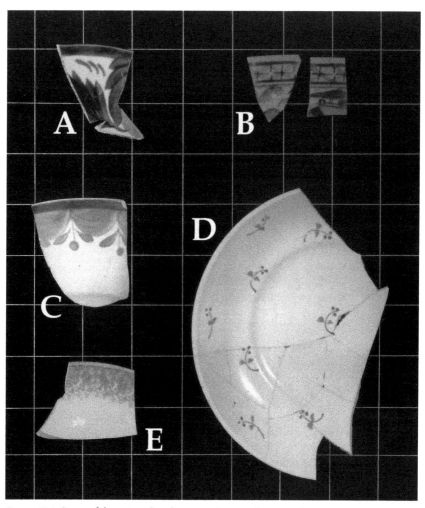

Figure 13.4. Some of the painted and sponge-decorated cups and saucers from the occupation levels. *A*, Hand-painted blue-on-white pearlware saucer with a floral motif, from upper and lower occupation levels. *B*, Hand-painted blue-on-white pearlware saucer with an oriental motif, from lower occupation level. *C*, Hand-painted blue- and red-on-white ironstone or whiteware cup, from upper occupation level. *D*, Hand-painted sprig motif saucer (red, green, and black-on-white) on whiteware or ironstone, from upper occupation level. *E*, Pink sponge-decorated whiteware or ironstone saucer, from upper occupation level. Note the sherds are photographed on a 1-inch grid. (Courtesy of HSMC.)

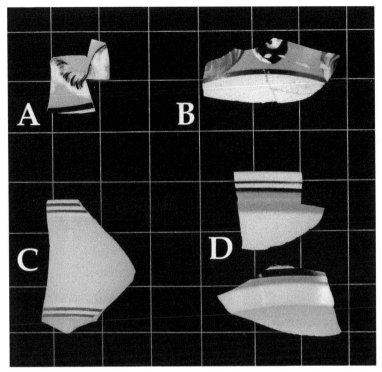

Figure 13.5. Dipt wares from the occupation levels. *A*, Mocha pearlware bowl with a strubbled worm motif (blue, brown, and white on a yellow drab brown band), from upper and lower occupation levels. *B*, Mocha whiteware bowl with a strubbled worm motif (brown, blue, and white on a tan band), from occupation level. *C*, Blue- and brown-banded pearlware bowl, from upper occupation level. *D*, Yellowware banded bowl with dark brown and blue bands, from upper occupation level. Note the sherds are photographed on a 1-inch grid. (Courtesy of HSMC.)

are from the 1830s to 1850s period. Vessel A has a broad blue painted floral pattern that was very common in the 1820s, when cobalt became more available from Saxony and Norway following the Napoleonic Wars.

Dipt Hollow Wares

Since publication of the 1974 article on the Tenant Farmer's Tableware, much has been learned about what the Staffordshire potters called dipt wares (e.g., descriptions of how they were created can be seen in Sussman 1997 and Rickard 2006). Dipt wares were the cheapest hollow wares with color decoration, and rarely have maker's marks. The decoration comes from colored liquid clay slips that are applied to the vessels before they are bisque fired. The hand application of the slip to the greenware ceramics means that no two vessels will be exactly alike. Dipt wares were very common from 1780 through most of the nineteenth century. Cobalt and chrome colors do not play much of a role in these wares. Cobalt does show up as blue-banded wares by the 1840s as a simpler version of the multicolored dipt wares. Figure 13.5 illustrates the dipt wares from the occupation levels, and table 13.2D provides the descriptions and updated information on the dipt wares. None of these bowls have a mocha decoration. The first two bowls were decorated using a three-chambered slip cup to create a pattern that the potters called "common cable." The three-chambered slip cup was patented in 1811 (Rickard 1993:185). Sherds to 15 bowls were recovered from the basement levels. None of them match, which again indicates a purchase pattern of one at a time, as replacements were needed. Other bowls included lead-glazed redware, plain creamware, and painted pearlware and whiteware.

A Second Look at the Tenant Farmer's Tableware

Documentation of the introduction of chrome colors into the Staffordshire potteries provides an insight into the dating of when the dirt ramp replaced the wooden steps into the Tabbs Purchase basement. The last chapter of Shaw's 1829 *History of the Staffordshire Potteries* describes the recent introduction of chrome colors. In his preface Shaw mentions a delay in publication was used to add additional information "entertaining to the present readers, and pregnant with interests to posterity" (Shaw 1829:vii). One of the notes was about the very recent introduction of printed wares using red, brown, and green colors, which came with the introduction of the chrome colors (Shaw 1829:235). Red or pink is the most obvious chrome color that can be identified in both printed and painted wares. Red or pink colors were produced by a combination of chrome and tin (Shaw 1837:527).

Table 13.3 shows that only two of the 15 vessels from the pre-ramp occupation assemblage were decorated with chrome colors, whereas 24 of the 52 vessels from the post-ramp occupation assemblage were decorated with chrome colors. Clearly the ramp was put in place sometime after 1830, and the vessels that postdate the ramp accumulated over a period of time. Perhaps the ramp was installed after the evaluation from the 1830 and 1833 guardian accounts in which the house was described as "in very bad repair" (Maryland State Archives 1841). The 1830 Administrative Accounts lists $8.87 paid to Merritt M. Kirby for work performed (Maryland State Archives 1833). This payment may relate to repairs to the Tabbs Purchase house.

The most datable vessel from the post-ramp upper occupation level is the brown printed plate of the Caledonia pattern that was registered by F. Morley

Table 13.3. Vessels from the Pre-ramp and Post-ramp Occupation Levels by Decorative Types

Decorative Type	Pre-ramp Occupation	Post-ramp Occupation	Pre-ramp Occupation%	Post-ramp Occupation%
Plain creamware	2	2	13.3%	3.8%
Green shell edge	3	3	20.0%	5.8%
Blue shell edge	2	10	13.3%	19.2%
China Glaze	1	0	6.7%	
Blue painted	3	3	20.0%	5.8%
Light blue printed	1	6	6.7%	11.5%
Dark blue printed	0	3	-	5.8%
Pre-chrome polychrome painted	1	1	6.7%	1.9%
Chrome colors painted	2	12	13.3%	23.1%
Chrome colors sprig painted	0	5	-	9.6%
Chrome colors sponged	0	6	-	11.5%
Chrome colors printed	0	1	-	1.9%
Total Vessels	15	52	100%	99.9%

& Company in 1846. They were in business until 1858 (Godden 1964:449). Thus, the plate could be from the period of occupation by William Crawly, who was listed as a tenant of Tabbs Purchase by at least 1850, or possibly from Edward or Mary Joy, who purchased the land in 1856. A couple of other vessels from the upper occupation levels indicate that assemblage continued to accumulate into the 1840s or possibly the 1850s. A flow blue printed saucer suggests a post-1845 date (Collard 1967:118). A blue willow plate has a printed lion and unicorn mark of a style that became common after Queen Victoria began her reign in 1837. No white granite vessels were recovered from the occupation levels. White granitewares became common after 1850. In summary, it appears that ceramics continued to accumulate in the basement well into the 1840s and possibly into the 1850s.

Conclusions

The ceramics from the lower and upper occupation levels from the Tabbs Purchase basement were, for the most part, manufactured in the period following the Napoleonic Wars into the mid-nineteenth century. The deflation and lower prices for Staffordshire ceramics following 1815 led to a transition from when plain creamware was the dominant type to a period that became dominated by decorated wares that included shell-edged tableware, painted teaware, dipt hollow ware, and printed wares. This is documented in "War and Pots," which was based on ceramics listed in 101 invoices from New York importers to country merchants from 1806 to 1886 (Miller and Earls 2008). Most of the vessels from the Tabbs Purchase assemblage were the cheapest type available with color decoration.

Despite four decades of continuing research on Staffordshire ceramics, the consumption pattern described in my 1974 article still holds. There was a period when green shell-edged plates were replaced by blue shell-edged ones and then by blue willow plates toward the end of the site's occupation. Almost none of these vessels match each other, which indicates that they were separate purchases that were made as vessels needed to be replaced. The tenants who occupied the site attempted to match plates, but they were frustrated by the rapidity with which molded rim patterns changed. These wares were not standardized so that the molded patterns of shell-edge plates from one potter commonly do not match those of another potter. It is clear that the tenants wanted their wares to look alike but were limited in the ability to achieve that because of their piecemeal purchase pattern.

My time as the St. Mary's City curator from 1972 to 1976 allowed me to expand my research on ceramics and the analysis of assemblages. My research on shell-edged wares after leaving St. Mary's City led to an article on them (Miller and Hunter 1990). This is also where my research on ceramic prices began that led to the creation of a set of CC index values that provided a tool for the study of costs and expenditure patterns of archaeological assemblages (Miller 1980).

It took some time for me to realize how good I had it at St. Mary's City. The research team of scholars there included Lois Green Carr, Russell R. Menard, Lorena S. Walsh, Cary Carson, and Garry Wheeler Stone. Little did I realize at the time what a powerhouse team this was and the impact they would have on the scholarship of the history of the Chesapeake.

14

The Archaeology of African American Mobility in Slavery and Freedom in Nineteenth-Century St. Mary's City

TERRY PETERKIN BROCK

Examining the nineteenth- and twentieth-century plantation landscape at St. Mary's City provides a look into the experience of African Americans during the transition from slavery to freedom in the United States. St. Mary's City, located in a slaveholding Union State and a pro-Confederacy county, is a unique context to study this transition. This chapter will examine how the negotiation of African American mobility was a critical component of this transition. It will look at how white planters intentionally restricted the mobility of African Americans during slavery, and how claiming mobility was a critical leverage point for African Americans following their emancipation. This chapter will use the plantation landscape to explore how these two groups negotiated mobility throughout the mid to late nineteenth century in St. Mary's City.

To date, archaeological studies asking questions about the transition from slavery to freedom in the United States are limited (Singleton 1985; Orser 1991; Orser and Nekola 1985; Singleton 1988, 2011; Barnes 2011; Reeves 2003; Boroughs 2013). Enslaved plantation landscapes, however, have received a great deal of study. These studies are important to our understanding of how plantation owners manipulated the cultural landscape to control their labor and maintain profits (Epperson 1999, 2000; Otto 1984). They range in scope from studying status (Lewis 1985), class and power (Delle 1999), race (Epperson 1999, 2000), and gender (Battle-Baptiste 2011; Delle 2000). They approach multiple scales, covering the entire plantation to areas surrounding slave dwellings, to single dwellings (Anderson 2004; Barile 2004; Battle-Baptiste 2010; Fesler 2010; Heath 2010; Heath and Bennett 2000). These studies examine how enslaved African Americans modified and changed the landscape of the household to create places of their own within the restrictive plantation landscape. The scholarship, therefore, investigates the landscape from the perspective of both the enslaver and the enslaved.

This chapter will examine these two forces: the plantation landscape as designed by the plantation owner, and as lived on by African American laborers. It will follow this from slavery to the Civil War and through the end of the nineteenth century, paying particular attention to how mobility was contested on these landscapes.

BACKGROUND

St. Mary's Manor, the name of the plantation home and surrounding acreage inherited by Dr. John Mackall Brome in 1839, occupied the site that was formerly the historic city of St. Mary's. Dr. Brome inherited the property from his stepfather, who had served as his guardian after Brome's father passed away in 1824. Brome immediately began increasing the plantation's acreage and its enslaved labor force. Brome's tenure lasted until his death in 1888. Throughout those almost 50 years, Brome made every effort to maximize his family's prestige and profits, making significant changes to the physical landscape to respond to the different challenges facing his plantation, the most dramatic being the transition following the Civil War.

Similarly, the enslaved African American community used creativity and perseverance to navigate the landscape of bondage and, following Emancipation, a landscape of Jim Crow to build their own homes and communities. Their population grew during Brome's tenure, reaching 65 individuals at some point during the Civil War. Following the war, African Americans living on the plantation leveraged their newfound freedom to navigate the changing economic landscape, and to create spaces on and off the plantation where they could build families and establish independent communities. The oldest surviving nineteenth-century photograph of the African American homes on the Brome Plantation dates to ca. 1890 and is seen in figure 14.1. It shows a single and duplex quarter that stood not far from Brome's house. Both Brome's home and the duplex quarter still exist today, although they were relocated in 1994.

HSMC archaeologists have collected a large volume of evidence about the nineteenth-century plantation. The Mattapany Path Road System Reconstruction Project was conducted in collaboration between HSMC and the State Highway Administration (SHA), and identified all the cultural resources within the 33-acre study area using Phase I controlled surface collection and shovel test pits (STP), and 90 Phase II 5 ft. by 5 ft. excavation squares

Figure 14.1. The double and single quarters of the Brome Plantation, ca. 1890 (Photograph from Howard Family Archives, courtesy of HSMC.)

(Miller et al. 2006). The project identified 63 archaeological site components, many of which related to the nineteenth-century plantation landscape and serve as the primary archaeological data set for this study (Miller et al. 2006).

Two slave and tenant dwellings were the subject of intensive excavations. Located along the St. Mary's River, the duplex quarter was moved in 1994, necessitating excavations along the building's interior and exterior walls. More excavations were conducted directly north of the duplex, where historical photographs identified a single room dwelling (see figure 14.1). Excavations from 1998 to 2003 revealed the remains of this dwelling, along with the remains of a seventeenth-century print shop beneath the dwelling. The foundation of the single quarter is shown in figure 14.2. The excavations also included a stratified, random sample fraction of 5 percent, resulting in 60 excavation units across the entire study area associated with these quarters (Riordan and Hurry 2015).

Mobility during Enslavement

Restricting the mobility of enslaved laborers ensured that enslavers like Brome could control their enslaved property. Similarly, enslaved laborers used different tactics to access family, goods, and information in spite of the

Figure 14.2. Archaeological excavations of the single quarter of the Brome Plantation, 2003. The quarter was supported by a shallow brick foundation, with a brick chimney on one gable and a brick-lined storage pit in front of the fireplace. (Figure by Henry M. Miller, courtesy of HSMC.)

restrictive context of their bondage. This negotiation is evident in the organization of the plantation landscape at St. Mary's Manor.

By 1860, this landscape had taken its full shape, a product of Brome's efforts to maximize his profits on the plantation. It consisted of three components: the Brome domestic household featuring his new manor home and outbuildings; a row of six enslaved African American dwellings; and the agricultural complex (Ranzetta 2010; Bureau of the Census 1860b; Brock 2014). His enslaved population had increased from 30 in 1840 to 42 in 1850 to 58 in 1860, and 59 during the Civil War, in addition to the six individuals owned by his mother, Ann Ashcom (Bureau of the Census 1840, 1850b, 1860b). His property value also increased from $10,000 in 1840 to $50,000 in 1860 (Bureau of the Census 1840, 1860a). Brome's fluctuations in labor, land, and property value corresponded to common agricultural practice in southern Maryland that relied on wheat as the staple crop and planting tobacco when it was in market demand (Marks 1979; Brock 2014).

Brome was a commanding force in the local community, reflected by his position on the Board of Trustees at the St. Mary's Female Seminary, his membership of the vestry at Trinity Church, and his construction of Brome's

Wharf (Fausz 1990; Neuwirth 1997). His physical association with the founding of St. Mary's City was important to his prestige (Brock 2013, 2014), an association his contemporaries had also established for St. Mary's County (King 2012).

Brome's position as an enslaver of African Americans was part of his elite social status. Controlling their mobility was one way he maintained his power over them. Brome used three tactics to do this: participating in the slave trade, designing a plantation that emphasized surveillance and racial separation, and relying on institutionalized slavery to ensure his property was protected off the plantation.

There are no direct records of sale that detail specific instances where Brome sold or purchased slaves. However, examining the 1850 and 1860 slave schedules and the 1867 list of lost enslaved property shows that he participated in the trade (Bureau of the Census 1850b, 1860b; Dent 1869:300–302). During these 25 years, he increased his enslaved labor force by 29 people, and comparative analysis shows that this increase was focused on purchasing women of child-rearing age and acquiring young men who could work in the fields for brief periods of time when additional labor was needed to harvest tobacco (Brock 2014).

The slave trade was the ultimate form of mobility control. Brome was able to choose the location where enslaved African Americans lived and to dramatically alter families and communities on the plantation. Even when enslavers did not sell their laborers, the threat of sale was a means to control behavior. The nature of slavery meant that African American property was tied to specific locations, meaning families were often divided across the landscape, either through sale, or by abroad marriages where spouses were enslaved on different plantations, sometimes at great distances (Nesbit 2011). These families were plentiful on Brome's plantation, shown by comparing the 1867 list to the 1870 census. In this case, a number of family members appeared in 1870 who were absent from families in 1867, indicating that they were separated by the slave trade or abroad marriage prior to the Civil War.

Brome's physical organization of the plantation's built environment also controlled mobility by separating white and black spaces, and constantly surveilling black spaces. Brome's design of the plantation reflected the social hierarchy, placing his home in a prominent location overlooking the river, and the quarters in a subservient position along a ravine (see figure 14.3A). This was standard practice in most plantation layouts (LaRoche 2013; Upton 1984; Lewis 1985; Delle 1999). It divided white and black spaces and ensured that the slave dwellings, the agricultural complex, and the people who lived and worked in those spaces were visible from the Bromes' home. Even

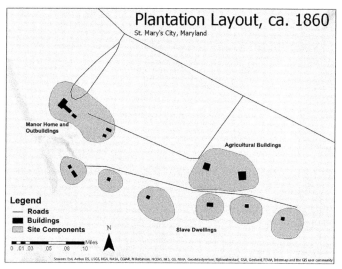

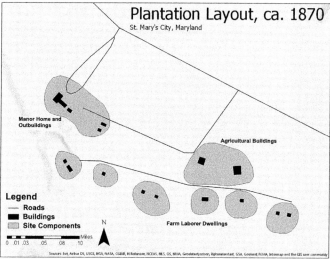

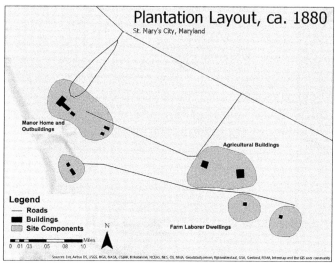

Figure 14.3. Maps of the buildings on the Brome Plantation through time. These cover three decades (1860, 1870, and 1880) and span the transition from slavery to freedom. They are based upon archaeological and documentary data. (Maps by Terry Peterkin Brock.)

though it might not have deterred resistance or covert activities, the proximity and line-of-sight from the Brome home ensured that any acts of resistance were done in secret and with extreme caution. Mention of a "manager" on the 1850 census suggests Brome may have also employed an overseer at some point, furthering his control over his enslaved laborers (Bureau of the Census 1850a).

Off the plantation, Brome relied on federal and state government support of slavery to protect his interests. When he permitted enslaved laborers to leave the plantation, it was the broader slave society that protected his property and limited the possibility that they might escape. Newspapers were one means by which Brome's interests were assured. In addition to communicating the opinions of slave owners and the politics of slavery, newspapers advertised runaway property between slave owners. Brome used the local newspaper at least once to advertise a runaway slave, putting an advertisement for William Washington Whalton in the paper on July 4, 1861 (*St. Mary's Beacon*). During the Civil War, Whalton was identified as present on the plantation, so he was either captured or returned on his own (Dent 1869:300–302). This shows how critical the newspaper was in controlling the mobility of enslaved African Americans: even when they did escape the boundaries of the plantation, slave owners used this communication tool to return them.

The enslaved community did not have many ways to exercise mobility within this controlled landscape. In practice, the strategies they used focused on reusing or exploiting the spaces to which they already had access and redefining them as places of their own. Counteracting the effects of the slave trade required the community to rely on other bonds in addition to familial ties to ensure survival. Archaeological analysis of the double quarter and single quarter indicates that these three dwelling spaces likely operated as a single household. Distributional data of ceramics suggest a shared swept yard between the two buildings, and shared refuse areas in the rear of the structures (Brock 2014). This is to be expected, because households were not defined by nuclear families with each living in a separate space. Households had to be flexible to compensate for the loss of individuals who were sold and accommodate the arrival of new members of the household. Children without parents on the plantation would need to be cared for or looked after by members of the community. This type of flexibility within the household structure was a necessary system to ensure survival on the plantation, particularly with Brome's participation in the slave trade.

The community accessed the river to supplement their diet and their income. Historians have noted that enslaved African Americans who lived near ferry stops or college campuses would often peddle goods and food to travelers or students (Penningroth 2003). The enslaved community at St. Mary's Manor had access to both these populations. The archaeological dis-covery of a mid-nineteenth-century homemade wooden skiff on the bank of the river just below the slave quarters suggests that African Americans living on the plantation accessed the river to collect crabs, oysters, and fish (Embrey 1999), and this would not have been unusual for enslaved laborers in Maryland (Douglass 1845; Twitty 2009). While faunal material is difficult to analyze at the slave quarter sites due to plowed contexts and the earlier long-term occupation of the site associated with the seventeenth-century print shop and residence, sealed contexts indicate that fish, oysters, and crabs were acquired by nineteenth-century inhabitants at the site (Brock 2014). Using natural resources improved the lives of the enslaved community in small but significant ways, providing modest incomes to engage in local economies. This allowed enslaved African Americans to purchase goods to decorate their homes and bodies, and to gain small pieces of freedom within the landscape of bondage.

William Whalton's escape attempt on Independence Day in 1861 is the only documented example of overt resistance at St. Mary's Manor. Most en-slaved laborers relied on smaller gestures to evoke the possibility of freedom. A pierced Spanish real, found in the single quarter, suggests how the yearn-ing for freedom may have been exercised in symbolic form (figure 14.4). The coin was pierced through its center, directly through the word *"Libertad"* on the liberty cap. This cap is of particular significance due to its classical association with freed slaves. By the 1850s, it was a symbol associated with the abolitionist movement, so much so that Jefferson Davis, in 1854, was op-posed to it being used on the Statue of Freedom that adorns the dome of the United States Capitol (Harden 1995; Scott 1995; Fischer 2005; Pasch 2020). The presence of this iconography on a possession of an enslaved African American, and the direct piercing of this portion of the coin, suggests an understanding of this meaning. A starburst behind the cap is also potentially symbolic. Recent scholarship has suggested that the celestial landscape is part of the social landscape (Sikes 2008). For African Americans, the iconog-raphy of the North Star was a symbol of freedom because it was the direc-tional guide for escaping enslaved individuals (Samford 2018). A starburst, therefore, may have represented the desire of this individual for freedom, despite the conditions of bondage that restricted their movement each day. In other cases, objects reflected the reality of restricted mobility and forced separation during slavery. A thimble, possibly a gift between a separated husband and wife, with the words "forget me not" indicates the importance

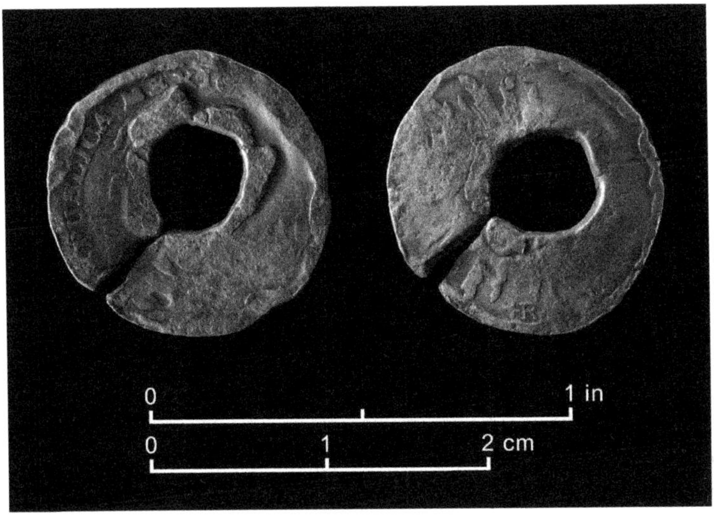

Figure 14.4. A Mexican Liberty real dated 1858, found in the single quarter. The coin was pierced directly through the word *Libertad* on the cap, perhaps suggesting a hidden yearning for liberty harbored by the enslaved individual who carried the coin. (Photograph by Donald L. Winter, courtesy of HSMC.)

of memory and remembering to people who had been forcibly separated through the slave trade.

THE CIVIL WAR

The opportunity for freedom came with the beginning of the Civil War. While St. Mary's County never saw military action, it was on the border of Virginia and was a primary location for smuggling. Therefore, the United States Army and Navy were present at various times throughout the war (Davidson 2000; Hammett 1977). This military presence directly impacted the institution of slavery in St. Mary's County and Brome's plantation in a variety of ways. Some evidence suggests that Brome, a Confederate sympathizer, allowed his land to be used for smuggling. The most direct record of this is the Union forces' destruction of his wharf, a tactic often used at places suspected of smuggling (*St. Mary's Beacon* 1874).

The regular presence of Union troops in St. Mary's County was the crack in the institution of slavery necessary for the enslaved community to resist more overtly. The Union Army arrested the editor and shut down the *St. Mary's Beacon*, closing the primary communication tool of the slaveholding elite. Union marches through the county and the arresting of Confederate sympathizers meant some enslaved laborers' owners were in prison

(Hammett 1977). Later in the war, when enslaved African Americans in the north could enlist in the US Colored Troops (USCT), many took the opportunity. Others were emboldened by the presence of African American troops and escaped to Point Lookout Prison on the southern tip of St. Mary's County, the fueling station on St. Inigoes Creek, or to the regularly patrolling ships of the Potomac flotilla (Davidson 2000).

This was the case on the landscape of St. Mary's Manor, and is demonstrated best through an 1867 document Brome submitted to the Maryland government in 1868 that lists first and last names, ages, and genders of each person enslaved on his property during the war (Dent 1869:300–302). It also notes the date and method by which the individual gained their freedom: left with military, enlisted, or freed by the state. Fourteen individuals left with the military, and two enlisted, representing a total of 30 percent of his enslaved property. This suggests the weakening hegemony of Brome and his fellow slave owners.

A deeper look into the historical documents and archaeology shows how invasive the Union forces were at St. Mary's. USCT recruiting parties, led by a white officer but otherwise comprising African Americans, were present at St. Mary's Manor. Two of Brome's slaves, Alexander Gough and William Gross, were recruited at two different times into the 38th USCT. Gross is documented in his Pension Records as saying he was recruited directly "out of the fields," indicating the parties visited the plantation (Department of Veteran Affairs 1910). While recruiting had to happen with Brome's permission, the fact that it happened at all is an indication of the limited power slaveholders had in St. Mary's County.

Archaeological evidence shows the presence of Union forces on Brome's property. One marine and two naval officer buttons were found near the manor home, in addition to a Union musket barrel band, a fragment of a cartridge box belt plate, a brass vent pick, and a pewter canteen spout. Considering Brome's local prominence and position on the water, it is no surprise that he was frequently visited by naval officers. Two additional buttons, one belonging to a member of the Artillery and another to a Dragoon, were found at the quarter. While it is possible that some of the buttons were part of uniforms later salvaged by post-Emancipation occupants of the site, the documented presence of Union forces at Brome's plantation and the diversity of accoutrements represented in the archaeological record strongly suggest that these artifacts belonged to troops who visited the plantation during their recruiting trips.

The presence of Union forces in St. Mary's County contributed significantly to the withering of Brome's power over his enslaved laborers. Brome maintained what control he could, but in the end was unable to restrict the mobility of his laborers. The fact that 30 percent of the enslaved population left suggests that each member of Brome's community had the option to leave in front of them: some chose to take it, and some chose to remain in their homes with their families. Nonetheless, the Civil War made the option to leave available and soon changed the entire way African Americans and white planters would negotiate the landscape. African Americans in Maryland were freed by a change to the state's constitution in 1864.

AFTER THE WAR

The end of the Civil War, alterations to Maryland's constitution, and the establishment of the 13th, 14th, and 15th amendments permanently changed the relationship between St. Mary's County planters and African American laborers. Freedom from bondage meant that African Americans could negotiate for more agreeable terms and could use their feet to leave situations that were untenable. Former enslavers responded in a variety of ways. Some in Southern Maryland attempted to use apprenticeship as a means of re-enslaving African American children, although this practice was rapidly ended by the courts. For others, this negotiation occurred on the plantation landscape.

This is evident at Brome's plantation, where he invested in agricultural labor to reinvigorate his profits immediately following the war. Brome placed 800 acres under improvement in 1870, more than ever before. He also spent $3,400 on labor, a cost that included housing, suggesting a new economic relationship between the Bromes and African American laborers (Bureau of the Census 1870a). If this reflects a wage labor system, it indicates that Brome was not engaging in the more exploitative systems such as sharecropping or tenant farming. Brome was not only competing for laborers with other planters, but was also attempting to stem African Americans' urge to migrate north to urban areas. Adopting a wage labor system was one of a number of different ways Brome attempted to make his plantation more appealing.

New family-sized houses are evident in the 1870 census and in the archaeological evidence. This was another accommodation made by Brome so that families could live in separate dwellings (see figure 14.3B). The 1870 census indicates nine dwellings on the landscape (Bureau of the Census 1870b). Likely many of them were reused slave dwellings, such as the single and double quarters, but some were new additions. The reunification of families was a critical part of the postwar experience for African Americans, and having a place for them to live was a part of this process. The 1870 census shows this was the case for laborers at St. Mary's City. Aside from one half of a duplex, which housed a number of single men, each dwelling was home to one family. A number of family names belonged to previously enslaved families, but with notable differences: the addition of spouses and children that were not listed on the 1867 list. Clearly, these families had been reunified and brought under one roof following the war (Bureau of the Census 1870b).

This was not the only concession Brome made. The archaeological and architectural evidence, for example, demonstrates that African Americans were able to make improvements on their homes. The thickness of window glass fragments found around the single dwelling, which correlates to time (Weiland 2009), shows that the glass was added in the late 1860s. Architectural analysis suggests that wooden floors were also added to the double quarter. These actions indicate that African Americans were making improvements to their homes that may have not been allowed when they were enslaved, and is a pattern that has been identified throughout St. Mary's County (McDaniel 1982).

The final example of negotiations occurring at St. Mary's was Brome's donation of a half acre in 1867 for the construction of an African American schoolhouse (St. Mary's County Circuit Court 1867). Next to family reunification, earning an education was one of the most pressing needs of African Americans in St. Mary's County (Unified Committee for Afro-American Contributions 2006). This was likely an urge Brome understood, considering his commitment to education as a trustee for the neighboring Female Seminary. However, the construction of these schoolhouses was largely due to the enthusiasm of the African American community, as made clear by the Freedman's Bureau Supervisor of Education, John Kimball (Kimball 1868). In addition to providing an opportunity for education, Brome donating the land for an African American schoolhouse made his property highly sought after, and likely attracted and retained African American families.

The immediate post-Emancipation landscape, therefore, reflected what was happening across the country, but in a slightly different manner. Brome made efforts to reestablish a landscape that was reminiscent of the period of enslaved labor, with large populations of African Americans doing agricultural labor, but he made concessions by providing housing and other accommodations such as access to schooling. African Americans were able to negotiate for better living conditions because they were able to leave unsatisfactory situations. This is not to suggest these systems pulled African Americans out of poverty, but leveraging their mobility did afford them new opportunities.

The 1870s marked another transition for the Brome family and the laborers who worked his plantation, which was visible on the built landscape,

particularly the dwellings. While Brome did increase the value of his plantation through a wage labor system, he continued to explore new avenues and
opportunities for investment—investments that focused less on controlling
black families and more on becoming less reliant upon their labor. One notable event was Brome's founding of the St. Inigoes chapter of the Grange in
1874 (Neuwirth 1997). This organization was developed following the Civil
War to introduce modernized agricultural methods, a need felt by many
former slave owners following the Civil War (Ayers 1992). Brome took the
things he learned from this organization and put them into practice, reduc-
ing his dependence on labor and agricultural output, and further diversify-
ing his investments.

This shift was reflected both in the 1880 agricultural census and in the
changing landscape. The census shows a reduction to only 275 improved
acres and an increase in the amount of money made from cattle and dairy
products. Of particular note is the increased value of his plantation machin-
ery, rising from $500 to $2,000, reflecting his investment in more modern
agricultural methods (Bureau of the Census 1880a). Brome also invested
heavily in county-level efforts to bring a railroad to St. Mary's City. This
would have helped farmers export food to urban areas such as Washington, D.C., similar to developments on Maryland's Eastern Shore at this time.
Brome gave land and money to the cause, going so far as to grade a portion
of the landscape for the terminus of the railroad. However, the investment
never came to fruition, and it eventually caused his bankruptcy.

By 1880 only two African American families are listed on the census as
living on the property (Bureau of the Census 1880b) (see figure 14.3C). One
family was listed at the site of the double quarter, which was inhabited until
the 1960s. The archaeological survey suggests that the second family's home
was near the agricultural buildings. The other buildings from the 1870 census
had disappeared from the landscape entirely, a fact validated by a reanalysis
of the Mattapany survey (Brock 2014). The year 1880 also marked the first
time a white family was listed as living on the property serving as both farm
laborers, and one person as a teacher for the group of cousins and relatives
that were living in Brome's home at the time (Bureau of the Census 1880b).

The smaller numbers of black families on the plantation landscape were
not entirely attributable to Brome's changing agricultural philosophy. They
also reflected simultaneous efforts by African American families to move off
plantations to form their own communities. In St. Mary's County, small African American towns emerged, centered around African American schools
and churches (Unified Committee for Afro-American Contributions 2006).
Freedom of mobility meant the opportunity to create greater separation

through new community institutions and purchasing of land. The formation of these communities changed the landscape of the county in significant ways. Many of the people who lived on Brome's property in 1870 are found in these communities in 1880 (Brock 2014).

Others chose to leave St. Mary's County. The two men who enlisted in the USCT were in Baltimore by 1880, relocating to join their fellow USCT veterans who lived in Baltimore following the war. Alexander Gough married a woman from St. Mary's County, and they were living in Baltimore with her two younger sisters. By 1900, the sisters had left, but her youngest brother was living with them (Bureau of the Census 1900). Mobility and family were intimately tied: family members were staying with relatives to get situated and build a community base. Using family was an important strategy for those seeking new opportunities in urban environments where communities of color were more prevalent and, in the case of Baltimore, better established.

Creating separate community spaces was critical for the survival of African Americans during the Jim Crow era. Building community, and establishing institutions such as schools, churches, burial societies, and businesses, ensured that African Americans were cared for, something that was not a guarantee elsewhere (Unified Committee for Afro-American Contributions 2006). The cultural landscape of the late nineteenth century was one where most African Americans became endangered as a new social system developed, ultimately resulting in Jim Crow laws, legalized racial segregation, and the threat of racial violence. While this constricted their ability to move across the landscape, they used the freedoms they did have to create separation between their own communities and white communities, and leveraged their proximity to major urban centers to migrate further north. They relied heavily on black institutions to provide protection and support. Building towns that consisted of churches and black-owned businesses was important to shield and protect members of the community.

PIECING TOGETHER THE TRANSITION FROM ENSLAVEMENT TO FREEDOM

Brome consistently used the landscape to ensure profitability and prestige by controlling black mobility on the plantation. During the 1840s and '50s, he shaped the landscape to reflect a contemporary, elite plantation home and agricultural complex. The landscape arrangement of the house and slave quarters followed patterning that was typical of other plantation estates. The landscape, and his participation in the slave trade, ensured that he controlled the mobility of African Americans. This control weakened during the Civil

War and is reflected in the number of African Americans who escaped from his plantation. However, immediately following Emancipation, Brome faced new challenges. Like all former slave owners, he had to recoup his financial losses from the Civil War and figure out how to renegotiate his economic relationship with African Americans whom he formerly enslaved. He had additional challenges due to the proximity of urban centers such as Baltimore and Washington, D.C., which African Americans eyed as places of opportunity. Therefore, Brome made significant accommodations, such as adopting a wage labor system, building a schoolhouse, and allowing laborers to make modifications to their homes. This ensured that a large number of families chose his plantation on which to live and work in the immediate years following the war and allowed him to recoup his losses and maintain a place among the county elite. By the 1880s, Brome began to adopt new agricultural methods and diversification to reduce his reliance on farm laborers. This effort was due in part to agricultural struggles being faced by Southern Marylanders, whose reliance on staple crop agriculture was being challenged by Midwestern farmers. In 1880, Brome had two African American families working on his plantation.

For African Americans, the exercise of mobility was critical to surviving within a racist society. During slavery, they had minimal opportunity to move about the landscape, although members of the enslaved community navigated these spaces to maintain relationships and marriages, pass information, and escape their bondage. The Civil War provided new opportunities for African Americans to navigate the landscape, and they took advantage by running away or enlisting in the USCT. Following Emancipation, the freedom to move across the landscape became essential to their ability to reunite families and improve their living conditions. This mobility became their primary negotiating tactic, forcing planters such as Brome to make broader accommodations to stem migration. When Reconstruction ended and Jim Crow laws became more prevalent, mobility became a critical means for African American families to build independent communities, in both rural and urban contexts. This afforded more security in an increasingly segregated and violent atmosphere that existed during this period.

Of course, the process of separation reflected the movement of national and local legislation. Segregation policies throughout the southern states reflected the continued efforts made by white Americans to control access to public spaces of African Americans. These policies ensured that blacks had limited access to quality education, living conditions, and other services. Creating separate institutions, be they towns, churches, schools, or businesses, provided alternatives for black communities. Such segregated spaces were even visible on the twentieth-century landscape at St. Mary's. Emma Hall, who grew up in the 1930s in the lone surviving double quarter, noted that there were separate entrances to the property that were accessed by the white descendants of John Brome and by her African American family (Henry M. Miller 2019, pers. comm.). Policies of segregation shaped the landscape of St. Mary's County on multiple scales throughout the county, in ways that are still visible today.

Examining how space and mobility is negotiated by both white and black families before, during, and after the Civil War shows how elite white families in Southern Maryland controlled landscapes to maintain power and control. It also shows how black families leveraged these contexts to carve out places of survival where they could build communities and maintain families despite the racism that surrounded them, or to migrate north to urban areas such as Baltimore, a process made possible only by their increased mobility and their proximity to these urban places that many African Americans in the Deep South did not have. Examining the actions of individuals and communities in Southern Maryland, therefore, demonstrates how mobility is a critical element in the way that whites and blacks negotiated power and control during and after slavery.

15

"Establish on that sacred spot a female seminary"

Archaeology of St. Mary's Female Seminary

MICHELLE SIVILICH, TRAVIS G. PARNO,
RUTH M. MITCHELL, AND DONALD L. WINTER

In the preamble to an 1840 law establishing a lottery to fund the creation of St. Mary's Female Seminary, the Maryland legislature commented that "the people of Maryland, and more especially the citizens of St. Mary's county, actuated by that delicate sensibility which prompts man to adorn and scatter flowers around the tombs of departed relatives and friends, desire to establish on that sacred spot a female seminary" (State of Maryland 1840:chapter 190). Six years later, following a successful fundraising campaign, the seminary opened, beginning a tradition of education that continues to this day. Although the early years of the seminary were marked with financial struggles and administrative challenges, the institution survived, transforming from a small women's secondary school into a four-year, coed college.

St. Mary's Female Seminary (today, St. Mary's College of Maryland) was founded as a monument to Maryland's first capital, meaning that it currently lies within the St. Mary's City National Historic Landmark (NHL). As a modern institute of higher education, St. Mary's College is driven to expand and improve their facilities to attract the next generation of students. This goal can, at times, result in impacts on cultural resources within the NHL, impacts which require archaeological mitigation. One such project occurred in 1997, prior to the installation of a utility corridor adjacent to Calvert Hall, the first building constructed as part of the seminary in the early 1840s. A mere four excavation units yielded more than 20,000 artifacts dating to the late nineteenth and early twentieth centuries. This chapter reviews the history of the school and analyzes the artifacts recovered from the 1997 excavations, in concert with the institution's documentary record, to explore what we can learn about life at the seminary at the turn of the century.

HISTORICAL OVERVIEW OF THE SEMINARY

In 1839, Colonel William R. Coad, Colonel James T. Blackistone, and Dr. Joseph F. Shaw began campaigning to create a secondary school for girls on the site of St. Mary's City as a living monument to the state's first capital. It was the first and only school designated for such a purpose. The school was further distinguished by virtue of the fact that it was nonsectarian and that one of the founders' goals was to make the institution affordable to its students. This would prove difficult initially because the State of Maryland was mired in an economic depression. But despite these difficulties, Governor William Grasan signed a law on March 21, 1840, allowing the school to be built. A lottery was held to raise the $30,000 required. A six-acre plot of Trinity Church land was purchased from the Vestry of William and Mary Parish. By 1845, the two-story seminary building was complete and the school was officially opened in October 1846 (Fausz 1990:29–37).

The seminary's early years were rocky, to say the least. Administrative infighting, teacher shortages, and financial woes during the 1840s and 1850s nearly scuttled the institution. The school was closed for three academic years in the mid-1850s, and after it was revived by renewed state support, it took time to rekindle belief in the institution's well-being among Marylanders. Enrollment continued to struggle, and as the nation was plunged into civil war, it seemed the school was doomed. Records are largely silent on the seminary's operation during the Civil War, although signatures inside two of the school's textbooks suggest that classes met in some capacity, however limited (Fausz 1990:44). Following the war, however, the Maryland General Assembly passed a series of legislation that allocated additional funds to the school, which allowed it to stabilize.

The school offered a nonsectarian, liberal arts secondary education at little to no cost. At the time of its opening, there were fewer than ten female students and three faculty members. Accommodations were sparse: furniture was minimal, the bedrooms lacked chests of drawers, and the girls had to store their clothes in the attic. The kitchen and dining area was located in the basement, which was heated via a fireplace. Other campus buildings included a bath house, storage sheds, a wash house, an ice house, and a stable (Fausz 1990:37). Despite the spare facilities, the seminary was highly thought of, at least locally. In 1867, the *St. Mary's Beacon* advertised that the seminary was able to enroll six students free of tuition fees (*St. Mary's Beacon* 1867).

Four years later, an editorial in the same newspaper declared that "there is no school in the State better managed than this Seminary . . . the course of study is very thorough and embraces all the branches which are taught in first-class academies" (*St. Mary's Beacon* 1871).

It cannot be overstated that during this period, and for many years afterward, St. Mary's City was a remote location. The road network was extremely rudimentary; steamboats provided the primary means of transportation to and from the seminary. As a result, the school's student population was composed almost entirely of boarders. Beyond Trinity Church, a wharf owned by local plantation owner Dr. James Brome, and the seminary itself, facilities and infrastructure were limited.

Archival records offer insight into how the students and teachers lived and what they owned, facts that would be useful when examining the archaeological record. Early records were sparse. By the 1880s the school was already aging and in need of constant repairs. The archives are replete with requests to remove old furniture and repair the heating system. There was also a mention of purchasing a piano, which suggests that despite needing repairs, the school was maintaining enrollment enough to warrant such a purchase. By the end of the 1880s, there was an effort to start recording the school's history, and investments made in a railroad company hint at a time of financial security and prosperity. Of interest archaeologically was that the riverbank was newly terraced and a new well was built during this period. In the 1890s, there are records of repairing a previously unmentioned carriage house, along with the stable, indicating the construction of new buildings on school property. Money for an annex was raised successfully, and when the addition was finished after the turn of the twentieth century, it was called Music Hall (now St. Mary's Hall). In 1903, an inspector found that the seminary's waste disposal system was unsatisfactory and suggested a system of "filtration and fire" (Fausz 1990:55). Thus it appears that in the early twentieth century the seminary changed its disposal methods and built an incinerator. In 1910, school officials commissioned the installation of acetylene gas lighting, replacing the existing whale oil fixtures (Fausz 1990:52).

Improvements were expensive and while the seminary was experiencing a period of stability in terms of administration and enrollment, its facilities remained a work in progress. In a 1913 report to the Maryland Board of State Aid and Charities, the Board's Secretary, William H. Davenport, wrote that "most of the equipment in the class rooms is very inadequate . . . the Recitation Rooms are also lacking maps, pictures and other paraphernalia for properly teaching . . . The furniture is fairly adequate but is exceedingly miscellaneous in character, there being hardly a complete set of furniture in any room . . . The girls are obliged to hang their dresses and suits on racks or nails in the walls without any protection from dust or sunlight" (Fausz 1990:55). The report contained recommended improvements and alterations designed to bring both the facilities and curriculum into alignment with the broader state system.

In 1924, tragedy struck when the 80-year-old Calvert Hall and its annex caught fire. John Whitmore, an eyewitness to the fire, described how "the typical St. Mary's County emergency plan" of phoning the only telephone operator at the local Great Mills exchange brought carloads of area residents to help salvage furniture, school records, and even bags of mail from the nearby post office (Whitmore 1979:2). Unfortunately, Calvert Hall could not be saved. Temporary housing referred to in records as the "Barracks" was erected for the students. Maryland citizens supported the cause of funding the rebuilding of the seminary, rallying around its status as a monument to the state's beginnings (Fausz 1990:66). The Barracks were in use at least until 1925 when Calvert Hall was rebuilt.

By 1926, the seminary added junior college courses to its curriculum, and to reflect this change, it soon came to be known as the St. Mary's Female Seminary–Junior College. The 1926 College Catalog, which included a list of required supplies that students were to bring with them upon enrollment, offers a useful glimpse into the material culture of student life (St. Mary's Female Seminary–Junior College 1926):

> Each pupil is required to provide the following: three sheets and a pair of blankets for a single bed, a colored couch cover, three pillow cases, 42 x 36, eight towels, a bureau scarf; six medium sized table napkins, a silver plaited knife, fork, teaspoon, soup or dessert spoon, and a napkin ring; a tumbler for the room; two laundry bags, hot water bag, over-shoes, umbrella, sweater; black bloomers, three white middies, black lisle stockings, and high white tennis shoes—the regulation Physical Education Costume. A small rug and window draperies will add to the comfort and attractiveness of the room.

The school continued to grow, and on March 21, 1941 (101 years to the day of the schools' founding), an $85,000 Gymnasium and Recreation Building was dedicated. Today this building is known as Kent Hall. As it navigated the postwar period, the seminary's leadership sought accreditation as a four-year college, recognition that would come in the late 1960s. A series of capital improvements, along with a name change to St. Mary's College of Maryland and the move to accept students of all genders, helped usher the institution into a new era of growth and prominence.

ARCHAEOLOGICAL INVESTIGATIONS

In 1997, St. Mary's College of Maryland staff determined that a new utility corridor needed to be installed on the east side of Calvert Hall. Archaeologists from Historic St. Mary's City (HSMC) performed limited excavations to mitigate the impact of the proposed corridor. A shovel test survey conducted near Calvert Hall in the previous year had identified a thick coal midden that contained artifacts dating to the nineteenth and twentieth centuries (Miller and Mitchell 1996). To learn more about the area that would be disturbed

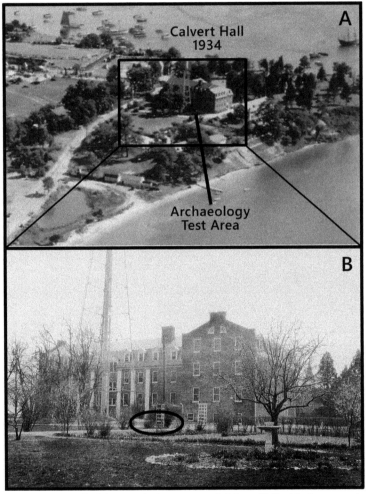

Figure 15.1. Aerial of the Female Seminary and Calvert Hall with the excavation area indicated. *A*, Aerial photograph from 1934. (Courtesy of HSMC.) *B*, View of the rear yard of Calvert Hall in 1931. (Image courtesy of St. Mary's College of Maryland Archives, P1931_0006b.)

by the utility installation, HSMC archaeologists excavated four 5×5-foot units in the area of impact. These excavations encountered the thick coal deposit, along with a high density of artifacts dating to the period spanning 1880–1940. The artifact assemblage from the coal deposit is reflective of an institutional setting. Figure 15.1 shows Calvert Hall in the 1930s and the area in which the test excavations were conducted. While archival records are not always complete and often do not provide information about mundane, everyday activities, archaeological data can be used to tell a richer story.

The primary artifact assemblage recovered from the coal midden offers a window into college life at the turn of the twentieth century. From the four excavation units, five proveniences were linked to the coal deposit. A total of 21,843 artifacts were found in the proveniences. While this is a significant quantity of material for five layers, roughly half of the assemblage ($n = 11,127$) consisted of fragments of unburned coal and coal slag (an additional 49.75 kg of coal was measured and discarded in the field). Faunal remains ($n = 3,332$), including oyster shell, composed the next most common type, followed by architectural materials ($n = 2,837$), including window glass, brick, tile, masonry, and other rubble. Glass artifacts ($n = 2,019$) were the next most common artifact type. Iron nails ($n = 1,405$) were next, followed by ceramics ($n = 658$), non-nail metal artifacts ($n = 345$), and lithics ($n = 29$). A subset of 84 artifacts was grouped into an "Other" type, which included floral, fossil, charcoal, and composite materials.

A minimum vessel count was completed for all ceramic and glass artifacts by isolating all the distinct rim, base, and body sherds (for more on the importance of vesselization, see chapters 5 and 13). Cross mends were identified, and individual vessels were hypothesized based on fragments of similar shape, color, and form. A full description was recorded for each vessel on individual vessel recording forms and assigned a unique number based on the provenience of the most representative sherd of the vessel.

Artifact Analysis

Ceramics

Based on a minimum vessel estimate, it was determined that there were 68 vessels present in the five coal midden contexts excavated (see table 15.1). The identifiable vessel forms included plates, saucers, small dishes, cups, and bowls. Fragments of what appear to be a tray were also found. These latter sherds were thin, suggesting that the tray was more likely a personal item and not related to food service. Therefore, they are not included in the minimal vessel tabulation. Several other non-vessel ceramic artifacts were found,

Table 15.1. Ceramic Vessels Recovered from the St. Mary's Female Seminary Excavations

	Plate	UID Hollow	UID Form	Saucer	UID Flat	Large UID Hollow	Cup	Bowl	TOTAL	% of Total
Ironstone	15	11	5	4	2	-	1	-	38	55.88
Whiteware	4	1	5	1	-	-	-	-	11	16.18
Porcelain	1	2	1	1	1	-	1	1	8	11.76
Stoneware	-	-	2	-	-	4	-	-	6	8.82
Yellowware	-	1	-	-	1	-	-	-	2	2.94
Semi-Porcelain	-	-	-	-	1	-	1	-	2	2.94
Earthenware	-	-	1	-	-	-	-	-	1	1.47
TOTAL	20	15	14	6	5	4	3	1	68	99.99
% of Total	29.4	22.06	20.59	8.82	7.35	5.88	4.41	1.47	99.99	

including a pamplin elbow pipe bowl, white clay pipe fragments, Prosser buttons, and a fragment of a porcelain bisque doll.

The different types of ceramics recovered include ironstone, whiteware, stoneware, various earthenwares, porcelain, semivitreous ware, and yellowware (see table 15.1). Ironstone vessels were the most abundant ceramic type recovered, comprising 55.88 percent of the total sherds. The least abundant ware was yellowware, comprising only 1.47 percent of the total vessel assemblage.

In conducting the MNV, there were many cases in which the vessel form could not be identified (20.59% of this assemblage). Another 27.94 percent were unidentified hollow wares and 7.35 percent were unidentified flatwares. Among the forms that could be identified, the most prevalent forms were plates (29.40%) and saucers (8.82%). The smallest categories of vessel forms were cups (5.88%) and bowls (4.41%). Of the flat vessels with measurable rim diameters, most ranged from 5 to 9 inches (i.e., saucers and small plates), with one 11-inch "dinner" plate. Sherds from two different American blue and gray stoneware vessels had measurable rim diameters of 7.5 inches and 9 inches. These were large storage vessels, likely crocks, with painted cobalt decorations.

Of the 68 vessels, 32 were decorated. The most common decoration types were blue and green transfer prints ($n = 5$ of each type). One blue transfer printed whiteware fragment featured the pattern called "Amoy," which was manufactured by Staffordshire firm William Ridgway and Company between 1834 and 1854. The fragment originates from an octagonal footed vegetable dish with a floral swag around the rim and a landscape with chinoiserie houses along a river in the vessel's center (Coysh and Henrywood 1982:302). Another blue transfer print decoration featuring a romantic landscape was identified as the "Lake" pattern by Staffordshire potters Francis Morley, Morley & Ashworth, and G.L. Ashworth & Bros. Morley, Ashworth, and various members of each man's family were in business beginning in 1836 and continuing into the early twentieth century (Larsen 1939:182–183). Three vessels made in two different flatware styles featured a green transfer-printed pattern that was used by New Jersey manufacturer Mercer Pottery Company and its subsequent permutations (including the International Pottery Co.) around the turn of the twentieth century. The pattern was popular from the mid-1890s to about 1920, although the pottery was active from 1868 to 1950 (Barber 1904:57–58). The two vessel form styles were differentiated by their rims: one was scalloped, while the other has a straight rim. The latter pattern has been found during previous surveys conducted throughout the St. Mary's City National Historic Landmark, suggesting it was at least popular locally, if not distributed as part of college-issue service. Other decorative styles found on tableware sherds recovered from the coal deposit included two different pink-edged ironstone vessels and saucers with various molded rim decorations.

Some sherds featured maker's marks that were helpful in dating the coal deposit. The first was the mark of East Liverpool, Ohio, potters Homer Laughlin China Company, which has been in operation since 1877. During the 1890s, the company began production of semivitreous porcelain. In 1914, after opening two new potteries, they started producing semivitreous dinner, hotel, and toilet wares (Gates and Ormerod 1982:126). Another sherd bore the mark of Baltimore potter Edwin Bennett. The mark was used between 1930 and 1936 (Holland 1973:24).

It is notable that of the 658 artifacts in the ceramic assemblage, 95 of them were discolored to a grayish hue, suggesting they had been burned. The 95 artifacts formed 18 vessels which were burnt.

Glass

A total of 2,019 glass sherds were found in proveniences associated with the coal deposit. From this total, 1,319 were bottle glass, 307 were lamp glass, and 209 sherds were table glass. Of the remainder, 91 could not be identified, and 16, curiously, were melted. Roughly 11 percent of the glass assemblage (or 212 sherds) could be vesselized into 76 unique vessels. Individual vessels were determined by sherds with diagnostic features such as measurable necks, closures, bases, manufacture techniques, or decoration. The most common vessel form were bottles ($n = 35$), although tumblers ($n = 22$), table glasses ($n = 11$), fruit jars ($n = 6$), and stemmed vessels ($n = 2$) were also present. There was one of each of the following forms: ink bottle, vial, milk bottle, and unidentified container. Other non-vessel glass artifacts included mirror fragments, three eyeglass lenses, four buttons, one shirt stud, and an electrical insulator.

The glass vessels were found at the site in varying conditions. One complete bottle was found: a 12-sided amber bottle, blown in a vented, three-piece mold. It has an applied, one-part patent lip and is embossed on the shoulder with "KENDALL'S SPAVIN CURE" and on the base with "ENOSBURGH FALLS, VT/10." The bottle held a patent medicine designed to treat joint pain that was produced between 1880 and 1913 (Fike 1987:101). In contrast to the complete Kendall's vessel, a bottle found in 21 separate sherds bore parts of an embossed label that read "SCOTT'S EMULSION\\COD LIVER OIL\\WITH LIME AND SODA." It has a two-piece post bottom mold and a tooled lip, and was manufactured beginning ca. 1899 (Fike 1987:196). Other diagnostic glass vessels include a colorless fruit jar base embossed with a ca. 1921 maker's mark of the Hazel-Atlas Glass Co. Fragments of another embossed bottle bore the label advertising a beef, iron, and wine tonic produced in Baltimore, MD. This may have been a bottle manufactured by Thomas & Thompson, Baltimore apothecaries practicing in the late nineteenth century (an advertisement for Thomas & Thompson's solution can be found in various issues of the Maryland Medical Journal in the 1880s, e.g., *Maryland Medical Journal: Medicine and Surgery* 1887:9). A light aqua bulk ink bottle base sherd embossed with capital letters is probably from a Carters Ink Bottle, most likely a 7.5 oz. container. Several other sherds bore individual letters or partial embossed designs that were too incomplete to be positively sourced to specific products or manufacturers.

Faunal Remains

The faunal assemblage included animal bone (n = 530) and oyster shell (n = 2,802). The bone assemblage was dominated by mammal bone (96.0%) (Miller 2019). The remaining fragments included bird (2.6%), fish (0.8%), and three reptile fragments (0.6%). Of these bones, most were not identifiable beyond class. Only 58 (10.94%) were identifiable to a genus or species level. There are nine cattle bones in the sample, and these came from two individuals. One is a mature animal and the other immature. Rib, vertebra, humerus, scapula, and femur sections are good meat quality elements, while two lower leg bones, a metatarsal, and navicular are less valued cuts, perhaps evidence of soup bones. Swine are the best represented species, with 34 identified elements comprising 3 individuals. However, 22 of the elements are teeth, including canines from a male and a female animal. One is a young animal. Other elements include a radius and tibia from an immature individual and three foot bones. Two sheep or goats are indicated by 12 identifiable elements, 8 of which are teeth. Most of these are deciduous teeth from a lamb while one molar is from a mature individual. Limb bones include a humerus and radius from a lamb.

Other animals identified were a sheepshead fish (one spine), and two carapace fragments of a common box turtle. The turtle is likely an incidental inclusion and not representative of diet. The sheepshead could have been eaten, but with only four fish bones recovered, fish do not seem to have been of much dietary significance. The assemblage includes many oyster shells, however, indicating they were consumed. None of the bird bones are identifiable, but the size of the specimens is within the range of domestic chicken.

With such a small faunal sample, no major conclusions can be drawn. It is clear that domestic species were the source of virtually all meat, with the

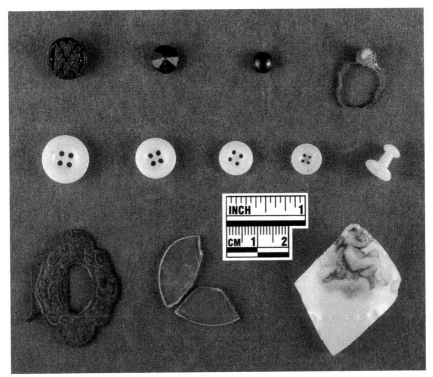

Figure 15.2. Personal items found during the excavations at St. Mary's Female Seminary. The top row includes black buttons and a finger ring with a pearl setting. The second row shows a variety of porcelain buttons and one collar stud. The bottom row contains a brass clothing buckle, a broken lens from a pair of eyeglasses, and a small porcelain vessel decal decorated with a cherub playing a flute. (Photograph by Donald L. Winter, courtesy of HSMC.)

exception of oysters that are well represented by shells. Consumption of both young and mature animals is indicated by the bones, including both lamb and veal. The presence of numerous teeth and some foot elements may indicate that butchery of some animals occurred at or near the seminary. Given the distance of the school from known markets (e.g., Leonardtown), these animals may have been obtained from local farms.

Other Artifact Types

Other objects discovered in the coal deposit included items associated with personal adornment such as buttons, a collar stud, combs, eyeglass lenses, a buckle, a ring, a copper-alloy straight pin, and mirror glass fragments. Some of these artifacts are shown in figure 15.2. Recreational items included parts from a ceramic doll and a clay marble. Evidence of the school's purpose was found in the form of 15 slate pencils. Architectural and furniture artifacts include slate roof fragments, furniture wheels, and tin lamp parts.

The most abundant artifact types included in the assemblage were coal (n = 9,152) and coal slag (n = 1,975). As mentioned above, an additional 49.75 kg of coal and coal slag was weighed and discarded in the field; no distinction was made between unburned coal and coal slag as part of this quantification. Given the intensity with which the coal industry expanded following the extension of the Baltimore and Ohio Railroad to Cumberland, Maryland, in 1842, it is likely that the coal used at the seminary was mined in Maryland (Lacoste and Wall 1989). The coal probably traveled to Baltimore by rail and canal, where it was then shipped to St. Mary's City via coal-fueled steamboats.

Discussion

The artifact assemblage from the Calvert Hall utility mitigation project sheds light on the daily lives of the seminary's residents at the turn of the twentieth century. The presence of the coal deposit suggests that the area behind Calvert Hall was a secondary space, one used for the stockpiling of coal near the basement furnace and discard of furnace leavings (and, occasionally, other refuse). Trash disposal at the institution was fairly rudimentary. In Davenport's 1913 report to the state Board of State Aid and Charities, he wrote that "the present method of disposing of garbage is to dump same in a chute which runs down into the River, where, in summer time . . . a flat boat is always kept anchored and . . . is pushed out into the . . . river and there dumped" (Fausz 1990:55). It seems that the coal-rich furnace waste was not dumped into the river, but was instead piled near the residence hall, where other refuse was occasionally tossed. The burned ceramics and melted glass fragments were likely evidence of objects that had been discarded into the furnace or incinerator, which was subsequently cleaned out and deposited behind Calvert Hall. The primary function of the midden was for stockpiling the coal necessary to heat the large building; the other artifacts that made up the midden assemblage seem to represent the space's secondary function of disposing of furnace leavings and domestic refuse. The majority of the seminary's waste was meant to be dumped into the river, but the midden offered a secondary target for the occasional disposal of dormitory refuse.

With artifacts dating back to the 1880s and a TPQ of 1936 provided by the Edwin Bennett ceramic maker's mark, it seems that the space behind Calvert Hall was in use for some time. An ending point in the late 1930s corresponds closely with the construction of the new gymnasium in 1941, which was built roughly 150 ft. northeast of Calvert Hall. It seems likely that the midden was leveled and covered after the construction of the new facility so that students and faculty would not have to pass it when traveling between the two buildings. Photographs from the period showing the rear of Calvert Hall suggest that college administration had begun the process of beautifying the area before the gymnasium was built (see figure 15.1). With the introduction of flower beds and walking paths by 1931, and a major new building 10 years later, the college gradually transformed the land behind Calvert Hall into a manicured space that would have been marred by a large coal pile and refuse midden.

When examining the artifact assemblage in greater detail, we turn first to Gibb and Beisaw's survey of excavations conducted at 19 primary and secondary schools in operation during the late eighteenth to early twentieth centuries (2000). They grouped the schools into three categories: private academies, rural common schools, and urban public schools. While the institutions differed in location, student demographics, and periods of operation, Gibb and Beisaw noted some similarities among the studies. The majority of each assemblage comprised brick fragments, window glass, and iron nails. Many of the sites showed evidence of architectural remodeling or infrastructural expansion. Gibb and Beisaw also highlighted artifacts related to "lighting, heating, furnishing, or sanitary facilities, issues of considerable concern to students, parents, teachers, local and state school officers, and writers on education" (2000:123). Domestic artifacts tended to be recovered only from school sites that boarded students or faculty.

The Calvert Hall assemblage generally fits with Gibb and Beisaw's observations. Other than coal, architectural materials (including brick, window glass, and nails) were the most frequently recovered artifacts. Objects related to the school's efforts to maintain or improve lighting, heating, and furnishings were seen in abundance. Coal and coal slag spoke to the primary method of heating the institution, and the 307 fragments of lamp glass, along with 19 tin lamp parts, suggested the most common form of lighting prior to (and perhaps, for a time, after) the installation of acetylene lighting in 1910. Glass and ceramic electrical insulators point to additional infrastructural upgrades.

Unlike the majority of the school assemblages reviewed by Gibb and Beisaw, the Calvert Hall materials shed light on the domestic side of seminary residency, particularly when it came to mealtime. Undecorated or molded ironstone vessels made up the majority of the assemblage, with plates appearing most commonly. While the ironstone vessels ostensibly matched in terms of their lack of decoration, it is interesting to note that of the 15 ironstone plates, there were no more than three of the same diameter. Of the whiteware vessels, blue and green transfer-printed patterns were found most frequently, although few vessels bearing the same pattern were identified. These stylistic trends suggest that the school attempted to provide a relatively uniform ceramic service, but that fully matching sets were uncommon. Mismatched, but similar ceramics represented a cost-saving measure, likely one of many to be found during the nineteenth and early twentieth century as the school navigated a series of financial ups and downs (Fausz 1990). Much like the school's furniture that Davenport's 1913 report characterized as "adequate," but "exceedingly miscellaneous in character," the tableware served its purpose without great expense. The one outlier to this observation was the transfer-printed footed vegetable dish, a vessel that is very specialized compared with others in the assemblage. Perhaps the vegetable dish was reserved for special occasions, such as holidays or important gatherings.

Another feature of the seminary ceramic assemblage was a lack of drinking vessels. Here it seems glass vessels were substituted for ceramic. The list of instructions provided in the 1926 College Catalog specifying what students should bring with them included "a tumbler for the room" (St. Mary's Female Seminary–Junior College 1926). The archaeological evidence suggests that this directive was followed closely: 22 tumblers representing a wide range of styles were found in the midden (figure 15.3). It seems that glass tumblers were used in place of ceramic drinking vessels, both in the residents' rooms and also possibly in the primary dining facilities. It might seem curious that no other items from the instructions, such as pieces of silverware, found their way into the midden, but the midden was used for small-scale trash disposal. Broken tumbler fragments would be swept up and discarded, while silverware was more likely to get lost, rather than to break and be intentionally discarded.

The seminary was not the only nineteenth-century institution using lowcost, mismatched tablewares. At the working-class industrial complexes of Lowell, Massachusetts, textile mills employed thousands of single, young women from throughout the region. These women worked side by side in the mills and lived together in nearby boardinghouses. Their workday was a stark contrast to that of the seminary girls; work in the mills was hot, loud, and often dangerous. The structure of their days, however, was quite similar. Both populations comprised young women who worked (in class or at the mills) during the day, ate meals together, and resided in communal housing. Excavations at a boardinghouse at the Boott Mill in Lowell revealed a ceramic assemblage dominated by whiteware, more than one-third of which was undecorated. Where vessels were decorated, colors matched while

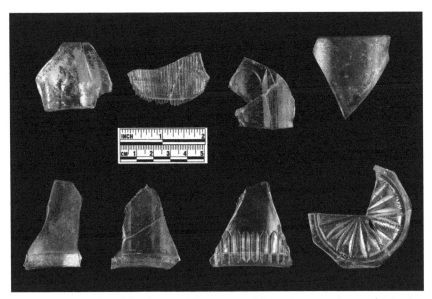

Figure 15.3. Examples of the glass tumblers recovered from the excavations at the Seminary. All are different with few matching vessels identified. This archaeological diversity is attributed to the school policy of having the students bring their own individual drinking vessels. (Photograph by Donald L. Winter, courtesy of HSMC.)

patterns did not. Mrozowski, Ziesing, and Beaudry argue that this indicated that "the motivating force behind tableware choice was cost" (1996:62). The authors are quick to point out, however, that while the ceramic service spoke to a "quiet humility," it was likely that meals were "lively, filled with talk of work, talk of family, and talk of leisure" (1996:62). One can imagine similar discussions during meals at the seminary.

Where the ceramic assemblages from the two institutions differed was in serving vessels. Meals at the boardinghouse were served from larger platters and plates, vessel forms that were all but absent from the seminary assemblage. It is possible that the small plates found most commonly in the Calvert Hall materials indicate that meals were apportioned directly from cooking vessels onto the residents' plates, without serving vessels acting as intermediaries, although this method would not teach the seminarians the proper etiquette associated with domestic dining rituals. It is also possible that metal serving vessels were used in place of ceramic platters and large bowls. The documentary record is largely silent on these questions.

Meals at both the Boott Mill boardinghouse and the seminary featured a variety of meats. At the Boott Mill boardinghouse, residents ate pork, sheep/goat, and chicken, but the most frequently consumed meat was beef. Faunal evidence suggests that the boardinghouse workers enjoyed an assortment of cuts ranging from mutton to sirloin (Mrozowski et al. 1996:62–63). At the seminary, the limited faunal assemblage indicates the residents consumed beef, pork, sheep/goat, fish, and oysters, with the latter being a dietary staple. Transportation challenges brought on by a poor road network and distance from local markets suggest that the seminary procured butchered meats or live animals from local farms. Oysters could be acquired economically from watermen working the St. Mary's River. Sourcing food locally offered an inexpensive provisioning solution. The lack of fish bone in the faunal assemblage may be a reflection of the seasonality of depositions rather than the seminarians' diet. In the warmer months when local fish would have been available, the coal pile would have seen less deposition. Residents were likely incentivized to dump rotting fish remains in the river rather than depositing them near the seminary where the odor would be obvious.

The seminary assemblage diverged from that of the Boott Mill boardinghouse when it came to expressions of its primary function: education. Fragments of at least 15 slate pencils were recovered during excavations, along with pieces of flat slate that likely functioned as writing surfaces (period photographs of the principal seminary structures show that their roofs were covered with metal rather than slate tiles). Sherds from a glass bulk ink bottle suggest the use of inkwells, although none were recovered. The three eyeglass lenses may have been part of necessary accessories to assist some of the seminary residents in reading their course materials.

The Calvert Hall assemblage also offers insight into the more personal aspects of life of the students at the seminary (see figure 15.2). Artifacts related to personal adornment, including glass and Prosser buttons, a copper-alloy buckle, a straight pin, a comb, bone toothbrush fragments, and sherds of mirror glass, illustrate the daily necessity of becoming clean and presentable in a scholastic environment. Residents countered illnesses and ailments with pharmaceutical tonics, including those designed to treat joint pain, indigestion, constipation, and iron deficiency. In their leisure hours, Seminarians played with ceramic marbles and porcelain dolls. This photograph shows some of the students in 1898 (figure 15.4). They also wrote letters and one composed that same year, dated September 24, 1898, was addressed from "St. Mary's Prison Cell No. 12." In it a distraught, homesick Grace Gibson begged her parents to allow her to return to the family home (Gibson 1898, as quoted in Fausz 1990:58). Grace lamented her challenging classes and the quality of the food ("All you have to eat is fish and I don't love it much as you know"; this complaint is another hint that fish may have been more common than what was found in the vicinity of the coal midden). At the bottom of

Figure 15.4. Some of the St. Mary's Seminary students posed in the front of Calvert Hall in 1898. (Image courtesy of St. Mary's College of Maryland Archives, P1898_0002.)

the letter was a note written by Grace's classmate, Ella Hodgson: "Don't let Grace come home. She will be alright in a few days. She has the blues right now. I'll take care of her." This letter, along with the artifacts described above, shows that seminary life was much like that of today's colleges and universities. It was a full-time experience that required personal upkeep, recreational distractions, and the emotional support of friends and family.

CONCLUSIONS

Excavations near Calvert Hall have revealed a wealth of information about the lives of students and faculty at St. Mary's Female Seminary at the turn of the twentieth century. More than 20,000 artifacts, when cast against the backdrop of the documentary record, show an institution that weathered administrative and financial struggles to provide quality education at reasonable costs. As the artifact assemblage demonstrates, costs were kept low by outfitting the school with inexpensive material culture such as ceramics that were stylistically similar, but not identical, and by sourcing food locally. Students also brought some of their own supplies from home, such as drinking vessels, bedding, and clothing, which also kept the seminary's costs down. The Calvert Hall material culture suggests that in terms of their living arrangements, the lives of the seminary residents were similar to those of boardinghouse workers. Despite the institution's frugality, it did make incremental improvements to its infrastructure, including shifts in the important areas highlighted by Gibb and Beisaw: heating, lighting, and sanitation. The archaeological work also illustrated changes to the seminary's landscape as the coal midden was abandoned following the construction of Kent Hall. Finally, artifacts related to personal adornment, hygiene, and recreation found near Calvert Hall can tell more personal stories about the private lives of the seminary's residents. This is the ultimate utility of historical archaeology: to shed light on the daily materiality of those from all walks of life and in doing so, learn about what typically goes undescribed and unreported.

16

Preserving the Cultural Memory of a Place

HENRY M. MILLER AND TRAVIS G. PARNO

In examining the nature of cultural heritage, Laurajane Smith describes it as "a multilayered performance—be this a performance of visiting, managing, interpretation or conservation—that embodies acts of remembrance and commemoration while negotiating and constructing a sense of place, belonging and understanding in the present" (2006:3). This definition beautifully captures the essence of heritage construction: a sense of place is created by the actions of people in the present, bestowing importance on a site's perceived historical significance. The ability of heritage to represent a place often necessitates a recognition and evaluation of authenticity, which is generally determined by either physical condition or, more conceptually, as a feeling or "a condition of an object that can be revealed insofar as it exists but cannot be willfully created" (Holtorf 2005:112). Indeed, the requirements for attaining protection under many national heritage organizations include an assessment of integrity and authenticity (Larson 1995; Lowenthal 1996; Holtorf 2005). Assessing authenticity can be challenging because it is often subjective, contextual, and culturally defined.

Historical archaeology is in many ways a tool of heritage. Archaeology unearths the material traces of the past, making history physical in a way that other disciplines cannot. Archaeology manufactures authenticity at historical sites, providing data sets on which interpretation and exhibition can be based. Artifacts and features invite the visitor to leap backward in time to see things "as they were" (despite the fact that the selection of materials and methods of exhibition are a deliberate process of editing, erasure, and revision). Archaeology, and the heritage construction it affords, is a form of "memory work," which Barbara Mills and William Walker define as "the many social practices that create memories, including recalling, reshaping, forgetting, inventing, coordinating, and transmitting" (2008:4).

St. Mary's City has been the subject of various forms of memory work beginning in the mid-nineteenth century (see King 2012). Yet while St. Mary's City is celebrated as a place of much historical significance, its prominence in human memory has varied greatly over time. Once its purpose was taken away with the movement of the provincial and county government, Maryland's first city was largely abandoned. Its former streets, dwellings, and outbuildings were dismantled or plowed away. By the mid-eighteenth century, most of the structures from the previous century had vanished, although the ruins of the prison and brick walls of St. Peter's mansion remained visible. A single building survived: the 1676 State House served as an Anglican place of worship. This lone survivor was finally dismantled in the 1830s and a new church built from its bricks.

Local residents did remember the place had an important history, as expressed by the then owner of what was left of St. Mary's City when he put the property up for sale in 1774. The newspaper advertisement for the sale noted that the location was "once the metropolis of Maryland, and flourishing city of St. Mary's" (*Maryland Gazette* 1774:1). But for the rest of Maryland, the old capital was largely forgotten. Indeed, the memory of Maryland's beginnings became so faint that no commemorative activities were conducted for the 200th anniversary of the founding of the colony in 1834. The efforts of one of America's first prominent historical novelists, John Pendleton Kennedy, began to change this situation.

In 1838, Kennedy, a resident of Baltimore, published the best seller *Rob of the Bowl: A Legend of St. Inigoe's*. It was an early example of American historical fiction, contemporary with volumes being composed by Kennedy's friends, Washington Irving and James Fenimore Cooper. Kennedy served in Congress, was a strong supporter of religious freedom, and an advocate for the abolition of slavery in Maryland. He set his novel in late seventeenth-century St. Mary's City based upon an unusually thorough study of surviving historical archives and other documents, local oral history, and a knowledge of the site. His biographer states that this exceptional fidelity to the historical record makes the book "a landmark in the development of the American historical novel" (Bohner 1961:103). Kennedy observed that "the very spot where the old city stood is known only to a few—for traces . . . have nearly faded away from the knowledge of this generation. An astute antiquarian eye, however, may define the site of the town by the few scattered bricks which the ploughshare has mingled with the ordinary tillage of the fields" (Kennedy 1965:35–36).

His lively and often humorous depiction of seventeenth-century life stirred interest in Maryland's beginnings throughout the state and beyond, with one scholar concluding that Kennedy "restored the forgotten Calvert capital to its rightful place in the minds of Marylanders" (Fausz 1990:29). Indeed, his novel is a powerful example of the ability of literature to influence the public and kindle interest in the past—a potent form of memory work. The following year, inspired by the novel, three St. Mary's County legislators devised a plan to belatedly commemorate Maryland's bicentennial at its founding site. The sentiment that inspired them was "the disposition to cherish the remembrance of great events and sacred places as connected with the early history of our ancestors [which] has ever been in all ages of the world considered praiseworthy and commendable" (State of Maryland 1840:chapter 190). From this came the act to "Establish a Female Seminary in Saint Mary's County, on the Site of the Ancient City of Saint Mary's," which was approved and signed into law in 1840. St. Mary's Female Seminary was to be a "Monument School" to the first city, the only school established as a memorial to and on the site of the founding place of one of the original colonies. It is today known as St. Mary's College of Maryland.

In 1844, interest in Maryland's history led to the establishment of the Maryland Historical Society in Baltimore. In the 1850s, as public knowledge of St. Mary's City's place in the state's history grew, St. Mary's became a site of historical pilgrimage with steamboat transport of visitors from Baltimore and Georgetown. Upon arrival, visitors enjoyed speeches, music, food, and the opportunity to walk the lands of the first capital. Among the visitors were Catholics of the Philodemic Society from Georgetown College, which organized trips from 1852. Despite the intense anti-Catholic sentiment of the time, land owner Dr. John Brome, an Episcopalian, allowed access to the sites for these events in recognition of the significance of the location for Catholics.

The year 1876 witnessed the destruction of the last witness to the events of the seventeenth century: an ancient mulberry tree. Reportedly 30 feet in circumference, tradition held that it was under this tree that the Charter was read to the first colonists. The mulberry tree also shaded Leonard Calvert's negotiations with the werowance of the Yaocomaco people to acquire the site of their village upon which to found the colony (Chandler 1855:19). This was again stated by historians William Cullen Bryant and Sidney Gay in their *Popular History of the United States* in which they wrote that "under this tree, according to well authenticated tradition, Leonard Calvert made a treaty with the Indians of the village" (Bryant and Gay 1876: 496). One source of this tradition was plantation owner Dr. John Brome, who they noted "has carefully preserved local traditions" (Bryant and Gay 1876:504). In the later 1600s, the tree served as a sign post for official notices, and a number of nails in the tree trunk were reportedly retrieved by relic hunters in the late nineteenth century (Thomas 1894:79). Supporting this story is a specimen of the original mulberry tree in the HSMC collection that has wrought nails driven into the wood. The trunk of the tree was toppled by a storm around 1876 and its wood fashioned into some of the furnishings of the nearby Trinity Church and a variety of collectible objects venerated by Marylanders (Marye 1944). Just as Plymouth, Massachusetts, has Plymouth Rock to symbolize its founding, the Mulberry Tree of St. Mary's played the same role as an idealized physical link to Maryland's beginning. Both objects were imbued with authenticity by virtue of having "been there," tied as they were to historical events by local myth-making.

While the storm that destroyed the mulberry tree was an act of providence, Marylanders' reactions to it were no coincidence. In that same year, celebrations across the country marked the United States' centennial anniversary. The nation had survived its revolutionary beginnings and more recently, a bloody Civil War. In the aftermath of conflict, Americans increasingly began to recognize the country's history as significant and worthy of preservation. Seeking physical manifestations of America's past, early preservationists turned to historic houses, particularly those associated with presidential figures and prominent (and almost always white) colonial citizens (West 1999). According to historian James Lindgren, these practices supported "the widespread belief that those early dwellings represented the unpretentious lives, rigorous thrift, and clear-headed resourcefulness of pioneers" (1995:69).

The salvage and sacralization of the St. Mary's mulberry tree were part of a countrywide period of memory work that in many places was designed to promote unity and nationalism, and counter concerns over contemporary cultural shifts, such as increases in immigration and urbanism that were occurring in the late nineteenth and early twentieth centuries. Plymouth Rock was also chipped away and pried apart by souvenir hunters looking to own a fragment of the past. That a scrap of rock, or a chunk of mulberry tree, could bear the significance of an entire nation speaks to the power of authenticity in constructing heritage narratives.

The former location of the famed mulberry tree was marked with a large granite obelisk by the State of Maryland in 1890 (figure 16.1). Bronze tablets attached to it declare that it is dedicated to the first governor, Leonard Calvert, and the monument is "Erected on the site of the old Mulberry Tree under which the first Colonists of Maryland Assembled to Establish a Government where the Persecuted and Oppressed of every Creed and of every Clime might Repose in Peace and Security, Adore their Common God, and Enjoy the Priceless Blessings of Civil and Religious Liberty." This was the first

Figure 16.1. The Leonard Calvert Monument erected in 1890 (*far left*) and the Copley Tomb Marker (*center*) in Trinity Church cemetery on Church Point, St. Mary's City. (Photograph by Henry M. Miller, courtesy of HSMC.)

marker erected to commemorate the site's seventeenth-century history, apparently being a delayed contribution for the 250th anniversary celebration of the founding. It is worth noting that the marker was dedicated one year after the National Monument to the Forefathers was dedicated in Plymouth, Massachusetts. The latter monument includes the names of those who traveled aboard the *Mayflower* along with text that reads "Erected by a grateful people in remembrance of their labors, sacrifices and sufferings for the cause of civil and religious liberty." The two monuments share more than the last four words of their inscriptions. Both were tributes to a national heritage that was being actively shaped to boldly declare that the country was healing, that its cause was built on a sacred foundation, and that its health would last long into the future. They offered a sense of permanence amid the rapidly shifting "changeful times" by "invoking an ersatz past to promise a real future" (Holleran 1998:6–7).

At some point in the late nineteenth century, the foundations of the 1676 State House were uncovered sufficiently for measurements to be taken and a conjectural drawing of the building produced, using both the physical evidence and the original 1674 architectural specifications written about it

(Browne 1884:404–407). This drawing was first published in the *Baltimore Sun* in 1894 and again in an important volume titled *Chronicles of Colonial Maryland* (Thomas 1913:31–32). Without doubt, this pre-1894 excavation is the first in Maryland for the purpose of obtaining evidence about a seventeenth-century building. Regrettably, no records have survived, and even the identities of the individuals who performed this work and produced the drawing have been lost to time.

The late nineteenth century saw two major developments that aided the study of seventeenth-century Maryland history. One was a legislative act in 1882 for transcribing and publishing the colonial records of the colony by the Maryland Historical Society. Under the direction of William Hand Browne, the *Archives of Maryland* project made the history of early Maryland available in a way never before possible. Today, the volumes may be found online through the Maryland State Archives. The second major event was the 1888 purchase in England of the Calvert Papers by the Maryland Historical Society. This collection of more than 1,300 documents is the only surviving archive of the Lords Baltimore and is invaluable for Maryland historical scholarship.

After the turn of the twentieth century, Maryland's 275th anniversary was celebrated on May 23, 1909, by the Maryland Pilgrims Association, which held a Catholic high mass at the Jesuit's St. Inigoe's estate followed by a "Civic Celebration at old St. Mary's City" (*America Magazine* 1909:193), but it received little statewide attention.

The 1920s witnessed two efforts to commemorate the history of St. Mary's. Both occurred at Church Point on land owned by Trinity Church. The first was the marking of the burial vault of Sir Lionel and Lady Anne Copley in 1922. The vault, which had been first opened in 1799, was reopened in May of that year. The lead coffins and skeletons were inspected by the rector of Trinity Church and precise dimensions of the vault recorded. Immediately afterward, an article about Governor Copley was published and the Maryland Society of the Colonial Dames of America sponsored construction of a permanent memorial (Siousett 1922). The Dames commissioned a memorial that outlined the brick vault with a granite border and erected a granite facade on the south side of the vault. Upon this facade is a bronze door bearing a plaque that identifies the Copleys' resting place and provides additional historical details (see figure 16.1).

The second effort involved the adjacent ruins of the 1676 State House. Workers relocated the original foundations, and the wall lines were demarcated with granite and each corner defined with a short pyramid-capped block of stone. These 12 stones made the cross shape of the first brick

Figure 16.2. The 1676 State House site marker placed in 1926 with Trinity Church built from its seventeenth-century bricks in the background. (Photograph by Henry M. Miller, courtesy of HSMC.)

statehouse visible again. They were accompanied by a massive granite block upon which is affixed a bronze plaque bearing the conjectural drawing of the structure published by Thomas (1913), and the dedication by the Major William Thomas Chapter of the Daughters of the American Revolution on October 21, 1926 (figure 16.2). These durable memorials remain important features of the site's historical interpretation in the twenty-first century.

The following year, Maryland governor Ritchie established a Tercentenary Commission to begin planning for the 300th anniversary of Maryland in 1934. The state would for the first time make a serious effort to properly acknowledge the founding in the appropriate year, not as a belated afterthought. Three goals were originally proposed: (1) erect a monument on St. Clement's Island where the colonists first landed; (2) erect a monument near the original State House site at St. Mary's City; and (3) build a Memorial Hall of Records in Annapolis to properly curate Maryland's government records

(Maryland Tercentenary Commission 1935). The first and third goals were achieved as proposed; a large stone cross was erected on St. Clement's Island and the Hall of Records became operational in 1935.

Among the many Tercentenary Commission members were Spence and Jeanette Brome Howard, who, along with her sister, had inherited the Brome Plantation at St. Mary's City. At the time, the plantation included most of the land that had made up the original city core. Spence Howard spoke with farmers, assembled the local traditions, conducted a land survey of the entire property, and consulted the limited historical records to produce the first map of the historic city in 1932. This map illustrated the city's main streets and some 60 sites of the original buildings. He publicly discussed this map in a *Washington Post* article on March 11, 1934, which noted that he had spent 23 years researching for it. Howard also proposed a major restoration effort that was discussed in a 1933 *Baltimore Sun* article headlined as "Plans to Raise St. Mary's City from Its Ruin" (*Baltimore Sun* 1933:1).

The original proposal for St. Mary's City was a stone arch with memorial plaques dedicated to the first three Lords Baltimore, and its preferred location was next to the original 1676 State House foundations. With continued discussions, the committee began to doubt that a simple monument would be adequate to commemorate the rich history of the first capital. Furthermore, because the suggested location was still an active cemetery, Trinity Church did not favor this idea. Another proposal following Howard's ideas was to rebuild the city's 1638 mill on its original site. While the site was known and its earthen dam survives, the location was hard to reach and a mill did not effectively convey the story of the early government. At that point, an alternative suggestion began gaining support: a full reconstruction of the 1676 State House. A key factor bolstering this proposal was the existence of the original building specifications found within the original 1674 act for its construction (Browne 1884:404–407). This is the only detailed construction document surviving from the seventeenth-century Chesapeake. There was one complication: the statehouse's original foundations upon which the reconstruction would be built lay within the active cemetery.

To overcome this problem, Dr. John Brome's two granddaughters, Susette Brome Bennett and Jeanette Brome Howard, offered to donate to the State 1.18 acres of their land immediately adjacent to the cemetery. The State accepted this offer, an architectural firm was hired, and design work began on the reconstruction. To verify the dimensions, Colonial Williamsburg archaeologist Herbert Shelton Ragland was hired to excavate the original site, although no report on this work has survived (Maryland Tercentenary Commission 1935). A building contract was issued in late December 1933

Figure 16.3. The 1676 State House as reconstructed in 1934 for Maryland's 300th Anniversary. (Photograph by Henry M. Miller, courtesy of HSMC.)

and work began immediately using original methods and materials, including oyster shell mortar and colonial brick salvaged from destroyed colonial homes in Southern Maryland. Flat roof tiles from the 1670s site of St. Peter's mansion provided a precedent for the roof covering. Skilled artisans completed the reconstruction on June 5, 1934, shortly before St. Mary's City was flooded with guests attending a major public celebration of Maryland's Tercentenary (figure 16.3).

The Tercentenary celebration featured three major events. The first, on November 22, 1933, celebrated the departure of the *Ark* and *Dove* bearing the first settlers from the Isle of Wight, England on that day in 1633. It was an event of international scope featuring a ceremony and plaque dedication at Cowes, Isle of Wight, accompanied by a transatlantic radio program on NBC and the BBC featuring Lord Fairfax, President Franklin Delano Roosevelt, and Maryland governor Albert Ritchie. Roosevelt concluded his remarks saying the Tercentenary celebrations would be "a reminder to people throughout the United States of the great fight that Lord Baltimore made three centuries ago for Religious Freedom in America" (Maryland Tercentenary Commission 1935:26). On March 25, 1934, a 40-foot-tall stone cross was

Figure 16.4. Aerial view of the Tercentennial Celebration at St. Mary's City in June 1934. Most of the event was held on the remaining portion of the Brome Plantation, owned by Brome's descendants, the Howards. The event included uncovering a portion of the seventeenth-century Van Sweringen site as an exhibit. (Photo purchased from the Baltimore Sun Archives by Henry M. Miller, 2013.)

dedicated on St. Clement's Island, 300 years to the day that the first settlers had erected a wooden cross there. The final event held at St. Mary's City on June 16–17, 1934, became a huge affair, attracting more than 100,000 people, a fleet of ships, and two days of pageantry. The Howard family allowed use of their farm for the event, as seen in figure 16.4. The reconstructed brick State House was officially dedicated and furnished as accurately as historical knowledge of the time allowed. Furthermore, collections of relics from St. Mary's and elsewhere in Southern Maryland were placed on display. A costume play about the founding of the colony performed by several hundred local residents entertained the crowd. Augmenting the event was the uncovering of a brick floor identified through tradition as the "Secretary's Office and Council Chamber." This was the first public display of a seventeenth-century archaeological site in Maryland. It is of note that later research confirmed that this tradition had been correct, it was indeed the Council Chamber site. In the following year, due to a production delay, a sculpture by prominent artist Hans Schuler was installed as a memorial to the counties of Maryland. It was intended to represent the idea of "Liberty of Conscience" and remains a highly visible piece of public art in the center of St. Mary's City.

In many ways, the Tercentenary captured Smith's definition of heritage as a "multilayered performance." The celebration was designed to honor Maryland's founding and it utilized various tools: a reconstructed building and other monumental installations, a radio program, antique shows, replicas of the two original ships, *Ark* and *Dove*, theatrical spectacle, and an archaeological exhibition. This mix of permanent and impermanent heritage devices called attention to the state's history and clearly excited people—even today, it is difficult to imagine 100,000 people descending on St. Mary's City at one time. The Tercentenary also fit hand-in-glove with the broader narrative of American history's importance during the interwar period in which the country emerged as an international power.

It is certainly true that as a result of the Tercentenary, the founding and early history of Maryland was more widely known, and a small stream of visitors began coming to the State House, which was staffed by a dedicated local caretaker named John Lancaster. The 1934 exhibits remained in place for several decades, invigorated by Lancaster's interpretations. Yet as is often the case with major anniversary celebrations, interest in the period and place tends to wane afterward, and St. Mary's City was no exception; it again receded into relative obscurity. The seventeenth-century Chesapeake was not a subject of intense scholarly interest at the time and the state allocated no resources aside from basic maintenance to enhance the State House or expand education. However, some local schools did begin bringing students to the building occasionally as part of a Maryland history curriculum.

There was one striking exception to the scholarly neglect during the post-Tercentennial period: the arrival of architectural historian Henry Chandlee Forman. With the support of Dr. Brome's descendants, especially his granddaughter Jeanette Brome Howard, Forman was given access to the land so he could explore St. Mary's City. This work culminated in the very popular volume titled *Jamestown and St. Mary's: Buried Cities of Romance* published in 1938, precisely 100 years after Kennedy's *Rob of the Bowl*. Forman conducted test excavations on a number of sites, including the Council Chamber, "Smith's Townhouse" (later identified by HSMC as the Leonard Calvert House), and the Chapel site, where he discovered the foundations of the cross-shaped Jesuit church of the 1660s. In 1940, Forman began testing Philip Calvert's mansion of St. Peter's and published a brief report on his findings (1942). World War II halted further work for a time, but in the 1950s, Forman returned and with the assistance of Spence Howard Jr., unsuccessfully attempted to find the 1640s house of early carpenter Philip West (Miller et al. 2004). The reason it failed is that Forman assumed it was a structure with brick foundations, but later investigations found that West's house was of earthfast construction. Forman's final excavation involved archaeological testing at the St. John's site in 1962.

Forman's efforts were vital in demonstrating the richness and significance of the archaeology at St. Mary's City, and his book became a valuable resource for people interested in seventeenth-century Maryland and Virginia. Local residents, especially members of the St. Mary's County Historical Society which was formed in 1951, desired greater public recognition for St. Mary's City, but there was little political support for any financial investment. This began to change in the early 1960s, inspired to a large degree by a Marine general with a deep interest in history who retired at St. Mary's City.

General Robert Hogaboom wrote an article in 1963 proposing that St. Mary's City become a "National Monument to Peace and Toleration." He noted the deep historical significance of the city and observed "that it should become almost blotted from man's memory is astonishing. It is a present day fact that few today, even in Maryland, know where St. Mary's is located, or that for 60 years (1634–1694) she was the proud capital of the Province" (Hogaboom 1963:33–34). This sentiment was echoed the following year by Secretary of the Interior Stewart Udall, who said that Maryland's "heritage matches that of any of the original states, and yet it is not appreciated by the rest of the country, or perhaps by some of your own citizens" (Udall 1964). He proposed that an energetic effort be made to develop St. Mary's City.

These calls finally were heard by Maryland's elected officials, and the governor established a study commission in 1965 to evaluate the future of St. Mary's. Led by delegate Louise Gore, the commission included noted historians, educators, descendants of the original settlers, and General Hogaboom. They recognized the value of the information provided by Henry Chandlee Forman, who pointed out the city's archaeological potential and the urgent need for its preservation. The committee reported that a permanent state commission should be created to protect and develop the site (Gore 1965). According to the report, this new commission should direct archaeological excavations, build select reconstructions based on sound research, and maintain to the extent possible the rural ambiance of the site.

One concern spurring the overall effort was the threat of residential, commercial, and academic development in the area. In particular, the growth of St. Mary's College, scheduled to become a four year college in 1967, was seen as an issue. Chandlee Forman and Spence Howard Jr. recognized this potential threat. To address it, they combined their knowledge of the site's history and archaeological remains and produced in the summer of 1965 a carefully conceived plan that proposed a preservation boundary that took into account most of the identified or suspected seventeenth-century

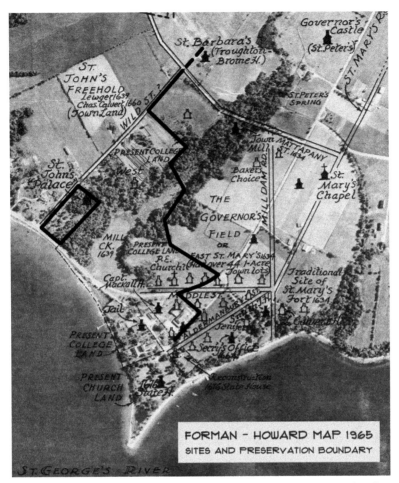

Figure 16.5. The preservation map of St. Mary's City prepared by Henry Chandlee Forman and J. Spence Howard Jr. in 1965. This map was a critical tool in guiding museum development and attempting to steer college growth away from the most significant archaeological areas of the first city. (Courtesy of HSMC Archives.)

archaeological resources (their map is reproduced in figure 16.5). The study commission gratefully accepted this map to suggest areas of preservation and development so that both public goals could be accomplished. The 1966 Legislature established the St. Mary's City Commission and its first meeting was held on August 3, 1966, with General Hogaboom serving as the chair. Forman was hired as a consultant soon afterward.

One of the commission's early priorities was to hire a professional staff, especially a historian and archaeologist. Lois Green Carr became the historian in late 1967. The search for an archaeologist was more difficult. Forman asked for advice from a vice president of Colonial Williamsburg in the spring of 1967 and was informed "colonial archaeologists are very scarce" (St. Mary's City Commission 1967). The first prospect was Stanley South, who entertained the opportunity but ultimately declined. Continued search and consultations with prominent archaeologists J. C. Harrington, John Cotter, and others led the Commission to Garry Wheeler Stone, who began work in late 1970.

For the new institution, the year 1969 proved significant. Based on Carr's early work, the first new exhibit since 1934 was designed and installed in the State House. Furthermore, a successful conclusion was achieved for the first major initiative of the Commission, which had begun in 1967. This was a nomination to the National Park Service to designate St. Mary's City as one of the nation's premier historic resources—a National Historic Landmark. The nomination was approved in August of 1969 based upon the location's exceptional history and its high degree of archaeological preservation. That same year, the new museum sponsored its first archaeological rescue excavation using the services of Contract Archaeology, Inc. on a threatened site on land owned by St. Mary's College of Maryland (see chapter 12).

Formal research excavations began in 1971, and archaeological exploration has continued annually since then. Some of these projects are presented in this book. Based upon the historical and archaeology work, reconstruction of a seventeenth-century tobacco plantation, a part of Garrett van Sweringen's Council Chamber site, and the marking of several of the most significant sites such as the Chapel and Leonard Calvert House were completed in time for the 350th anniversary of Maryland's founding in 1984. Maryland's governor and the Duke and Duchess of Kent formally opened the Historic St. Mary's City museum as part of these celebrations. Since then, many thousands of schoolchildren visit the museum annually along with a steady flow of tourists. Archaeology has continued as an indispensable element of museum development with reconstructed seventeenth-century buildings, traditional exhibit galleries, the re-creation of the colonial capital's street system, period fencing, and the installation of "ghost frames." These are timber-framed outlines of buildings designed to populate the city with structures without the investment or evidence required for full-scale reconstructions (for more on the museum's experiences interpreting archaeology, see Hurry and Bodeman 2007; Miller 2007).

CONCLUSION

Maryland's first city has faded from and returned to public memory multiple times over the past four centuries. Except for local residents who retained some traditional knowledge, St. Mary's City was almost completely forgotten by the public for more than a century after ca. 1725. Historical novelist John Pendleton Kennedy briefly returned the old city to the public imagination in 1838, and this inspired the state to create the St. Mary's Female Seminary as a "Monument School" to the founding of Maryland in 1840. Pilgrimages to the site began in the mid-1800s as steamboats made St. Mary's City accessible from both Baltimore and Washington, D.C. While a few markers were installed as part of late nineteenth-century memory work devoted to vestiges of early American history, no major effort to acknowledge the former capital was made until the approach of the 300th anniversary of Maryland's founding in 1934. The Tercentenary was a multilayered heritage performance, one of many occurring during this period that were tied to America's rise on a global stage. The permanent contribution of this event was the first seventeenth-century reconstruction in the state—the 1676 State House. Nevertheless, the site and its history once again were largely forgotten within a few years of the ceremonies.

Renewed interest by local citizens and the threat of site destruction from development in the early 1960s once again spurred action. A 1966 Maryland act created the St. Mary's City Commission to preserve, investigate, and interpret St. Mary's City for the benefit of the citizens of Maryland. That same year, Congress passed the National Historic Preservation Act, also in response to the destruction of irreplaceable historic sites throughout the country. More than 250 years after its abandonment, Maryland's first city began to be restored to permanent public memory by this legislative act. But it took energetic private citizens with a strong sense of history, along with the promise of tourism, to convince legislators to take this step.

From the museum's beginning in the 1960s, historical archaeology has been central in the development of St. Mary's City. Archaeologists have located sites, explored the architecture and landscapes of the first capital, and revealed the lives of the people who have lived at St. Mary's City over millennia. Archaeology is essential for creating high quality exhibits because it retrieves the crucial information to both reconstruct and interpret the sites. It is also uniquely capable of making history tangible, unearthing the physical traces of the past for the consumption of modern audiences. Archaeology at St. Mary's City is a continuing act of memory work that allows us to reinforce the importance of Maryland's history through its ongoing study. This volume presents some of the highlights of these explorations over the first 50 years of research. We firmly believe that the second 50 years will be just as productive and archaeology will remain a vital tool to ensure that the cultural memory of this historic city will not again be lost.

REFERENCES

Abrahams, Peter W., Jane A. Entwistle, and Robert A. Dodgshon
2010   The Ben Lawers Historic Landscape Project: Simultaneous Multi-element
         Analysis of Former Settlement and Arable Soils by X-ray Fluorescence Spec-
         trometry. *Journal of Archaeological Method and Theory* 17(3):231–248.
Adams, William Hampton, and Sarah Jane Boling
1989   Status and Ceramics for Planters and Slaves on Three Georgia Coastal Planta-
         tions. *Historical Archaeology* 23(1):69–96.
Agbe-Davies, Anna S.
2010   Social Aspects of the Tobacco Pipe Trade in Early Colonial Virginia. In *Social
         Archaeologies of Trade and Exchange,* Alexander A. Bauer and Anna Agbe-
         Davies, editors, pp. 69–98. Left Coast Press, Walnut Creek, CA.
2015   *Tobacco, Pipes and Race in Colonial Virginia: Little Tubes of Mighty Power.* Left
         Coast Press, Walnut Creek, CA.
Alden, Harry
2005   *Analysis of the Smith's Ordinary Charcoal Samples.* Revised from 1996 edition.
         Report to Department of Research and Collections, Historic St. Mary's City,
         St. Mary's City, MD, from Charcoal Identification Service, Edgerton, WI.
America Magazine
1909   Celebration of Maryland 275th Anniversary. *America Magazine* 1:193.
Anderson, Nesta
2004   Finding the Space between Spatial Boundaries and Social Dynamics: The Ar-
         chaeology of Nested Households. In *Household Chores and Household Choices:
         Theorizing the Domestic Sphere in Historical Archaeology,* Kerri S. Barile and Ja-
         mie C. Brandon, editors, pp. 109–120. University of Alabama Press, Tuscaloosa.
Arber, Edward, and A. G. Bradley
1910   *Travels and Works of Captain John Smith, President of Virginia, and Admiral of
         New England, 1580–1631.* John Grant, Edinburgh, Scotland.
Armstrong, Douglas V.
1990   *The Old Village and the Great House: An Archaeological and Historical Exami-
         nation of Drax Hall Plantation, St. Ann's Bay, Jamaica.* University of Illinois
         Press, Urbana.
Ayers, Edward L.
1992   *The Promise of the New South: Life after Reconstruction.* Oxford University
         Press, Oxford, UK.

Bair, Daniel A., and Richard E. Terry
2018   Soil Phosphate Chemistry. In *The Encyclopedia of Archaeological Sciences*, Sandra L. López Varela, editor. Wiley Online Library. https://doi/10.1002/9781119188230. saseas0538. Accessed 2 May 2019.

Baker, William Joseph
1988   *Sports in the Western World*. University of Illinois Press, Champaign.

Baltimore City
1828   *The Ordinances of the Mayor and City Council of Baltimore, passed at the extra sessions in 1827, and at the January session 1828. To which is annexed, Sundry Acts of Assembly, a List of the Officers of the Corporation, the Summary of the Register, the Annual Reports of the Health Commissioners, City Commissioners, and Wardens of the Port. Also, the Returns of the Officers of the Corporation.* Benjamin Edes, Baltimore.

Baltimore Sun
1933   Plans to Raise St. Mary's City from Its Ruin. *Baltimore Sun* 3 February: 1: Baltimore.

Banning, E. B.
2002   *Archaeological Survey Methods*. Manuals in Archaeological Method, Theory, and Technique. Springer, New York.

Barber, Edwin Atlee
1904   *Marks of American Potters*. Patterson & White, Philadelphia, PA.

Barile, Kerri S.
2004   Hegemony within the Household: The Perspective from a South Carolina Plantation. In *Household Chores and Household Choices: Theorizing the Domestic Sphere in Historical Archaeology*, Kerri S. Barile and Jamie C. Brandon, editors, pp. 121–137. University of Alabama Press, Tuscaloosa.

Barley, M. W.
1961   *The English Farmhouse and Cottage*. Routledge and Kegan Paul, London.

Barnes, Jodi A.
2011   Introduction: The Materiality of Freedom, Archaeologies of Postemancipation Life. In *The Materiality of Freedom: Archaeologies of Postemancipation Life*, Jodi A. Barnes, editor, pp. 1–25. University of South Carolina Press, Columbia.

Battle-Baptiste, Whitney
2010   Sweepin' Spirits: Power and Transformation on the Plantation Landscape. In *Archaeology and Preservation of Gendered Landscapes*, Sherene Baugher and Suzanne Spencer-Wood, editors, pp. 81–94. Springer, New York.
2011   *Black Feminist Archaeology*. Left Coast Press, Walnut Creek, CA.

Beaudry, Mary C., Janet Long, Henry M. Miller, Fraser D. Neiman, and Garry Wheeler Stone
1983   A Vessel Typology for Early Chesapeake Ceramics: The Potomac Typological System. *Historical Archaeology* 17(1):18–43.

Beckett, J. V.
1981   *Coal and Tobacco: The Lowthers and the Economic Development of West Cumberland, 1660–1760*. Cambridge University Press, Cambridge, UK.

Blackmore, Howard L.
1961   *British Military Firearms, 1650–1850.* Herbert Jenkins, London.
Bohner, Charles H.
1961   *John Pendleton Kennedy: Gentleman from Baltimore.* Johns Hopkins University Press, Baltimore.
Boring, Karin
1975   A Survey of Ceramic Advertisements in the *National Daily Intelligencer,* 1827–1837. Manuscript, Department of Research and Collections, Historic St. Mary's City, St. Mary's City, MD.
Boroughs, Jon Jason
2013   Gathering Places, Cultivating Spaces: An Archaeology of a Chesapeake Neighborhood through Enslavement and Emancipation, 1775–1905. Doctoral dissertation, Department of Anthropology, College of William and Mary. University Microfilms International, Ann Arbor, MI.
Bourdieu, Pierre
1977   *Outline of a Theory of Practice.* Cambridge University Press, Cambridge, UK.
Brock, Terry Peterkin
2013   "Once the Capital of Maryland": Connecting a City's Past to a Plantation's Present. Paper presented at the 8th Society of Early Americanists Biennial Conference, Savannah, GA.
2014   "All of Us Would Walk Together": The Transition from Slavery to Freedom at St. Mary's City, Maryland. Doctoral dissertation, Department of Anthropology, Michigan State University. University Microfilms International, Ann Arbor, MI.
Brown, Gregory J., Thomas F. Higgins III, David F. Muraca, S. Kathleen Pepper, Roni H. Polk, Joanne Bowen Gaynor, and William E. Pittman
1990   *Archaeological Investigations of the Shields Tavern Site, Williamsburg, Virginia.* Department of Archaeological Research, Colonial Williamsburg Foundation, Williamsburg, VA.
Browne, William Hands (editor)
1883   *Archives of Maryland, Vol. 1, Proceedings and Acts of the General Assembly of Maryland, January 1637/8–September 1664.* Maryland Historical Society, Baltimore.
1884   *Archives of Maryland, Vol. 2, Proceedings and Acts of the General Assembly of Maryland, April 1666–June 1676.* Maryland Historical Society, Baltimore.
1885   *Archives of Maryland, Vol. 3, Proceedings of the Council of Maryland, 1636–1667.* Maryland Historical Society, Baltimore.
1887a   *Archives of Maryland, Vol. 4, Judicial and Testamentary Business of the Provincial Court, 1637–1650.* Maryland Historical Society, Baltimore.
1887b   *Archives of Maryland, Vol. 5, Proceedings of the Council of Maryland, 1667–1675.* Maryland Historical Society, Baltimore.
1889   *Archives of Maryland, Vol. 7, Proceedings and Acts of the General Assembly of Maryland, October 1678–November 1683.* Maryland Historical Society, Baltimore.

1891   *Archives of Maryland, Vol. 10, Judicial and Testamentary Business of the Provincial Court, from 1649/50–1657.* Maryland Historical Society, Baltimore.

1900   *Archives of Maryland, Vol. 20, Proceedings of the Council of Maryland, 1693–1696/1697.* Maryland Historical Society, Baltimore.

1902   *Archives of Maryland, Vol. 22, and Acts of the General Assembly of Maryland, March 1697/8–July 1699.* Maryland Historical Society, Baltimore.

1903   *Archives of Maryland, Vol. 23, Proceedings of the Council of Maryland, 1696/7–1698.* Maryland Historical Society, Baltimore.

Brownstein, Oscar Lee

1963   Stake and Stage: The Baiting Ring and the Public Playhouse in Elizabethan England. Doctoral dissertation, Theater Department, University of Iowa. University Microfilms International, Ann Arbor, MI.

Brush, Grace S.

2001   Forests Before and After the Colonial Encounter. In *Discovering the Chesapeake: The History of an Ecosystem*, Philip D. Curtin, Grace S. Brush, and George Fisher, editors, pp. 40–59. Johns Hopkins University Press, Baltimore.

Bryant, William Cullen, and Sidney H. Gay

1876   *A Popular History of the United States from the First Discovery of the Western Hemisphere by the Northmen to the End of the Civil War.* Four volumes. Charles Scribner's Sons, New York.

Bureau of the Census

1810   United States Federal Census, St. Mary's County, Maryland. National Archives, Washington, DC.

1820   United States Federal Census, St. Mary's County, Maryland. National Archives, Washington, DC.

1840   United States Federal Census, St. Mary's County, Maryland. National Archives, Washington, DC.

1850a   United States Federal Census, St. Mary's County, Maryland. National Archives, Washington, DC.

1850b   United States Slave Schedules, St. Mary's County, Maryland. National Archives, Washington, DC.

1860a   United States Federal Agricultural Census, St. Mary's County, Maryland. National Archives, Washington, DC.

1860b   United States Slave Schedules, St. Mary's County, Maryland. National Archives, Washington, DC.

1870a   United States Federal Agricultural Census, St. Mary's County, Maryland. National Archives, Washington, DC.

1870b   United States Federal Census, St. Mary's County, Maryland. National Archives, Washington, DC.

1880a   United States Federal Agricultural Census, St. Mary's County, Maryland. National Archives, Washington, DC.

1880b   United States Federal Census, St. Mary's County, Maryland. National Archives, Washington, DC.

1890   United States Federal Census, St. Mary's County, Maryland. National Archives, Washington, DC.

1900 United States Federal Census, St. Mary's County, Maryland. National Archives, Washington, DC.

Canuto, Marcello A., and Jason Yaeger

2000 Introducing an Archaeology of Communities. In *The Archaeology of Communities: A New World Perspective,* Marcello A. Canuto and Jason Yaeger, editors, pp. 1–15. Routledge, London.

Carr, Lois Green

1969 St. John's Tract History. Manuscript, Department of Research and Collections, Historic St. Mary's City, St. Mary's City, MD.

1973 Ceramics from the John Hicks Site, 1723–1743: The St. Mary's Town Land Community. In *Ceramics in America,* Ian M. G. Quimby, editor, pp. 75–102. University Press of Virginia, Charlottesville.

1974 The Metropolis of Maryland: A Comment on Town Development along the Tobacco Coast. *Maryland Historical Magazine* 69:124–145.

1978 The Foundations of Social Order: Local Government in Colonial Maryland. In *Town and County: Essays on the Structure of Local Governments in the American Colonies,* Bruce C. Daniels, editor, pp. 72–110. Wesleyan University Press, Middletown, CT.

1992 Chancellor Philip Calvert (1626–1682) and Anne Wolseley Calvert (1610?– ca. 1679). Manuscript, Department of Research and Collections, Historic St. Mary's City, St. Mary's City, MD.

1994 The Country's House Documentation. Manuscript, Department of Research and Collections, Historic St. Mary's City, St. Mary's City, MD.

Carr, Lois Green, J. Glenn Little, and Stephen Israel

1971 *Salvage Archaeology of a Dwelling on the John Hicks Leasehold, 2 Volumes.* Contract Archaeology. Alexandria, VA.

Carr, Lois Green, and Russell R. Menard

1979 Immigration and Opportunity: The Freedman in Early Colonial Maryland. In *The Chesapeake in the Seventeenth Century: Essays on Anglo-American Society,* Thad W. Tate and David L. Ammerman, editors, pp. 206–242. W. W. Norton and Company, New York.

Carr, Lois Green, Philip D. Morgan, and Jean B. Russo

1988 *Colonial Chesapeake Society.* University of North Carolina Press, Chapel Hill.

Carr, Lois Green, and Lorena S. Walsh

1977 The Planter's Wife: The Experiences of White Women in Seventeenth-Century Maryland. *William and Mary Quarterly* 34:542–571.

1980 Inventories and the Analysis of Wealth and Consumption Patterns in St. Mary's County, Maryland 1658–1777. *Historical Methods* 15:81–104.

1994 Changing Lifestyles and Consumer Behavior in the Colonial Chesapeake. In *Of Consuming Interests: The Style of Life in the Eighteenth Century,* Cary Carson, Ronald Hoffman, and Peter J. Albert, editors, pp. 59–166. University Press of Virginia, Charlottesville.

Carr, Lois Green, Russell R. Menard, and Lorena S. Walsh

1991 *Robert Cole's World: Agriculture and Society in Early Maryland.* University of North Carolina Press, Chapel Hill.

Carroll, Kenneth L., and Orlando Ridout V

1984   *Three Hundred Years and More of Third Haven Quakerism.* Queen Anne Press, Easton, MD.

Carroll, Lynda

1999   Could've Been a Contender: The Making and Breaking of "China" in the Ottoman Empire. *International Journal of Historical Archaeology* 3(3):177–190.

Carson, Cary

1994   The Consumer Revolution in Colonial British America: Why Demand? In *Of Consuming Interests: The Style of Life in the Eighteenth Century,* Cary Carson, Ronald Hoffman, and Peter J. Albert, editors, pp. 483–697. University Press of Virginia, Charlottesville.

2011   Plantation Housing: Seventeenth Century. In *The Chesapeake House,* Cary Carson and Carl R. Lounsbury, editors, pp. 86–103. University of North Carolina Press, Chapel Hill.

2017   *Face Value: The Consumer Revolution and the Colonizing of America.* University of Virginia Press, Charlottesville.

Carson, Cary, Norman F. Barka, William M. Kelso, Garry Wheeler Stone, and Dell Upton

1981   Impermanent Architecture in the Southern American Colonies. *Winterthur Portfolio* 16 (2/3):135–196.

Carson, Cary, Ronald Hoffman, and Peter J. Albert (editors)

1994   *Of Consuming Interests: The Style of Life in the Eighteenth Century.* University Press of Virginia, Charlottesville.

Carson, Cary, and Carl Lounsbury (editors)

2013   *The Chesapeake House: Architectural Investigations by Colonial Williamsburg.* University of North Carolina Press, Chapel Hill.

Chandler, Joseph R.

1855   *Civil and Religious Equality: An Oration Delivered at the Fourth Commemoration of the Landing of the Pilgrims at Maryland, celebrated May 15, 1855, under the auspices of the Philodemic Society of Georgetown College.* J. B. Chandler, Philadelphia, PA.

Christie's

1986   *The Nanking Cargo: Chinese Export Porcelain and Gold; European Glass and Stoneware.* Christie's Auction Catalogues, Amsterdam, Netherlands.

Clemens, Paul G. E.

1980   *The Atlantic Economy and Colonial Maryland's Eastern Shore.* Cornell University Press, Ithaca, NY.

Collard, Elizabeth

1967   *Nineteenth-Century Pottery and Porcelain in Canada.* McGill University Press, Montreal, Canada.

Collins, Tony, John Martin, and Wray Vamplew (editors)

2005   *Encyclopedia of Traditional British Rural Sports.* Routledge, London.

Cooke, Ebenezer

1708   *The sot-weed factor: or A Voyage to Maryland. A Satyr. In which is describ'd, the laws, governments, courts and constitutions of the country; and also the build-*

ings, feasts, frolicks, entertainments and drunken humours of the inhabitants of that part of America: In burlesque verse. B. Bragg, London.

Cotter, John L.
1958   *Archaeological Excavations at Jamestown, Virginia.* National Park Service, Washington, DC. Reprinted 1994 by Archaeological Society of Virginia, Richmond.

Cotton, Charles
1674   *The compleat gamester, or, Instructions how to play at billiards, trucks, bowls, and chess together with all manner of usual and most gentile games either on cards or dice: to which is added the arts and mysteries of riding, racing, archery, and cock-fighting.* Printed by A.M. for R. Cutler, London.

Cox, C. Jane
2002   Skipworth's Addition (1664–1682): Tobacco Pipes from an Early Quaker Homelot. In *The Clay Tobacco Pipes in Anne Arundel County, Maryland (1650–1730),* Al Luckenbach, C. Jane Cox, and John Kille, editors, pp. 66–71. Anne Arundel County Lost Towns Project, Annapolis, MD.

Coysh, A. W., and R. K. Henrywood
1982   *The Dictionary of Blue and White Printed Pottery, 1780–1880.* Antique Collectors' Club Ltd., Woodbridge, UK.

Culver, Francis Barnum
1922   *Blooded Horses of Colonial Days: Classic Horse Matches in America before the Revolution.* Francis Barnum Culver, Baltimore, MD.

Curry, Dennis C.
1999   *Feast of the Dead: Aboriginal Ossuaries in Maryland.* Maryland Historical Trust, Crownesville.

Custer, Jay F.
2019   Smoking Pipes and Time at 18QU30, Queen Anne's County, Maryland. *Maryland Archaeology* 52(1–2):41–59.

Custer, Jay F., Ellis C. Coleman, Wade P. Catts, and Kevin W. Cunningham
1986   Soil Chemistry and Historic Archaeological Site Activity Areas: A Test Case from Northern Delaware. *Historical Archaeology* 20(2):89–94.

Davidson, Roger A., Jr.
2000   Yankee Rivers, Rebel Shore: The Potomac Flotilla and Civil Insurrection in the Chesapeake Region. Doctoral dissertation, Howard University. University Microfilms International, Ann Arbor, MI.

De Lotbiniere, Seymour
1980   English and Gunflint Making in the Seventeenth and Eighteenth Centuries. In *Colonial Frontier Guns,* T. M. Hamilton, editor, pp. 154–159. The Fur Press, Chadron, NE.

De Vries, David P.
1912   The Korte Historiael ende Journaels Aenteyckeninge. In *Narratives of Early Pennsylvania, West New Jersey and Delaware, 1630–1707,* Albert Cook Myers, editor, pp. 1–30. Charles Scribner's and Sons, New York.

Deetz, James
1977   *In Small Things Forgotten: The Archaeology of Early American Life.* Anchor Books/Doubleday, Garden City, NY.

Delle, James A.

1999   The Landscapes of Class Negotiation on Coffee Plantations in the Blue Moun-
           tains of Jamaica: 1790–1850. *Historical Archaeology* 33(1):136–158.

2000   Gender, Power, and Space: Negotiating Social Relations under Slavery on
           Coffee Plantations in Jamaica, 1790–1834. In *Lines That Divide: Historical Ar-
           chaeologies of Race, Class, and Gender,* James A. Delle, Stephen A. Mrozows-
           ki, and Robert Paynter, editors, pp. 168–201. University of Tennessee Press,
           Knoxville.

Dent, George B.

1869   *Record of Slaves in St. Mary's County, July 2, 1867–April 16, 1869.* Maryland State
           Archives, Maryland Hall of Records, Annapolis.

Department of Veterans Affairs

1910   William H. Gross (Pvt., Co. D, 38th US Colored Troops Infantry, Civil War).
           Records of the Veterans Administration, National Archives, Washington, DC.

Deutsch, Clayton V., and Andre G. Journel

1998   *GSLIB: Geostatistical Software Library and User's Guide.* Oxford University
           Press, Oxford, UK.

Dickey, Stephen

1991   Shakespeare's Mastiff Comedy. *Shakespeare Quarterly* 42(3):255–275.

Dinwiddie, William

1899   *Puerto Rico: Its Conditions and Possibilities.* Harper & Brothers Publishers,
           New York.

Douglass, Frederick

1845   *Narrative of the Life of Frederick Douglass, an American Slave.* The Anti-Slavery
           Office, Boston.

Egan, Geoff, Susan D. Hanna, and Barry Knight

1986   Marks on Milled Window Leads. *Post-Medieval Archaeology* 20:303–309.

Egloff, Keith, and Stephen R. Potter

1982   Indian Ceramics from Coastal Plain Virginia. *Archaeology of Eastern North
           America* 10:95–117.

Embry, James W.

1999   A Search to Identify the Seventeenth-Century Shoreline of St. Mary's City,
           Maryland. Masters dissertation, Department of Anthropology, East Carolina
           University. University Microfilms International, Ann Arbor, MI.

Emerson, Matthew

1988   Decorated Clay Pipes from the Chesapeake. Doctoral dissertation, Depart-
           ment of Anthropology, University of California, Berkeley. University Micro-
           films International, Ann Arbor, MI.

1994   Decorated Clay Tobacco Pipes from the Chesapeake. In *Historical Archaeol-
           ogy of the Chesapeake,* Paul A. Shackel and Barbara J. Little, editors, pp. 35–49.
           Smithsonian Institution Press, Washington, DC.

Epperson, Terrence W.

1999   Constructing Difference: The Social and Spatial Order. In *"I, Too, Am Ameri-
           ca": Archaeological Studies of African-American Life,* Theresa A. Singleton, edi-
           tor, pp. 159–172. University Press of Virginia, Charlottesville.

2000   Panoptic Plantations: The Garden Sights of Thomas Jefferson and George Ma-
            son. In *Lines That Divide: Historical Archaeologies of Race, Class, and Gender,*
            James A. Delle, Stephen A. Mrozowski, and Robert Paynter, editors, pp. 58–77.
            University of Tennessee Press, Knoxville.

Fairbanks, Jonathan L., and Robert F. Trent
1983   *New England Begins: The Seventeenth Century.* Museum of Fine Arts, Boston.

Farman, Edgar
2006   *The Bulldog: A Monograph.* Beech Publishing House, West Sussex, UK.

Fausz, J. Frederick
1990   *Monument School of the People: A Sesquicentennial History of St. Mary's College
            of Maryland 1840–1890.* St. Mary's College of Maryland, St. Mary's City.

Federal Assessment List
1798   Federal Direct Tax Assessment List, St. Mary's County, Maryland State Papers,
            Maryland State Archives, Maryland Hall of Records, Annapolis.

Federal Gazette and Baltimore Daily Advertiser
1796   The Citizens of Baltimore. *Federal Gazette and Baltimore Daily Advertiser.* 8
            October, 1:1. Baltimore, MD.

Feest, Christian F.
1978   Nanticoke and Neighboring Tribes. *Handbook of North American Indians*
            15:240–252.

Fesler, Garrett
2010   Excavating the Spaces and Interpreting the Places of Enslaved Africans and
            Their Descendants. In *Cabin, Quarter, Plantation: Architecture and Landscapes
            of North American Slavery,* Clifton Ellis and Rebecca Ginsburg, editors, pp.
            27–49. Yale University Press, New Haven, CT.

Fike, Richard E.
1987   *The Bottle Book: A Comprehensive Guide to Historic, Embossed Medicine Bot-
            tles.* Gibbs M. Smith, Inc., Peregrine Smith Press, Salt Lake City, UT.

Fischer, David Hackett
2005   *Liberty and Freedom: A Visual History of America's Founding Ideas.* Oxford
            University Press, Oxford, UK.

Fithian, Charles H.
1991   Earthworks of the Chesapeake and Delaware Regions, 1600–1700. Paper pre-
            sented at the 24th Annual Conference on Historical and Underwater Archae-
            ology, Richmond, VA.

Forman, Henry Chandlee
1938   *Jamestown and St. Mary's: Buried Cities of Romance.* Johns Hopkins University
            Press, Baltimore, MD.
1942   The St. Mary's "Castle," Predecessor of the Williamsburg "Palace." *William and
            Mary Quarterly* 22(2):135–143.

Gadsby, David, and Rosemarie Callage
2002   Homewood Lot through Four Generations: Tobacco Pipes from 18AN871. In
            The Clay Tobacco Pipes in Anne Arundel County, Maryland (1650–1730), Al
            Luckenbach, C. Jane Cox, and John Kille, editors, pp. 18–27. Anne Arundel
            County Lost Towns Project, Annapolis, MD.

Garratt, Michael W., and R. Kirk Steinhorst

1976   Testing for Significance of Morisita's, Horn's and Related Measures of Overlap. *American Midland Naturalist* 96(1):245–251.

Gates, William, Jr., and Dana E. Ormerod

1982   The East Liverpool Pottery District: Identification of Manufacturers and Marks. *Historical Archaeology* 16(1–2):128–138.

Gems, Gerald, Linda Borish, and Gertrud Pfister

2008   *Sports in American History: From Colonization to Globalization.* Human Kinetics, Champaign, IL.

Gibb, James G.

1994   "Dwell Here, Live Plentifully, and Be Rich": Consumer Behavior and the Interpretation of 17th-Century Archaeological Assemblages from the Chesapeake Bay Region. Doctoral dissertation, Department of Anthropology, State University of New York–Binghamton. University Microfilms International, Ann Arbor, MI.

Gibb, James G., and April M. Beisaw

2000   Learning Cast Up from the Mire: Archaeological Investigations of Schoolhouses in the Northeastern United States. *Journal of Northeast Historical Archaeology* 29:107–129.

Gibson, Grace L.

1898   Letter to Mama, 24 September. *Alumni Newsletter,* 16(3), St. Mary's City: St. Mary's College of Maryland, 1967.

Giddens, Anthony

1979   *Central Problems in Social Theory: Action, Structure, and Contradiction in Social Analysis.* University of California Press, Berkeley.

Gilbey, Walter Bartholomew

1912   *Sport in the Olden Time.* Vinton, London.

Giles, Colum

1985   *Rural Houses of West Yorkshire 1400–1830.* Royal Commission on the Historical Monuments of England, Supplementary Series 8. Her Majesty's Stationery Office, London.

Glassie, Henry

1972   Eighteenth-Century Cultural Process in Delaware Valley Folk Buildings. *Winterthur Portfolio* 7:29–57.

Glover, Thomas

1676   An account of Virginia, its scituation, temperature, productions, Inhabitants, and their manner of planting and ordering tobacco &c. communicated by Mr. Thomas Glover, an ingenious chirurgion that hath lived some years in that country. *Philosophical Transactions of the Royal Society* 11(126).

Godden, Geoffrey A.

1964   *Encyclopedia of British Pottery and Porcelain Marks.* Bonanza Books, New York.

Goldstein, Erik, and Stuart Mowbray

2010   *The Brown Bess: An Identification Guide and Illustrated Study of Britain's Most Famous Musket.* Mowbray Publishing, Woonsocket, RI.

Goodwin, Lorinda B. R.
1999   *An Archaeology of Manners: The Polite World of the Merchant Elite of Colonial Massachusetts.* Kluwer Academic/Plenum Publishers, New York.

Goovaerts, Pierre
1997   *Geostatistics for Natural Resources Evaluation.* Oxford University Press, Oxford, UK.

Gore, Louise
1965   Report of the Commission to Study the Feasibility and Desirability of Restoring Historic St. Mary's City: A Report to the Governor and General Assembly. Manuscript, Department of Research and Collections, Historic St. Mary's City, St. Mary's City, MD.

Graham, Clare
2003   *Ordering Law: The Architectural and Social History of the English Law Court to 1914.* Ashgate, Burlington, VT.

Graham, Willie, Carter L. Hudgins, Carl R. Lounsbury, Fraser D. Neiman, and James P. Whittenburg
2007   Adaptation and Innovation: Archaeological and Architectural Perspectives on the Seventeenth-Century Chesapeake. *William and Mary Quarterly* 64(3):451–522.

Green, Mary Anne E.
1875   *Calendar of State Papers, Domestic Series, 1649–50, Preserved in the State Papers, Department of Her Majesty's Public Record Office.* Her Majesty's Stationery Office, London. Reprinted in 1965 by Kraus Reprint, Vaduz, Liechtenstein.

Gryczkowski, Carolyn
2002   Tobacco-Pipes from Rumney's Tavern at London Town (ca. 1700–1730). In *The Clay Tobacco Pipes in Anne Arundel County, Maryland (1650–1730),* Al Luckenbach, C. Jane Cox, and John Kille, editors, pp. 92–99. Anne Arundel County Lost Towns Project, Annapolis, MD.

Hall, Charles L.
2013   *Points in Time: Formal Biface Typology in Maryland.* Maryland Archaeology Month Contribution. Maryland Historical Trust, Crownsville.

Hammett, Regina Combs
1973   My Search for the Great Mill. *Chronicles of St. Mary's* 21(3):7–8 and 21(4):1.
1977   *History of St. Mary's County, Maryland.* Regina Combs Hammett, Ridge, MD.

Hansen, Denise
1986   *Eighteenth Century Fine Earthenwares from Grassy Island.* Environment Canada Parks, Research Bulletin, 247. Ottawa.

Hanson, Carl A.
1981   *Economy and Society in Baroque Portugal, 1668–1703.* University of Minnesota Press, Minneapolis.

Harden, J. David
1995   Liberty Caps and Liberty Trees. *Past & Present* 146(1):66–102.

Harrington, Peter
2003   *English Civil War Fortifications, 1642–51.* Fortress Series 9. Osprey Publishing, Oxford, UK.

Harrison, Barry, and Barbara Hutton

1984   *Vernacular Houses in North Yorkshire and Cleveland.* John Donald, Edinburgh, Scotland.

Hawley, Jerome, and John Lewger

1910   A Relation of Maryland. In *Narratives of Early Maryland 1633–1684,* Clayton C. Hall, editor, pp. 63–112. Barnes and Noble, New York.

Hayes, Katherine

2013   Parameters in the Use of pXRF for Archaeological Site Prospection: A Case Study at the Reaume Fort Site, Central Minnesota. *Journal of Archaeological Science* 40(8):3193–3211.

Hayes-McCoy, G. A.

1964   *Ulster and Other Irish Maps, ca. 1600.* Stationery Office for the Irish Manuscripts Commission, Dublin, Ireland.

Heath, Barbara J.

2010   Space and Place within Plantation Quarters in Virginia, 1700–1825. In *Cabin, Quarter, Plantation: Architecture and Landscapes of North American Slavery,* Clifton Ellis and Rebecca Ginsburg, editors, pp. 157–176. Yale University Press, New Haven, CT.

Heath, Barbara J., and Amber Bennett

2000   "The little Spots allow'd them": African-American Yards. *Historical Archaeology* 2:38–55.

Heikkenen, Herman J., and Mark R. Edwards

1983   The Key-Year Dendrochronology Technique and Its Application in Dating Historic Structures in Maryland. *Association of Preservation Technology Bulletin* 15(3):3–25.

Henry, Susan L.

1979   Terra-cotta Tobacco Pipes in 17th-Century Maryland and Virginia: A Preliminary Study. *Historical Archaeology* 13:14–37.

Herman, Lynn L., John Sands, and Daniel Schecter

1973   Ceramics in St. Mary's County, Maryland during the 1840s: A Socioeconomic Study. *The Conference on Historic Site Archaeology Papers* 8:52–93.

Hester, Thomas, Harry Shafer, and Kenneth Feder

2009   *Field Methods in Archaeology,* 7th edition. Routledge, London.

Hewitt, Cecil A.

1970   Some East Anglian Prototypes for Early Timber Houses in America. *Post Medieval Archaeology* 3:100–121.

Historic St. Mary's City

[1975]   Innkeeping. Manuscript, Department of Research and Collections, Historic St. Mary's City, St. Mary's City, MD.

Hogaboom, Robert E.

1963   St. Mary's City: National Monument to Peace and Toleration. *The Chronicles of St. Mary's* 11(4):32–35.

Holland, Eugenia Calvert

1973   *Edwin Bennett and the Products of His Baltimore Pottery.* Maryland Historical Society, Baltimore.

Holleran, Michael
1998   *Boston's "Changeful" Times: Origins of Preservation and Planning in America.* Johns Hopkins University Press, Baltimore, MD.

Holtorf, Cornelius
2005   *From Stonehenge to Las Vegas: Archaeology as Popular Culture.* AltaMira, Walnut Creek, CA.

Horn, James
1988   Adapting to a New World: A Comparative Study of Local Society in England and Maryland, 1650–1700. In *Colonial Chesapeake Society,* Lois Green Carr, Philip D. Morgan, and Jean B. Russo, editors, pp. 133–175. University of North Carolina Press, Chapel Hill.
1994   *Adapting to the New World: English Society in the Seventeenth-Century Chesapeake.* University of North Carolina Press, Chapel Hill.

Horning, Audrey
1995   "A Verie Fit Place to Erect a Great Cittie": Comparative Contextual Analysis of Archaeological Jamestown. Doctoral dissertation, Department of Anthropology, University of Pennsylvania. University Microfilms International, Ann Arbor, MI.

Hudde, Andries
1877   A Brief, But True Report of the Proceedings of Johan Printz, Governor of the Swedish Forces at the South-River of New Netherland, Also of the Garrisons of the Aforesaid Swedes, Found on that River, The First of November, 1645. In *Documents Relating to the History of the Dutch and Swedish Settlements on the Delaware River, Vol. 12,* Berthold Fernow, editor, pp. 28–39. Argus, Albany, NY.

Huey, Paul R.
2008   From Bird to Tippett: The Archaeology of Continuity and Change in Colonial Dutch Material Culture after 1664. In *From De Halve Maen to KLM: 400 Years of Dutch-American Exchange,* Margriet Lacy, Charles Gehring, and Jenneke Oosterhoff, editors, pp. 41–55. Nodus Publikationen, Munster.

Hurry, Silas D., and Dorsey Bodeman
2007   The Whole Site Is the Artifact: Interpreting the St. John's Site, St. Mary's City, Maryland. In *Past Meets Present: Archaeologists Partnering with Museum Curators, Teachers and Community Groups,* John H. Jameson and Sherene Baugher, editors, pp. 53–68. Springer, New York.

Hurry, Silas D., and Henry M. Miller
1992   The Varieties and Originals of Chesapeake Red Clay Pipes: A View from the Potomac Shore. Manuscript, Department of Research and Collections, Historic St. Mary's City, St. Mary's City, MD.

Inomata, Takeshi, and Lawrence S. Coben
2006   Overture: An Invitation to the Archaeological Theater. In *Archaeology of Performance: Theaters of Power, Community, and Politics,* Takeshi Inomata and Lawrence S. Coben, editors, pp. 11–46. Altamira Press, Lanham, MD.

Jackson, Thomas Penfield
2008   Maryland Design: The First Wall between Church and State. St. Mary's Col-

lege of Maryland, Center for the Study of Democracy, *Occasional Papers of the Center for the Study of Democracy* 3(1). St. Mary's City, MD.

Jackson, William
1878   Whitehaven: Its Streets, Its Principal Houses and Their Inhabitants. *Transactions of the Cumberland & Westmoreland Antiquarian and Archaeological Society* 3:348–381.

Jordan, David W.
1979   Political Stability and the Emergence of a Native Elite in Maryland. In *The Chesapeake in the Seventeenth Century: Essays on Anglo-American Society*, Thad W. Tate and David L. Ammerman, editors, pp. 243–273. W. W. Norton and Company, New York.
1987   *Foundations of Representative Government in Maryland 1632–1715*. Cambridge University Press, Cambridge, UK.

Kalof, Linda
2007   *Looking at Animals in Human History*. Reaktion Books, London.

Keeler, Robert W.
1978   The Homelot on the Seventeenth Century Chesapeake Tidewater Frontier. Doctoral dissertation, Department of Anthropology, University of Oregon. University Microfilms International, Ann Arbor, MI.

Kelly, James
2014   *Sport in Ireland, 1600–1840*. Four Courts Press, Portland, OR.

Kelso, Gerald K., and Henry M. Miller
2016   Pollen Analysis of Three Seventeenth-Century Lead Coffins. *Journal of Archaeological Science: Reports* 6:160–169.

Kelso, William M.
1984   *Kingsmill Plantations, 1619–1800*. Academic Press, San Diego, CA.

Kelso, William M., and Edward Chappell
1974   Excavation of a Seventeenth Century Pottery Kiln at Glebe Harbor, Westmoreland County, Virginia. *Historical Archaeology* 8(1):53–63.

Kelso, William M., and Beverly Straube
2004   *Jamestown Rediscovery, 1994–2004*. Association for the Preservation of Virginia Antiquities, Richmond.

Kennedy, John Pendleton
1965   *Rob of the Bowl: A Legend of St. Inigoe's*. William S. Osborne, editor. College & Universities Press, New Haven, CT.

Kent, Bretton W.
1988   *Making Dead Oysters Talk: Techniques for Analyzing Oyster Shells from Archaeological Sites*. Maryland Historical and Cultural Publications, Crownsville.

Keys, Marcus M., Jr., Leslie P. Milliman, Michael A. Smolek, and Silas D. Hurry
2016   Sourcing a Stone Paver from the Colonial St. Inigoes Manor, Maryland. *Northeast Historical Archaeology* 45:18–41.

Kimball, John
1868   *Records of the Education Division of the Bureau of Refugees, Freedmen, and Abandoned Lands, 1865–1871*. National Archives, Washington, DC.

King, Julia A.

1988   A Comparative Midden Analysis of a Household and Inn in St. Mary's City, Maryland. *Historical Archaeology* 22(2):17–39.

1990   An Intrasite Spatial Analysis of the Van Sweringen Site, St. Mary's City, Maryland. Doctoral dissertation, Department of American Civilization, University of Pennsylvania. University Microfilms International, Ann Arbor, MI.

1996   The Patuxent Point Site. In *Living and Dying on the 17th-Century Patuxent Frontier,* Julia A. King and Douglas H. Ubelaker, editors, pp. 15–46. Maryland Historical Trust, Crownesville.

2012   *Archaeology, Narrative, and the Politics of the Past: The View from Southern Maryland.* University of Tennessee Press, Knoxville.

King, Julia A., and Henry M. Miller

1987   The View from the Midden: An Analysis of Midden Distribution and Composition at the Van Sweringen Site, St. Mary's City, Maryland. *Historical Archaeology* 21(2):37–59.

King, Julia A., and Scott M. Strickland

2016   *The Search for Zekiah Fort: Tracing Piscataway History on the Ground.* St. Mary's College of Maryland, St. Mary's City, MD.

Kirby, Michael X., and Henry M. Miller

2005   Response of a Benthic Suspension Feeder (*Crassostrea virginica* Gmelin) to Three Centuries of Anthropogenic Eutrophication in Chesapeake Bay. *Estuarine, Coastal and Shelf Science* 62:679–689.

Klingelhofer, Eric

1987   Aspects of Early Afro-American Material Culture: Artifacts from the Slave Quarters at Garrison Plantation. *Historical Archaeology* 21(2):112–119.

Kostro, Mark

2005   *The 2003 Archaeological Excavations at the Peyton Randolph Property, Williamsburg, Virginia.* Colonial Williamsburg Archaeological Reports. Colonial Williamsburg, Williamsburg, VA.

Kraft, John C., and Grace S. Brush

1981   A Geological-Paleoenvironmental Analysis of the Sediments in St. John's Pond and the Nearshore Zone Near Howard's Wharf at St. Mary's City, Maryland. Manuscript, Department of Research and Collections, Historic St. Mary's City, St. Mary's City, MD.

Krugler, John

2004   *English and Catholic: The Lords Baltimore in the Seventeenth Century.* Johns Hopkins University Press, Baltimore, MD.

Lacoste, Kenneth C., and Robert D. Wall

1989   *An Archeological Study of the Western Maryland Coal Region: The Historic Resources.* Maryland Geological Survey, Baltimore.

LaMotte, Charles E.

1864   Charles E. LaMotte to His Mother, May 8, 1864. LaMotte Papers, RG 9200-L02-000. Delaware Public Archives, Dover.

Land, Aubrey C.

1965   Economic Base and Social Structure, the Northern Chesapeake in the Eighteenth Century. *Journal of Economic History* 25(4):639–654.

LaRoche, Cheryl Janifer

2013   *Free Black Communities and the Underground Railroad: The Geography of Resistance.* University of Illinois Press, Chicago.

Larsen, Ellouise Baker

1939   *American Historical Views on Staffordshire China.* Doubleday, Doran & Company, New York.

1975   *American Historical Views on Staffordshire China,* 3rd edition. Dover Books, New York.

Larson, Knut Einar (editor)

1995   *Nara Conference on Authenticity.* Tapir, Trondheim, Norway.

Lavin, James D.

2000   *Arms and Armor of 17th-Century Virginia.* Jamestown-Yorktown Foundation, Williamsburg, VA.

Leone, Mark P., and Silas D. Hurry

1998   Seeing: The Power of Town Planning in the Chesapeake. *Historical Archaeology* 32(4):34–62.

Lewis, James F., and James Motley Booker

1967   *Northumberland County, Virginia, Wills and Administrations, 1713–1749.* James F. Lewis and James Motley Booker, Lottsburg, VA.

Lewis, Kenneth E.

1985   Plantation Layout and Function in the South Carolina Lowcountry. In *The Archaeology of Slavery and Plantation Life,* Theresa A. Singleton, editor, pp. 35–66. Academic Press, San Diego, CA.

Lindgren, James

1995   *Preserving Historic New England: Preservation, Progressivism, and the Remaking of Memory.* Oxford University Press, Oxford, UK.

Lipski, Louis L., and Michael Archer

1984   *Dated English Delftware.* Sotheby's, London.

Litten, Julian

1991   *The English Way of Death: The Common Funeral since 1450.* Robert Hale, London.

Lounsbury, Carl R.

2005   *Courthouses of Early Virginia: An Architectural History.* University of Virginia Press, Charlottesville.

2011   *Essays in Early American Architectural History: A View from the Chesapeake.* University of Virginia Press, Charlottesville.

Lowenthal, David

1996   *Possessed by the Past: The Heritage Crusade and the Spoils of History.* Free Press, New York.

Luckenbach, Al, and C. Jane Cox

2002   Tobacco-Pipe Manufacture in Early Maryland: The Swan Cover Site (c. 1660–1669). In *The Clay Tobacco Pipes in Anne Arundel County, Maryland (1650–*

1730), Al Luckenbach, C. Jane Cox, and John Kille, editors, pp. 46–63. Anne Arundel County Lost Towns Project, Annapolis, MD.

Luckenbach, Al, and Taft Kiser

2006 Seventeenth-Century Tobacco Pipe Manufacture in the Chesapeake Region: A Preliminary Delineation of the Makers and Their Styles. In *Ceramics in America, Vol. 6,* Robert Hunter, editor, pp. 160–177. Chipstone Foundation, Milwaukee, WI.

Luckenbach, Al, and Paul Mintz

2002 The Broadneck Site (18AN818): A 1650's Manifestation. In *The Clay Tobacco Pipes in Anne Arundel County, Maryland (1650–1730),* Al Luckenbach, C. Jane Cox, and John Kille, editors, pp. 12–17. Anne Arundel County Lost Towns Project, Annapolis, MD.

Mackinder, Anthony, Lyn Blackmore, Julian Bowsher, and Christopher Phillpotts

2013 *The Hope Playhouse, Animal Baiting, and Later Industrial Activity at Bear Gardens on Bankside: Excavations at Riverside House and New Globe Walk, Southwark, 1999–2000.* Museum of London Archaeology, London.

Main, Gloria L.

1982 *Tobacco Colony: Life in Early Maryland, 1650–1720.* Princeton University Press, Princeton, NJ.

Mann, Robert W., and Sean P. Murphy

1990 *Regional Atlas of Bone Disease: A Guide to Pathologic and Normal Variation in the Human Skeleton.* Charles C. Thomas, Springfield, IL.

Marks, Bayly

1979 Economics and Society in a Staple Plantation Economy: St. Mary's County, Maryland. Doctoral dissertation, Department of History, University of Maryland. University Microfilms International, Ann Arbor, MI.

Martin, Anne Smart

1989 The Role of Pewter as Missing Artifact: Consumer Attitudes toward Tablewares in Late 18th Century Virginia. *Historical Archaeology* 23(2):1–27.

Marye, William B.

1944 The Historic Mulberry Tree of St. Mary's City. *Maryland Historical Magazine* 39(1):73–80.

The Maryland Gazette

1774 "To be sold . . ." *The Maryland Gazette,* 3 February. Annapolis, MD.

Maryland Medical Journal: Medicine and Surgery

1887 Thomas & Thompson: Advertisement. *Maryland Medical Journal: Medicine and Surgery* 17(8):9. Baltimore.

Maryland State Archives

1671 Inventory of the Estate of Robert Slye. Testamentary Proceedings, 5:152–190, Maryland State Archives, Maryland Hall of Records, Annapolis.

1678a Inventory of the Estate of Michael Rochford. Inventories and Accounts, 6, f. 2, Maryland State Archives, Maryland Hall of Records, Annapolis.

1678b Inventory of the Estate of Richard Chilman. Inventories and Accounts, 5, f. 383, Maryland State Archives, Maryland Hall of Records, Annapolis.

1679   Inventory of the Estate of Thomas Notley. Inventories and Accounts, 5, f. 383, Maryland State Archives, Maryland Hall of Records, Annapolis.

1687   Inventory of the Estate of John Baker. Inventories and Accounts, 10, f. 111–124, Maryland State Archives, Maryland Hall of Records, Annapolis.

1689   Inventory of the Estate of Justinian Gerard. Inventories and Accounts, 10, f. 223, Maryland State Archives, Maryland Hall of Records, Annapolis.

1693   Inventory of the Estate of Governor Lionel Copley. Inventories and Accounts, 12, f. 45–60, Maryland State Archives, Maryland Hall of Records, Annapolis.

1698   Inventory of the Estate of James Pattison. Inventories and Accounts, 16, f. 34–36, Maryland State Archives, Maryland Hall of Records, Annapolis.

1701   Inventory of the Estate of Garrett van Sweringen. Inventories and Accounts, 20, f. 96–98, Maryland State Archives, Maryland Hall of Records, Annapolis.

1753   Inventory of the Goods and chattels of John Hicks, Inventories and Accounts, 55, f. 27–30, 57, f. 59, Maryland State Archives, Maryland Hall of Records, Annapolis.

1779   Will of Moses Tabbs. Patent Liber BC & GS 38, f. 235; St. Mary's County Wills, J.J. no. f. 94, Maryland State Archives, Maryland Hall of Records, Annapolis.

1780   St. Mary's County Valuations and Indentures, 1780–1808, f. 1, Maryland State Archives, Maryland Hall of Records, Annapolis.

1799   Will of George C. Tabbs. St. Mary's County Will Book J.j.2, 1791–1805 no. 723, Maryland State Archives, Maryland Hall of Records, Annapolis.

1803   Will of William Kirby. St. Mary's County Wills, Liber J.J. No. 3; f. 24, Maryland State Archives, Maryland Hall of Records, Annapolis.

1826   St. Mary's County Valuations 1807–1826, ff. 94–95, Maryland State Archives, Maryland Hall of Records, Annapolis.

1830   Will of Daniel Campbell. St. Mary's County Wills, E.M. N0.1, F.145, Maryland State Archives, Maryland Hall of Records, Annapolis.

1833   St. Mary's County Administration Accounts, Liber E.J.M. 1831–1833:15, Maryland State Archives, Maryland Hall of Records, Annapolis.

1839   St. Mary's County Guardian Accounts 1835–1839, pp. 353–354, Maryland State Archives, Maryland Hall of Records, Annapolis.

1841   St. Mary's County Annual Valuations of Real Estate and Personal Property 1826–1841:125–201, Maryland State Archives, Maryland Hall of Records, Annapolis.

1851   Release of Sarah Ann Golly Burch dower rights, St. Mary's County Deed Book W.M.T. No. 2:327, Maryland State Archives, Maryland Hall of Records, Annapolis.

1853   Deed, John and Sarah Campbell to Jane Biscoe. St. Mary's County Deed Book J.T.B. No. 1:501–502, Maryland State Archives, Maryland Hall of Records, Annapolis.

1856   Deed, Jane Biscoe to Edward Joy. St. Mary's County Deed Book J.T.B. No 2:324, Maryland State Archives, Maryland Hall of Records, Annapolis.

1858   St. Mary's County Annual Evaluation of Real and Personal Property 1841–1864,

Liber G.C. 1, f. 262, Maryland State Archives, Maryland Hall of Records, Annapolis.

1866   St. Mary's County Administrative Accounts 1863–1869:12 and 45, Maryland State Archives, Maryland Hall of Records, Annapolis.

Maryland Tercentenary Commission

1935   *Report of the Maryland Tercentenary Commission.* State of Maryland, Annapolis.

McDaniel, George

1982   *Hearth and Home: Preserving a People's Culture.* Temple University Press, Philadelphia, PA.

McIlvoy, Karen E.

2009   The Ceramics Assemblage from the Kingsley Plantation Slave Quarters. Archeology Program, National Park Service, U.S. Department of the Interior https://www.nps.gov/archeology/sites/npsites/kingsleyCeramics.htm. Accessed 4 June 2019.

McKnight, Matthew D.

2019   The Piscataway Trail: Clues to the Migration of an Indian Nation. In *The Archaeology of Colonial Maryland,* Matthew D. McKnight, editor, pp. 74–78. Maryland Historical Trust Press, Crownsville.

McMillan, Lauren K.

2015   The Multiple Interaction Spheres of 17th-Century Tobacco Pipes at the John Hallows Site, Westmoreland County, Virginia. *Middle Atlantic Archaeology* 31:1–22.

McMillan, Lauren K., Scott Stickland, Rebecca Webster, and Julia King

2017   *Phase I and II Archaeological Investigations of a Portion of the St. Barbara's Tract.* Report to St. Mary's College of Maryland, St. Mary's City, MD, from St. Mary's College of Maryland, St. Mary's City, MD.

McNamara, Martha J.

2004   *From Tavern to Courthouse: Architecture and Ritual in American Law, 1658–1860.* Johns Hopkins University Press, Baltimore, MD.

Menard, Russell R.

1973   Farm Price of Maryland Tobacco, 1659–1710. *Maryland Historical Magazine* 68(1):80–85.

1975   Economy and Society in Early Colonial Maryland. Doctoral dissertation, Department of History, University of Iowa. University Microfilms International, Ann Arbor, MI.

1977   From Servants to Slaves: The Transformation of the Chesapeake Labor System. *Southern Studies* 16:355–390.

1984   Population, Economy, and Society in Seventeenth-Century Maryland. *Maryland Historical Magazine* 79(1):71–92.

Merritt, Elizabeth (editor)

1952   *Archives of Maryland, Vol. 41, Proceedings of the Provincial Court of Maryland, 1670/1–1675.* Maryland Historical Society, Baltimore.

Meyers, Allan D., Allison S. Harvey, and Sarah A. Levithol

2008   Houselot Refuse Disposal and Geochemistry at a Late 19th-Century Hacienda Village in Yucatán, Mexico. *Journal of Field Archaeology* 33(4):371–388.

Middleton, Arthur Pierce, and Henry M. Miller

2008   "Mr. Secretary": John Lewgar, St. John's Freehold, and Early Maryland. *Maryland Historical Magazine* 103(2):132–165.

Miller, George L.

1974   A Tenant Farmer's Tableware: Nineteenth-Century Ceramics from Tabbs Purchase. *Maryland Historical Magazine* 69(2):197–210.

1980   Classification and Economic Scaling of 19th Century Ceramics. *Historical Archaeology* 14:1–40.

1986   Ode to a Lunch Bowl: The Atlantic Lunch as an Interface between St. Mary's County, Maryland and Washington, DC. *Northeast Historical Archaeology* 13:2–8.

1991   A Revised Set of CC Index Values for Classification and Economic Scaling of English Ceramics from 1787 to 1880. *Historical Archaeology* 25(1):1–25.

Miller, George, and Amy C. Earls

2008   War and Pots: The Impact of Economics and Politics on Ceramic Consumption Patterns. In *Ceramics in America, Vol. 8,* Robert Hunter, editor, pp. 67–108. Chipstone Foundation, Milwaukee, WI.

Miller, George L., and Robert Hunter

1990   English Shell Edged Earthenware: Alias Leeds Ware, Alias Feather Edge. In *The Consumer Revolution in 18th Century English Pottery, Proceedings of the Wedgwood International Seminar,* 35th Annual Wedgwood International Seminar, pp. 107–136. Birmingham Arts Museum, Birmingham, AL.

Miller, George, and Robert R. Hunter

2001   How Creamware Got the Blues: The Origins of China Glaze and Pearlware. In *Ceramics in America, Vol. 1,* Robert Hunter, editor, pp. 135–161. Chipstone Foundation, Milwaukee, WI.

Miller, Henry M.

1978   Analysis of the Window-Related Artifacts at the St. John's Site—18-ST1-23. Manuscript, Department of Research and Collections, Historic St. Mary's City, St. Mary's City, MD.

1983   *Search for the "Citty of Saint Maries": Report on the 1981 Excavations in St. Mary's City, Maryland.* Historic St. Mary's City, St. Mary's City Research Series, No. 1, St. Mary's City, MD.

1984   Colonization and Subsistence Change on the Seventeenth Century Chesapeake Frontier. Doctoral dissertation, Department of Anthropology, Michigan State University. University Microfilms International, Ann Arbor, MI.

1986   *Discovering Maryland's First City: A Summary Report on the 1981–1984 Archaeological Excavations in St. Mary's City, Maryland.* Historic St. Mary's City, St. Mary's City Archaeology Series, No. 2. St. Mary's City, MD.

1988a   Baroque Cities in the Wilderness: Archaeology and Urban Development in the Colonial Chesapeake. *Historical Archaeology* 22(2):57–73.

1988b   An Archaeological Perspective on the Evolution of Diet in the Colonial Chesapeake, 1620–1745. In *Colonial Chesapeake Society,* Lois Green Carr, Philip Morgan, and Jean Russo, editors, pp. 176–199. University of North Carolina Press, Chapel Hill.

1994   The Country's House Site: An Archaeological Study of a Seventeenth-Century Domestic Landscape. In *Historical Archaeology of the Chesapeake,* Paul A. Shackel and Barbara J. Little, editors, pp. 65–83. Smithsonian Institution Press, Washington, DC.

1999   Archaeology and Town Planning in British North America. In *Old and New Worlds: Historical/Post Medieval Archaeology Papers from the Societies' Joint Conferences at Williamsburg and London 1997,* Geoff Egan and R. L. Michael, editors, pp. 72–83. Oxbow, Oxford, UK.

2000   The Forts of St. Mary's City. Manuscript, Department of Research and Collections, Historic St. Mary's City, St. Mary's City, MD.

2001   Living along "Great Shellfish Bay": The Relationship between Prehistoric Peoples and the Chesapeake. In *Discovering the Chesapeake: The History of an Ecosystem,* Philip D. Curtin, Grace S. Brush, and George W. Fisher, editors, pp. 109–126. Johns Hopkins University Press, Baltimore, MD.

2006   Analysis of the Aisled Outbuilding in the Backyard of the St. John's Site (18ST1-23). Manuscript, Department of Research and Collections, Historic St. Mary's City, St. Mary's City, MD.

2007   When the Digging is Over: Some Observations on Methods of Interpreting Archaeological Sites for the Public. In *Past Meets Present: Archaeologists Partnering with Museum Curators, Teachers and Community Groups,* John H. Jameson and Sherene Baugher, editors, pp. 35–52. Springer, New York.

2008   "To Serve the Countrey": Garrett Van Sweringen and the Dutch Influence in Early Maryland. In *From De Halve Maen to KLM: 400 Years of Dutch-American Exchange,* Margriet Bruijn Lacy, Charles Gehring, and Jenneke Oosterhoff, editors, pp. 85–104. Nodus Publikationen, Münster, Germany.

2016   Some Comparisons of the Ceramic Vessels from St. Mary's City Sites. Manuscript, Department of Research and Collections, Historic St. Mary's City, St. Mary's City, MD.

2019   Faunal Remains from 18ST1-130. Manuscript, Department of Research and Collections, Historic St. Mary's City, St. Mary's City, MD.

Miller, Henry M., and Robert W. Keeler
1986   *An Analysis of Gunflints, Tools and Flint Debitage from the St. John's Site (18ST 1-23) in St. Mary's City, Maryland.* Historic St. Mary's City, St. Mary's City Research Series, No. 2. St. Mary's City, MD.

Miller, Henry M., Ruth M. Mitchell, Timothy B. Riordan, Patricia Dance, James W. Embrey, Silas D. Hurry, Donald Winter, and Ilene J. Frank
2006   *Archaeological Survey and Testing for the 17th-Century "Mattapany Path" Road System, St. Mary's City, Maryland, 18ST1.* Archaeological Report No. 160. Report to Maryland Department of Transportation, Baltimore, MD, from Department of Research and Collections, Historic St. Mary's City, St. Mary's City, MD.

Miller, Henry M., Ruth M. Mitchell, Wesley R. Willoughby, and Donald L. Winter
2004   *Archaeological Investigations in West's Field (18ST1-29), St. Mary's City, Maryland.* Report to St. Mary's College of Maryland, St. Mary's City, MD, from Department of Research and Collections, Historic St. Mary's City, St. Mary's City, MD.

Mills, Barbara J., and William H. Walker

2008   Introduction: Memory, Materiality, and Depositional Practice. In *Memory Work: Archaeologies of Material Practices,* Barbara J. Mills and William H. Walker, editors, pp. 3–23. School of American Research Press, Santa Fe, NM.

Mitchell, James T., and Henry Flanders (editors)

1896   *The Statutes at Large of Pennsylvania from 1682 to 1801, Vol. 2: 1700 to 1712.* Clarence M. Busch, State Printer, Harrisburg, PA.

Mitchell, Ruth M. and Henry M. Miller

1996   A Phase 1 Archaeological Survey of Portions of the St. Mary's College of Maryland Campus in St. Mary's City, Maryland. Manuscript, Department of Research and Collections, Historic St. Mary's City, St. Mary's City, MD.

Mitchell, Ruth M., Henry M. Miller, Edward Chaney, and Donald Winter

1999   *A Phase 1 Archaeological Survey and Selective Phase 2 Testing of Sites in the Athletic Field Area, St. Mary's College of Maryland, St. Mary's City, Maryland.* Report to St. Mary's College of Maryland, St. Mary's City, MD, from Historic St. Mary's City, St. Mary's City, MD.

Mitchell, Vivienne

1976   Decorated Brown Clay Tobacco Pipe Bowls from Nominy Plantation: A Progress Report. *Quarterly Bulletin of the Archaeological Society of Virginia* 31(2):83–92.

Moorrees, Coenraad F. A., Elizabeth A. Fanning, and Edward E. Hunt Jr.

1963   Formation and Resorption of Three Deciduous Teeth in Children. *American Journal of Physical Anthropology* 21(2):205–213.

Morgan, Edmond

1952   *Virginians at Home: Family Life in the Eighteenth Century.* Colonial Williamsburg Foundation, Williamsburg, VA.

Morisita, Masaaka

1959   Measuring of the Dispersion and Analysis of Distribution Patterns. Kyushu University, *Memoirs of the Faculty of Science,* Biology, Series E, 2:215–235, Fukuoka, Japan.

Morrison II, Alexander H.

1985   A New Way of Looking at Old Holes: Methods for Excavating and Interpreting Timber Structures. In *Structure and Process in Southeastern Archaeology,* Roy S. Dickens and H. Trawick Ward, editors, pp. 119–134. University of Alabama, Tuscaloosa.

Mouer, Daniel L., Mary Ellen N. Hodges, Stephen R. Potter, Susan L. Henry Renaud, Ivor Noël Hume, Dennis J. Pogue, Martha W. McCartney, and Thomas E. Davidson

1999   "Colono" Pottery, Chesapeake Pipes, and "Uncritical Assumptions." In *"I, Too, Am America": Archaeological Studies in African American Life,* Theresa A. Singleton, editor, pp. 105–166. University Press of Virginia, Charlottesville.

Mountford, Arnold R.

1971   *The Illustrated Guide to Staffordshire Salt-glazed Stoneware.* Praeger, New York.

Mrozowski, Stephen A., Grace H. Ziesing, and Mary C. Beaudry

1996   *Living on the Boott: Historical Archaeology at the Boott Mills Boardinghouses, Lowell, Massachusetts.* University of Massachusetts Press, Amherst.

Mungeam, Gerald I.

1968   Contracts for the Supply of Equipment to the New Model Army in 1645. *The Journal of the Arms and Armor Society* 6(3):53–115.

Museum of London

n.d.   Die. Collections Online, Museum of London. https://collections.museumoflondon.org.uk/online/object/30413.html. Accessed 21 May 2019.

Neiman, Fraser

1980a   Field Archaeology of the Clifts Plantation Site, Westmoreland County, Virginia. Robert E. Lee Memorial Association, Stratford, VA.

Neiman, Fraser D.

1980b   *The "Manner House" Before Stratford.* Robert E. Lee Memorial Association, Stratford, VA.

Nesbit, Scott

2011   Scales Intimate and Sprawling: Slavery, Emancipation, and the Geography of Marriage in Virginia. Southern Spaces. https://southernspaces.org/2011/scales-intimate-and-sprawling-slavery-emancipation-and-geography-marriage-virginia/. Accessed 29 January 2020.

Neuwirth, Jessica Loren

1997   Landscapes of Authority and Nostalgia: Modernization of a Southern Maryland Plantation, St. Mary's City, Maryland, 1840–1930. Doctoral dissertation, Department of American Civilization, University of Pennsylvania. University Microfilms International, Ann Arbor, MI.

Nicholson, Kate

2005   Medieval Deposits and a Cockpit at St. Ives, Cambridgeshire. *Proceedings of the Cambridge Antiquarian Society* 94:103–115.

Noël Hume, Audrey

1978   *Food.* Colonial Williamsburg Foundation, *Colonial Williamsburg Archaeological Series* 9. Williamsburg, VA.

Noël Hume, Ivor

1968   *Historical Archaeology.* Alfred A. Knopf, New York.

1970   *A Guide to Artifacts of Colonial America.* Alfred A. Knopf, New York.

1978   The Rise and Fall of English White Salt-Glazed Stoneware, Parts I and II. In *English Pottery and Porcelain: An Historical Survey,* Paul Atterbury, editor, pp. 16–29. Universe Books, New York.

1979   First Look at a Lost Virginia Settlement. *National Geographic* 155(6):735–767.

1982   *Martin's Hundred: The Discovery of a Lost Colonial Virginia Settlement.* Alfred A. Knopf, New York.

Noël Hume, Ivor, and Audrey Noël Hume

2001   *The Archaeology of Martin's Hundred, Parts 1 and 2.* Colonial Williamsburg Foundation, Williamsburg, VA.

Oonk, S., C. P. Slomp, and D. J. Huisman

2009   Geochemistry as an Aid in Archaeological Prospection and Site Interpretation: Current Issues and Research Directions. *Archaeological Prospection* 16(1):35–51.

Orser, Charles E.

1991   The Continued Pattern of Dominance: Landlord and Tenant on the Postbellum

Cotton Plantation. In *The Archaeology of Inequality*, Randall H. McGuire and Robert Paynter, editors, pp. 40–54. Basil Blackwell, Cambridge, MA.

Orser, Charles E., and Annette M. Nekola

1985   Plantation Settlement from Slavery to Tenancy: An Example from a Piedmont Plantation in South Carolina. In *Archaeological Studies of the Plantation System*, Theresa A. Singleton, editor, pp. 67–96. Academic Press, New York.

Ortner, Donald J., and Walter G. J. Putschar

1981   *Identification of Pathological Conditions in Human Skeletal Remains.* Smithsonian Institution, Smithsonian Contributions to Anthropology, No. 28. Washington, DC.

Ortner, Sherry B.

1989   *High Religion: A Cultural and Political History of Sherpa Buddhism.* Princeton University Press, Princeton, NJ.

Oswald, Adrian

1982   *English Brown Stoneware, 1670–1900.* Faber & Faber, London.

Otto, John Solomon

1984   *Cannon's Point Plantation, 1794–1860: Living Conditions and Status Patterns in the Old South.* Academic Press, New York.

Outlaw, Alain C.

1990   *Governor's Land: Archaeology of the Early Seventeenth-Century Virginia Settlements.* University of Virginia, Charlottesville.

Owoc, Mary Ann

2005   From the Ground Up: Agency, Practice, and Community in the Southwestern British Bronze Age. *Journal of Archaeological Method and Theory* 12(4):257–281.

Owsley, Douglas W., and Karin S. Bruwelheide

n.d.   Osteological Analysis of Human Remains from the Chapel Field, Historic St. Mary's City, Maryland. Manuscript, National Museum of Natural History, Smithsonian Institution, Washington, DC.

Oxford English Dictionary

1971   Trumpery. *The Compact Edition of the Oxford English Dictionary.* Oxford University Press, Oxford, UK.

Panich, Lee M., Emilie Lederer, Ryan Phillip, and Emily Dylla

2018   Heads or Tails? Modified Ceramic Gaming Pieces from Colonial California. *International Journal of Historical Archaeology* 22:746–770.

Papenfuse, Edward, Alan Day, David Jordan, and Gregory Stiverson

1979   *A Biographical Dictionary of the Maryland Legislature, 1635–1789.* Johns Hopkins University Press, Baltimore, MD.

Parno, Travis G.

2011   *Report of the Second Season of Archaeological Testing at the Fairbanks House Property, 511 East Street, Dedham, Massachusetts.* Report to the Massachusetts Historical Commission, Boston.

Pasch, Christopher

2020   Enslaved below the Temple of Liberty: Exposing the Hidden Landscape of the Temple and Icehouse at James Madison's Montpelier. Masters dissertation,

Department of Archaeology and Ancient History, University of Leicester. University Microfilms International, Ann Arbor, MI.

Pearce, Jacqueline

1992   *Post-Medieval Pottery in London, 1500–1700, Volume 1: Border Wares.* HMSO, London.

Pearson, Sarah

1985   *Rural Houses of the Lancashire Pennines 1560–1760.* Her Majesty's Stationery Office, London.

Penningroth, Dylan C.

2003   *The Claims of Kinfolk: African American Property and Community in the Nineteenth-Century South.* University of North Carolina Press, Chapel Hill.

Percy, George

1922   "A Trewe Relacyon": Virginia from 1609 to 1612. *Tyler's Quarterly Historical and Genealogical Magazine* 3:259–282.

Peterson, Harold L.

1956   *Arms and Armor in Colonial America, 1526–1783.* The Stackpole Company, Harrisburg, PA.

1969   *Round Shot and Rammers: An Introduction to Muzzleloading Land Artillery in the United States.* Bonanza Books, New York.

Pogue, Dennis J.

1987   Seventeenth-Century Proprietary Rule and Rebellion: Archaeology at Charles Calvert's Mattapany-Sewall. *Maryland Archaeology* 23(1):1–37.

1988   Anthrosols and the Analysis of Archaeological Sites in a Plowed Context: The King's Reach Site. *Northeast Historical Archaeology* 17:1–15.

1991   Clay Tobacco Pipes from Four 17th-Century Domestic Sites in the Lower Patuxent River Valley of Maryland. In *The Archaeology of the Clay Tobacco Pipe XII: Chesapeake Bay,* Peter Davey and Dennis J. Pogue, editors, pp. 3–26. BAR International Series 566, Oxford, UK.

2005   Measuring the Advent of Gentility. Paper presented at the 38th Annual Conference on Historical and Underwater Archaeology, York, UK.

Polglase, Christopher, Michael B. Hornum, Andrew D. Madsen, Christian Davenport, John Clarke, Kathleen M. Child, and Martha Williams

2001   *Phase III Archaeological Data Recovery at Site 18SM704, Naval Air Station, Patuxent River, St. Mary's County, Maryland.* Report to Tams Consultants, Inc., Arlington, VA, from R. Christopher Goodwin and Associates, Frederick, MD.

Potter, Stephen R.

1993   *Commoners, Tribute and Chiefs: The Development of Algonquian Culture in the Potomac Valley.* University Press of Virginia, Charlottesville.

Powell, Richard E.

1993   Sport, Social Relations, and Animal Husbandry: Early Cock-Fighting in North America. *International Journal of the History of Sport* 10(3):361–381.

Pritchard, Edward T.

2013   *Bird Medicine: The Sacred Power of Bird Shamanism.* Simon and Schuster, New York.

Puype, Jan Piet

1985   *Proceedings of the 1984 Trade Gun Conference, Part 1: Dutch and Other Flint-locks from Seventeenth-Century Iroquois Sites.* Research Records No. 18. Research Division, Rochester Museum & Science Center, Rochester, NY.

Rafferty, Sean, and Rob Mann

2004   *Smoking and Culture: The Archaeology of Tobacco Pipes in Eastern North America.* University of Tennessee Press, Knoxville.

Ranzetta, Kirk E.

2010   *I'm Goin' Down County: An Architectural Journey Through St. Mary's County.* Maryland Historical Trust Press, Crownsville.

Reeves, Matthew B.

2003   Reinterpreting Manassas: The Nineteenth-Century African American Community at Manassas National Battlefield Park. *Historical Archaeology* 37(3): 124–137.

Reich, David, Kristin Stewardson, Iosif Lazaridis, Swapan Mallick, Nadin Rohland, and Douglas Owsley

2016   Ancient DNA Analysis of St. Mary's City Lead Coffin Burials. Department of Genetics, Harvard University Medical School. http://genetics.med.harvard. edu/reich/Reich_Lab/Datasets.html. Accessed 30 April 2019.

Rice, James D.

2009   *Nature and History in the Potomac Country: From Hunter-Gatherers to the Age of Jefferson.* Johns Hopkins University Press, Baltimore, MD.

Rice, Kym

1983   *For the Entertainment of Friends and Strangers: The Role of the Tavern in 18th Century Life.* Fraunces Tavern Museum, New York.

Rickard, Jonathan

1993   Mocha Ware: Slip-Decorated Refined Earthenware. *The Magazine Antiques* 144(2):182–189.

2006   *Mocha and Related Dipped Wares, 1770–1939.* University Press of New England, Hanover, NH.

Ricketts, Mac Linscott

1966   The North American Trickster. *History of Religion* 5(2):320–350.

Riordan, Timothy B.

1988   The Interpretation of 17th-Century Sites through Plow Zone Surface Collections: Examples from St. Mary's City, Maryland. *Historical Archaeology* 22(2):2–16.

2000   *Dig a Grave Both Wide and Deep: An Archaeological Investigation of Mortuary Practices in the 17th-Century Cemetery at St. Mary's City, Maryland.* Historic St. Mary's City, St. Mary's City Archaeology Series, No. 3. St. Mary's City, MD.

2004a   Philip Calvert: Patron of St. Mary's City. *Maryland Historical Magazine* 99(3):329–350.

2004b   *The Plundering Time: Maryland in the English Civil War, 1645–1646.* Maryland Historical Society, Baltimore.

Riordan, Timothy B., and Silas D. Hurry

2015   Archaeological Excavations of the Print House Building, Slave Quarter Site

(18ST1-14), St. Mary's City, Maryland. Manuscript, Department of Research and Collections, Historic St. Mary's City, St. Mary's City, MD.

Riordan, Timothy B., Henry M. Miller, and Silas D. Hurry

1994 Birth of an American Freedom: Religion in Early Maryland. Report to the National Endowment for the Humanities, Washington, DC, from Historic St. Mary's City, St. Mary's City, MD.

Ritz, Casey, and William Merka

2004 *Maximizing Poultry Manure Use through Nutrient Management Planning.* Bulletin 1249. University of Georgia Cooperative Extension Service, Athens.

Rivington's New York Gazetteer

1774 Bull-Baiting. *Rivington's New York Gazetteer.* 21 July, 1:2. New York.

Robertson, Ross M.

1973 *History of the American Economy,* 3rd edition. Harcourt, Brace, Jovanovich, New York.

Roth, Rodris

1961 *Tea Drinking in 18th-Century America: Its Etiquette and Equipage.* United States National Museum, Contributions from the Museum of History and Technology: History Paper 14:61–91.

Rountree, Helen C.

1989 *The Powhatan Indians of Virginia: Their Traditional Culture.* University of Oklahoma Press, Norman.

Ruport, Arch

2008 *The Art of Cockfighting: A Handbook for Beginners and Old Timers.* Read Books, London.

Russell, Aaron

1997 Material Culture and African American Spirituality at the Hermitage. *Historical Archaeology* 31(2):63–80.

Russo, Jean B., and J. Elliott Russo

2012 *Planting an Empire: The Early Chesapeake in British North America.* Johns Hopkins University Press, Baltimore, MD.

Salinger, Sharon V.

2002 *Taverns and Drinking in Early America.* Johns Hopkins University Press, Baltimore, MD.

Samford, Patricia M.

1997 Response to a Market: Dating English Underglaze Transfer-Printed Wares. *Historical Archaeology* 31(2):1–30.

2018 Following the Drinking Gourd: Considering the Celestial Landscape. Paper presented at the 51st Annual Conference on Historical and Underwater Archaeology, New Orleans, LA.

Scott, Pamela

1995 *Temple of Liberty: Building the Capitol for a New Nation.* Oxford University Press, Oxford, UK.

Scott-Warren, Jason

2003 When Theaters Were Bear-Gardens; or, What's at Stake in a Comedy of Humors. *Shakespeare Quarterly* 54(1):63–82.

Secord, William

1992   *Dog Painting, 1840–1940: A Social History of the Dog in Art.* Antique Collectors Club, Woodbridge, UK.

Seib, Rebecca, and Helen C. Rountree

2014   *Indians of Southern Maryland.* Maryland Historical Society, Baltimore.

Shakespeare, William

1992   *Hamlet.* Washington Square Press, New York.

Shaw, Simeon

1829   *History of the Staffordshire Potteries; and the Rise and Progress of the Manufacture of Pottery and Porcelain.* Hanley, Staffordshire, UK. Reprinted 1968 by Beatrice C. Weinstock, Great Neck, NY.

1837   *Chemistry of the several Natural and Artificial Heterogeneous Compounds used in Manufacturing Porcelain, Glass and Pottery.* W. Lewis and Son, London. Reprinted 1900 by Scott, Greenwood and Co., London.

Shepard, Anna O.

1956   *Ceramics for the Archaeologist.* Carnegie Institution of Washington, Washington, DC.

Shepard, E. Lee

1995   "This Being Court Day": Courthouses and Community Life in Rural Virginia. *Virginia Magazine of History and Biography* 103(4):459–470.

Shlasko, Ellen

2002   Frenchmen and Africans in South Carolina: Culture Interactions on the Eighteenth-Century Frontier. In *Another Country: Archaeological and Historical Perspectives on Cultural Interactions in the Southern Colonies,* J. W. Joseph and Martha Zierdon, editors, pp. 133–144. University of Alabama Press, Tuscaloosa.

Sikes, Kathryn

2008   Stars as Social Space? Contextualizing 17th-Century Chesapeake Star-Motif Pipes. *Post-Medieval Archaeology* 42(1):75–103.

Singleton, Theresa A.

1988   An Archaeological Framework for Slavery and Emancipation, 1750–1880. In *The Recovery of Meaning: Historical Archaeology in the Eastern United States,* Mark P. Leone and Parker B. Potter Jr., editors, pp. 345–370. Smithsonian Institution Press, Washington, DC.

2011   Epilogue: Reflections on Archaeologies of Postemancipation from a Student of Slavery. In *The Materiality of Freedom: Archaeologies of Postemancipation Life,* Jodi A. Barnes, editor, pp. 277–285. University of South Carolina Press, Columbia.

Singleton, Theresa A. (editor)

1985   *The Archaeology of Slavery and Plantation Life.* Academic Press, San Diego, CA.

Siousett, Annie Leaken

1922   Lionel Copley: First Royal Governor of Maryland. *Maryland Historical Magazine* 17(1):163–191.

Smith, B. Holly

1991   Standards of Human Tooth Formation and Dental Age Assessment. In *Ad-*

vances in Dental Anthropology, Marc A. Kelley and Clark Spencer Larsen, editors, pp. 143–168. Wiley-Liss, New York.

Smith, Frederick H.
2008   *The Archaeology of Alcohol and Drinking.* University Press of Florida, Gainesville.

Smith, Frederick H., and Karl Watson
2009   Urbanity, Sociability, and Commercial Exchange in the Barbados Sugar Trade: A Comparative Colonial Archaeological Perspective on Bridgetown, Barbados in the Seventeenth Century. *International Journal of Historical Archaeology* 13(1):63–79.

Smith, John
1624   *The Generall Historie of Virginia, New England, and the Summer Isles.* Readex, Microprint, 1966.

Smith, Laurajane
2006   *Uses of Heritage.* Routledge, London.

Smith, Paige, and Charles Daniel
2000   *The Chicken Book.* University of Georgia Press, Athens.

Snyder, Jeffrey B.
1995   *Historical Staffordshire: American Patriots and Views.* Schiffer Publishing, Atglen, PA.

Sonderman, Robert C., Matthew R. Virta, Marilyn W. Nichels, and Stephen R. Potter
1993   *Archaeology at Harmony Hall: Exploring the Late Seventeenth-Century Frontier of Maryland.* Occasional Report #9. Regional Archaeology Program, National Capital Region, National Park Service, Washington, DC.

Sperling, Christopher I., and Laura Galke
2001   *Phase II Archaeological Investigations of 18ST233 and 18ST239, Aboard Webster Field Annex, Naval Air Station, Patuxent River, St. Mary's County, Maryland.* Occasional Papers No. 13. Jefferson Patterson Park and Museum, St. Leonard, MD.

St. Giles in the Fields
1692   Burial Registry, St. Giles in the Fields, London.

St. Mary's Beacon
1861 $50 Reward. *St. Mary's Beacon* 4 July 1861:2. St. Mary's City, MD.
1867   St. Mary's Female Seminary. *St. Mary's Beacon.* 28 November 1867:2. St. Mary's City, MD.
1871   St. Mary's Female Seminary. *St. Mary's Beacon.* 31 August 1871:2. St. Mary's City, MD.
1874   Correspondence of the Beacon St. Inigoe's. *St. Mary's Beacon.* 20 June 1874:2. St. Mary's City, MD.

St. Mary's City Commission
1967   St. Mary's City Commission Meeting Minutes, June 1967. Manuscript, Department of Research and Collections, Historic St. Mary's City, St. Mary's City, MD.

St. Mary's County Circuit Court
1867   Deed, John M. and Susan M. Brome to James Stevenson, William Kelly, John Bush, John Baley, and John Holly, 3, f. 114–115, St. Mary's County Circuit Court, Maryland State Archives, Annapolis.

St. Mary's Female Seminary–Junior College
1926   Catalog of Courses. St. Mary's Female Seminary–Junior College, St. Mary's
            City, MD.

Stacy, Carl C., Henry M. Miller, and Richard C. Froede
1990   Surface Analysis of a Musket Shot Dated between 1645 and 1655 Found in
            Historic St. Mary's City, Maryland. *Journal of Forensic Sciences* 35(3):753–761.

Stallybrass, Peter, and Allison White
1986   *The Politics and Poetics of Transgression.* Cornell University Press, Ithaca, NY.

Stanley, Harvey
1853   *Pilate and Herod: A Tale. The Early History of the Church of England in the
            Province of Maryland.* H. Hooker, Philadelphia, PA.

State of Maryland
1840   *Laws Made and Passed by the General Assembly of the State of Maryland.* Wil-
            liam M'Neir, Annapolis.

Steen, Carl
1999   Stirring the Ethnic Stew in the South Carolina Backcountry: John de la Howe
            and Lethe Farm. In *Historical Archaeology, Identity Formation, and the Inter-
            pretation of Ethnicity,* Maria Franklin and Garrett Fessler, editors, pp. 93–120.
            Colonial Williamsburg Research Publications, Williamsburg, VA.

Steiner, Bernard Christian (editor)
1918   *Archives of Maryland, Vol. 38, Acts of the General Assembly Hitherto Unprinted,
            1694–1698, 1711–1729.* Maryland Historical Society, Baltimore.
1922   *Archives of Maryland, Vol. 41, Proceedings of the Provincial Court of Maryland,
            1658–1662.* Maryland Historical Society, Baltimore.

Stephenson, Robert, Alice L. Ferguson, and H. G. Ferguson
1963   *The Accokeek Creek Site: A Middle Atlantic Seaboard Culture Sequence.* Anthro-
            pology Papers No. 20. Museum of Anthropology, University of Michigan, Ann
            Arbor.

Steponaitis, Laurie Cameron
1980   *A Survey of Artifact Collections from the Patuxent River Drainage, Maryland.*
            Maryland Historical Trust Monograph Series No. 1. Maryland Historical Trust,
            Annapolis.

Stone, Garry Wheeler
1974   St. John's: Archaeological Questions and Answers. *Maryland Historical Maga-
            zine* 69(2):146–168.
1975   Inventoried Ceramics and Society. Paper presented at the 8th Annual Confer-
            ence on Historical and Underwater Archaeology, Charleston, SC.
1976   Analysis of the Kitchen at St. John's. Manuscript, Department of Research and
            Collections, Historic St. Mary's City, St. Mary's City, MD.
1978   *Dutch Wall Tile from St. Mary's City Excavations.* Historic St. Mary's City, St.
            Mary's City Research Series, No. 3. St. Mary's City, MD.
1982   Society, Housing, and Architecture in Early Maryland: John Lewger's St. John's.
            Doctoral dissertation, Department of American Studies, University of Penn-
            sylvania. University Microfilms International, Ann Arbor, MI.
1983   Garrett van Sweringen's "Council Chamber" Lodging House (1677–1699): A

Historic Structures Report and Restoration Analysis. Manuscript, Department of Research and Collections, Historic St. Mary's City, St. Mary's City, MD.

1987   The Key-Year Dendrochronology Pattern for the Oaks of Maryland's Western Shore 1570–1980. Manuscript, Department of Research and Collections, Historic St. Mary's City, St. Mary's City, MD.

1988   Artifacts Are Not Enough. In *Documentary Archaeology in the New World*, Mary C. Beaudry, editor, pp. 68–77. Cambridge University Press, Cambridge, UK.

Stone, Garry Wheeler, J. Glenn Little III, and Stephen Israel

1973   Ceramics from the John Hicks Site, 1723–1743: The Material Culture. In *Ceramics in America*, Ian M. G. Quimby, editor, pp. 103–140. University Press of Virginia, Charlottesville.

Stone, Lyle M.

1974   *Fort Michilimackinac 1715–1781: An Archaeological Perspective on the Revolutionary Frontier.* The Museum, Michigan State University, East Lansing.

Straube, Beverly A.

1995   The Colonial Potters of Tidewater Virginia. *Journal of Early Southern Decorative Arts* 21(2):1–40.

Streibel MacLean, Jessica

2015   Sheltering Colonialism: The Archaeology of a House, Household, and White Creole Masculinity at the 18th-Century Little Bay Plantation, Montserrat, West Indies. Doctoral dissertation, Department of Archaeology, Boston University. University Microfilms International, Ann Arbor, MI.

Strickland, Scott M.

2019   Native Settlement and Colonization: AD 900–1712. In *The Archaeology of Colonial Maryland*, Matthew D. McKnight, editor, pp. 140–179. Maryland Historical Trust Press, Crownesville.

Strutt, Joseph

1801   *The Sports and Pastimes of the People of England, from the Earliest Period, including the Rural and Domestic Recreations, May Games, Mummeries, Pageants, Processions and Pompous Spectacles, Illustrated by Reproductions from Ancient Paintings in which are Represented Most of the Popular Diversions.* Methuen & Co., London.

Sussman, Lynne

1997   *Mocha, Banded, Cat's Eye, and Other Factory-Made Slipware.* Council for Northeast Historical Archaeology, Studies in Northeast Historical Archaeology, No. 1. Boston.

Thomas, Gertrude Z.

1965   *Richer Than Spices: How a Royal Bride's Dowry Introduced Cane, Lacquer, Cottons, Tea, and Porcelain to England, and So Revolutionized Taste, Manners, Craftsmanship, and History in Both England and America.* Alfred A. Knopf, New York.

Thomas, James Walter

1894   The First Capital of Maryland. In *Celebration of the Two Hundredth Anniversary of the Removal of the Capital of Maryland From St. Mary's To Annapolis, March 5 1894*, Elihu Reiley, editor, pp. 62–83. King Bros., Annapolis, MD.

1913   *Chronicles of Colonial Maryland.* Eddy Press, Cumberland, MD. Reprinted
            1995 by Genealogical Publishing, Baltimore, MD.

Tucker, John, and Lewis Winstock

1972   *The English Civil War: A Military Handbook.* Stackpole Books, Harrisburg, PA.

Twitty, Michael

2009   *Fighting Old Nep: Foodways of Enslaved Afro-Marylanders, 1634–1864.* Michael
            Twitty, Maryland.

Ubelaker, Douglas H.

1989   *Human Skeletal Remains: Excavation, Analysis, Interpretation,* 2nd edition. Ta-
            raxacum, Washington, DC.

Udall, Stewart

1964   Restoring St. Mary's City: Refurbish Heritage, Stimulate Economy. *The St.
            Mary's Beacon* 20 February 1964. St. Mary's City, MD.

Unified Committee for Afro-American Contributions

2006   *In Relentless Pursuit of an Education: African American Stories from a Century
            of Segregation (1865–1967).* Unified Committee for Afro-American Contribu-
            tions of St. Mary's County, Lexington Park, MD.

Upton, Dell

1984   White and Black Landscapes in Eighteenth-Century Virginia. *Places* 2(2):59–72.

Van Der Lingen, Bert

2013   PKN: Stichting voor onderzoek historische tabakspijren. *JaarBoek* 2013:59–64.
            https://www.tabakspijp.nl/publicaties/pkn-publicaties/jaarboek-2013-digita-
            al/. Accessed 20 January 2020.

Veblen, Thorstein

1899   *The Theory of the Leisure Class: An Economic Study of Institutions.* Macmillan,
            New York.

Voss, Barbara L., and Rebecca Allen

2010   Guide to Ceramic MNV Calculation Qualitative and Quantitative Analysis.
            Technical Briefs in Historical Archaeology 5:1–9.

W.G.S.

1895   Racing in Colonial Virginia. *The Virginia Magazine of History and Biography*
            2(3):293–305.

Wagner, Eduard

1979   *European Weapons and Warfare, 1618–1648.* Artia, Prague, Czechoslovakia.

Walsh, Lorena S.

1977   Charles County, Maryland, 1658–1705: A Study of Chesapeake Social and Po-
            litical Structure. Doctoral dissertation, Department of History, Michigan State
            University. University Microfilms International, Ann Arbor, MI.

1985   Land, Landlord, and Leaseholder: Estate Management and Tenant Fortunes in
            Southern Maryland, 1642–1820. *Agricultural History* 59:373–396.

1988   Community Networks in the Early Chesapeake. In *Colonial Chesapeake Soci-
            ety,* Lois Green Carr, Philip D. Morgan, and Jean B. Russo, editors, pp. 202–241.
            University of North Carolina Press, Chapel Hill.

2010   *Motives of Honor, Pleasure, & Profit: Plantation Management in the Colonial
            Chesapeake, 1607–1763.* University of North Carolina Press, Chapel Hill.

Walsh, Lorena, and Russell R. Menard

1974   Death in the Chesapeake: Two Life Tables for Men in Early Colonial Maryland. *Maryland Historical Magazine* 69(2):211–227.

Walsham, Alexandra

1989   Godly Recreation: The Problem of Leisure in Late Elizabethan and Early Stuart Society. In *Grounds of Controversy: Three Studies in Late 16th and Early 17th Century English Polemics*, D. E. Kennedy, editor, pp. 7–48. University of Melbourne History Department, Melbourne, Australia.

Walthall, John A.

1991   *French Colonial Archaeology: The Illinois Country and the Western Great Lakes.* University of Illinois Press, Chicago.

Wanser, Jeffrey

1982   *A Survey of Artifact Collections from Central Southern Maryland.* Maryland Historical Trust Manuscript Series 23. Maryland Historical Trust, Annapolis.

Weiland, Jonathan

2009   A Comparison and Review of Window Glass Analysis Approaches in Historical Archaeology. *Technical Briefs in Historical Archaeology* 4:29–40.

West, Patricia

1999   *Domesticating History: The Political Origins of America's House Museums.* Smithsonian Books, Washington, DC.

Wheaton, Thomas R.

1987   Slave Architecture at Yaughan and Curriboo Plantations, Berkeley County, South Carolina. Manuscript, Department of Research and Collections, Historic St. Mary's City, St. Mary's City, MD.

Wheaton, Thomas R., Amy Friedlander, and Patrick Garrow

1983   *Yaughan and Curriboo Plantations: Studies in Afro-American Archaeology.* Report to the National Park Service, Southeast Regional Office, from Soil Systems, Inc.

White, Andrew

1910   A Brief Relation of the Voyage Unto Maryland. In *Narratives of Early Maryland 1633–1684*, Clayton C. Hall, editor, pp. 29–45. Barnes and Noble, New York.

White, Gregory, and Thomas King

2007   *The Archaeological Survey Manual.* Routledge, London.

Whitmore, John M.

1979   Interview by Marcia W. Keen, June. Manuscript, Alumni Association of St. Mary's College of Maryland, St. Mary's City, MD.

Wilkins, Andrew P.

2015   Appendix 5: Final Report on Soil Chemistry Analysis of Wingo's Quarter Site, Bedford County, Virginia. In *Archaeological Excavations at Wingo's Quarter (44BE0298), Forest, Virginia, Results from the 2000–2012 Seasons*, Barbara J. Heath, Eleanor E. Breen, Crystal Ptacek, and Andrew Wilkins, editors, pp. 345–401. University of Tennessee Archaeological Reports, Knoxville.

Willoughby, Wesley R.

2015   The Country's House: Examining Public Spaces and Community in St. Mary's City's Seventeenth-Century Town Center. Doctoral dissertation, Department of Anthropology, Syracuse University. University Microfilms International, Ann Arbor, MI.

Wood, Anthony à

1813   *Athenae Oxonienses.* 4 Volumes. Reprinted 1813–1820 by F. C. Rivington et al., London.

Yentsch, Anne

1990   Minimum Vessel Lists as Evidence of Change in Folk and Courtly Traditions of Food Use. *Historical Archaeology* 24(3):24–53.

Zimmerman, Michael R., and Marc A. Kelley

1982   *Atlas of Human Paleopathology.* Praeger, NY.

CONTRIBUTORS

Terry Peterkin Brock is assistant director for archaeology at the Montpelier Foundation in Orange, Virginia. He received his PhD from Michigan State University in anthropology and conducted his research for his dissertation at Historic St. Mary's City. He is the author of various publications and papers discussing plantations in the Middle Atlantic and how archaeologists communicate the past to the public.

Karin S. Bruwelheide is a skeletal biologist / forensic anthropologist at the National Museum of Natural History, Smithsonian Institution. Her research emphasizes forensic examination of modern and historic remains including skeletal studies of seventeenth- and eighteenth-century Americans, iron coffin burials, and Civil War military remains.

Charles H. Fithian is lecturer in anthropology at Washington College. He is coauthor with Daniel R. Griffith of "The Roosevelt Inlet Shipwreck, An Eighteenth-Century British Commercial Vessel in the Lower Delaware Valley: A Framework for Interpretation," in *Historical Archaeology of the Delaware Valley, 1600–1850* and author of "An Archaeological Analysis of the Armaments of H. M. Brig *DeBraak*," *Journal of the Company of Military Historians*.

Silas D. Hurry has served as curator of collections and archaeological laboratory director for Historic St. Mary's City for the past 32 years. He is the author or editor of numerous articles and essays on the archaeology of St. Mary's City including *Our Towne we Call St. Maries,* "*. . . once the Metropolis of Maryland,*" and "The Whole Site Is the Artifact: Interpreting the St. John's Site, St. Mary's City, Maryland."

Stephen S. Israel is retired from the U.S. Army Corps of Engineers, Baltimore district, planning division, where he was a staff archaeologist from 1976 to

2003. He received his M.A. from the Department of Anthropology at the University of Oklahoma. He is coauthor, with Frank J. Mosca and O'Brien Wolff, of "The School in Rose Valley: Digging Our Past Project: A Case Study in Public Archaeology and Progressive Education," *Pennsylvania Archaeologist*, Fall 2017.

Robert Keeler is professor of anthropology at Clackamas Community College. He conducted his doctoral dissertation work in St. Mary's City and received his PhD from the University of Oregon. His dissertation was the first systematic analysis of seventeenth-century English colonial artifact spatial distributions in America, focused on the 1638–1715 St. John's site.

George L. Miller is a retired archaeologist. He worked mostly as a lab man for half a century for several institutions, including serving as the first laboratory curator for the Historic St. Mary's City Commission. His research interests and publications were centered on ceramics and glass with a focus on changes in technology, chronology, price histories, and how the economic conditions and wars affected consumption prices. Miller was awarded the J. C. Harrington Medal in Historical Archaeology in recognition of a lifetime of contributions to the field in 2012.

Henry M. Miller is the Maryland Heritage Scholar for Historic St. Mary's City. He received his PhD from Michigan State University and served as curator and director of research for the museum from 1977 to 2017. His research includes zooarchaeology, environmental archaeology, seventeenth-century architecture, spatial analysis, and material culture studies. Miller was awarded the J. C. Harrington Medal in Historical Archaeology in recognition of a lifetime of contributions to the field in 2020.

Ruth M. Mitchell is the senior staff archaeologist for Historic St. Mary's City. She earned her M.A. in anthropology from the American University in Cairo, Egypt. She has more than 25 years of experience excavating American Indian, colonial, and postcolonial sites. She has worked primarily on domestic colonial period sites and burial grounds.

Alexander "Sandy" H. Morrison II received an M.A. in anthropology from the University of North Carolina at Chapel Hill, working under Joffre Coe. Morrison became assistant archaeologist for Historic St. Mary's City in 1972 and co-directed the Tolle-Tabbs, St. John's, and Van Sweringen site excavations, and the initial Town Center excavations. He helped pioneer new methods of investigating post-in-the-ground buildings, and played a major role in developing and enhancing formal archaeological excavation procedures for the museum. He passed away in 1983.

Douglas W. Owsley is a curator of biological anthropology at the National Museum of Natural History, Smithsonian Institution. He is the coeditor of *Kennewick Man: The Scientific Investigation of an Ancient Skeleton*.

Travis G. Parno is director of research and collections at Historic St. Mary's City. He earned a PhD in archaeology from Boston University and is the author/editor of publications including, with Mary C. Beaudry, *Archaeologies of Mobility and Movement* and, with Brent Fortenberry, "Catholic Artifacts in a Protestant Landscape: A Multi-Vocal Approach to the Religiosity of Jamestown's Colonists," a chapter in *Historical Archaeologies of Cognition: Explorations of Faith, Hope, and Charity*.

Timothy B. Riordan received his PhD in anthropology from Washington State University. From 1985 to 2015, he was chief archaeologist at Historic St. Mary's City. He is author of *The Plundering Time: Maryland and the English Civil War, 1645–1646*. Retiring from St. Mary's City in 2015, he currently volunteers with the City of Boston Archaeology Program and pursues his interest in tombstones and the materiality of death.

Michelle Sivilich is executive director of Gulf Archaeology Research Institute in Florida. She is an alumni of St. Mary's College of Maryland, received her M.S. from Indiana State University, and her PhD from the University of South Florida. Her publications include "KOCOA Considerations in Asymmetrical Warfare: Education and Environment in the Second Seminole War, 1835–1842," a chapter in *Partisans, Guerillas, and Irregulars: Historical Archaeology of Asymmetric Warfare*, and "An Archaeological Investigation for the Reconstruction of Fort King, and Fort King Road: Battlefields and Baggage Trains."

Garry Wheeler Stone is a retired archaeological historian. From 1971 to 1987, he was archaeologist, then director of research, at Historic St. Mary's City. He founded the archaeological research program at HSMC and guided the first seventeenth-century reconstructions for the museum. Among his publications are "The Roof Leaked, but the Price Was Right: The Virginia House Revisited" and, with Mark Edward Lender, *Fatal Sunday: George Washington, the Monmouth Campaign, and the Politics of Battle*.

Wesley R. Willoughby is an archaeologist for the Bureau of Land Management and serves as the Cultural Resources Program Lead and Tribal Liaison for the Northeastern States District Office based in Milwaukee, Wisconsin. He earned a PhD in anthropology from Syracuse University where he focused on the historical archaeology of the Colonial Chesapeake.

Donald L. Winter serves as media specialist at Historic St. Mary's City. He previously worked for 25 years as a professional archaeologist, including serving as chief archaeology lab assistant at HSMC. He lends his expertise in graphic design and 45 years of photography to design layouts for exhibits as well as photograph artifacts and events for publication.

INDEX

Page numbers in italics refer to illustrations.